MEDIUM ÆVUM MONOGRAPHS
NEW SERIES

MEDIUM ÆVUM MONOGRAPHS
NEW SERIES 25

# STUDIES IN THE METRE OF ALLITERATIVE VERSE

by

**AD PUTTER, JUDITH JEFFERSON, & MYRA STOKES**

The Society for the Study of
Medieval Languages and Literature
Oxford
2007

THE SOCIETY FOR THE STUDY OF
MEDIEVAL LANGUAGES AND LITERATURE

OXFORD, 2007

http://mediumaevum.modhist.ox.ac.uk



British Library Cataloguing Publication Data

A catalogue record for this book
is available from the British Library

ISBN-13: 978-0-907570-18-9 (pb)

First published 2007
This digital reprint first issued 2015

# CONTENTS

# PREFACE

This book is the product of a three-year research project on the metre of alliterative verse, carried out at the University of Bristol between October 2002 and September 2005, and generously sponsored by the Arts and Humanities Research Council. The research could not have been completed without their financial backing, and we are thankful for their support. We are also grateful to the University of Bristol for an award from the Arts Faculty Research Fund — which made it possible for Judith Jefferson to travel to Princeton in order to consult Princeton University Library, MS Taylor Medieval 11 — and for a term of sabbatical leave granted by the English department to Ad Putter to expedite the completion of the book.

The book consists of five case studies, each of them originally written independently of the others. Some material previously published in the journals *Medium Aevum*, *Parergon* and *Studies in Philology* has been included, and we thank the publishers for granting us permission to re-use that material here. Chapter One was written jointly by Ad Putter and Myra Stokes; the second section is largely based on their essay entitled 'Spelling, Grammar and Metre in the Works of the *Gawain*-poet', in *Medieval English Measures: Studies in Metre and Versification*, ed. Ruth Kennedy, special issue of *Parergon*, 18 (2000), 77–95. Chapter Two was written by all three authors; it incorporates a previously published article by Judith Jefferson and Ad Putter, 'The Distribution of Infinitives in *–e* and *–en* in Some Middle English Alliterative Poems', *Medium Aevum*, 74 (2005), 221–47. The remaining chapters were written by Judith Jefferson and Ad Putter. Parts of Chapter Three were previously published in their article 'Alliterative Patterning in the *Morte Arthure*', *Studies in Philology*, 102 (2005), 415–33. The Introduction and Conclusion were written by Ad Putter, who had overall responsibility for the research project and the related publications.

It is a pleasure to thank those who have helped us in our writing and research and in the process of publication, especially Ruth Kennedy, who read a version of this book for Medium Aevum Monographs, John Burrow, Hoyt Duggan, Ralph Hanna, Noriko Inoue, Donka Minkova, Rick Russom, Thorlac Turville-Petre, Nicolay Yakovlev, and all the participants of the Bristol 2005 Conference on the Metre of Alliterative

Verse. We also thank the staff of the University Library, and the Editorial Board of the Medium Aevum Monograph Series, particularly Corinne Saunders, and Anthony Lappin, who heroically prepared the manuscript for publication.

No doubt, even the help of our many readers will not have saved us from mistakes and misapprehensions; for these we alone are responsible.

# ABBREVIATIONS

The following abbreviations are used in reference to Middle English poems:

| | |
|---|---|
| *A* | *Alexander A* |
| *ABC* | *The ABC of Aristotle* |
| *B* | *Alexander B* or *Alexander and Dindimus* |
| *BD* | Chaucer, *Book of the Duchess* |
| *C* | *Cleanness* |
| *CA* | Gower, *Confessio Amantis* |
| *CT* | *Canterbury Tales* |
| *D* | *Death and Liffe* |
| *DT* | *The Destruction of Troy* |
| *E* | *Saint Erkenwald* |
| *G* | *Sir Gawain and the Green Knight* |
| *HF* | Chaucer, *House of Fame* |
| *LGW* | Chaucer, *Legend of Good Women* |
| *MA* | *Morte Arthure* |
| *P* | *Patience* |
| *PP* | Langland, *Piers Plowman* |
| *P3A* | *The Parlement of Three Ages* |
| *SJ* | *Siege of Jerusalem* |
| *T&C* | Chaucer, *Troilus and Criseyde* |
| *WA* | *Wars of Alexander* |
| *WP* | *William of Palerne* |
| *WW* | *Wynnere and Wastoure* |

The following dictionaries, reference works, and series titles, are referred to in abbreviated form:

| | |
|---|---|
| EETS (OS, ES, SS) | Early English Text Society (Original Series, Extra Series, Supplementary Series) |
| *LALME* | *A Linguistic Atlas of Late Mediaeval English*, ed. A. I. McIntosh, M. L. Samuels, and Michael Benskin, with the assistance of Margaret Laing and Keith Williamson, 4 vols (Aberdeen, 1986) |

| | |
|---|---|
| *MED* | *Middle English Dictionary*, ed. Hans Kurath, Sherman M. Kuhn, and Robert E. Lewis (Ann Arbor, Mich., 1954–1996) |
| *OED* | *Oxford English Dictionary. The Compact Edition of the Oxford English Dictionary*, 2 vols (Oxford, 1971) |

Other symbols and abbreviations used:

| | |
|---|---|
| AF | Anglo-French |
| EME | Early Middle English |
| OE | Old English |
| (L)OE | (Late) Old English |
| OF | Old French |
| OI | Old Icelandic |
| ON | Old Norse |
| (E)ME | (Early) Middle English |
| ModE | Modern English |
| MS(S) | Manuscript(s) |
| adj. | adjective |
| adv. | adverb |
| ind. | indicative |
| inf. | infinitive |
| n. | noun |
| pl. | plural |
| p.p. | past participle |
| pres. | present tense |
| pret. | preterite tense |
| *rh* | rhyming line(s) |
| SE | South East |
| sg. | singular |
| v. | verb |
| < | develops from |
| > | evolves into |
| / / | encloses phonemes |
| [ ] | encloses editorial additions or emendations |
| < > | encloses spelling forms |
| : | rhyming with |
| + | one of a number of attestations |
| * | reconstructed form or example |

# INTRODUCTION

The study of Middle English alliterative metre is now in a period of such rapid change and development that there are few specialists in the area who would agree with each other on some quite fundamental questions concerning the metrical rules and norms of the alliterative long line. The main cause of the present turmoil is a paradigm shift in our understanding of the metrical system underlying the poems of the 'alliterative revival'. To simplify, it used to be thought that what matters in the metre of the alliterative long line is simply number of beats and alliteration, and that '[n]on-stressed, non-alliterating syllables are not metrically significant'.[1] But recent research, of which Hoyt Duggan's is an outstanding example,[2] suggests that unstressed syllables do in fact play a crucial part in the metre of alliterative verse. Yet while confidence in the old paradigm has gone, the shape of the paradigm that will replace it is uncertain. In the words of Stephen Barney, 'we know too much to rest content with the earlier consensus about the prosodies of the alliterative poets, but not enough to rest content with what we now know.'[3]

To illustrate the inadequacies of our current knowledge, consider the opening lines of *Patience*:

> Pacience is a poynt,  þaȝ hit displese ofte.
> When heuy herttes ben hurt  with heþyng oþer elles,
> Suffraunce may aswagen hem  and þe swelme leþe,
> For ho quelles vche a qued  and quenches malyce. (1–4)[4]

A large number of problems regarding the metre of these lines remains at present unsolved. Barney gives a comprehensive list of them; below are the six problems that will concern us most:

[1] R. W. Sapora, *A Theory of Middle English Alliterative Meter with Critical Applications*, Speculum Anniversary Monographs (Cambridge, Mass., 1977), p. 20.
[2] See especially Hoyt Duggan, 'The Shape of the B-Verse in Middle English Alliterative Poetry', *Speculum*, 61 (1986), 564–92.
[3] Stephen A. Barney, 'Langland's Prosody: The State of Study', in *The Endless Knot: Essays on Old and Middle English in Honor of Marie Borroff*, ed. M. Teresa Tavormina and R. F. Yeager (Cambridge, 1995), pp. 65–85.
[4] *Patience*, ed. J. J. Anderson (Manchester, 1969).

(1) In all these lines the minimal alliterative pattern is *aaax* (*a* stands for an alliterating stave and *x* for an non-alliterating one), at least if we can assume initial stress on *Suffraunce* at l. 3. Was that *aaax* pattern obligatory in the poems of the classical corpus (as the poets, rather than the scribes, wrote them) or was it merely an optimum, and is there any evidence to be gleaned one way or the other from single-manuscript poems? If the *aaax* pattern was obligatory then how do we explain and emend exceptions to this rule?

(2) What is the status of final *–e* in this and other comparable poems? (And is that status the same across all the major alliterative poems?) In the lines before us, is final *–e* to be sounded in the words at line ending (*ofte, leþe, malyce*)? And what about final *–e* in words within the line (*displese,*[5] *suffraunce, swelme*)?

(3) How many beats (or 'lifts') are there in the alliterative long line: 4, 5, or possibly even more? The question is raised by the second line of *Patience*: is this a line with five beats ('When héuy hérttes ben húrt with héþyng oþer élles') or four? On what basis and what evidence do we determine which words take the beat and which ones do not? If adjective-noun combinations (in this instance 'heuy herrtes') can take a single beat, does the noun or the adjective carry the beat and what empirical procedures allow us to educate our intuitions about such matters?

(4) Hoyt Duggan and Thomas Cable have argued, convincingly in our view, that the metre of the b-verse (i.e. the second half of the line) is constrained not only by the number of beats (two) but also by the number of long dips it may contain: the b-verse must contain *one and only one* long dip (a long dip is a sequence of two or more

[5] Elision of final *–e* is normal before vowels, but it is not in our view inevitable, for even careful metrists such as Chaucer and Hoccleve seem to permit hiatus: e.g. *CT* IV.2233, VI.772, VIII.1266, *BD* 99, 903. References are to *The Riverside Chaucer*, gen. ed. Larry D. Benson, 3rd edn (Boston, 1987). As Elizabeth Solopova has shown in 'Metre and Scribal Editing in the Early Manuscripts of *The Canterbury Tales*', in '*The Canterbury Tales*' *Project: Occasional Papers*, vol. II, ed. Norman Blake and Peter Robinson (London, 1997), pp. 153–65, lines such as 'That made his facë often reed and hoot' (*CT* III.540) are overwhelmingly supported by the MS tradition: 'there is no indication that the rules for elision were absolutely strict in Chaucer's verse' (p. 160). See also below, p. 104, n. 77.

unstressed syllables; a short dip a single unstressed syllable).[6] The syllabic patterns shown by the b-verses above are all permissible patterns according to this rule. Using x for an unstressed syllable, (x) for a *possible* unstressed syllable (depending on the status of final –*e*), and / for a beat, we can scan the b-verses as follows:

xxx/(x)/(x)
x/xx(x)/x [7]
xx/(x)/(x)
x/xx/(x)

The scansion of line 4 assumes second-syllable stress on *malyce*, as distinct from the 'English' pronunciation of the word later on in the poem ('And her *malys* is so much, I may not abide', l. 70). (A further question: could differences in spellings, such as *malyce* versus *malys*, have been intended to direct us towards the required pronunciations?) Not all recent editors of alliterative poems seem to have been convinced by Duggan and Cable. For example, the text printed by Andrew and Waldron in their recently revised edition of the *Pearl* poems shows no regard for the b-verse rule posited by Duggan and Cable.[8] Is there any evidence from single-manuscript poems that might persuade future editors that b-verses that do not meet the long dip requirement are scribal?

(5) If there are metrical constraints for the b-verse (two beats, one and only one long dip), then what about the a-verse? Are there any rules that govern the distribution of unstressed syllables, or can we speak only of tendencies and preferences?

(6) As our scansion of these b-verses indicates, it is possible that they end in one and only one unstressed syllable. It has been argued that masculine line endings were strictly avoided by alliterative poets: is that true for any of them? What evidence is there for this and are there any exceptions?

[6] See Duggan, 'Shape of the B-Verse' and Thomas Cable, *The English Alliterative Tradition* (Philadelphia, 1991).
[7] *Oper* may be subject to syncopation.
[8] Malcolm Andrew and Ronald Waldron (eds), *The Poems of the Pearl Manuscript*, 4th edn (Exeter, 2002).

What makes these questions so complicated is that the answer to any one of them will depend on the answers we give to the others. For example, to study the distribution of unstressed syllables in a-verse dips it will be necessary to have some hypothesis about which (if any) final *–es* should be counted as syllables; the scansion will further be affected by the number of lifts we deem to be permissible in the a-verse, for what is a lift in a three-beat theory of the a-verse may be a dip, or part of one, in a two-beat theory. This interdependency of hypotheses is inevitable in the study of metre and not a cause for despair. Understanding in metrics, as in any hermeneutic enterprise, 'is always a movement ... from the whole to the parts, and vice versa'.[9] The question is therefore not how do we avoid the hermeneutic circle but, rather, how do we make sure that we enter it at an appropriate point?

We have decided, in each chapter, to provide a full examination of one or two particular metrical problems in a number of selected alliterative poems, and then to set these case studies in the context of a larger corpus. In presenting the evidence, we have tried to adopt the principle of 'disclosure', as described by Stephen Barney: '*Disclosure*, to use the legal jargon [means] the presentation of evidence such that it can be assessed by others ... Exceptions, irregularities, counterexamples, the "rare" cases, instances requiring manipulation to make them fit, require full review.'[10] Compliance with this principle imposes restrictions on the amount of material that can be covered and digested, both by the 'prosecution' and the 'jury', so to speak; and we shall therefore be concentrating on a small number of poems quite closely. This case-by-case procedure also safeguards against the danger of over-generalisation, a danger that makes the selection of texts a hermeneutic as well as a practical problem.

If one took a broad view, Middle English poems in the alliterative long line could be said to include a wide range of different forms and traditions, including Early Middle English works (e.g. Laȝamon's *Brut*), later Middle English works in the 'looser' tradition (e.g. *Joseph of Arimathie*), the rhymed tradition in stanzaic and non-stanzaic form (e.g. *The Awntyrs off Arthure* and *The Song of the Husbandman*) and the classical tradition (e.g. *Cleanness*).[11] Needless to say, anyone trying to posit metrical

[9] Hans-Georg Gadamer, *Truth and Method* (London, 1975), p. 167.

[10] Barney, 'Langland's Prosody', p. 70.

[11] For a survey of the tradition in this wider sense, see J. P. Oakden, *Alliterative Poetry in Middle English*, 2 vols (Manchester, 1930–35), and (focusing more on the

regularities that would apply uniformly across all alliterative poems in these different traditions is unlikely to come up with anything more than some broad generalisations that bear only a remote relation to the finer rules with which individual poets actually composed their verse. In his studies of alliterative metre, Hoyt Duggan reasonably restricted himself to the 'classical corpus' of unrhymed alliterative verse, excluding *Piers Plowman* [*PP*] (which may be not just metrically idiosyncratic, but also differently so in its various versions),[12] but including the following:

> *Alexander A* [*A*]
> *Alexander B* or *Alexander and Dindimus* [*B*]
> *Cleanness* [*C*]
> *Death and Liffe* [*D*]
> *The Destruction of Troy* [*DT*]
> *Saint Erkenwald* [*E*]
> *Mum and the Sothsegger* [*M*]
> *Morte Arthure* [*MA*]
> *The Parlement of Three Ages* [*P3A*]
> *Patience* [*P*]
> *Siege of Jerusalem* [*SJ*]
> *Sir Gawain and the Green Knight* [*G*]
> *Wars of Alexander* [*WA*]
> *Wynnere and Wastoure* [*WW*].[13]

'classical' tradition) Thorlac Turville-Petre, *The Alliterative Revival* (Cambridge, 1977).

[12] See Hoyt Duggan, 'The Authenticity of the Z-Text of *Piers Plowman*: Further Notes on Metrical Evidence', *Medium Aevum*, 56 (1987), 27–45.

[13] References will normally be made to the following editions: *A*: *The Gests of King Alexander of Macedon*, ed. Francis Peabody Magoun (Cambridge, Mass., 1929); *B*: *The Alliterative Romance of Alexander and Dindimus*, ed. W. W. Skeat, EETS ES 31 (London, 1878); *C*: *Cleanness*, ed. J. J. Anderson (Manchester, 1977); *D*: *Death and Liffe*, ed. Joseph M. Donatelli, Speculum Anniversary Monographs 15 (Cambridge, Mass, 1989); *DT*: *Destruction of Troy*, ed. George A. Panton and David Donaldson, EETS OS 39, 56 (London, 1869, 1874); *E*: *Saint Erkenwald*, in *A Book of Middle English*, ed. J. A Burrow and Thorlac Turville-Petre, 2nd edn. (Oxford, 1996); *M*: *Mum and the Sothsegger*, in *The Piers Plowman Tradition*, ed. Helen Barr (London, 1993); *MA*: *Morte Arthure*, ed. Mary Hamel (New York, 1984); *P3A*: *Parlement of Three Ages*, ed. M. Y. Offord, EETS OS 246 (Oxford, 1959); *P*: *Patience*, ed. Anderson; *SJ*: *Siege of Jerusalem*, ed. Ralph Hanna and David Lawton, EETS OS 320 (Oxford, 2003); *G*: *Sir Gawain and the Green Knight*, ed. J.

In this 'classical corpus', Duggan argues, *aa/ax* alliteration is a condition of metricality, as is a single long dip in the b-verse. However, there are grounds for suspecting that even Duggan's stricter 'classical' corpus may be too broad to reveal the specific metrical rules and grammars that are at work in particular poems or groupings of poems within the corpus. Chronologically, the poems span a period ranging from the middle of the fourteenth century (e.g. *WW*)[14] to the early fifteenth or later (*DT*),[15] and in terms of authorial dialect they range from the southern end of the West Midland area (e.g. *A*: from Gloucestershire) to the counties bordering on the North (e.g. *WA*: from Lancashire?).[16] When it comes to the scribal copies in which the poems have come down to us, the chronological and dialectal span is even more extreme.[17] The earliest extant manuscripts of classical alliterative poems are from the end of the fourteenth century.[18] They are:

R. R. Tolkien and E.V. Gordon, rev. Norman Davis (Oxford, 1967); *WA*: *Wars of Alexander*, ed. Hoyt Duggan and Thorlac Turville-Petre, EETS SS 10 (Oxford, 1989); *WW: Wynnere and Wastoure*, ed. Stephanie Trigg, EETS OS 297 (Oxford, 1990)

[14] We find persuasive Gollancz's dating of the work to 1352, as argued in the preface to his edition (London, 1920). For a different view see Trigg (ed.), *Wynnere and Wastoure*, pp. xxii–xxvii, and Elizabeth Salter, 'The Timeliness of *Wynnere and Wastoure*', *Medium Aevum*, 47 (1978), 40–65. For a defence of Gollancz's argument see Thorlac Turville-Petre, '*Wynnere and Wastoure*: When and Where?', in *Loyal Letters: Studies on Mediaeval Alliterative Poetry and Prose*, ed. L. A. R. J. Houwen and A. A. MacDonald (Groningen, 1994), pp. 155–66

[15] On the dating of *DT* see the remarks by Ralph Hanna and David Lawton (eds), *The Siege of Jerusalem*, EETS OS 320 (London, 2003), pp. xxxvi–xxxvii. A much later date has been suggested by Edward Wilson, 'John Clerk, Author of the *Destruction of Troy*', *Notes and Queries*, n.s. 37 (1990), 391–6.

[16] Gloucestershire and Lancashire are the provenances suggested for respectively *A* and *WA* in the editions cited in n. 13.

[17] For a general discussion of the manuscripts of alliterative verse see Ian Doyle, 'The Manuscripts', in *Middle English Alliterative Poetry and Its Literary Background*, ed. David Lawton (Cambridge, 1982), pp. 88–100.

[18] For an up-to-date description of Bodley 264 see K. I. Scott, *Later Gothic Manuscripts, 1390–1490*, 2 vols (London, 1996), II, pp. 68–73. For datings and descriptions of the other manuscripts see the editions listed in n. 13.

King's College Cambridge, MS 13 (*c.* 1375, containing *WP*, a poem which may or may not belong to the 'classical' tradition)[19]

British Library, MS Cotton Nero A.x. (*c.* 1400, containing the *Gawain* poems)

Bodleian Library, MS Bodley 264 (*c.* 1400, containing *B*)

Bodleian Library, MS Laud Misc. 656 (late fourteenth-century, containing *SJ*)

Princeton University Library, MS Taylor Medieval 11 (late fourteenth-century, also containing *SJ*)

The latest witnesses are centuries removed from the period in which the alliterative poems they contain were originally composed. Thus *A* and *D* (both from the second half of the fourteenth century) survive only in seventeenth-century texts: the former in Oxford, Bodleian, MS Greaves 60 (*c.* 1600), the latter in the Percy Folio, London, British Library, MS Add. 27897 (*c.* 1650). Some poems (e.g. *B*) were copied by professional London scribes; others by amateurs (e.g. *MA*, copied by the Yorkshire gentleman Robert Thornton).

Since the metrical rules that poets observed were ultimately based on the possibilities of their language, it seems dangerous to assume that identical norms and rules can be extrapolated from poems written (and copied) in languages belonging to different generations and different dialects, especially where such rules are predicated on factors (such as final *–e* or inflectional *–n*) that were subject to dialectal variability and rapid historical change. Nevertheless that is the assumption that holds sway in current work. Hoyt Duggan, for example, seems to attribute an identical grammar of final *–e* to all the poems in his selected corpus (except *PP*), and posits and admits as the conditions of their metricality only such rules as obtain in each and every one of these poems. By contrast, Karl Luick suggested that the classical tradition was not homogeneous, but could be roughly divided into two main groups based on dialect and date: first, an early Central West Midland group (as represented by e.g. the Alexander fragments *A* and *B*), and second a later and distinctly North-West Midland Group (represented by e.g. *DT*). He

19 Duggan excludes it from his corpus without explanation; the proportion of lines with irregular alliteration (as judged by the standards of the 'classical corpus') is higher than normal (around eleven percent), but the commixture of dialects indicates a lengthy scribal tradition. For discussion, see the edition by G. H. V. Bunt, *William of Palerne* (Groningen, 1985), pp. 77–92.

considered various other poems (e.g. the Cotton Nero poems and *E*) to be chronologically and dialectally transitional.[20] In the first group, Luick argued, final *–e* retained syllabic status; in some of the poems belonging to the latter final *–e* had become obsolete, with important consequences for alliterative line endings (strictly feminine in the former, but masculine or feminine in the latter). Luick's research, now more than a century old, has been forgotten by many (and sometimes misread by those who still refer to it), but it seems to us that students of alliterative metre are slowly re-discovering, often without knowing it, what Luick said all those years ago. Even the most important breakthrough in recent work, namely the discovery (made independently by Duggan and Cable) of the long-dip requirement in the b-verse was anticipated by Luick, who as early as 1889 argued that b-verse patterns of the types xx/xx/(x) and x/x/(x) were irregular and inauthentic.[21] His warning that the linguistic and metrical systems of the later Middle English alliterative poems may not be identical seems to us worth bearing in mind. As a precaution against over-generalisation, we therefore prefer to test the validity of metrical hypotheses by concentrating on a few specific poems, and to turn our attention to the corpus as a whole only after some intensive case studies.

The poems that we focus on in our case studies are *B*, *C*, *E*, *G*, *MA*, *P* and *SJ*. It may strike the reader as odd that, with the exception of *SJ*, none of these poems is extant in more than one manuscript, given Duggan's warnings about what he believes to be 'the inherent weak-

[20] Karl Luick, 'Der mittelenglische Stabreimvers', in *Grundriss der Germanischen Philologie*, ed. Hermann Paul, 2 vols (Strasbourg, 1905), II, pp. 141–80 (§40–§44).

[21] See Karl Luick, 'Die englische Stabreimzeile im XIV., XV. und XVI. Jahrhundert', *Anglia*, 9 (1889), 392–443, 553–618. See particularly §24. Luick's position was developed by Julius Thomas, who shared Luick's view that b-verses without a long dip were inauthentic but held that two long dips were permissible (*Die alliterierende Langzeile des Gawayn-Dichters* (Jena, 1908), p. 45). Luick himself changed his mind: in his 1905 chapter for Paul's *Grundriss*, §43 (see n. 20), he suggested the possibility that verses without long dips might after all be authorial. That Luick has not been given the credit for first discovering the metrical rules of the b-verse is a historical injustice; Duggan's suggestion (in 'Final *–e* and the Rhythmic Structure of the B-Verse in Middle English Alliterative Poetry', *Modern Philology*, 86 (1988), 119–45) that Luick naively trusted that metrical rules were faithfully reflected in scribal copies (121) cannot be based on a careful reading of Luick's work, Luick being not only the first to regard b-verses without one and only one long dip as unmetrical but also the first to use that knowledge as a basis for emendation.

nesses which undermine studies based on single-manuscript witnesses'.[22] At the heart of Duggan's distrust of single-manuscript poems is the knowledge that scribal corruption is liable to distort the practices of the original poets; since none of the extant poems is preserved in an autograph copy, it is, as Duggan warns, unwise to proceed on the assumption that the texts as we have them will faithfully reflect the author's metrical system. We entirely agree with him on this point. But while a poem extant in more than one manuscript certainly offers the scholar the benefit of multiple scribal opinions, it does not follow that these opinions (and the best opinion that can be formed on their basis) will necessarily give us a better insight into authorial practice than can be derived from a single witness. What matters supremely is the quality of a witness's testimony — and it is clearly possible to arrive at an informed judgment about that, regardless of the presence or absence of other scribal testimonies. To give an example, since in *C* (a single-manuscript poem) the regular pattern *aa/ax* (and *aa/aa*) obtains in over 98 percent of all cases,[23] there is good reason to be suspicious about deviations. Consider, for example, the following lines:

Þen he wendeȝ his way, *wepande* for care,
Toward þe mere of Mambre, *wepande* for sorewe. (777–8)[24]

Here the second *wepande* is suspect, and all sensible editors emend to *mornande*, knowing as they do that this type of error (i.e. the substitution of synonyms) is extremely common, and was in this instance apparently prompted by *wepande* in the preceding line. Let us suppose that there was

[22] Duggan, 'Final *-e*', 123.
[23] The statistics are based on Noriko Inoue, 'The A-Verse of the Alliterative Long Line and the Metre of *Sir Gawain and the Green Knight*' (PhD Dissertation, University of Bristol, 2003), p. 202, though we revise her calculation (2.7%) downward since she includes among her list of 49 irregularities (to which list should be added 228 and 515), various lines that have an acceptable alliterative pattern by our understanding of beat and alliteration (as explained in the next chapter): (*C* 285, 303, 447 [MS *Mararach*], 513, 526, 610, 653, 659, 758, 1245, 1291). See ch. 3 for further discussion. We accept as irregular (and corrupt) the following: *C* 67, 105, 175, 228, 299, 315, 327, 345, 427, 464, 515, 520, 608, 735, 770, 779, 958, 993, 1073, 1101, 1205, 1261, 1483, 1518, 1571, 1573, 1618, 1622, 1655, 1727, 1807.
[24] We follow the editors' practice of expanding MS abbreviations silently, except where the words at issue are problematic and the orthography matters to our argument.

another manuscript of *C*: if that manuscript had *mornande* the emendation would be confirmed; but even if it read *wepande*, there would be compelling grounds for the emendation, unless of course that manuscript turned out to be a holograph, for that, and that alone, would prove absolutely that *wepande* was authorial. Editors (including Hoyt Duggan and Thorlac Turville-Petre in their edition of *WA*, and Ralph Hanna and David Lawton in their edition of *SJ*) quite properly exercise their judgement independently of multiple scribal opinions when they choose to emend lines with irregular alliteration or b-verse rhythms even when the witnesses agree. If one really believed that the evidence of other manuscripts *proves* anything, as Duggan at times suggests,[25] one should not be making these emendations. However, what justifies these editors' emendations of various shared errors is the probability that the extant witnesses ultimately go back to a single archetype *that is not the author's original*[26] — which of course means that the ultimate evidential basis for students of multiple-manuscript poems is itself the single-manuscript witness, with all its 'inherent weaknesses'. Additional witnesses provide a further check on the dependability of a manuscript reading and a useful introduction to the kinds of errors that scribes make, but to regard the evidence of single-manuscript poems as inherently inferior or flawed is both to overestimate the evidential value of an additional witness and to underestimate the importance of other methods of checking the quality of a 'witness report'.

One such check is the witness's temporal and geographical proximity to the author's original, especially if the evidence under investigation is diachronically and dialectally unstable. In this respect, the evidence provided by the earliest extant poems seems to us potentially more dependable than that provided by the double-manuscript poems *WA* and *P3A*, which survive in texts that are much later (mid-fifteenth-century and later) and dialectally impure, their scribal languages being significantly further north than those of the original poets.

For reasons of date and dialect, we have in our studies devoted particular attention to *B*, *C*, *P*, *G*, and *SJ*, and we shall briefly introduce these sources. The Cotton Nero poems *C*, *P* and *G* not only survive in a

[25] E.g. in 'Alliterative Patterning as a Basis for Emendation in Middle English Alliterative Poetry', *Studies in the Age of Chaucer*, 8 (1986), 73–105: 'the evidence of other manuscripts proves Thornton's text corrupt' (76).

[26] Hanna and Lawton are explicit about this in their edition (see the stemma on p. lcvii).

relatively early manuscript but are also written in a language which (according to Angus McIntosh) is 'reasonably homogeneous',[27] i.e., there is little evidence of dialectal scribal translation.

*B* is also early, though we know that the poem has travelled. The codex (Oxford, Bodley 264), which is roughly contemporary with Cotton Nero A.x, is a *de luxe* manuscript, containing a finely illuminated copy of the Old French *Roman d'Alexandre* (produced in Flanders, *c.* 1340), to which the alliterative English romance was subsequently added by an English scribe who wrongly thought that the French text was incomplete. Kathleen Scott characterises the style of the manuscript illuminations accompanying *B* as late fourteenth-century, and suggests they were produced in London.[28] That localisation is consistent with the ownership history of the manuscript, which belonged to Lord Rivers in London in 1466,[29] and also consistent with the language of the scribe who (as appears from a short scribal rubric) wrote in a South East Midland dialect.[30] The original language of the poet has been localised to Gloucestershire.[31] If this is correct, it is slightly further south than Langland's.

*SJ* has a very complicated textual history and it is hard to be sure about the dialect of the original. The most recent attempt at localisation is that of Hanna and Lawton, who propose the area of Barnoldswick, West Yorkshire.[32] Their localisation seems to us unsafe. The comment by the editors that 'we construe the appearance of a specific form, rather than the overwhelming frequency of its record, as a sign that such a form is a possible representation within the locale of record' suggests they had some difficulty identifying an area encompassing all the forms which they select as diagnostic, a problem which appears to originate with the selection process itself. In particular, the use of forms of 'shall' in /s/ (*sall etc.*) for diagnostic purposes, something which sets a firm southern limit on any possible placement, is based on the flimsy foundation that

27 A. I. McIntosh, 'A New Approach to Middle English Dialectology', *English Studies*, 44 (1963), 1–11 (4–5). See also the qualifications by Putter and Stokes, 'The Linguistic Atlas and the Dialect of the *Gawain* Poems', forthcoming in *Journal of English and Germanic Philology*, 106 (2007), 468–91.

28 Scott, *Later Gothic Manuscripts*, II, pp. 68–73.

29 Turville-Petre, *Alliterative Revival*, p. 43.

30 *Alexander and Dindimus*, ed. Skeat, p. xxvi.

31 Magoun (ed.), *Gests*, pp. 78 and 112.

32 Hanna and Lawton (eds), *Siege*, pp. xxvii–xxxvii.

such forms of the auxiliary occur three times in positions where initial /s/ rather than /ʃ/ would provide a third metrical stave in the a-verse.[33] Since the number of these examples is so small; since auxiliaries do not usually take the beat; and since third staves, if they exist at all, are not a metrical requirement, it seems unwise to place quite so much reliance on evidence which the editors themselves admit is 'ambiguous'. Once this particular diagnostic form is discounted, forms of 'or' in 'other', forms of 'them' with initial *h*–, forms of 'church in *ch*–, past participles with prefix –*y* (all more satisfactorily evidenced from the metre) suggest a more southerly placement. We accept Kölbing and Day's suggestion that the poet's original dialect was North West Midland.[34]

In some of our case studies, we also draw on *WP*, *E*, and *MA*, and a few more words about these three witnesses may be helpful. *WP* has the merit of being early, but despite the early date of the manuscript, it evidently had a lengthy scribal transmission. The poem may originally have been composed in Gloucestershire but the language of the extant copy is mixed, containing West-Midland features, with East-Midland and Northern admixtures. The complicated scribal tradition might explain the high proportion of lines with irregular alliterative patterns (there are 717 non-*aa/ax* lines according to J. P. Oakden).[35] The editor Gerrit Bunt inclines to the view that many of these irregular lines are authentic, and lists numerous *aa/xx* lines for which 'no … emendation readily suggests itself' (p. 83). Even though some of Bunt's 'non-emendable' lines could be corrected without much difficulty,[36] many apparently 'unemendable' lines remain; and without further research, it is hard to be sure whether or nor such lines are scribal. The manuscript of *E* (Harley 2250) is late (*c.*

[33] For some further objections to Hanna and Lawton's localisation, see Ad Putter's review in *Speculum*, 81 (2006), 523–5.
[34] Eugen Kölbing and Mabel Day (eds) *The Siege of Jerusalem*, EETS OS 188 (London, 1932), p.xv. For further discussion see Allen Bond Kellog, who, in what is still the most detailed analysis of the language of *SJ*, concluded that 'the MSS as a group are not decidedly Northern', and that 'the western characteristics of L may be taken ... to be survivals of the dialect of the poet': 'The Language of the Alliterative *Siege of Jerusalem*' (PhD Dissertation, University of Chicago, 1943), pp. 61–2.
[35] Oakden, *Alliterative Poetry*, I, pp. 184–6.
[36] To give a couple of examples, the b-verses of 388 and 389 can be transposed to create metrically regular *aa/ax* patterns. At 4410, *keuer* for *graunt* would restore the alliteration and b-verse metre.

1475); both the language of the poet and the scribe belong to Cheshire; indeed, *E* does not appear to have travelled outside Cheshire until after the single extant manuscript was copied.[37] *MA*, a single-manuscript poem, late and linguistically messy (due to the complicated scribal transmission that took it from the North-Midlands to the East Riding of Yorkshire)[38] is of very limited use in a study of alliterative metre, yet we include it in one of our studies because we have — even in this desperate case — found it possible to develop procedures for testing the authenticity or inauthenticity of departures from metrical norms without the benefit of a second manuscript witness. These procedures allow us to check the reliability of the evidence given by a single-manuscript poem

After these preliminary remarks about the corpus and our general procedure, we can move on to a brief outline of the chapters, whose order will indicate how we intend to negotiate the 'hermeneutic circle'.

We start at the alliterative line ending. This is the juncture where two critical problems are encountered. The first is: are feminine line endings preferred or obligatory in the poems of this corpus? The second, related, question is: was final *–e* pronounced at line ending? In attempting to answer these two questions we shall adopt two complementary approaches. One of them is to examine all words that occur at line ending in a substantial poem, *B* (1140 lines), with particular attention to final *–e* in nouns and adjectives with monosyllabic stems. Having made full and open 'disclosure' of exceptions and special cases, we shall show that only nouns and adjectives with historically justified final *–e* occur at line ending. Final *–e* at line ending therefore occurs only under those conditions where it would have been operative in the prosody of such careful contemporary poets as Chaucer and Gower. We conclude from this that the *B* poet must have expected final *–e* to be pronounced at line ending. The other approach focuses on apparent 'strategies of evasion', i.e., ways

37 Internal evidence shows that the poem was composed by a poet from Cheshire (see J. A. Burrow, '*St Erkenwald*, line 1: "At London in Englond"', *Notes and Queries*, n.s. 40 (1993), 22–3) and external evidence that it was also copied there: manuscript marginalia and the companion pieces firmly connect the codex with Cheshire. See Claude Luttrell, 'Three North-West Midland Manuscripts', *Neophilologus*, 42 (1958), 38–50.

38 See A. O. Andrew, 'The Dialect of *Morte Arthure*', *Review of English Studies*, 4 (1928), 418–23, and A. I. McIntosh, 'The Textual Transmission of the Alliterative *Morte Arthure*', in *English and Medieval Studies Presented to J. R. R. Tolkien*, ed. Norman David and C. L. Wrenn (London, 1962), pp. 231–40.

in which alliterative poets avoided masculine line endings. Here we focus on the *Gawain* poems and *E*, which, of all the poems in the classical corpus, show the highest degree of resourcefulness in this regard. After considering the problem cases in these poems, we look at the evidence of some other poems and discuss a few examples of how the feminine-line-ending rule can help future editors to establish and gloss their texts.

In the second chapter we look at final *–e* within the alliterative long line. The best place to begin our inquiry is the b-verse, where metrical research has made more headway than in the a-verse. According to Cable and Duggan (and Luick before them), the rhythm of the b-verse is defined by the rule that it should have one and only one long dip. After surveying the evidence for this rule in the earliest poems, we examine the role of syllabic final *–e* in b-verse rhythms. Did alliterative poets pronounce historical *–e* within the b-verse? We focus on two specific grammatical contexts as they occur in the earliest extant poems (*B*, *C*, *G*, *P*, *G*, *SJ*, *WP*). The first is infinitives, where (as we show) inflectional *–e* was alive and well and, as far as we can tell, regularly sounded by alliterative poets. The second category comprises adverbs and adjectives in *–lych(e)* (e.g. *luflyche*); we hope to demonstrate that the *–lyche* ending was disyllabic in accordance with historical grammar and was deliberately used by alliterative poets as a metrical variant for monosyllabic *–ly*. A final section extends our findings into other alliterative poems and other syntactical contexts.

It is alliteration that connects the two halves of the long line, and in the third chapter we make the transition to the a-verse by looking into the question of the authenticity (or otherwise) of statistically abnormal patterns (e.g. *aabb* or *aaxa* patterns). In the case of multiple-manuscript poems, comparison with other manuscripts tends to suggest that such minority patterns are 'scribal'; in the case of single-manuscript poems such comparison is not available, and 'no evidence has so far been adduced that would persuade a conservative editor that adequate grounds exist for emendation'.[39] As we have already indicated, we think that single-poem manuscripts can be made to yield such evidence. The criterion of self-consistency can be applied not merely to identify statistical inconsistencies; it can in turn expose *consistencies* within these inconsistencies. As we shall show, uncommon alliterative patterns often turn out have other things in common: alliteration frequently breaks

[39] Duggan, 'Alliterative Patterning', p. 75.

down on a generic word (e.g. *man*) for which alliterative poets employed a range of synonyms; often other grounds, such as sense or sources, may render non-*aaax* patterns doubly suspect. Our case study deals with a difficult case (*MA*); we also discuss some irregular lines in other single-copy poems (*P*, *C* and *G*), lines that are likewise suspect on other grounds.

In the final two chapters we turn our attention to the a-verse. Unlike the rhythm of the b-verse, which is known to be rule-bound, the rules (if there are any) that govern the prosody of the a-verse have remained elusive. Progress on this front has been hampered by a number of uncertainties. One of these, the problem of final *–e*, will have been addressed in the second chapter; the remaining difficulty concerns the number of beats in the a-verse. The current consensus is that the a-verse can have three beats (and perhaps more). We argue that so-called extended a-verses are a myth, based on a poor understanding of how accentuation actually works. The traditional position that stress will fall on most major-category words (i.e., 'open-classed words') and not on grammatical or closed-class words (such as prepositions, pronouns, conjunctions, *etc.*) is an oversimplification: we shall show that the theory is unworkable in practice (where it would lead to three-beat b-verses and four-beat a-verses) and that it fails to correspond with the way we stress words in normal language. Whether words have 'content' or not is determined, not primarily by their lexical class, but by their relative semantic importance in the utterance, and that importance is reflected by the degree of stress they receive in pronunciation. In connected speech there are also rhythmical factors that tend to reduce the stress of a word surrounded by strongly stressed words. By analysing some so-called extended a- and b-verses with these semantic and rhythmical influences in mind, we develop an approach that avoids the complications that beset a theory of stress-assignment based on a hierarchy of word-classes.

Having argued for a two-beat a-verse (and for the functionality of final *–e*), we are able in the final chapter to specify the minimum conditions of metricality for the a-verse:

> the syllabic structure of the a-verse must be different from that of the b-verse. A-verses must contain a long dip. Normally they have a long initial *and* long medial dip; failing that, they must contain either an extra-long dip (four or more unstressed syllables) or a long or heavy final dip (a heavy dip consisting of a syllable with secondary stress).

This rule is tested against *B*, *P* and *SJ*. We shall also occasionally invoke it to explain unusual forms in the preceding chapters

In a short conclusion, we summarize our findings and pose the question of why alliterative poetry should have developed the rules that we have described.

At the end of this introduction we should like to say just a few words to students and teachers of English literature who wonder what the point is of research into such technicalities. Although we have not written the book with the purpose of answering that larger question — being content, for the most part, to study metre for metre's sake — we do believe that the analysis of metre has something meaningful to contribute to other areas of Middle English studies, particularly to editing and literary appreciation. Advances in our knowledge of the metrical practices of alliterative poets have already led to improved texts of alliterative poetry, just as surely as current misunderstandings (as we see them) have led to mistaken editorial policies and emendations. Since this book will contain many new suggestions for editors of alliterative poems, we hope that readers interested in textual problems will see the relevance of our studies.

Metre is also relevant to literary criticsm, insofar as it is concerned with the verbal art of alliterative and other poets, the measure of whose achievement lies in part in the ability to communicate within and by means of self-imposed formal constraints. Robert Frost famously said that 'Writing free verse is like playing tennis without a net'.[40] Writing alliterative poetry, to adapt Frost's saying, is like playing tennis with a net and with various other constraints besides. In the case of the classical alliterative poets, the 'net' may be thought of as the four-beat alliterative pattern (*aaax* or *aaaa*), verse play being further constrained by various other rules governing line endings and the syllabic requirements and restrictions of the a- and b-verse. To anyone coming new to the art of alliterative verse, the discovery of such rules should be as revelatory as the realisation that tennis players are deliberately hitting the ball between particular white lines. Could we really say that we had understood their skilfulness without such a realisation? Because no English alliterative

[40] Robert Frost, 'Address to Milton Academy, Milton, Massachusetts', 17 May 1935. We owe the reference to George Kane, 'Music Neither Unpleasant nor Monotonous', in *Medieval Studies for J. A. W. Bennett* (1981), repr. in his *Chaucer and Langland: Historical and Textual Approaches* (London, 1989), pp. 77–89 (n. 9).

poet ever articulated how the game should be played, and because the lines have been partially effaced in scribal transmission, the precise rules of alliterative verse have not been visible to the modern reader. The discoveries made by scholars such as Luick, Duggan and Cable, and such discoveries as we believe we have made in our own research, have certainly opened our eyes to the verbal agility of alliterative poets and that of their greatest champion, the *Gawain* poet. Perhaps others will similarly find their own appreciation of alliterative verse enhanced by the better understanding of alliterative metre to which we hope this book will contribute.

# 1. THE LINE ENDING IN ALLITERATIVE VERSE

In a seminal article on the metre of alliterative verse in 1896, Karl Luick proposed a number of rules for the alliterative long line.[1] One of these, that the b-verse should contain one and only one long dip (a dip of two or more syllables), has recently been rediscovered by Thomas Cable and by Hoyt Duggan.[2] But Luick also suggested that the line must (in most, though not all, of the unrhymed alliterative poems) end in one and only one unstressed syllable; and that proposition has proved controversial. Marie Borroff, in her study of the metre of *G*,[3] argued that the masculine line ending was a legitimate, if infrequent, variant in that poem, just as it is in *DT* (where, Luick had argued, masculine line endings had become acceptable because of the mutescence of final –*e*). But Borroff's evidence is unpersuasive, consisting merely of three examples (taken from a longer list provided by Luick himself):

> so sware and so þik (138b; the antecedent noun is singular)
> to fonge þe kny3t (816b)
> wapped a flone (1161b)

None of these examples is convincing: etymological final –*e* is present in *þik* (< OE *þicce*), which is disyllabic in Chaucer and Gower in both strong and weak flexions; *kny3t* could well represent scribal substitution of an unmarked form for a marked form like *wy3e* (such scribal subsitution is evident elsewhere in the poem);[4] and *flone* is from an OE noun (*flan*) which, although masculine, could also be feminine, and it is known that many feminine nouns developed alternative forms in –*e* in Early Middle English.[5]

[1] Luick, 'Stabreimzeile'.
[2] See Cable, *Alliterative Tradition*; Duggan, 'The Shape of the B-Verse'.
[3] Marie Borroff, *'Sir Gawain and the Green Knight': a Stylistic and Metrical Study* (New Haven, 1962), pp. 188–9.
[4] As Borroff notes (*'Sir Gawain*', p. 160), 'þe kny3t wel þat tyde' (736) is the only rhymed line where clashing stress occurs. Both the iambics and the alliteration normal to the bob-and-wheel lines indicate emendation to *wy3e* here too.
[5] See Samuel Moore, 'Earliest Morphological Changes in Middle English', *Language*, 4 (1928), 238–66, and most recently Janet Cowen and George Kane (eds), *The Legend of Good Women* (East Lansing, Mich., 1995), pp. 116–7, n. 8.

In their investigations into line endings, Hoyt Duggan and Thomas Cable arrived at different conclusions. In *The English Alliterative Tradition* (1991), Cable assumes final *–e* where it is grammatically or etymologically justified, and finds that under two percent of lines in *Cleanness* are masculine. By contrast, Duggan argues that final *–e* was no longer pronounced by alliterative poets (except by Langland) and points to the findings of historical linguists, who have concluded that in Midland dialects final *–e* ceased to be pronounced by about the middle of the fourteenth century.[6] In the light of these findings, Duggan considers it improbable that such final *–es* were still pronounced in these areas at line endings,[7] concluding that, in the corpus of poems he examines, the feminine line ending that may once have been a rule has become a mere tendency; there is 'sufficient evidence that ... a final unstressed syllable ... was no longer required by the time these poems were composed'. The following words, which appear at line ending, are cited in support of that claim:

> *lord(e), D* 38, *MA* 3798, *WA* 848, *etc.*; *queen, B* 194, *WA* 238, 525, etc.; *stronde, B* 140; *astate, WA* 723; *wame* < OE *wamb, WA* 538; *ost(e), WA* 2153; *tole WA* 3373; *might A* 169; *Cryste, MA* 257, 320, etc.; *birthe, WA* 2522; *none, C* 262; *mynd WA* 269; *stour DT* 5758.[8]

[6] See e.g. Karl Brunner, *An Outline of Middle English Grammar,* trans. G. K. W. Johnston (Oxford, 1963), p. 32, and Tauno F. Mustanoja, *A Middle English Syntax* (Helsinki, 1960), pp. 95, 314. A survey of the literature on final *–e* can be found in Donka Minkova, *The History of Final Vowels in English: the Sound of Muting* (Berlin, 1991), pp. 15–34.

[7] This is a simplification of a position to which Duggan admits some exceptions, particularly weak and plural adjectives whose stem is monosyllabic: see his 'Final *–e*'. He thinks that Langland did voice final *–e*, but that in this and other matters he was 'a good deal more conservative ... than ... any of the other alliterative poets': 'Langland's Dialect and Final *–e*', *Studies in the Age of Chaucer*, 12 (1990), 157–91 (191). In 'Some Aspects of A-Verse Rhythms in Middle English Alliterative Poetry', in *Speaking Images: Essays in Honor of V. A. Kolve,* ed. R. F. Yeager and Charlotte Morse (Asheville, NC, 2001), pp. 479–503, Duggan states that there is some evidence that alliterative poets 'occasionally made use of ... inflectional and etymological *–e*'s on stressed stems for metrical convenience' (485), but does not seem to have abandoned the basic position he took up in his article on 'Final *–e*'.

[8] Duggan, 'Final *–e*', p. 140, n. 51.

Duggan's position has been accepted by Ralph Hanna and David Lawton, who consider Duggan's view on final *–e* to be superior to Cable's (given the 'probable loss of [final] *–e* in the spoken dialects one might associate with alliterative poets from early in the fourteenth century'[9]), and who edit the *Siege* without any special regard for the line ending, presumably because, like Duggan, they do not believe it was metrically constrained.

However, a closer look at Duggan's wordlist shows the slipperiness of the problem. Firstly, research cannot proceed on the assumption that final *–e* can be justified only by etymology or grammar. As we have already remarked, many words (especially feminine nouns) acquired final *–e* in Early Middle English by a process of analogy; Duggan inadvertently includes such words amongst his counter-examples: *queen* and *wame* ('womb') were feminine nouns in OE, as (usually) was *mynd*: all acquired analogical final *–e* in EME and can be disyllabic in Chaucer's verse. *Might* is also a feminine noun with unetymological *–e* in EME,[10] though it is monosyllabic in Chaucer's verse; *birthe* (of uncertain origin) is always disyllabic in Chaucer, as also is the neuter noun *stronde.* There is also the fact that some words can be referred to more than one etymon. Thus *estate* had two distinct forms in Old French, one with, and one without, final *–e*,[11] which therefore cannot be regarded as inorganic in *astate* (*WA* 723) or in *state* (*C* 1708), as it is assumed to be by both Duggan and Cable.[12] *None* can be used substantivally ('nothing') or as a singular pronoun 'no one', with unjustified final *–e* (< OE *nān*), but it is clearly a plural pronoun with grammatical *–e* (< OE *nāna*) at *C* 262 ('Forþy so semly to see syþen wern none), as the plural verb shows. *Lorde* has the conservative disyllabic forms *louerd*, Northern *lauerd* (< OE *hlaford*), and Cable accordingly argues that *lorde* may be 'read as disyllabic'. This may be hard to believe without manuscript evidence, so it is worth pointing out that *louerd* is sporadically found in the corpus of alliterative verse, and that it appears precisely at line ending, where the unstressed syllable

[9] Hanna and Lawton (eds), *Siege*, p. xciv.

[10] On disyllabic *mihte,* see Minkova, *History of Final Vowels*, p. 60, and cf. *Ormulum*, ed. Robert Holt, 2 vols (Oxford, 1878), where both *mahhte/mihhte* and *mahht/mihht* occur.

[11] See A. Tobler and E. Lommatzsch, *Altfranzösisches Wörterbuch* (Berlin, 1915–), s.v. *estat* and *estate.*

[12] See Cable, *Alliterative Tradition*, p. 168, n. 7.

appears to be metrically required.[13] Finally, caution and discrimination are required in the extrapolation from a single text to the larger corpus (which may have been composed by poets from different generations and different dialect areas), especially with regard to linguistic factors subject to recession, as final *–e* most certainly was. For instance, according to Luick, the poet of *DT* no longer avoided masculine endings because inflectional *–e* had lost its value to the poet as well as the scribe.[14] Given *DT*'s northerliness (Lancashire)[15] and lateness (the most recent dating by Hanna and Lawton puts it 'at the earliest, toward 1400'),[16] this would not be surprising. If *DT* were indeed atypical, masculine endings in that poem (e.g. *stour DT* 5758) cannot be used as evidence of their authenticity in the corpus as a whole.

Anyone trying to decide what to believe about line endings also faces the problem that the evidence so far adduced has been patchy. Cable treats only *C* thoroughly, and provides no evidence to substantiate his claim that his findings 'can be generalized to the ends of lines in other poems, including *Sir Gawain and the Green Knight*, *Piers Plowman*,[17] *Morte Arthure*, *The Parlement of the Thre Ages*, *William of Palerne*, *Alexander A*, and

[13] See *MA* 3918 and *SJ* 185 (MS P).

[14] Luick's opinion is based on the spelling of adjectives such as 'lief' – which would normally vary, acording to grammar, between forms with intervocalic /v/ and word-final /f/ (i.e. *lef* / *leue*). These adjectives are consistently spelt with <f> in the manuscript, suggesting that /f/ was authorial, and hence that inflectional *–e* had been lost, at least in adjectives. See Luick, 'Stabreimzeile', 406–8, 414. His point can be extended to include nouns such as *life*, which, as far as we can tell, was not used by the poet in the form *liue* (excepting adverbial *beliue* and of course plural *liues*).

[15] This is where J. P Oakden located the dialect in his *Alliterative Poetry*. He was proved right by Thorlac Turville-Petre's discovery of the author's name ('John Clerk of Whalley') in an acrostic. See Turville-Petre, 'The Author of *The Destruction of Troy*', *Medium Aevum*, 57 (1988), 264–9.

[16] Hanna and Lawton (eds), *Siege*, p. xxxvii.

[17] Some interesting preliminary research on Langland's line endings has been carried out by Stephen Barney, who produces facts and figures that provide 'strong support for Cable's Theory'. See 'Langland's Prosody: the State of Study', in *The Endless Knot: Essays on Old and Middle English in Honor of Marie Borroff*, ed. M. Teresa Tavormina and R. F. Yeager (Cambridge, 1995), pp. 65–85 (p. 85). A. V. C. Schmidt, in his edition of the B-Text (*The Vision of Piers Plowman* (1978, rev. London, 1995)), emends 'in order to provide the feminine ending habitual at the end of the line' (p. lxxx).

*The Wars of Alexander*'.[18] Duggan lists some examples of masculine line endings, but, as we have seen, these are far from unproblematic: many may end in authentic *–e*. But the question of whether even authentic *–e*s should be sounded is itself a contentious one. Their presence or absence in manuscript spelling is of limited use in resolving the question, partly because of the vagaries of scribal transmission and partly because final *–e* was routinely written for reasons that had nothing to do with its phonetic value, and *–e* may or may not be represented in a final flourish at word- or line-ending. Moreover, arguing for the value of final *–e* on metrical grounds risks begging the question. As Marie Borroff points out:

> In attempting to argue one way or the other about lines in which the feminine ending would be constituted by the sounding of final *–e*, one is all too likely to find oneself going in a circle. The poet sounded *–e* at the end of the line because he preferred the feminine ending; the poet must have preferred the feminine ending because he almost always uses words ending on *–e* at the end of the line.[19]

In this chapter, we provide a systematic account of line endings, using two complementary approaches which we believe will avoid the danger of such circular arguments. We examine all lines in *B* where the presence or absence of final *–e* at line ending would make the difference between feminine or masculine ending and we consider whether the particular *–e*s in question would be historically justified (by etymology, syntax or analogy). If, for instance, it can be shown that at line ending the poet used nouns with historically justifiable *–e* (e.g. *herte, grace*), but not nouns where final *–e* would be unhistoric (e.g. *bok, king*[20]), then it seems likely that the poet chose his words deliberately to produce a feminine line ending. We then consider whether there are observable strategies for avoiding masculine line endings in *C*, *P*, *G* and *E*, by examining the distribution of 'minimum metrical pairs' (words or forms identical in sense but differing in syllable count). For the most part, the collection of such data requires no prior assumptions about the value of final *–e*. In the final section we briefly survey other major alliterative poems, focusing on the small number of problem cases and exceptions.

[18] Cable, *Alliterative Tradition*, p. 68.

[19] Borroff, '*Sir Gawain*', p. 188.

[20] In nominative and accusative cases. After prepositions, inflectional *–e* for dative case will need to be considered.

## Line Endings in *Alexander and Dindimus* (1139 lines)

Although this poem (often referred to as *Alexander B*) has been neglected in studies of alliterative poetry, its unique textual history gives it a special value with regard to metrical research. The poem was copied *c* 1400 into an illuminated *de luxe* manuscript containing a French Alexander romance,[21] apparently in order to remedy what was mistakenly believed to be a lacuna in the French. The language of composition is usually localised to Gloucestershire. Discrimination between scribal and authorial usage is assisted by the fact that the scribe also wrote a short rubric showing South East Midland features,[22] which is consistent with the probability that the illuminations were the product of a London workshop.[23] There is no evidence of a lengthy chain of scribal transmission, and the text as it appears in the two published editions (by Skeat and Magoun) contains little obvious corruption. We also know the poet's source: the *Historia de preliis* by Archpresbyter Leo. The Middle English poem can most usefully be checked against the J[2] recension of the *Historia*.[24] *B* was not studied by Cable, but Duggan included it in the corpus on which his conclusions about alliterative metre and final *–e* rest. If those conclusions were correct, we should expect to find no compelling evidence for either the sounding of final *–e* or the exclusion of masculine endings. But that, as we shall see, is not what we do find.

We begin with some straightforward categories of words that occur at line ending in this poem. In the first place, we find there numerous plurals that turn monosyllabic nouns into disyllables, as well as nouns that are disyllabic in the singular *and* in the plural due to syncope:[25] e.g. *cauys*, 7; *somerus*, 8; *lettres*, 20; *children*, 53; *daies*, 76; *kinguus*, 82; *þoughtus*, 95; etc. These need no further discussion, since the feminine line ending is uncontroversial in such cases. Also unproblematic are disyllabic words with

[21] On the manuscript, see Kathleen L. Scott, *Later Gothic Manuscripts 1390–1490*, 2 vols (London, 1996), II, pp. 68–73.

[22] Skeat (ed.), *Alexander*, pp. xxv–xxvi.

[23] See Scott, *Later Gothic Manuscripts*, n. 14.

[24] See the discussion by Magoun (ed.), *Gests*, pp. 76–77. Magoun provides a Latin text at the foot of the Middle English text.

[25] Syncope will normally affect words with two consecutive unstressed syllables: in later Middle English, one of the two weak vowels was normally lost (see Karl Luick, *Historische Grammatik der englischen Sprache* (Leipzig, 1921–9), 3 vols, I, pp. 534–6). This rule affects the syllable count of words such as *keuered*, 351, *deuelus*, 608, *punched* (= punished), 679, *etc.*, which regularly occur at line ending.

accent on the root syllable (e.g. *þedirre*, 2; *manie*, 26; *drihten*, 88; *oþur*, 103; *gena* (= Ganges) 141; *iuli* (= July) 154;[26] *aftur*, 167), where the feminine line ending is also beyond doubt. Interestingly, words ending in two unstressed syllables, or words with secondary stress at line ending such as compounds, or words ending in a suffix (e.g. *–ly*, *–les*, *–ship)*, do not occur at line ending. This appears to be the case for all the major alliterative poems,[27] with the exception of *Piers Plowman* and *Destruction of Troy*.[28]

Verbs also end in an unstressed syllable. This is uncontroversial for present tense verbs with 2nd sg. inflection in *–est*, 3rd sg. in *–eþ* and *–es*, indicative and subjunctive plurals in *–en*, and pret. and p.p. in *–ed*, e.g. *called*, 11, *wreten*, 24, *heren*, 27, *graunted*, 73, *knowist*, 77, *stinteþ*, 91, *arereþ*, 92, *folweþ*, 155, *vsen*, 202, *writes*, 253, *hihten*, 418, *tellen*, 902.

As far as words with possible final *–e* are concerned, we propose to adopt the following procedure. We will examine all words at line ending to determine whether the use of final *–e* on those particular words would be historically justified. These words will be considered under the relevant grammatical categories; lists introduced by 'e.g.' introduce a sample; otherwise the lists are intended to be comprehensive, items occurring more than once being indicated by a plus sign. Justification of *–e* will be determined mainly with reference to historical grammatical inflexions, etymological derivation and history of the word in EME, in which, as we have already mentioned, final *–e* was added to a number of words (mostly feminine nouns) by a process of analogy, and for which a good source of evidence is the *Ormulum* (whose special and consistent spelling system and distinct and regular metre, the septenary, give a clear indicatation about the status of *–e*). Another good source of evidence is Chaucerian usage, which has been well documented by scholars such as Bernhard ten Brink, Ruth McJimsey, E. T. Donaldson, Stephen Barney, Janet Cowen and George Kane.

[26] The pronunciation with stress on the final syllable is modern (see headnote in *OED* s.v July).

[27] For example, in *E* all paroxytonic words at line ending terminate in an unstressed vowel, inflection, or schwa + consonant. The single exception is *bishop*, which had presumably developed the modern pronunciation.

[28] On the line endings of *PP*, see Hoyt Duggan, 'Notes on the Metre of *Piers Plowman: Twenty Years On*', forthcoming in *The Metres of Alliterative Verse*, ed. Judith Jefferson and Ad Putter, Leeds Studies in English (2008), and on *Destruction of Troy*, see below, pp. 69–70.

Our approach differs from that of Cable in a number of ways. In the first place, Cable reconstructs his 'phonology of final *–e*' on historical principles without regard to manuscript spellings. So he argues that *–ly* (< ON *liga*, OE *lice*) is always disyllabic in *C*, even though it *never* appears with final *–e* in the MS. Because Cable sees no obstacle to his theory in MS spellings, he also sees no reason to emend them; in his phrase, MS forms 'cover' any *–e* that should be present in accordance with the underlying rules. This approach seems to us problematic. That a poet would normally encode metrical distinctions in his own orthography is apparent from the holograph poems that we possess (Hoccleve being a case in point), and some of these orthographic-metrical distinctions are likely to survive the process of scribal transmission. We therefore do attach some significance to MS spellings, not of course to the point of trusting them to be an always secure guide to the prosody but certainly to the point of assuming that, but for scribal corruption, they might have been. Hence, in the list of words below, any final *–e*s that are historically justified but not reflected in the MS spelling are signalled as conjectural emendations by enclosure in square brackets. In the second place, we make provision for a category of dative nouns. Cable makes allowances for final *–e* only in petrified datives (e.g. *on grounde*), but Barney's work on *Piers Plowman* suggests that the net needs to be cast wider: nouns following prepositions are 'a business that needs study' (85). In the sections below we provide such a study.

*I: Verbs*

(1) 1st singular present verbs: e.g. *graunte*, 68, *haue*, 84, *warne*, 205

(2) 1st and 3rd singular pret. of weak verbs: e.g. *hadde*, 1, *wiste*, 14, *saide*, 64. We include here verbs that were strong in OE but developed weak formations in ME: e.g. *dradde*, 192, *radde*, 819

(3) present and pret. plurals: e.g. *warne*, 30, *hadde*, 41, *ferde*, 54, *haue*, 72

(4) subjunctives: e.g. *were*, 318, *founde*, 337, *conne*, 571

(5) infinitives: e.g. *sende*, 18, *haue*, 25, *fare*, 28

(6) strong past participles: e.g. *helde*, 5, *founde*, 32

In all these instances, final *–e* is both historically justified and a regular feature in Chaucerian metrical usage. We may note that there are only two cases in which such inflectional *–e*s are not represented in the orthography of the manuscript: *shew[e]* (inf.), 572, *red[e]* (inf.), 971.

There is also one instance of a strong 2nd sg. pret. at line ending: 'as þou þeiself *badé*' (511). Final *–e* is historically justified in this grammatical category and still optional (though not invariable) in Chaucerian usage: e.g. mid-line *bigonne*, *CT* VIII.442; mid-line *fownde*, T&C 3.362.[29]

Verb forms without historical *–e* do not appear to be used at line ending. Conspicuous by their absence are present sg. forms of the preterite-present verbs *can*, *may*, *shall*, *mot*. These verbs occur at line ending only in the plural (e.g. *schulle*, 1106, *mowe*, 290, 619), where final *–e* is historically justified, but not in the singular, where *–e* is not justified. Also absent at line endings are present and preterite indicative sg. and pl. forms of the irregular verbs 'to do' (pres. pl. *do* and *don*; pret. *dide*), 'to go' (pres. pl. *go* and *gon*; pret. *wente*) and 'to be' (pres. plural *ben*, *arn*, *ar*), except for plural preterite *were* (412). The present plural form of the verb 'have' used at line end is invariably *hauen* (543, 951, 953) or *haue* (72, 344, 1008), even though the form *han* is quite cleary the unmarked form (it is used twenty-three times in auxiliary and non-auxiliary usages, but never at line end).[30]

Strong verbs do occur at line ending in the past tense plural (*sie* 'saw', 126; *knewe*, 397), and in these cases *–e* is grammatical. But 1st and 3rd sg. pret. of strong verbs do not, with one exception:

> For eueri grene growe tre þat on þe ground *spronge*
> Hadde bremliche a brid þe braunchus alofte. (133–4)

[29] It appears that in Chaucer final *–e* in 2nd ps. sg. pret. was possible only in a small class of strong verbs (Bernhard ten Brink, *The Language and Metre of Chaucer*, rev. F. Kluge, trans. M. B. Smith (London, 1901), p. 110). In Gower, there is no such restriction. See G. C. Macaulay (ed.), *John Gower's English Works*, *John Gower's English Works*, 2 vols, EETS ES 81–82 (London, 1900–01), I, xcv.

[30] The hypothesis that *haue* and *hauen* are prompted by metrical constraints is confirmed by the use of these forms within the line. *Hauen* occurs only once mid-line, where the final *–n* is needed to protect the inflectional syllable (which contributes to the required long dip in the b-verse) against elision: '& þat we happili her hauen of kynde' (35). *Haue* occurs more frequently mid-line (7 x), but not usually without cause: it is an alliterative stave in lines 62, 299; at 189 (subj.), 314 and 353 a-verse metre requires a disyllable by our rules (see ch. 5). The only anomalous cases are 281 and 346 (contrast 434, 742), both containing an uncontracted negation that may well be scribal (see below, p. 228, 230–31). If the poet intended contracted negations, disyllabic *haue* would also be metrically required at 281 and 346.

It is relevant to note, however, that where *every* has the distributive sense of 'all', it is occasionally found with a plural verb (see OED s.v. *every* adj. I.1.a, headnote).[31] Note, for example, *WP* 5412–3:

> At emperour and emperice euereche on at ones
> Loveli *lauȝten* here leue to here lond to wend.

It is therefore possible that *spronge* at 133 should be understood as a plural verb.[32]

There is only one other anomalous verb form, and that is the weak p.p. *by-taughte*:

> For-þi boþe for hur bost ben y-brend nouþe,
> Wiþ fir in þe fir-hil to fendus by-tauhte. (1068–9)

Although final *–e* is historically justified, the past participle was, according to standard grammars, 'rarely inflected even in early ME'.[33] But, as noted by Ten Brink, §234, the inflected p.p. did in fact on occasion constitute a metrical recourse:

> Bitwixe hem thre, syn they been thus *ymette* (*CT*.2.1115; rhyming with inf. *lette* [delay] and past plural *sette*)[34]

> Thilke that *unbrende* were (*House of Fame*, 173)

> ... As the briddes to the flihte
> Ben *made* so the man is bore (*Confessio Amantis* IV, 2343)[35]

What these instances have in common with *B* 1069 is that the p.p. is construed with the verb *to be*, and thus analysable as a plural adjective.[36]

[31] For further examples specific to alliterative verse see Herbert Koziol, *Grundzüge der Syntax der Mittelenglischen Stabreimdichtungen* (Vienna, 1932), 164–5.
[32] Luick suggests a subjunctive ('Stabreimzeile', p. 564).
[33] Joseph Wright and Elizabeth Mary Wright, *An Elementary Middle English Grammar*, 2nd edn. (Oxford, 1967), p. 177.
[34] Cf. *Ladd y the daunce a Myssomur day* (c1400?), ed. Thomas G. Duncan, *Late Medieval English Lyrics and Carols, 1400–1530* (London, 2000), no. 110, l. 33: 'whan we were *mette*' (rhyming with 3rd sg. pret. *by-hette* and *sette*).
[35] Citations from Gower ate taken from *John Gower's English Works*, ed. G. C. Macaulay, 2 vols, EETS ES 81–82 (London, 1900–01).
[36] A plural inflection could also explain p.p. *sett* at line ending in *A* 708 and *WW* 335, but the verb *set* developed an alternative p.p. *sete*, either by confusion with the verb 'sit' or (as Macaulay suggests) by analogy with *gete*. See Macaulay (ed.), *English Works*, p. cxix.

*II: Adjectives, Adverbs and Prepositions*

The following adjectives and adverbs are used at line ending:

(1) (a) Weak adjectives, e.g. 'europ þe grete', 518; 'Minerua þe falce', 653. Line 474b ('on þe loft heie') would be problematic if interpreted (with Skeat) as an adjective rather than as an adverb, since an adjective not immediately preceded by the definite article does not normally take the weak form; but the adverb is also possible ('far up in the heavens').

(b) Plural adjectives: e.g. *wise*, 2, *alle*, 44, *snelle*, 437, *i-like*, 792. *Bare*, 33, may also belong here, but Chaucerian usage suggests that *bare* acquired final –*e* in EME.

(2) Strong adjectives with etymological final –*e*: *quainte*, 12 (pl.), *sterne,* 52+, *clene* 496, *þikke*, 500, *huge* (sg.), 530, *kene*, 536 (sg.), *i-sene*, 666 (sg.),[37] *noble,* 697+, *one* 'alone', 698 (sg.), *more* 'bigger', 704 (sg.), *werse*, 737 (sg.), *riche*, 744 (sg.)+, *unbliþe,* 929, *riue*, 935, *schene*, 1027+, *newe*, 1074.

(3) Adverbs and prepositions with historical final –*e*: *inne*, 10+, *sone*, 19+, *wiþ-inne*, 38+, *longe*, 78, *romme* (< OE *rūme*), 80, *iliche*, 102, *aboute*, 122+, *alofte*, 134+[38], *raþe*, 136, *alone*, 169+, *þerinne*, 164+, *þanne*, 175, *ʒorne*, 179, *ofte*, 199+, *more*, 289+, *wiþoute*, 340, *biside*, 341, *rede*, 479,[39] *alse*, 549+, *aliue*, 557, *stille*, 574, *nede*, 859, *foule*, 1065, *clene*, 1099. *Vppe* (< OE *up* and *uppan*), 861, is never disyllabic in Chaucer, but Orm similarly alternates between *upp* (monosyllabic) and *uppe* (disyllabic), depending on metrical requirements;[40] and the manuscript spelling in *B* confirms the disyllabic form as a metrical option: 'up' in *B* is always spelt *vp*, except at 861, where it appears at line ending. The pattern of distribution should be compared with that of *in/inne* (OE *in/innan*), which is equally striking: there are over 200 instances

[37] 'For þere þe miht of man most is *isene*'. Adjectival. *isene* < OE *gesene* occurs after the verb *to be* and is distinct from the past participle *iseie.* Chaucer makes the same distinction. See Ten Brink, *Language*, p. 115.

[38] The grammatical distinction between ON *a lopt* (motion) and *a lopti* (position) was lost in ME; in Chaucer's usage *alofte* and *o-lofte* invariably have final –*e*, regardless of sense.

[39] Skeat glosses this as a plural adjective ('þe sonne ... & þe seue sterres ... [shining] rede'); but at 121 — 'As raþe as pe sonne ros & reed gan schine' — the b-verse requires a long dip and hence the adverb (read *rede*).

[40] See the glossary to *Ormulum*, ed. Holt, s.v. *uppe*.

of *in* initially and medially (always spelt *in*), but at line ending (4x) the form is invariably *inne* (10, 435, 489, 597).[41] The adverb *nouþe* with historical final *–e* (< OE *nū þa*) likewise occurs exclusively at line ending (71, 239, 583, 651 (spelt *nowþe*), 1007, 1068); mid-line the word *now* is used (e.g. 12, 34, 67).

(4) Adverbs and prepositions with unetymological final *–e*: *þere*, *þare*, 250+, *tille*, 166+, *here*, 384+, *ille*, 786, *lite*, 886. That a number of these words acquired final *–e* in EME is evident from Chaucerian usage, where *ille* (adj. and adv.), *alofte*, and *lyte* are regularly pronounced with final *–e*, while final *–e* in *here* and *there* is optional .[42] *Tille* ('to' in postposition) is northern and does not occur in Chaucer. Skeat dismisses the form as 'badly spelt' in his glossary, but the evidence suggests that it is a disyllabic variant of *til*: in *B* the form *tille* is only ever found at line ending (166, 590, 802, 1041), while *til* and *tyl* (the unmarked forms) occur elsewhere (48, 148, 314, etc.).

At line 93 an emendation is required. The context is as follows:

> Men seþ wel þat þe see     seseþ and stinteþ,
> But whan ['except when'] þe wind on þe watur     þe wawus arereþ.
> So wolde .i. reste me raþe ['at once']     and ride *ferþe*,
> Neuere to gete more good     n[e] no gome derie, [MS and Skeat *no*]
> Bute as þe heie heuene godus     wiþ herteli þouhtus
> So a-wecchen my wit     and my wil chaungen,
> Þat i mai stinte no stounde     stille in o place ... (91–7)

Skeat and Magoun gloss *ferþe* as 'forth' and retain the MS reading, but this seems unlikely for several reasons. Firstly, the adverb is otherwise always spelt *forþ* and *forth* in the MS. Secondly, the sense of these lines must be that, just as the sea is still except when the winds strike it, so Alexander would stay still if it were not for the fact that the gods make him restless. Thirdly, the metre of 93b is defective (the long dip is missing). The line should obviously be emended to: *and ride [no] ferþ[er]*.

[41] The pattern does not obtain when *–in* is preceded by prefixes such as *wiþ–* and *þer–*, which always attract the emphatic form (as in OE).

[42] See Ten Brink, *Language*, pp. 155 (on *ille*, *lyte*) and 174 (on variously monosyllabic and disyllabic *here* and *there*).

*III: Nouns*

The nouns that occur at line ending in *Alexander* belong to three categories: (1) nouns which historically ended in a vowel[43] or in a syllable reducible to a vowel; (2) nouns which acquired final *–e* in EME (unless otherwise indicated, these nouns are also variably or invariably disyllabic in Chaucerian usage); (3) nouns with inflectional *–e*, i.e. datives.

(1) nouns with etymological final *–e*: *peple*, 4+, *wede*, 6, *wise*, 12+, *prynce* (also *prince*), 16+, *kynde*, 35, *erþe*, 39, *sawe*, 42, *fare*, 48+, *speche*, 65+, *tale*, 66, *ende*, 75+, *side*, 86, *trouþe*, 81+, *chere*, 83+, *place*, 97+, *molde*, 101+, *hiȝþe*, 123, *name*, 139+, *Inde*, 142, *tyme*, 145+, *haste*, 168+, *wille*, 170+, [*ioie*], 197+,[44] *praie*, 204, *ensaumple*, 233+, *herte*, 272+, *werre*, 282+, *enuie*, 283+,[45] *faute*, 303, *tente*, (< OF *atente*) 305+, *age*, 331+, *hete*, 328, *fode*, 354+, *tonge*, 358+, *paine*, 390+, *spouce* 393, *face*, 408, *sonne*, 424+, *scole*, 453+, *iangle*, 458, *gile*, 464+, *bourde*, 469, *purþe*, 482, *strenke*, 532+, *oxe*, 612, *regne*, 642, *pride*, 637+, *wraþþe*, 662, *grace*, 673+, *welþe*, 700+,[46] *temple*, 714+, *oule*, 723, *wreche*, 772, *tene*, 873+, *ere*, 948, *elde*, 943, *swete*, 952, *skaþe*, 990, *ese*, 1010, *glose*, 1016, *yle*, 1088, *byleue*, 1113, *marbre*, 1134.

(2) nouns with analogical final *–e* in ME: *sonde*, 21+, *nede*, 62+, *ȝifte*, 69, *miȝhte*, 85+,[47] *stronde*, 140, *monþe*, 153,[48] *quene*, 194+, *while*, 270+, *slyhþe*, 301+, *wombe*, 317+, *soule*, 329+, *blisse*, 330+, *while*, 336+, *sinne*, 386+, *dede*, 400+,

[43] We include under this heading nouns that had double forms in the parent language, with and without a final syllabic vowel, such as *trouþe* (< OE *treowđ*, *treowđe*) and *speche* (< OE *spræc*, *spræce*).
[44] This obvious emendation (suggested by Skeat in his glossary) for MS *gon* is also adopted by Magoun (ed.), *Gests*.
[45] Here and in 373 b-verse metre indicates stress on the second syllable.
[46] The word occurs only once in Chaucer, in eliding position, but voiced final *–e* is probable, since the word is formed by analogy with *helþe,* regularly disyllabic in Chaucer and Gower, who repeatedly rhymes *helþe* with *welþe*. Cf. also *PP* A 1.53b, 'ȝoure welþe to kepe', where b-verse metre requires disyllabic pronunciation (*Piers Plowman: the A Version*, ed. George Kane (London, 1960)).
[47] Monosyllabic in Chaucer, but with analogical *–e* in EME (see p. 21 above). Since in *B* the word at line ending is always preceded by a preposition (*of mi(ȝ)hte*, 85, 1004), the final *–e* may be a dative inflection.
[48] The word is always followed by a vowel in Chaucer, where its syllable count is thus unknowable, but it is regularly disyllabic in Gower (see e.g. *Confessio Amantis*, 4.776, 4.781). The variant form 'monyth' (< OE *monađ*) is found in the Cotton Nero poems, where it is evidently disyllabic; see *Cleanness* 493b, 'monyth þe fyrst', and 1030b, 'broþely a monyth'. Since the word occurs only once in *B*, it is difficult to be be sure what the poet's form was.

*mirthe*, 465, *ore*, 525, *heste*, 528, *sorwe*, 624, *minde*, 756, *bone*, 764, *stalþe*, 788, *drynke*, 791, *mede*, 869, *warde*, 1035.

(3) prepositional phrases in which nouns with inflectional *–e* occur: *of witte*, 23+, *to gronde*, 119 (Ch), *of (þe) lande*, 172+ (Ch), *in (þe) ȝere*, 203+ (Ch), *wiþoute long dwelle*, 275,[49] *to harme*, 365+ (Ch), *to goode*, 366+(Ch), *in oure lande*, 381, *by rihte*, 416, *in(to) þis worde* (= world), 430+, *in hure liue*, 551 (Ch), *to a litil wordle* [*sic*], 645, *of iubiterus hede*, 656, *of þe breste*, 665, *in wante*, 867, *of mouþe*, 947 (Ch),[50] *by day[e]*, 995.

A number of these datives (followed by 'Ch' in parentheses) are petrified ones that are also used with inflectional *–e* in similar constructions by Chaucer and Gower. Others seem to attest to a more extensive use of dative *–e*. And although Chaucer provides no parallels for these, we are certain that dative *–e* continued to be used extensively by alliterative poets. As Barney has noted, in *PP*, too, words without etymological *–e* 'occur at line ending mostly or only as objects of prepositions'.[51] In *Gawain*, rhyme evidence confirms the poet's use of dative forms. For instance, the word 'staff' (spelt *staf* at *G* 214) appears as inflected dative at *G* 2137 (*with staue*, rhyming with *saue*); the noun 'knife' (spelt *knyf* at 1331) must be inflected at 2042 ('withoute dabate of bronde hym to were / oþer knyffe'), because the rhymes (with *bilyue* and *ryue* adv.) indicate that the poet wrote *knyue*. The careful spelling in the MS of *B* provides further evidence of dative use. For example, *lond* and *land* are always spelt without *–e*, except at line ending, where they are always preceded by a preposition, with one similar instance at the end of the a-verse (665a: 'He is alosed in lande'). *Harme* occurs with written final *–e* only at line ending (365, 771), with preposition, and is otherwise spelt *harm* (40, 46, etc.), with one exception, again a dative: 'to harme hit ȝou turnus' (765b). Mid-line *hed* (408) and *mouþ* (951) similarly alternate with line-ending *of hede* (656) and *of mouþe* (947), as do mid-line *riht/ryht* (82, 507, 593, 789, 907,

[49] The word (a ME formation from the verb *dwellen*) is not well-attested; forms with final *–e* seem to be restricted to the phrase 'without delay'. *MED* cites various examples, including *SLeg.Inf.Chr* (Ld) 1079: 'He with oute duelle / Þis dede gan wide telle'.

[50] Ruth McJimsey, *Chaucer's Irregular –E* (New York, 1942), would explain final *-e* in *mouthe* as due to OE *muđa* [river mouth, estuary], a variant of *muđ* [mouth]; but this seems an unnecessary hypothesis, in view of the fact that disyllabic 'mouth' is found only after prepositions in Chaucer (*HF* 2.250, 3.589, 3.595, 3.986) and in Gower (*CA* 1.1642, 1.2433, 1.3187, 2.485, 3.484, 3.925, 4.40).

[51] Barney, 'Langland's Prosody', p. 84, n. 40.

916) with line ending *by rihte* (416) and *of rihte* (909). 'Wit' is always spelt *wit* (96, 211, 534, 573, 924, 930, 946, 1002), except at line ending, where, again, it is always preceded by a preposition (23, 260, 905, 966). 'World' is normally spelt without final *–e* (23x), the ten spellings with final *–e* being, with a single exception (105), datives used mid line (359, 548) or at line ending (430, 645, 779, 877, 983, 993). Exept in the case of *by day* (995), the dative *–e* is always present in the MS spelling.

A couple of cases (*(a)* and *(b)*) merit special attention:

*(a)* and tel me *þe soþe* (207b)

Luick believed that *soþ* (< OE neuter n. *soð*) developed final *–e* (by analogy with feminine nouns in *–þe*),[52] but this explanation misses a metrical finesse. In the major alliterative poems, *soþ* occurs at line ending only:

i) in the petrified dative *for soþe* (not attested in *B*);
ii) when it is preceded by the definite article (*þe soþe*),[53] in which context it is treated as an adjective (used substantivally) and so appears in the weak form normal to adjectives following the definite article.

In these two contexts *sothe* is also disyllabic in Chaucer, where it is otherwise monosyllabic. Compare *T&C* 1.12, 'For wel sit it, the *sothe* for to seyne', with *T&C* 4.1407, 'And for o *soth* they tellen twenty lyes'.[54]

[52] Luick, 'Stabreimzeile', §53.

[53] For examples of *for soþe,* see *P* 212, *G* (at end of alliterative long line and bob-and-wheel) 820, 2359, *MA* 1087, 1097, 2631, 2638, 3030, 3364, 3369, 3422, *P3A* 107, 159. For examples of *þe soþe,* see *WW* 257, *A* 401, *MA* 2593, 2637, 3329, 3287, 3556, 3867, *G* 355, 1786, *P3A* 166, 250, 307, 412.

[54] The spelling with and without *–e* is consistent in the manuscripts. *T&C* 4.1303 as printed in *The Riverside Chaucer*, 'The *soth* is this, that twinning of us tweyne', may give the impression that Chaucer's spelling was haphazard, but it is entirely possible that Chaucer wrote the noun with final *–e* (naturally elided before vowel), as did most of his scribes (Cl soþe; Cp soth; Gg soþe; J soth; H[1] sothe; H[3] sothe). The only clear exception of monosyllabic *soth* after the definite article seems to be *BD* 520, 'I herde the not, to seyn the soth'. The rhyme, with 'wroth' (strong adj.) indicates monosyllabic *soth*, even as the definite article suggests final *–e* (duly reflected in the spelling of the witnesses, which read *sothe*). It is worth considering the possibility that 'the', in *to seyn the soth*, represents the personal pronoun rather than the article (cf. *BD* 513–4).

This distinction between *soþ* and *soþe* is accurately reflected in *B*'s spelling. The word is spelt *soþ* on all occasions (27, 44, 206, 209, 386, 451, 459, 552, 840, 902) except the only (above-quoted) one on which it is preceded by the definite article, where it appears as *soþe.*

*(b)* We no spende no speche but what we speke weele
We ne sain but soþ & sesen by time. (367–8; repunctuated).

Skeat's explanation of *weele* ('apparently an error for *wel*') is dubious. The form *wele* occurs in the poem for the plural subjunctive of 'will': 'Now liþus, ȝe þat listene *wele,* þe lettrus to þe ende' (820); and this makes good sense in 367: 'We do not waste words, but whenever we wish to speak we say nothing apart from the truth and stop speaking in good time'. The Latin source is closer to our interpretation of these lines: 'Non loquimur multum, sed cum locuti fuerimus non dicimus nisi ueritatem et statim tacemus' ('We do not speak much but when we have spoken we have said nothing but the truth and then are silent at once').[55]

*IV: Pronouns*

Personal pronouns are only infrequently found at line ending. The only instances are *ȝoure* (271), *oure* (273), *þe* (342) and *ȝou-siluen* (795). All these produce regular feminine line endings. At 271 and 273 the pronouns are used predicatively and absolutely with plural antecedents ('For oure lif and oure lawe vnlich is to ȝoure', 271, and 'Al þe dedes þat ȝe don discorden til oure', 273), and final *–e* is thus justifiable (and in accord with Chaucerian usage).[56] In the corrupt b-verse at 342, 'ay berest wiþ þe' (emend to 'berest ay wiþ þe'?), the preposition is stressed, and the enclitic pronoun forms the last unstressed syllable — as is not uncommon in alliterative verse (e.g. *P* 171, *G* 1828). The avoidance of masculine endings is indicated by the distribution of the forms *–self/ silf* and *–silue(n).* The normal form of the suffix is *–silf/self,* in both subject and oblique case, singular and plural (e.g. 33, 61, 74, 511, 763, 872, 917); *silue(n)* is the form selected at line ending (795) and to create a long dip in the b-verse at 454, 'vs silue to wisse'.

The general pronoun *echone* occurs repeatedly at line ending (627, 646, 874, 888, 1086). Historically final *–e* is not strictly speaking justified in *one* except where it means 'alone', but trisyllabic pronunciation of *echone* was

[55] Cited from Magoun (ed.), *Gests*, p. 185.
[56] See Ten Brink, *Language*, pp. 166–7.

clearly an option for Chaucer (who rhymes *echone* with *allone* at *T&C* 4.218, for instance, and *everichone* with *allone* and *grone* (inf.) at *T&C* 1.912). In *B*, as in Chaucer, it appears that trisyllabic *echone* is only ever used at line ending. Mid-line the form is always *echon* (750, 851, 1053).

The above analysis provides strong evidence in favour of the strict observance in *B* of a rule dictating that line endings should be feminine. Where a final unstressed syllable would depend on final *–e*, that *–e* is justified, by grammar, etymology, or the development of analogical *–e* in EME. Monosyllabic nouns without justified *–e* are conspicuous by their absence: words such as 'man', land', 'ground', 'life' (though of frequent occurrence elsewhere in the poem) are not selected at line ending, unless they follow a preposition, and so have *–e* for dative case. Discounting the already-discussed *spronge* at 133, which may be plural (see above, at p. 27), adjectives and verbs confirm the pattern: there are none at line ending that do not have either organic or grammatical *–e*. The spelling of the manuscript thus reflects the poet's metrical and grammatical choices with remarkable accuracy: with rare exceptions, final *–e* is written where it is metrically required. We believe that in this respect, as in others,[57] MS Bodley 264 is the most reliable of the manuscript witnesses to the alliterative poems in the classical corpus.

## Strategies of Avoidance in *Cleanness*, *Patience*, *Sir Gawain* and *St Erkenwald*

In our analysis of *B* we have drawn attention to some doublet forms — *now*/*noupe*, *–self* (or *–silf*)/*–silven*, *til*/*tille*, *echon*/*echone* — that appear to be used *metri causa*: the disyllabic forms occur less frequently than the monosyllabic ones and are invariably found at line ending, where, as Luick and Cable argue, a single unstressed syllable is obligatory.

This kind of evidence, based on the poet's selection from metrical 'minimal pairs', is sparse in *B* and in most other poems in the corpus; but a remarkable resourcefulness in this matter is observable in the poems to be considered in this section. *C*, *P*, and *G* are by the *Gawain* poet, who needs no introduction. The single extant MS is again early (*c.* 1400). For our purposes it is important to note that *Pearl* and *G* are metrically different from other poems in the classical corpus. *Pearl* is written in rhymed iambic tetrameter, *G* in stanzas of alliterative long lines con-

[57] See below, pp. 111, 245.

cluded by a bob-and-wheel using rhyme and iambic rhythm.[58] The MS of *E* (Harley 2250) is much later (*c.* 1470). The poem was at one time attributed to the *Gawain* poet, but its authorship is irrelevant to our present purpose, namely to demonstrate that the *Gawain* poet and the poet of *E* exploited lexical and grammatical variants in a way only to be explained by their studious avoidance of stressed line endings.[59] The data in question will, moreover, supply a body of evidence as to line-ending practice that is usefully independent of the vexed question of final *–e*, which is by and large not at issue here.

We shall begin with some examples of grammatical variants whose distribution is determined by their position in the alliterative line. In ME a number of verbs derived from OE could be conjugated either as strong verbs (as in OE) or as weak verbs.[60] One crucial consequence of the latter option is that in many cases it results in an additional unstressed syllable in the past tense (*–de*) and past participle (*–ed*). In comparison with other alliterative poets, the *Gawain* poet was the readiest to exploit this flexibility. For, instance, 'wax' was clearly for him normally a strong

[58] On the iambic metre of *Pearl*, see Hoyt Duggan, 'Libertine Scribes and Maidenly Editors: Meditations on Textual Criticism and Metrics', in *English Historical Metrics*, ed. C. B. McCully and J. J. Anderson (Cambridge, 1996), pp. 219–37. Duggan successfully demonstrates the poet's avoidance of clashing stress. However, if 'iambic' is to be used in the strict sense, the case for iambic metre in *Pearl* and the bob-and-wheel of *G* would also need to show that the poet tends to avoid sequences of two unstressed syllables and/or that such sequences are resolvable by such traditional prosodic factors as syncope, elision, apocope, and synizesis. This case cannot be made here, but it is relevant to note that spelling again provides some suggestive evidence of reductions *metri causa* (which is not to say that the poet never allowed himself the licence of a double off-beat). Thus the selection of *mas* rather than *makes* (' Much mirthe he mas withalle') is one factor in the regular iambics of the bob-and-wheel at *G* 103–06, and may be contrasted with 'makes much ioye' (*C* 1304b), where the disyllabic form is required to provide a long dip for the b-verse.

[59] Some of the evidence here marshalled was published in Ad Putter and Myra Stokes, 'Spelling, Grammar and Metre in the Works of the *Gawain* Poet', in *Medieval English Measures: Studies in Metre and Versification*, ed. Ruth Kennedy, *Parergon* 18 (2000), 77–95. This article also discusses evidence of meaningful spelling variation found in *Pearl.* We were not aware at the time of writing of Saburo Ohye, 'Metrical Influences in the Grammar of the Four Poems Preserved in MS. Cotton Nero A.x', *St Paul's Review* (Tokyo) 11 (1962), 75–97, which contains a number of similar observations.

[60] Wright, *Grammar*, p. 179.

verb, with past singular *wex* (*C* 204, 235, *G* 319, *P* 410, *Pearl* 538, 648) or *wax* (*C* 375, *P* 499, *Pearl* 649), past plural *wexen* (*C* 1198) and past participle *waxen* (*P* 497). The single exception occurs on the only occasion on which the verb appears at the end of a line:

> Bi þat þe flod to her fete  floȝed and *waxed* (*C* 397)

This uncharacteristic form has clearly been chosen to produce a feminine line ending. The verb 'speak' provides a parallel example. For the *Gawain* poet, as for most later Middle English speakers, *speken* was a strong verb. The *Gawain* poet has *spek(e)* for the preterite singular and *speken* for the plural (*C* 646, 845, 1220, *G* 1117, 1288, *Pearl* 438). Once, at *Pearl* 938, the preterite singular is *spakk*, for the purposes of rhyme with *sake*, *etc.* However, there is one instance where the poet treats *speken* as a weak verb:

> With glopnyng of þat ilke gome þat gostlych *speked* (*G* 2461).

Again this happens to be the only place where the verb occurs at the end of a line. The variants for the past tense of the verbs 'rise', 'shine', and 'lie' show an identical distributional pattern. The preterite singular of 'rise' appears as *ros* in fourteen of its twenty occurrences (e.g. *C* 797, 893, *etc.*), but in the six remaining line-ending cases the poet opts for the weak past tense *rysed* (*C* 509, 838, 971, 1203, 1778, *G* 1313). The strong past tense form *schon* (*G* 772, 956, *Pearl* 166, 213, 982, 1018, 1057) is only twice replaced, *metri causa*, by a weak form: *schynde* at *Pearl* 80 provides a rhyme with *kynde*, *Ynde*, etc., and *schyned* at *C* 1532, 'In contrary of þe candelstik, þer clerest hit schyned', ensures an unstressed syllable at the end of an alliterative long line. Finally, there is the verb 'to lie'. Both in *E* and in the Cotton Nero poems this verb is used mostly as a strong verb with a monosyllabic preterite singular, *leȝ*, *lay(e)*, *lyȝe* (as in *G* 1195, 2006, 2088, *C* 609, *E* 281, 314),[61] and a monosyllabic present singular, *lys*, *lis*, *lies/lyes* (as in *G* 1469, *Pearl* 360, 602, *E* 99, 179). But on occasion the geminated form with weak preterite is used:

> & a blissful body  opon þe bothum *lyggid* (*E* 76)
> Into þe boþem of þe bot,  and on a brede *lyggede* (*P* 184)

[61] The plural preterite is monosyllabic at *C* 460b ('þer costese lay drye'), but disyllabic at *C* 936b ('þay leȝen ful stylle'), where the inflectional syllable is metrically required (to provide a long dip in the b-verse).

Moreover, as in Chaucer, who also varies modern forms of the verb 'to lie' (with vocalic stem) with conservative ones with <gg>,[62] so in these poems the monosyllabic present singular alternates with a disyllabic variant (*lygges*, *ligges*, *lygge3*). This variant occurs exclusively at line ending (*C* 99, 1126, 1792, *G* 1179, *E* 186).

These variations seem to be clear cases of deliberate strategies for avoiding masculine line endings. That objective may also be achieved by exploiting lexical choices between pairs of verbs with overlapping meanings but belonging to different conjugations. For example, ME possessed, as well as the strong verb 'spring' (< OE *springan*), a weak verb *sprengen* (< OE *sprengan*), whose usual sense was 'sprinkle, disperse'. The latter is found twice in the Cotton Nero MS:

> Þe douthe dressed to þe wod    er any day *sprenged* (*G* 1415)
> Deliuerly he dressed vp    er þe day *sprenged* (*G* 2009)

These lines from *G* provide the only two attestations in the *MED* (s.v. *sprengen* (f)) of the verb *sprengen* in the sense of 'dawn'. The likely explanation for the poet's unusual wording is that the obvious choice of *springen* — the verb normally used of the breaking of day (see *MED* s.v. *springen* 3(a)) — was ruled out, since the strong preterite (*sprong*/*sprang*(*e*)) would result in a stressed final syllable. Another interesting pair is ME *clingen* < OE *clingan*, a strong verb in ME, and *clengen* ('adhere') < OE *clengan*, which is weak. Editors have generally assumed that the *Gawain* poet uses only the former, deriving spellings with <e> (e.g. *G* 505, *C* 1034) from OE *clingan*.[63] In fact, however, the poet uses both 'cling' (spelt *clynge* and rhyming with *bryng*, *mynge*, at *Pearl* 857) and 'cleng'. The decisive point is that, unlike 'cling', which is invariably strong in ME (see *MED* s.v. *clingen*), 'cleng' can, as a weak verb, provide an unstressed line-ending syllable:

> Ferly fayre watz þe folde,    for þe forst *clenged* (*G* 1694)

In the treatment of weak verbs, too, some interesting patterns emerge. A number of weak verbs had reduced preterite and past-

[62] See Ad Putter, 'Chaucer's Verse and Alliterative Poetry: Grammar, Metre, and Some Secrets of the Syllable Count', *Poetica*, 67 (2007), 19–35.

[63] See the glossaries in the Tolkien-Gordon edition of *G* and in Anderson's of *C*.

participle forms in *–t–* or *–d–*.[64] In this body of poems, the unreduced forms will be used when an extra syllable is needed for metrical purposes. Thus *E* has pret. pl. *kepten* at 66, but the verb appears unreduced in order to secure the b-verse long dip at 266b ('has kepyd vnwemmyd'). Similarly, *caȝt* is the usual preterite and past-participle form in the Cotton Nero poems (see, e.g. *P* 485, *C* 1296, *G* 2508); it is replaced only twice by *cached,* again in order to create the required long dip in the b-verse ('watȝ cached as swyþe', *C* 1619b;[65] 'and cached þerinne', *C* 1800b). Such unreduced forms are also exploited in the Cotton Nero poems at line ending. For example, 'deal' has the reduced pret. *dalt(en)* (e.g. *G* 1114, 1662, 2418) and p.p. *dalt* (*G* 452); but once, at line ending, the participle *deled* is preferred:

Sone haf þay her sortes sette and serelych *deled* (*P* 193)

Similarly, the p.p. of 'keep' is *keppte* mid-line (*C* 89), but *keped* at line ending (*G* 2016). The verb 'latch' normally has the reduced form *laȝt* in the pret. and p.p., but at line ending the p.p. is *lachched* or *lached* (*C* 1186, *P* 266).[66]

The p.p. of 'depaint' is *depaynt* at *Pearl* 1102 ('Depaynt in perleȝ and wedeȝ qwyte') but *depaynted* at *G* 649b ('hir ymage depaynted'). Finally, the pret. form of *make* is *mad(e)*, with historically justified *-e*, sometimes *maden* for the plural; the p.p. is *mad(e)*, where the final *–e* is not historically justified. But the Cotton Nero poems also preserve the older form *maked*, used exclusively at line ending.[67] In that position, pret. *maked* is found (*P* 303, *G* 1142, 1324), as well as pret. sg. *made* (*C* 198, 212, *etc.*) and pret. pl. *maden* (*G* 542, 1405) — for both forms of the preterite create feminine line endings. In the case of the past participle, however, only *maked* does so; and, significantly, that is the form in which the past participle occurs at line ending (*C* 1071, 1308, 1799, *G* 1112).

The avoidance of masculine line ending also explains some peculiarities concerning the common verbs 'can', 'take', 'have' and

[64] See Albert H. Marckwardt, *Origin and Extension of the Voiceless Preterit and the Past Participle Inflections of the English Irregular Weak Verb Conjugation* (Ann Arbor, Mich., 1935).

[65] MS *cached as as swyþe.*

[66] *Laȝt* does occur as pret. at line ending (*G* 2061), but not as p.p. (for which final *–e* would not be historically justified).

[67] In *E* 43 'makkyd' occurs mid-line ('& as þai makkyd and mynyd a mervayle þai founden'); here too, *mad* would be unmetrical by our a-verse rules (see ch. 5).

'speak' in the *Gawain* poems. In the poet's normal usage 'can' (in the sense of 'know how to') conforms to the Northern paradigm, where the plural present was generalised from the singular, without any change in the stem vowel. Hence 'con' is used in both the singular and the plural. However, there are two examples of the unlevelled plural. One occurs at the end of *P* 510 ('disserne noȝt *cunen*'), where *con* would produce a stressed ending; the other occurs at *Pearl* 521 ('Gos into my vyne, dotȝ þat ȝe conne'), where the rhymes (with p.p. *wonne*, *sunne*, and p.p. *runne*) show that the <o> in *wonne* and *conne* is scribal or at least graphical, *u* being conventionally written as *o* before nasals to avoid minim confusion.[68] The forms of 'take' also show some fluctuation between Northern and Midland usages. The shortening typical of Northern dialects is especially prevalent in the past participle, which is usually *tan* in the Cotton Nero MS.[69] *Taken* is the minority form, and occurs only four times, once (for no apparent reason) in *C* 943a ('Lest ȝe be taken in þe teche'), once to avoid clashing stress in *Pearl* 830 ('Twyeȝ for lombe watȝ taken þare') — and twice at line ending (*C* 1131 and *G* 2448). In the case of 'have' it is remarkable that the poems retain — alongside the 'modern' forms (inf. and 1st sg. *haue*, *haf*, 2nd and 3rd sg. *hatȝ*, pl. *han*, *haf*, *hauen*[70]) — the conservative *habbe* forms. For, though the *habbe* forms are common in the South-West Midlands, they are apparently not otherwise attested in the North-West Midlands.[71] They are thus probably dialect borrowings, explicable as metrical expedients. For the 2nd sg. the normal form is *hatȝ*; *habbeȝ* is used exclusively at line ending to provide the

[68] See F. Knigge, *Die Sprache des Dichters von Sir Gawain and the Green Knight* (Marburg, 1885), p. 27.

[69] There is also the curious form *tone* (rhyming with *grone*, *G* 2157), comparable with 3rd pres. sg. *totȝ* (rhyming with *clos*, *þos*, *Pearl* 513). Both forms are unparalleled according to E. V. Gordon (see his note to *Pearl* 513) and *LALME*. There are in fact some examples of the form in *Sir Perceval of Galles* (Lincoln Cathedral, MS 91, copied by Robert Thornton), where *tone* can be found alongside *tane*. As Gordon observes, the forms are probably analogical form ations, based on such pairs as *broþ* and *braþ*, *loþ* and *laþ*, and thus confirm a dialect region where Northern /a/ was heard alongside non-Northern /o/.

[70] Plural *hauen* is rare: it occurs once in *G* 1255, where context might indicate a subjunctive, and otherwise only in *Pearl* 859 ('We þurȝoutly hauen cnawyng'), where monosyllabic *han* would fit the metre better, since *cnawyng* (rhyming with 'bryng', 'mynge', *etc*) bears second-syllable stress.

[71] See *LALME*'s county dictionary.

feminine line ending (*G* 327, 452, *C* 95). This is also true for the 3rd sg: *habbes* occurs only at line ending (*C* 995), as do *habbeȝ* (*G* 626) and *habbe* — usually emended to *habbeȝ* (*G* 2339). Plural *habbe(ȝ)* also occur only at line ending: see *C* 75, 105, (and at 308 and 325, where the verb, with subject *alle*, could be singular or plural). The only apparent anomaly is 1st sg. *habbe*, which occurs mid-line at *G* 1251–2: '... þat leuer were nowþe / Haf þe, hende, in hor holde, as I þe *habbe* here'; in this line it may be used to attract the beat.[72] For the verb 'to say', there is similarly the modern singular 'says' (usually spelt *saytȝ*), but also the older form *seggeȝ*, which appears once, at the end of *C* 621, where the normal *saytȝ* would result in a stressed-syllable line ending.

The distribution of inflected and uninflected forms of the pronominal suffix *–self* provides particularly strong confirmation both of the iambics intended in *Pearl* and of the unstressed closure preferred for the alliterative long line.[73] *Myself* (once *myselfe*: *G* 1052) is invariably the form used mid-line in alliterative verse (*C* 291, *P* 503, *G* 1540) and where the iambic metre requires a disyllable with final stress in *Pearl* (414, 1175); *myseluen* only occurs in line-ending position in the alliterative poems (*C* 194, 691, 700, 1572, *P* 386) and where the trisyllabic stress pattern x/x contributes to the iambics of *Pearl* (52). The distinction between *himself* and *himseluen* is likewise metrical, not grammatical: *himseluen* occurs at line endings only (*C*1237, 1591, *G* 1046).[74] In *E*, too, the suffix is *–selfe* (170, 197), except once, at line ending (*þi seluen*, 185).

72 See below, p. 187.

73 Mustanoja's discussion of the 'indiscriminate use [of nominative *self* and oblique *selven*] ... in later Middle English' (*Middle English Syntax*, p. 147) is flawed by the failure to consider metre. In all three examples he quotes — 'myselven can not telle why' (Chaucer, *BD* 34), 'as thou saist thiselven here' (Gower, *CA* II.555) and 'himselve grieveth alther werst' (Gower, *CA* I.326) — the choice of the inflected form is plainly influenced by the iambic metre.

74 The avoidance of *–self* at line ending applies to other works in the alliterative tradition. In the Thornton manuscript (BL, Add. 31042) of the *Parlement of the Three Ages*, ed. M. Y. Offord, EETS OS 246 (London, 1959), *myself(e)* and *hymself(e)* are found medially, while *myseluen* and *hymseluen* are found only at the end of the line. The pattern has disappeared in the fragment of the poem in the later Ware manuscript (BL Add. 33994), where line-terminal *–seluen* is sometimes replaced by *–self* (526, 599, 609, *etc.*) and where line-terminal *–e* is systematically dropped (287, 233, 237, *etc.*). The poem illustrates how the rule on feminine endings could be lost with time and/or by scribal ignorance or inattention.

The kinds of variation we have observed (between inflected and uninflected pronouns, strong and weak declensions, regular and irregular weak conjugations, modern and conservative forms of 'have', 'say', 'lie', *etc.*) provide a strong indication that both the *Gawain* poet and the poet of *E* avoided masculine line endings. We have deliberately confined ourselves thus far to evidence that does not involve the sounding of final *–e*, in order not to beg that vexed question. We shall now consider variations that do depend on final *–e*, beginning with some further examples of inflected and uninflected forms. The word 'life' usually appears as *lyf* in the Cotton Nero poems and as *lyf(e)* / *life* in *E*. This uninflected form (indicated by the unvoiced medial consonant) also appears mid-line after prepositions (e.g. *G* 355, 675, *Pearl* 247, *C* 325), except in the tag *(vp)on lyue* (*P* 51, *G* 1786, 2054, 2095), though even here the uninflected form (*G* 1719, *E* 150) may be found. However, at the end of the alliterative line, and for purposes of rhyme in the bob-and-wheel of *G*, we encounter the inflected form *lyue* (*G* 385*rh*, 706, 1717*rh*, 2480, *C* 173, 293, 356, 1321, *P* 293, *E* 236). Its presence there is always justified by a preceding preposition (*on*, *vpon*, *in*, *of*), except in the case of *C* 1321:

Þat ryche in gret rialté   rengned his lyue

In this context, however, *his lyue* is adverbial ('during his life'), with a justified final *–e* that is paralleled in Chaucerian usage (see, e.g. *T&C* 2.205, 2.1056). Given that final *–e could* be pronounced by the *Gawain* poet — *to þe* rhymes with *for soþe* (*G* 413, 415), *waþe* rhymes with *ta þe* (*G* 2355, 2357) — and given that the poet appears to avoid masculine endings by using grammatical resources, we may safely suppose that the poet opted for *lyue* (rather than his normal *lyf*) at line ending because the final inflection mattered to his metre: i.e., final *–e* should here be pronounced. The same applies to the metrical variant *halue* (n.).[75] Mid-line the inflected and uninflected forms *half* and *halue* alternate without regard to historical grammar: thus 'on Godeȝ half' (*G* 2149), but 'on Godeȝ halue' (*G* 692); 'vpon ayþer half' (*P* 450) but 'on nawþer halue' (*G* 1552). At line ending, however, only the inflected form (justified by preceding preposition) seems to be permitted: see *G* 326, 2070, 2119, 2165, and *E* 181 ('in his behalue').

[75] The adjective *half* (occasionally used substantively) is not without interest. Mid-line it appears as *half* and is not inflected for plural or weak form (see *G* 185, 1543); but at line ending the poet does take advantage of grammatical *–e*: 'Þat were to tore for to telle of tryfles þe halue' (*G* 165).

It appears from the cases of *half* and *life* that the poet was more inclined to use conservative and obsolescent grammatical forms at line ending. In this context, the choice between subjunctive and indicative is of especial interest. The standard view is that by the fourteenth century the subjunctive was no longer used as extensively as in OE and survived only to indicate 'the presence of some modal colour'.[76] Against this background, the use of the subjunctive in alliterative verse seems curious:

Þe brethe of þe brynston   bi þat hit blende *were*,
Al þo citees and her sydes   sunkken to helle. (*C* 967–8)

And alle hende þat honestly   moȝt an hert glade,
Aboutte my lady watȝ lent,   quen ho delyuer *were*. (*C* 1083–4)

Hit is tolde me bi tulkes   þat þou trwe *were* (*C* 1623)

Fale oþir folk ben   þat fillen hure wombe
And nimen more þan inow   whan no ned *were*. (*B* 317–8)

For vch wyȝe may wel wit   no want þat þer were. (*G* 131)

Fyrst to say the þe soþe   quo myselfe were (*E* 197)

'Dere sir,' quod þe dede body,   'deuyse þe I thenke,
Al was hit neuer my wille   þat wroght þus hit *were*...' (*E* 225–6)

In the first two examples from *C*, the subjunctive is used for events that occurred in the past (though arguably the narrative orientation is forward-looking). This seems unusual both by the standards of fourteenth-century English and by the poet's own standards, for everywhere else in this corpus *bi þat* and *when* take the indicative (see e.g. *G* 20, 1365, 1912). The subjunctives at *C* 1623, *G* 131 and *E* 197 are historically correct (the clauses being dependent on verbs of saying and knowing), but would be unexpected at this date in non-hypothetical clauses.[77] At *B* 318 *whan* might be said to have concessive force ('although'); but, even so, the past subjunctive has plainly been induced by metrical needs which the present subjunctive *be* would not meet. A finer point concerning *E* 197 and *E* 225–6 is the use of the past subjunctive (where the present tense might be expected). At *E* 197 it matters that the speaker is a dead corpse (poin-

[76] Mustanoja, *Middle English Syntax*, p. 461.

[77] Indeed, Anderson and other editors construe *were* at *C* 1623 as an indicative. But as Gösta Forsström has pointed out, the form for the 2nd sg. ind. pret. is *watȝ*, so 'the example is better taken as a subj.': *The Verb 'To Be' in Middle English: a Survey of the Forms* (Lund, 1948), p. 163.

tedly referred to as *hit*) until a miracle brings him back to life; it is therefore apt that he should speak of himself in the past tense. Thus in *E* (in contrast to *B* 318) both sense and metre benefit from the avoidance of the present subjunctive *be*. At *E* 226, the subjunctive is more explicable ('Although it was never my will that this (i.e. the honouring of his body) should have been done'); but it remains striking that the subjunctive mood does not extend to the concessive clause of the a-verse ('Al *was* hit'), where it would be more normal.[78] Metrical considerations therefore seem to be of crucial importance in understanding some line-ending choices between indicative and subjunctive moods.[79]

Choice between inflected and uninflected infinitive is also influenced by metre. As in Chaucer, so in alliterative verse the inflected infinitive with *–e* (historically the dative inflection on infinitives preceded by *to*) survives only for a small number of verbs (*see, do, be, say*).[80] Although in texts from the West Midlands the inflected infinitive seems to have all but disappeared from normal usage after the thirteenth century,[81] alliterative poets could still access it *metri causa*. In the Cotton Nero poems it occurs three times in rhyme position. At *Pearl* 45 *to sene* is used to rhyme with words ending in etymological or grammatical final *–e*, *grene* (adj. < OE *grene*) : *kene* (adj. < OE *cene*) : *bytwene* (adv. < OE *betweonan*) : *wene* (1st sg. vb.) : *schene* (adv. < OE *schene*). At *Pearl* 914 *to done* rhymes with *bone* (n. < ON fem. *bon*, with analogical *–e* from EME)[82] : *won* (inf.;

[78] See E. Einenkel, *Geschichte der englischen Sprache: II: Historische Syntax*, Grundriss der Germanischen Philologie (Strasbourg, 1916), pp. 43–5.

[79] Metrical considerations also explain variations in mood that have puzzled historical linguists (see e.g. Mustanoja, *Middle English Syntax*, p. 460, and Davis's appendix on language in the Tolkien-Gordon edition of *G*, p. 146):

> If any so hardy in þis hous *holdez* hymseluen,
> *Be* so bolde in his blod, brayn in hys hede... (*G* 285–6)
>
> I hadde wondre what she *was* and whos wif she *were* (*PP* B 2.18)

In the first example, indicative *holdez* varies with subjunctive *be*. The reason is that subj. *holde* would deprive the b-verse of the obligatory long dip (final *–e* being subject to elision); in the second example, the subj. furnishes the final unstressed syllable.

[80] See Ten Brink, *Language*, p. 135, and Luick, 'Stabreimzeile', p. 553.

[81] See Forsström, *The Verb 'To Be'*, p. 158.

[82] Hence the word is disyllabic in Chaucer: see Ten Brink, *Language*, p. 147.

the omission of final *–e* is presumably scribal)[83] : *trone* (n. < OF *trone*) : *hone* (inf.) : *mone* (n. < OE *mona*). It may reasonably be assumed that *sene* and *done* are in these instances disyllabic.[84] Finally, at *G* 712 *myȝt sene* rhymes with *grene* and *vnbene* (of uncertain origin); in this instance the inflected infinitive is strictly speaking incorrect, since it is not preceded by *to*. Apart from these rhyme usages, the only other example of an inflected infinitive occurs at line ending:

Bot mon most I algate  mynn hym to *bene* (*G* 141)

The explanation for *bene* is, we suggest, that *be* would be unmetrical in this position.

The metrical variants evident in *C*, *G*, *P* and *E* include the smaller number of those observable in *B* (which is less resourceful in this respect), to wit, *now*/*nouþe*, *self* (or *silf*)/*silven*, *til*/*tille*, *echon*/*echone*. On the evidence of *LALME*, it seems that the forms *nouþe* and *nowþe* — with organic final *–e* (< OE *nū þa*) — are typical of the southern and central, rather than the northern, parts of the West Midlands. In the Cotton Nero poems they are, accordingly, metrical expedients, used exclusively at line ending to create feminine closure (*G* 1251, 1784, 1934, 2466, *P* 414). Mid-line the adverb for 'now' is *now*/*nov*. In the case of *til* the statistics clearly suggest that the *Gawain* poet, like the *B* poet, employed a disyllabic variant for the sake of metre. There are some forty-three occurrences of *til*/*tyl*, as against only six of *tille*/*tylle*, which always figures at line ending, five times in the alliterative poems (*C* 882, 1064, 1174, 1752, *G* 1979) and once at *Pearl* 676, where the rhymes — with *skylle*, *hylle*, *dylle*, *ille*, *stylle* — suggest that the final *–e* was indeed sounded.[85] For 'each one'

[83] Cf. E. V. Gordon: 'it seems reasonable to suppose that in some cases where there is no final *–e* in the MS. its omission is scribal and not original' (p. 107).

[84] Again we concur with E. V. Gordon: 'And in *Pearl* when all the rhyme-words in a group have an *–e* that is organic ... it may be assumed with some probability that it was sounded' (p. 107).

[85] Neither *skille* nor *ille* have etymological final *–e* but they are normally disyllabic in Chaucer. On disyllabic *ille* see n. 42 above; there is some uncertainty about the disyllabic pronunciation of *skille* in Chaucer, mainly because of conflicting evidence from *Romaunt of the Rose* (see McJimsey, *Irregular –E*, p. 211), but the *Romaunt*'s disregard for final *–e* is notorious, and the word is invariably disyllabic in Gower (see *CA* 4.3439, 7.1867, 8.2027, 2047). Hence the use of *skill* at line ending (*G* 1509) is not irregular, nor is it surprising that Barney should find *skill* to be the only ON noun with inorganic *–e* which Langland uses at line ending

the majority form is *vchon* (10x), but as in *B* a special form with final –*e* is used at line ending only (*G* 1113, *C* 71, 394, 825, 1024, 1221, *P* 173, 198).

But the *Gawain* poet's repertoire of metrical expedients is much more extensive than is that of *B*. It seems, for example, that he had metrical variants for a range of other prepositions and adverbs. The adverb *out* (< OE *ut(e)*) occurs only once with final –*e* mid-line (*Pearl* 3); however, it is always spelt with final –*e* at line ending (*C* 41, 881, 1046, 1205, *G* 1511), where it presumably represents an emphatic variant exploited for metrical reasons. 'Upon' is always spelt *vpon* (or *vp on*) in the manuscript, except at line ending in *C* 1665 and at *Pearl* 1054 where *vpone* is used to rhyme with *mone* (< OE *mona*). Although final –*e* in *vpone* is not organic, disyllabic *onne* is securely attested in the *Ormulum*, where it is also used *metri causa* as an emphatic variant of *on*. Similarly, 'far' (< OE *feorr(an)*) is always spelt *fer*, except on the one occasion where it occurs at line ending (*G* 1093), with written, and presumably sounded, final –*e*.

A further example concerns the courts of Arthur and Bertilak, each of which is referred to mid-line as a *won* ('dwelling'): *G* 257, 764, 906, 2490. However both become *wones* at line ending and once mid-line for the sake of b-verse metre: 'soȝt fro þo woneȝ' (685), 'me hade fro þo woneȝ' (1051), 'þis woneȝ wythinne' (1386), 'aȝayn to my woneȝ' (2400). One might be tempted to explain these plural usages by assuming, with *MED* (see *won(e* n.(2) 1(c)), that *won* in these cases has the sense 'room or chamber'. But that would not account for the application of the plural to the surely unicameral Green Chapel ('þe roffe of þo roȝ woneȝ', 2198) and would not fit *Cleanness* 779 ('And þere in longyng al nyȝt he lengeȝ in wones') where *wones* corresponds to *locum suum* in Genesis 18.33. We are obviously dealing here with a plural with contextual singular sense ('quarters'), a usage resorted to or coined by this poet exclusively where metre requires a second unstressed syllable.

This requirement would also explain the unusual plural *fotez*, which is found only once in this corpus (normal is *fete*), at the line end of *G* 574b: 'vpon þe segge fotez'. Again we seem to be dealing with a metrical ploy. The same variation occurs in *Wars of Alexander*, where the plural for 'foot' is *fe(e)te* in the middle of the line, yet *fotes* at the end (199, 4978).

Two final instances of the poet's lexical adaptiveness are provided by the numerals 'two' and 'three'. The normal forms for these numerals, *two*

('Langland's Prosody', p. 82). Actually, another such noun is *sleighte* (e.g. *PP* B 18.162, C 20.165).

and *þre*, have the disadvantage of being inescapably monosyllabic, but the poet had at hand the disyllabic alternatives *twayne* or *tweyne* (< OE *twegen*)[86] and *þrynne* (with historical *–e* < LOE *þrinna*, from ON *þrinnr*). *Twayne* and *tweyne* are only ever found at line ending (*G* 1864, *C* 674, 782, 788, 1749), with the single exception of *G* 962, 'þe tweyne yȝen and þe nase, þe naked lyppez'; but in that line, too, *tweyne* is metrically motivated, the linking alliteration of *–ne yȝen* providing the first alliterating stave on *n–*. *Þrynne* is also used excusively *metri causa*: it is found at line ending (*C* 606, 645, 1727), to prevent clashing stress in the bob-and-wheel of *G* 1968 ('Bi þat on þrynne syþe'), and once in an extended a-verse where the poet needs to ensure the quantifier rather than the noun alliterates:

Þús upon þrýnne wyses I haf you þro schewed (*C* 1805)[87]

The above survey of the *Gawain* poet's exploitation of variants makes it obvious that he deliberately avoided stressed monosyllables at the end of alliterative long lines. As we hope to have shown, this conclusion is indicated by various features of grammatical usage that do not depend on any assumptions about the value of final *–e*. In the context of those findings, we have examined other lexical variants (e.g. *two/twayne*, *haf/habbe*, *vchon/vchone*, *now/nowþe*) and grammatical variation between inflected and uninflected nouns and infinitives, between indicative and subjunctive moods, levelled and unlevelled plurals: in each of these cases the variant with justified *–e* was used at line ending or at other positions in the line where the extra syllable was metrically required. The only reasonable conclusion to be drawn from this evidence is that the poet did pronounce final *–e* at line ending. Although inflectional markers may well have been recessive in his dialect, the poet seems to have had a perfectly accurate sense of more conservative usages that were still selectable in literary and metrical contexts.

If these observations are true, a further conclusion about the reliability of the Cotton Nero MS is warranted. As Duggan notes in his study of *Pearl*, there is good evidence that the Cotton Nero scribe (and/or the scribe(s) of his examplar) did not always retain final *–e* where the poet wrote it.[88] In this respect the *Gawain* poems are less dependable witnesses than *B*, which seems to us the single most accurate manuscript

[86] The numeral *tweyne* is also disyllabic in Chaucer.
[87] Common quantifiers (e.g. *two*, *many*) tend to be of low alliterative rank. See below, pp. 199, 209.
[88] See Duggan, 'Libertine Scribes', p. 226.

guide to the metrical practices of an alliterative poet. Nevertheless, the Cotton Nero manuscript preserves a large number of quite subtle metrical-orthographic distinctions. Since these distinctions are unlikely to have survived frequent re-copying, the Cotton Nero MS is unlikely to be very far removed from the archetype. Duggan's view that single-manuscript poems provide an unreliable basis for metrical investigation seems to us mistaken in this particular case: the absence of manuscript variants does not rule out the possibility that a single manuscript witness is consistent and reliable enough for informed judgments to be made about particular readings.

**Case Studies**

We will now examine the number and the nature of the exceptions to the rule dictating that lines should end in one and one only unstressed syllable. The total number of lines of each text is included in each section title. This will make it obvious that the total number of problematic line endings is statistically insignificant. By identifying and concentrating on problem cases despite their numerical insignificance we hope to decrease the workload of future editors of these poems, who will have to decide what to do with these exceptions: whether to explain or to emend them. Further linguistic research may show that an apparent exception may not in fact be one; otherwise, the manuscript must be assumed to be in error. We will suggest for each text some possible types of explanation and emendation. We cannot, in the space available, undertake a fresh and systematic investigation of alliterative line endings in all the major alliterative poems. We have therefore limited ourselves to a cross-section of significant texts of different lengths and textual histories (taking advantage, wherever possible, of existing studies of their metre and line endings): *C* and *P*; *G* (which seems to have had a longer textual history than *C* and *P*, and the text of which may therefore be slightly less reliable[89]), *E*, *P3A*, *WA*, *SJ* and *DT*.

*Cleanness* (1812 lines)

As the second section will have suggested, we think that the *Gawain* poet avoided masculine line endings in his alliterative long lines; but we have not dealt with the question of exceptions to the rule. Work by Cable (on

89 See Putter and Stokes, 'The Linguistic Atlas'.

*C*) and Luick (on *G*) provides a useful starting point, and in looking at these poems we provide a fresh review of their findings.[90]

According to Cable, 98 percent of the alliterative lines in *C* end on an unstressed syllable (assuming historically justified final *–e*). Before we look at Cable's list of exceptions, it should be noted that his omission from it of certain lines appears inconsistent with his contention that dative *–e* is relevant only in the case of certain 'petrified datives: *on lyue, to grounde, on fete, of (in) gold*' (p.79). This formulation obviously covers line-ending phrases such as *to honde* (*C* 174), *on honde* (*C* 1412) and *in honde* (*C* 1704), but must be stretched to account for 'in his fayre honde' (*C* 1106b), where the noun does not immediately follow the preposition. Emendation to *hondeʒ* would be a possible solution, but is probably unwarranted, in view of the fact that such non-petrified or independently created datives appear to be widespread in *C* and its companion pieces. Thus *P* 512b reads 'bitwene þe ryʒt hande' (and here context rules out plural) and *G* 957 ends 'by the lyft honde'. These line endings cannot be accounted for by Cable's declared assumption of 'petrified' datives only (or by his declared assumption of historically justified *–e*, since *hand* did not belong to that phonological category of feminine nouns (OE *ō–*, *jō–*, *wō–*, and *i–*stems) that characteristically developed final *–e*[91] and is not treated by Orm or Chaucer as a disyllable). Omissions likewise unaccounted for as petrified datives are *C* 1590b, 'and gos to þe kyng', matched by *G* 343, 'quoþ Wawan to þe kyng', all datives, but clearly not petrified ones; *C* 1488, 'al of brende golde'; and *C* 1669 'wonnen of his mowþe' (cf. *G* 1778).[92] Another probable example is *C* 869, where Lot says of his daughters: 'Hit arn ronk, hit arn rype, and redy to manne'. *Manne* has surely been misunderstood by some of the poem's editors.

[90] Less reliable is Julius Thomas, *Die alliterierende Langzeile des Gawayn-Dichters* (Jena, 1908). Thomas also argues (p. 10) that the line endings are feminine and lists problem cases, but he is less well-informed about historical *–e*. For example, since final *–e* is organic in *fest(e)* (*C* 81, 1364, 1393), *wrath* (*C* 690, *C* 746), *hast* (*C* 599), *help* (*C* 1345 [< OE *help* and *helpe*; cf. the variant forms *help* and *helpe* in Gower]), dative *–e* seems irrelevant; it is also irrelevant for *drynk* (*C* 182) and *syʒt* (*P* 530, *C* 706, 1548), which both developed *–e* in EME. The adjective *quoynt* (*C* 160, *C* 871) has organic *–e* and so requires no special pleading.

[91] See Wright, *Grammar*, pp. 141-2.

[92] Perhaps Cable assumes derivation from *muða* ('estuary, river-mouth), but see p. 32, n. 50 above.

According to Robert Menner[93] and Anderson, *manne* is the passive infinitive of the verb 'to man', i.e. to be manned, wielded. Anderson's editorial note reads:

> 869. *manne*. Probably a verb, OE *mannian* (Menner); there is no parallel in the MS for *manne* as a variant spelling for the noun *man* 'man'.

However, ME *mannen* is not recorded in the sense proposed by Anderson,[94] and it seems simpler to construe *man* as dative and *redy to manne* as 'ready for a man'.[95] The final *–e* given to a noun that does not otherwise figure in the MS with *–e* is consistent with a dative used *metri causa* — and consistent with the other evidence that points to the line ending as a locus for dative *–e* in prepositional phrases and for other special or conservative grammatical forms.

That the grammar of alliterative poets was retentively receptive to archaic usages, particularly at line ending,[96] is a point that receives further confirmation from the way in which the word 'head' figures in the Cotton Nero poems. Unlike *B* — which has just one form, *hed* (with one dative *hede* at line ending at 656: 'of iubiterus hede') — the Cotton Nero MS evinces two forms: *hed(e)* and *heued*. The normal form is *hed*(e), which, when it occurs at line ending, is always spelt with *–e* and always follows a preposition:

| | |
|---|---|
| at þe hede (*G* 217) | on his hede (*G* 1721) |
| in hys hede (*G* 286) | ouer his hede (*G* 2217) |

These are obviously datives, but not petrified ones; and there is no reason to assume that a scribe consistently replaced *heued* by *hede*, for, if anything, the iambic metre of *Pearl* would suggest that the Cotton Nero scribe (or his predecessor) sporadically wrote *heued* for *hed*.[97] *Heued* occurs only once after a preposition at line ending (*P* 319) and is otherwise used

[93] Robert J. Menner (ed.), *Purity* (New Haven, Conn., 1920).

[94] In Middle English one can 'man' (= 'staff' or 'populate') ships, places, or countries, but one cannot 'man' (= 'provide a mate for') women.

[95] Cf. the line ending at *PP* B 1.82 'þat wroȝte me to man', emended to *manne* in A. V. C. Schmidt's edition.

[96] Something similar may be true for poets such as Chaucer, who, for example, retains dative *–e* in *yere*, but only at line ending.

[97] *Hed* is the form in *Pearl* 209, and *heued* (confirmed by rhyme) at *Pearl* 974. But at *Pearl* 459 ('As heued and arme and legg and naule') and *Pearl* 465 ('Þy heued hatȝ nauþer greme ne gryste'), the metre favours *hed*.

in that position only where dative *hede* is ruled out: at *C* 876 and *P* 486 the noun is in the accusative, and the form it appears in is *heued*. Only once does *heued* occur midline in the alliterative poems of this MS: to create a long dip in the b-verse: 'his heued watʒ couered' (*C* 1707). The poet plainly not only understood, but also generated, dative cases, as his alternation between dative *hede* and accusative *heued* at line ending testifies, and that alternation was equally plainly prompted by the need for a trochaic word in that position.

Turning now to Cable's list of exceptions, we find further reason to posit a more extensive use of dative case than he assumes:

> *Cam* (299), *nere* prep. (414), *are* adv. (438+), *day* (494), *bete*, imp. (627), *vale* (673), *toune* (721), *blake* adj. (747), *dispyt* (821), *tylle* (882b+), *beste* adj. (913), *lawe* (992) *rounde* (1121), *olde* adj. (1123), *scole* (1145), *away* (1241), *lyȝt* (1272), *þere* (1336), *þalle* 'wooden platform' (1384), *þerwyth* (1406+), *among* (1414), *clere* (1456), *þerof* (1499+), *þertylle* (1509), *wowe* (1531), *þurʒoute* (1559), *schal* (1571), *þervpone* (1665), *state* (1709), *Gode* (1730), *felde* (1750).[98]

Strikingly, all the native nouns in this list occur where dative case –*e* would be historically correct and would (if supplied and/or sounded) provide the lacking unstressed syllable:

> Myryly on a fayr morn, monyth þe fyrst
> Þat falleʒ formast in þe ʒer, and þe fyrst day (493–4)
>
> wer founde *in* ʒonde *toune* (721b)
>
> þat sat *on* a *lawe* (992b)
>
> charged *with* þe *lyʒt* (1272)
>
> *vpon* þe playn *wowe* (1531b)
>
> in borʒe and *in felde* (1750b)

It is difficult to regard these as either anomalous or scribal, since comparable line endings are frequent in the MS. The noun *day*, for instance, occurs at line ending only in adverbial constructions of time and duration:

> Þe lede wiþ þe ladyez layked alle day (*G* 1560)
> I haf meled with þy maystres mony longe day (*P* 329)

[98] We amalgamate the three separate lists in Cable, *Alliterative Tradition*, pp. 70, 73, and 168n.

Emendation to *daye* is obviously indicated — especially since, where dative *daye* occurs in rhyme, the rhyme companions also have justified final *–e* (G 80, 686, 1075, *Pearl* 1210). *Toun* likewise only ever occurs at line ending in dative regimen (*G* 1049, *P* 458) and is only spelt with final *–e* after a preceding preposition (*G* 614*rh*,[99] *C* 721, 763, *P* 458). And the dative *lawe* at *C* 992b (quoted above) is paralleled by *G* 2175b, 'and com *to* þe *lawe*'.

Some of Cable's other anomalies are in our view regular: in addition to *state*, *-vpone*, and *-tylle*, which we have already discussed,[100] we note *pere* (optionally disyllabic in Chaucer, due to an extension of French usage where *per* and *pere* marked a difference in gender),[101] *palle* (< OF *pal*), which also has inorganic *–e* in Chaucer (cf. *pale* : *tale* at *House of Fame* 1840),[102] *–oute* (< OE *ut(e)* and *utan*), *away* (*way* being optionally disyllabic in Orm (*weȝȝe*) and in Chaucer.[103] *Scole* (< ON *skal*) seems to have undergone merger with *scale* (< Latin *scala*), with the result that *scale* came to be used in the sense of 'cup' (see *MED* sense 3); the lexical items are also interchanged in the two versions of Laȝamon's *Brut*, which alternate between *scole* and *scale* (592–3). Thus the *–e* on *scole* in *C* may be not merely graphical, but represent what was assumed to be an organic *–e*. *Nere* (< OE *near*) is optionally disyllabic in Chaucer, as rhymes show.[104] This is presumably due to the encroachment of adverbial *–e*, a process that would also explain *are* adv. (*C* 438+) and *ere* at *Pearl* 164 (rhyming with *mere* < OE *mere*, *rere* inf., *debonere* < OF *debonaire*, *schere* inf., *þere*). *Bete* in 'þou þe fyr bete' (*C* 627) is construed as an imperative by Cable; since *bete* is a weak verb, final *–e* would be perfectly regular in Chaucerian usage (where imperative singular *–e* was lost in strong verbs only),[105] but in this case *bete* could equally well be a subjunctive.[106] Finally, apropos of

[99] Final *–e* has been scribally lost from the rhyme companions *croun* (< OF *corone*) and *broun* (pl. adj.).

[100] See above, pp. 21, 30, 45.

[101] Ten Brink, *Language*, p. 150.

[102] See McJimsey, *Irregular –E*, p. 60. McJimsey cannot find an explanation. It appears from the forms such as *pali* (sg.) and *palleyz*, *palys* (pl.) that the word was re-analysed as a singular form of *palis* (< OF *paliz*). *Pale* also occurs at line ending in *SJ* 681.

[103] See Ten Brink, *Language*, p. 142, and McJimsey, *Irregular –E*, pp. 105–6.

[104] See for instance Chaucer, *Romaunt*, 2003.

[105] See Ten Brink, *Language*, p. 134.

[106] See Mustanoja, *Middle English Syntax*, p. 456.

*þerof* (1499+), we note that the disyllabic forms *offe/offen* are well attested in *Ormulum* and *Genesis and Exodus*,[107] where they function as metrical variants of *of*. Presumably the addition of inorganic *–e* in this and other prepositions and adverbs (cf. *on* and *onne* in Orm) is due to analogy with inherited variants like *vp/vppe, in/inne*. This development has been invoked to explain *þerwyth* (1406),[108] but there is little dictionary evidence to support the form *þerwyþþe*;[109] the solution adopted by alliterative poets was usually *þer-mydde* (see *OED* s.v. *ther(e)-mide*), routinely altered by scribes to *þer-wyth* (see e.g. the variants at *PP B* 15.316, *SJ* 192, and *MED* s.v. *ther-mid*).

Some of the remaining anomalies are suspect on other grounds. At *C* 299, 'Sem soþly þat on  þat oþer hyȝt Cam', the alliterative pattern is defective (perhaps read 'þat oþer Cham hyȝte').[110] At 1730, b-verse 'as maynful Gode' also lacks the required long dip; read *as maynful[le] Dryȝtyn*.[111] *C* 1571, 'And of my þreuenest lordeȝ þe þrydde he schal', is suspect on the grounds of (a) grammar, since auxiliary *schal*, corresponding to Latin *eris* (Daniel 5.16), lacks a main verb; (b) alliteration, since there are only two alliterating staves; and (c) b-verse metre, since inflectional *–e* in *þrydde* would normally elide before unstressed *h–*. 'And of my þreuenest þayneȝ  þe þryyde he schal worþe' is one possible reconstruction of the original line.

Future editors of *C* are probably justified in considering possible emendations to the few irregular line endings that remain. For example, at *C* 55, 'For my boles and my bores  arn bayted and slayne', the poet may have written *slawe(n)* (< OE *slagen*) rather than *slain* (< OE *slægen*); Chaucer also used the two forms *slayn* and *slawe(n)* as metrical variants,

107 See *Genesis and Exodus*, ed. Richard Morris, EETS OS 7 (London, 1865), l. 2403.

108 Cable, *Alliterative Tradition*, p. 73.

109 *MED* cites only the rhyme *pith* (varying with *pithe* in Chaucerian usage) : *þer with* [var. *þere wiþþe*] (*CT*, III, 476).

110 *Cham* would then alliterate on /sh/. Cf. the alliteration on /sh/ and /s/ at *C* 58 and 566. In a still valuable study of alliteration (*Studien über den Stabreim in der mittelenglischen Alliterationsdichtung*, Bonner Studien zur englischen Philologie 11 (Bonn, 1914), pp. 99–100), Karl Schumacher concluded that /sh/ and /s/ alliteration was not permitted by the *Gawain* poet, but his conclusions are based on the unsafe assumption that the a-verse needs only one alliterating stave.

111 Adjectives before proper names (including 'God') are weak.

though the scribes did not always maintain the distinction.[112] In the case of 1414b, 'tulket among', emendation of 'among' to 'amonges' provides the simplest solution. The latter form appears as a metrical expedient in a number of alliterative poems. In *C*, *G*, and *MA* it occurs exclusively in the following verses:

> inmongeȝ mankynde (*C* 278b)
> blende þeramongeȝ (*G* 1361b)
> the vines imangez (*MA* 3169b)

In the Cotton Nero poems, the forms *agaynes* and *aȝaynes* are similarly usually employed at line ending (*G* 971, *G* 1661, *C* 611, but see *C* 1711), where the regular form *agayn* would be unmetrical.

*Patience (531 lines)*

The following line endings in *P* require consideration:[113]

> *gode* 'goodness' (20), *layde* p.p. (37), *hyȝe* adj. (93), *sterne* n. 'stern' (149), *bote* n. 'help' (163) *hens* (204), *borne* (205), *drede* (255), *myȝt* (257), *fissche* (262), *beste* adj. (277), *myre* (279), *day* (329), *swete* n. (364), *wronge* (376), *þynk* 3rd sg. (427), *ȝet* (432), *nyȝt* (442), *soyle* (443), *cole* adj. (454), *toune* (458), *ryȝt* n. (493).

Supplying and/or pronouncing dative *–e* would, here too, account for a number of native nouns. Besides the cases of *day* and *toune* (discussed above), note the following:

> of þat fissche (262b; contrast the spelling *fysch* at 251 and 337).
> on her wronge (376)
> al nyȝt (442)[114]
> to ryȝt (493)

*Yet* is monosyllabic in Chaucer, but the OE forms *gieta* and *geta* would explain a variant form with *–e*, and the spelling *ȝette* does once occur, at line ending at *C* 867; compare *WP*, where forms with final *–e* are restricted to line ending (1955, 2274, 4484). The origin of *sterne* (='stern

[112] On these variants see Wright, *Grammar*, p. 58, and Joseph Bihl, *Die Wirkungen des Rhythmus in der Sprache von Chaucer und Gower* (Heidelberg, 1916), p. 17, and Friedrich Wild, *Die sprachlichen Eigentümlichkeiten der wichtigeren Chaucer-Handschriften und die Sprache Chaucers* (Vienna, 1915), p. 339.

[113] We have not included words that require such pronunciations, common in ME, as *malýcë* (4), *pouértë* (13), *meknéssë* (15), on which see Ten Brink, *Language*, pp. 145 and 149.

[114] The noun *nyȝt* occurs at line ending in this corpus only in durational sense or after prepositions: *G* 751, *G* 1887, *G* 1922, *G* 2347, *P* 442.

of a ship') is uncertain: *MED*, s.v. *stern(e* n.2, compares OI *stjorn* and Old Frisian *stiarne*, *stiorne*. Analogical *–e* is probable in *drede*, *myre* and *bote* (all disyllabic in Chaucer) and possible in *myȝt* (optionally disyllabic in Orm).[115] For *borne* read *boren*, for *hens* either *hennes* or *hethen* (see *G* 1794, 1879), and for *layde* ('arn in teme layde') *layed*. *Swete* n. 'sweat' is derived by Anderson from OE *swat*, but this yielded ME *swot*; ME *swete* derives either from OE *swætan* (v.) or from OI *sveiti*, and so has justified *–e*.[116] *Soyle* has no organic *–e* if it represents AF *soil* 'ground, earth', but note also ME *soile* (< OF *soille*, *souille* 'miry or muddy place'), giving ModE *soil* 'dirt'. The latter word may be the one intended, if indeed *soil* and *soile* were always distinct in ME.

What Anderson sees as two adjectives are better regarded as adverbs:

> 'Oure syre syttes', he says,  'on sege so hyȝe' (93)
> Þat euer wayued a wynde  so wyþe and so cole (454)

The first of these lines is based on the idiom *sitten heighe* adv. (often followed by *in se, in sete*) 'be pre-eminent' (see *MED* s.v. *sitten* 1(i)), in which 'high' is adverbial;[117] *wyþe* and *cole* may also be adverbs (cf. þat schaded ful cole, 452).

*Good* is a special case; it occurs at alliterative line ending as noun and adjective in the following contexts:

> and Lucan þe gode (*G* 553)
> of leudeȝ ful gode (*G* 849)
> wrast alway to god (*G* 1482)
> þat woldeȝ my gode (*G* 2127)
> For þay schal frely be refete  ful of alle gode (*P* 20)

Final *–e* is grammatical in the weak and plural adjectives at *G* 553 and *G* 849 and in the phrase *to god* (a familiar petrified dative). No secure explanation offers itself for 'my gode', but at *P* 20 *gode* is a pl. adjective

[115] See above, p. 21 and n. 10. But note that in this MS as in *B* the noun is used at line ending only in dative constructions (as here at *P* 257 'þurȝ his honde myȝt', and *G* 1546) or in the plural (*C* 1699).

[116] Note e.g. the rhyme *swete* (n.) : *bete* (inf.) at *Sir Tristrem* 2904.

[117] See also David Burnley's discussion of constructions such as 'hye on hors he sat', and 'He pleyeth Herodes on a scaffold hye', in 'Inflexion in Chaucer's Adjectives', *Neuphilologische Mitteilungen*, 83 (1982), 169–77.

used as substantive and means 'good things',[118] in which usage sounded final *–e* is regular in Middle English.[119] Compare:

> And thus cam ferst to mannes ere
> The feith of Christ and alle goode
> Thurgh hem that thanne weren goode ... (*CA* Pr. 236–8)
>
> The hihe god, which alle goode
> Purveied hath for mannes foode ... (*CA* 4.6961–2)[120]

In sum, *P* presents very few exceptions to the unstressed line-ending rule, and such seeming exceptions as do exist are nearly all explicable.

*Sir Gawain and the Green Knight (2530 lines)*

The irregular line endings in *G* were examined by Luick, who found that the number of masculine endings was rather higher than in other alliterative poems, though not significantly so.[121] He lists thirty-nine problematic line-ending words (some of them ending more than one line), and we would add *broȝt* p.p. (567), *horne* (1601), *sele* n. (1938), *gode* n. (2127), *mo* (2322), *maye* pl. (2396). The list is short enough in itself to warrant his conclusion that the poet wrote only feminine line endings, and can be reduced even further by such considerations as have already been exemplified. *I* at 1991 is perfectly regular (say[e] ne dár I),[122] as are the following words with organic *–e*: *bonk* (700) < *ON *banke*,[123] *þikke* (138) < OE *þicce*, *wors* (726) < OE *wyrsa*, *knot* (662, 1334) < OE *cnotta*, *wylde* (741) < OE *wilde*, *oute* (1140+) < OE *ut(e)*, *utan*, *poynt* (2284) < OF *point* 'prick' and *pointe* 'extremity', *lace* (1851) < OF *las* and *lace* (although *point* and *lace* are monosyllabic in Chaucerian usage). The noun *rest* (1990)

[118] Although the poet's immediate source is the fourth beatitude, 'quoniam ipsi satuabantur' (Matt. 5.6), the addition 'full of all gode' recalls the *Magnificat*, 'Esurientes implevit *bonis*' (Luke 1.53).

[119] See McJimsey, *Irregular –e*, p. 152.

[120] Cf. *P3A* 257, 'schall wake for þi gode' (in the Ware MS; Thornton has *gudes*).

[121] Luick, 'Langzeile', p. 577. The subject is also discussed in a valuable study by Nicolay Yakovlev, 'On Final *–e* in *Sir Gawain and the Green Knight*', forthcoming in *The Metres of Alliterative Verse*.

[122] For other examples of the use of a personal pronoun at line ending, see above, p. 34.

[123] Because 'bank' is always in eliding context in Chaucer, his pronunciation cannot be determined, but the word is evidently disyllabic in Gower (*CA* 2.144, 2.720).

had acquired analogical *–e; drynk* n. (1935) is regularly disyllabic in Chaucer; and (as Luick himself pointed out) analogical *–e* is also probable in the cases of *eke* (90),[124] *innoghe* adv. (219),[125] *ere* adv. (527), *þere* (1640+), *here* (2194), and *waye* (1876+; see above, p. 52), all with optional or regular *–e* in Chaucerian usage. Northern *sele* (< OE *sæl*) is a feminine noun that may have developed final *–e*; pronounced final *–e* would certainly be the most natural way of explaining the b-verse at *P* 5, 'sele wolde folȝe'.[126] We have already discussed *lorde, tylle, of, wyth, flone* and *knyȝt*. Dative *–e* would explain a number of anomalies, not merely, as Luick suggested, *golde* (found at line ending (190+) only after prepositions), but also *flet* in 'stif on þis flet (294b), 'ouer þe flet' (568b), *noȝt* in 'þen britned to noȝt' (680b), and several other nouns not mentioned by Luick, such as 'on þe grounde' (426), 'on þe flor' (834), 'of þe ȝere' (1072), 'in his bedde' (2006), 'in þe fyrst nyȝt' (2347), 'in þis londe' (2445).[127]

Some of the remaining cases may be acceptable. Final *–e* in *helme* (2407) < OE *helm* (monosyllabic in Chaucer) may be influenced by OF *helme, heaume*. For p.p. *borne* (996, 2394) read etymological *boren* (cf. *B* 598). P.p. *bene* (677) also occurs at line ending in *WP*; since it is only in that position spelt with final *–e* we may be dealing with a genuine 'emphatic variant' (in G. H. V. Bunt's words),[128] though the isolated instance gives cause for doubt.[129] The past participle *cast* at 878b is acceptable with final *–e(n)*, for, although the verb is historically weak, the strong past participle was also used in ME (see e.g. Chaucer, *CT* VII.606).[130] Luick suspected analogical *–e* in *honde* (369 < OE *hand*, fem.),

[124] See Ten Brink, *Language*, p. 273.

[125] Cf. *ynowë*, *CT* VIII, 860; *ynowhë*, *CA* 2.3226.

[126] The other solution would be to assume voiced final *–e* in *wolde*. But mid-line auxiliary *wolde* is normally monosyllabic (as indicated by the iambic metre of *Pearl* (304, 390, 391, *etc.*) and of the bob-and-wheel of *G* (1976) and by b-verse metre: note *P* 113, 'Lo, þe wytles wrechche,  for he wolde noȝt suffer'). The only possible counter-indication is (plural) *wolde G* 1537, 'Þat so worþy as ȝe wolde wynne hidere' (which appears to be corrupt).

[127] See also *kyng, ryȝt, mouþ*, and *hond*, discussed above, pp. 32–33, 49.

[128] See Bunt (ed.), *William of Palerne*, p. 63.

[129] We suspect scribal transposition: read *had ben wyt more* for *had more wyt bene*. The apparent avoidance of p.p. *ben* at line ending has consequences for *C* 659, 'Fro mony a brod day byfore  ho barayn ay byene', emended by Anderson to *ay had bene*, by Andrew and Waldron (following Gollancz) to *ay bydene*. Another possibility is *ay byleued*.

[130] See Wild, *Eigentümlichkeiten*, p. 303.

but this is unlikely for the reasons already given (see above, p. 49). *Hand/hond* occurs at line ending only after prepositions, except for two instances in *G*: *hond* at 494 ('stafful her hond') may represent an original plural in *–e* (a well-attested plural form) or *–es*, but we can offer no explanation for 'lyfte vp his honde' (369).[131] We suspect scribal error in the anomalies that remain. Plausible emendations could be made to *and alle were þay broȝt* (567) — read *and alle þay broȝte*; to *may* (380) and *maye* (2396) — read *mowe*;[132] to *horne* — read *hornez*; to *bade* (1699) — read *bydez* (cf. *Traylez* 1700). At 2322, 'bede me no mo', (i.e. no more than the one axe-stroke: cf. 2324a, 'And if þow recheȝ me any mo'), emendation to *more* is possible. Although the emendation would elide the usual distinction made in this MS between *mo* (numerically more) and *more* (further; greater in extent or degree), the poet did once for the sake of rhyme allow himself the reverse licence of substituting *mo* (in the sense of 'greater') for *more* (at *Pearl* 340: 'For dyne of doel of lureȝ lesse, Ofte mony mon forgos þe mo').

*Saint Erkenwald (352 lines)*

From the Cotton Nero poems we move to *E*, the line endings of which have been cursorily examined by Joseph Fischer (who argued that the poem was in septenary metre, with a single off-beat at line ending).[133] *E* contains remarkably few exceptions to the regular trochaic line ending. Of these, analogical *–e* accounts for *quile* (105) 'while' and *speche* (152), as also for *grave* n. (153), *pyne* (188), *routhe* (240), and *rode* (290).[134] To the petrified datives such as 'in his honde' (84) and 'in golde' (248) may be added 'opon slepe' (92), 'on fyrste' (207), 'to holde hom to riȝt' (232), 'to glent out of ryȝt ' (241), 'on benche' (250) — all of which have parallels in Chaucer's usage.

[131] Scribal substitution of *hand* for *looue* (as at *WA* 923) is unlikely here, since 'lift up the hand' was idiomatic in the context of blessing, and *looue* would yield an *aaaa* line, a pattern generally avoided.
[132] *May* is subjunctive at 380 (*as* = so that) and plural at 2396 (where alone the plural form occurs with final *–e*). On the poetic use of the unlevelled form in preterite-present verbs, cf. our observations regarding *cunen* (see above, p. 40) and note the rhyme expedient *mowe* at *G* 1397. Like *can*, *may* appears to be monosyllabic in the plural in the poet's usage.
[133] Joseph Fischer, *Die stabende Langzeile in den Werken des Gawaindichters*, Bonner Beiträge zur Anglistik, 11 (1901), 1–64.
[134] All disyllabic in Chaucer: see McJimsey, *Irregular –E*, pp. 39, 40, 65.

This leaves some fourteen line endings that require some explanation. The proper name *Paule* (113) < *Paulus* is also disyllabic at 35b: 'of Saynt Paule mynster' (alliterating on *s*). Dative *–e* is possible in *of yrne* (71), but the poet's form may well have been *yren* (< OE *iren*). Similarly, at 177, *corce* — spelt *cors* mid-line (110, 317) — is a potential prepositional dative, but the word has ME forms based on both OF *cors* and L. *corpus* (*cors, corce, corps, corsus, corpus*). For *hatte* (4, 38) Fischer would read *hates*, but *E*'s form is not the preterite (ME *het*, *hette*) but the passive 'is/was called' (< OE *hatte*), with historical *–e*. At 285–6, 'Nas I a paynym vnprest þat neuer thi plite knewe' / Ne þe mesure of þi mercy ...?', *knewe,* occurring here in a relative clause subordinate to a question, might well be a subjunctive,[135] rather than an apparently anomalous singular preterite of a strong verb. At 134, 'to herken hit', syncope of *–en* in *herken* or emendation of *herken* to *herk* is necessary to prevent two unstressed syllables at line end. *His* at 174, 'I schal auay ȝow so verrayly of vertues His', would not be historically incorrect, but the pronoun is regularly monosyllabic (and normally unstressed) and scribal corruption is probable. At 271 the lack of concord between the plural subject and the singular also indicates corruption: 'And if *renkes* for riȝt þus me arayed *has*, [read *haue*] / He has lant me to last...' *Riȝt* at 301 ('Quat wan we with oure wele-dede þat wroghtyn ay riȝt') could possibly be an adverb. Adverbial *–e* on *best* (272) is conceivable, but the evidence for this is slender,[136] and the same applies to *noȝt* (261). The possibility that p.p. *bene* (26) may have had a disyllabic variant has been mentioned before (see above, p. 57), but the half line is a little too odd to inspire confidence. At 117, 'and day belle ronge', the otherwise anomalous strong singular preterite could be regularized by emending to 'and day belles rongen' (cf. 352).

*Parlement of the Three Ages* (665 lines)

For *P3A*, *SJ*, and *WA*, we have the advantage of variant readings, since these texts are preserved in more than one manuscript. For *P3A* there are two MSS to consider: T, the London Thornton MS (BL Add. 31042) and W, the Ware MS (BL Add. 33994). According to the editor, M. Y. Offord, the MSS 'are obviously not closely connected, but there are a

[135] Cf. Mustanoja, *Middle English Syntax*, p. 461.

[136] The adverb is always monosyllabic in Chaucer, with the doubtful exception of the apocryphal *RR* 2261, which in the Globe edition, gen. ed. Alfred Pollard (London, 1913), reads 'Of hym that kan [hem] beste do' (Riverside: 'Of hym that kan best do').

few indications that they may be descended from a common original (which was perhaps not far removed from the author's copy)' (p. xvi). As might be expected, the loss of final *–e* is more pervasive in W (late fifteenth-century) than in T (mid-fifteenth-century). Thus in many cases T preserves an organic *–e* or an inflection which W omits, e.g. *ȝerne* adv. (227), *to þe dethe*, dat. (233), *holde* inf. (237), *beste* weak & pl. adj. (297), *erþe* (298), *a-waye* (504), *hym-seluen* (609; W *hym self*). Conversely, the feminine line ending appears on occasion only in W's form: thus W *elles* (260, 445; T *ells*); W *wille* (465: T *will*), W *þerynne* (437, 608; T *þer-in*).

The majority of nouns at line ending have a weak ending in the parent language. At 279b, the metrically irregular reading of W, '& made up my hows' is confirmed as an error by T: 'and made vp my howses'. A large group of other nouns are known to have acquired analogical *–e*: *while* (T23+), *sighte* (T96), *hewe* (155+), *haulle* (T253, W *halle*), *gloue* (TW 232),[137] *dussypere* (T 348; W errs with *duke pere*),[138] *sonde* (T 442; W errs with *found*), *rode* (T555; W transposes), *nede* (TW565), *riste* (T 572; W *rest*), *emperour* (T 597; *W emperoure*),[139] *ȝouþe* (TW 652), *graue* (TW 623), *blysse* (TW 663), *synn* (T664, W *mysse*[140]), *rigge* (T 78),[141] *myghte* (T 479, W *myght*).[142] More doubtful cases of analogical *–e* are *faythe* (T 547, W *faith*), and *therewith* (259; W *þer with*) — the last two ocurring at line ending also in *C* (see above, p. 53).

[137] Analogical *–e* is not demonstrable in Chaucer, but evident in Gower: e.g. *gloue* : *behoue*, *CA* Prol. 357–8.

[138] Affected by variable pronunciation of *pere* (see above, p. 52).

[139] With final *–e* in ME verse in the form *emperére* (e.g. *Castle of Love*, ed. Kari Sajavaari, *The Middle English Translations of Robert Grosseteste's 'Chateau d'Amour'* (Helsinki, 1967), 745–6, rhyming 'emperere' with 'chayȝere'). The two forms are due to variation between *emperere* (subject) and oblique *emperour* in OF.

[140] From OE & ON *mis* fem. n. (cf. OI *missa*), the word is monosyllabic in Chaucer, Gower, and *Gawain* poet (with the possible exception of *Pearl* 382, where *mysse* rhymes with *blisse,* which is monosyllabic or disyllabic in the poet's usage, as in Chaucer).

[141] Northern, from OE *hrycg* masc. n., inflected *hrygge*; note analogical *–e* in comparable OE masculine nouns such as *wedge* and *midge* – on which see Ten Brink, *Language*, p. 142, and Wright, *Grammar*, p. 138. At T 78 the construction would give a dative, but the word also occurs at line ending in accusative case at *MA* 900.

[142] See above, p. 21 and n. 10.

Seventeen lines show dative *–e*, and in only one case is the *–e* not represented in the spelling of either MS (T659 'towarde townn', W 'toward þe town'). The only two clear cases of unjustified *–e* are the following:

And one swyftely with a swerde   swapped of his hede (T 551; W *his hed*)
There Sir Rowlande the ryche Duke   refte was his lyfe (T 563; W *his lyf*)

At T 551 the form *heued* is required. The situation may be compared with *MA* (also copied by Thornton), where *heued*/*hevede* is used at line ending (note 1354b, 'he strykes of his heued', and 2445, 3351) with the single exception of 2129b: 'he strake ofe his hede'.[143] Both here and in *P3A*, the deviation from the metrical norm suggests that Thornton (or a preceding scribe) inadvertently introduced his normal form *hede*. T 563b requires emendation, e.g. to *refte was of lyue*.

The adjectives, adverbs and prepositions used at line ending generally have etymological or inflectional *–e*, e.g. *fele* (T1), *riche* (T9), *longe* (T28), *beste* (TW 458). *Tame* at TW 342 is regular, since it belongs to a small group of adjectives to which *–e* had been added.[144] There are only four apparent exceptions:

and of body grete (T 32)
the sone was so warme (T 100) (read *schon* for *was*?)
yn A shawe faire (W 661) (T *in þe schawes faire* is correct)[145]
And be thou doluen and dede thi dole schall be *schorte* (258)

At 258, Offord assumes that *thi dole* means 'grief for you', but the context favours 'dole' (< OE *dale* 'alms', ME pl. *dole* and *doles*): 258b means 'the alms-giving ceremonies conducted for you' will be *shorte* (pl. adj). There are two apparent cases of adverbial *most* (without preceding *the*), but these are ambiguous, since *moste* may represent 'must' (cf. 653):

And now es dethe at my dore   that I drede moste (292) [W *most*]
By cause of Dame Cand[ac]e   that comforthed hym moste (396)
[W *þat comforth hym moste*]

[143] See above, pp. 50.
[144] The group includes *tame*, *bare*, *evene*, *lyte*, *ille*, *lowe*, *meeke*, *holwe* and possibly *smale*: see Ten Brink, *Language*, p. 155, and (on *lowe* and *smale*) Burnley, 'Inflexion', p. 177.
[145] Ten Brink includes *fair* in the group of adjectives which acquired *–e* (see previous note). But *faire* occurs in Chaucer only before proper names without preceding article, where it is in effect a weak form.

We find a small number of metrically irregular verbs at line ending. Singular preterites of strong verbs occur at T 53 (1st sg. *smote*),[146] T 332 and 473 (3rd sg. *wanne*; W *wan*), and T 439 (3rd sg. *bere*; W *bare*), but there is also evidence that strong sg. preterites were not welcome at line ending. A striking example of their avoidance is provided by lines 567–70:

Then *suede* he the Sarazenes seuen ȝere and more
And the Sowdane at Saragose sothely he *fyndis*
And there he bett downn þe burghe and Sir Merchill he *tuke*
[W: *And þere he betes down þe burgh and Balam he takes*]
And that daye he dide [hym] to the dethe als he had wele seruede.

The shift into the historic present at 569 obviates *found*,[147] and *takes* (W 570) avoids *took*. At 439, the curious form *bere* (W *bare*) for the preterite may be explicable as a trace of an original historic present. We might compare T 494, 'The gates to-wardes Glassthenbery full graythely he *rydes*; / And ther Sir Mordrede hym mett ...' (where W errs with *ride* for *rydes*). Other revealing MS variations are W 603b, 'þat yn Erth *was*', where T is metrically regular: *that euer wonnede in erthe*, and W640b '& vanyte es', where T reads *and vanyte es alle*, translating '*& omnia vanitas*' (which shows the *–e* in *alle* to be the inflection indicating plural number).

Irregular line endings caused by non-finite verb forms are rare. We find only *hade mysdone* (TW 359; read *mysdone hade*?), *to see* (TW 363; read *to sene*?), and *scholde be* (TW 483; read *be scholde*?). On two occasions, a masculine line ending caused by a past participle in T is disputed by a superior reading in W:

and a kyng *made* (p.p.) T 443; W *& a king makid* (cf. *maket* TW 594)
now dethe has þam *boghte* T 617; W *now dethe hath þem bothe*

The MS evidence is thus consistent with the hypothesis that the line endings as the poet wrote them were feminine. In a number of cases the readings of one of the two MSS confirm error in the other, though on occasion the two MSS agree on a metrical irregular reading, which presumably goes back to the common exemplar (not the author's original) from which T and W derive.

[146] Assuming the verb is strong; weak conjugation (pret. *smitte*, *smotte*) is possible: see Wright, *Grammar*, p. 181.

[147] *Found* does occur at line ending in the Ware MS at 442b, where, however, Thornton more intelligibly as well as more metrically reads *sonde* (with analogical *–e*).

*Wars of Alexander (5803 lines)*
Like *P3A*, *WA* survives in two fifteenth-century MSS: A and D, both mid-fifteenth-century; D from Durham, A possibly somewhat further to the North. Both are thus in a scribal language removed in time and place from the dialect of the poet (around Lancashire). Whatever the author's practice in the writing and pronunciation of final –*e*, 'it was not', according to the editors Duggan and Turville-Petre, 'grammatically or phonetically significant for the scribe' (p.xxvii). Spelling is thus in this case a poor guide to metre: historical –*e* at line-ending is sometimes omitted (e.g. *tell* inf. (67), *myȝt* 3rd sg. pret. (68)), and at other times it appears where it has no justification.

Steffens analysed line endings in a substantial sample (ll. 1124–2131 in Duggan and Turville-Petre's edition).[148] In this sample, to which we restrict ourselves, Steffens demonstrated, to our minds convincingly, that masculine line endings were avoided by the poet. A particular strength of Steffens's study is that he draws attention to relevant MS variation at line ending. Regrettably, some of this information is filtered out from the apparatus by Duggan and Turville-Petre, who do not regard final –*e* as metrically significant. Thus not all the following variants can be recovered from their edition:

| A | D | *line* |
|---:|---|---:|
| had | *hadde* | 1162 |
| was meruale to sene | *to see* | 1185 |
| swappis of hes hede | *heued* | 1355 |
| quen þai sa many see | *so mony seen* (pret. pl.?) | 1376 |
| þaire frynde (acc.) | *frendes* | 1381 |
| þaimselfe | *þaimseluen* | 1398 |
| | | cf. 1876, 1914, 1993, *etc.* |
| many threuyn berne | *knyghteȝ* | 1530 |
| into þe wild streme | *stremes* | 1555 |
| arayd | *atired* | 1756 |
| store-ben ('large-boned') | *store-baned* | 1826 |
| he hauys | *he hase*[149] | 1933 |

[148] H. Steffens, *Versbau und Sprache des mittelenglischen stabreimenden Gedichtes 'The Wars of Alexander'*, Bonner Beiträge zur Anglistik, 9 (Bonn, 1901).
[149] *Hauys* and *haues* are clearly line ending specialities (comparable to the *Gawain* poet's *habbe* forms). They occur only in A, in place of normal *hase*, at line ending: 428, 1852, 1933, 2106, 3228 (D *fonges*), 4475) — and 2837b, 'þat þou acheued

| | | |
|---|---|---|
| agayne | *ayayns* (read *agaynes*?)[150] | 2068 |
| fais | *athellis* | 2071 |

To these cases of corrections recoverable from the variants may be added some straightforward petrified datives: *at the last* (1131), *out of lyfe* (1143), *on first* (1152), *to þe gronde* (1338) *to dethe* (1386), *on his brest* (1722), *to dede* (1915), *in hand* (2056); and some datives also susceptible of other explanations *with his hede* (1092, or *heved*?), *all daye* (1928; or pl.?), *on þe morne* (1476 < OE *morgen*, or etymological *–e(n)* in *morwe*(*n*)?).

This leaves only eleven problematic cases.[151] *Lorde* (1775), *helme* (1839), *vaile* (1328; D *wale*), *flayne* (1893)[152] have already been discussed. *Werd* 'world' (2011 dative; 2024 accusative) has various disyllabic forms (< OE *woruld*) but the word is also a common scribal misreading for *erde* or *erþe*.[153] Steffens would emend *durand* (MS D *endurand*) *his lyfe* (1311) to *all hys lyf-daies* (after 369b), but inflected *lyue* is correct after prepositional *durand*. He also suggests the possibility of a disyllabic form of *hert* 'hart' (1193), from OE *heorot*, but the word may here have been substituted for original *beste*. Generic *men* (1292) may well be a substitute for a poetic synonym: Steffens suggests *athils*, and points to the scribal substitution of *athils* by *men* at 49 (see Duggan and Turville-Petre's note to 49 for other

hase', may be emended to accord with this pattern. Mid-line *haues* occurs only once, not for *hase*, but as imp. pl. (2895).

150 As in the Cotton Nero poems, so in *WA agaynes* (or *ayaynes*) is the line-ending form, though original *–es* appears variously in A are *ayaynez* (830), *agayne* (918), *agaynes* (1077, 1624, 1859, 2004, 2045), *agayne* (2068), *agaynes* (2921), and *agayne* (4168). Mid-line *agaynes* occurs once to secure a long b-verse dip (2099), and twice in a-verses without anacrusis (2483, 3977).

151 Steffens unnecesarily finds fault with *emperoure* (see n. 139 above) and with *thinke* at 1762 ('how so me dere thinke') and 1972 ('surely me thinke'), both of which he would emend to *þinkes*. But the former is subjunctive (cf. 3074) and the latter a personal construction (with justified final *–e* in the first person) influenced by the impersonal one (a consequence of the incipient collapse of the distinction between personal and impersonal 'think'), paralleled by e.g. (*as*) *me þynk* at *Pearl* 267 and *P* 427.

152 Steffens thinks a plural is intended and would emend to *flanes* (cf. 2337, 5574).

153 See *WA* 189 and the editors' note to 18. The same error may be responsible for the defective alliteration at *C* 228, 'On vche syde of þe worlde aywhere ilyche'.

examples). The etymology of *ryft* (1880; D *drifte*)[154] is uncertain (cf. OI *ript*); *Troy Book*, 2.1002, 'Þat in þe werk þer was no rifte sene', might suggest that the word had a disyllabic form in ME, though Lydgate's metre is notoriously problematic. *Ost(e)* (1172, 1297, 1573) also occurs at line ending at 2157, where *D* has plural *ostez*; conversely, at 2441 A reads *ostes*, but D *ost*; emendation to the plural is therefore possible, though it may well be that the noun *host* (army) was confused with *hoste* (host), the latter with organic *–e*.

*Siege of Jerusalem (1340 lines)*

*SJ* is extant in nine copies, of which the oldest are L (Bodleian Library, MS Laud Misc 656, from Oxfordshire) and P (Princeton UL, MS Taylor Medieval 11, from Yorkshire). Hanna and Lawton use L as the base-text for their recent edition. Like Duggan and Turville-Petre, they give no special consideration to line endings in recording manuscript variants, so differences as between masculine and feminine line endings are not systematically recorded in the apparatus. This makes it difficult to investigate the question properly on the basis of their edition. We have supplemented the MS variants recorded in Hanna and Lawton's apparatus with an independent consultation of P (which terminates at 1143 and is illegible towards the end). Where P departs from L, we shall give the variant reading below. Readings from other MSS are provided selectively; references to these MSS are by the sigla as used in Hanna and Lawton's edition.

The poem as edited by Hanna and Lawton appears to have remarkably few masculine endings. Where the final unstressed syllable at line ending depends on the status of final *–e* in nouns with monosyllabic stems, that *–e* is either organic or grammatical. In addition to petrified datives, there are again cases which indicate an active ability to generate, not merely a passive ability to repeat, dative constructions: *on his breste* (475; P *hreste*), *myd chaf* (806 < OE *ceaf* n.), *with a pryuande kny3t* (437), and *Of [Iosue] þe noble Iewe and Iudas þe kny3t* (480), *in þe werke* (990), *in þe fuste* (1144).

Apart from some cases where the MSS disagree — which we reserve for later — the only noteworthy anomalies in the category of noun are:

[154] The reading of D is disproved by the source; see Duggan and Turville-Petre's illuminating note to the line.

*lord* (185; P *louerde*), *vale* (604; P omits),[155] *oste* 'army' (733),[156] *dynte* (1202 acc. < OE *dynt* m.), and *Holy Goste* (107; 115, P *hegh halygast*).[157]

Adjectives also have either grammatical *–e* (for plural) or organic *–e*, the *–e* being absent in MS L only in the case of *twey* (137+), *out* (96) and *few* (1114). The only clearly non-feminine line-ending adjective on which the MSS agree is *þre* (935); the source confirms the number (*tribus mensibus*), though the poet may have written *þrynne*. In the analogous case of *two*, the distribution of forms is similar to that of the Cotton Nero poems: *two* appears mid-line (134, 140, 1173), *twey* < OE *twegen* appears at line ending (137, 273, 711), though it has lost the *–e* that almost certainly put it there to begin with. The exception is 705a, 'Twey apys at his armes', which is metrically irregular by our a-verse rules (see chapter 5) and contradicted by MSS UEC (*And two*).

Adverbs and prepositions are likewise unproblematic. They have historical or analogical *–e,* which is missing from L in only a few cases: *þan* 173 and 181 (*þan* at 173, emended by Hanna and Lawton to *emperour*, following PAUDE), *ynow* (208; P *many*), *awey* (257), *withyn* (452), *hey* (650), and *hard* (841, 1030). For *þeraȝens* (219) read *þeraȝenes* (cf. Hanna and Lawton's emendation at 1219). The only other problematic adverb is *noȝt* (19), which also occurs at line ending in *E*.

Pronouns confirm the preference for feminine line endings. In L the suffix *–self* always appears in this form in the middle of the line (17x), and it is only at the end of the line that we find traces of the inflected form — *vsselue* (876; P omits), *ȝourselfen* (1217), *myselue* (1235) — a fact which justifies emendation to *–selue* of line-terminal *hemself* (1074) and *hymself* (1298). *None* at 641 is construed as sg. 'no one' by Hanna and Lawton, but pl. 'none, no persons' is equally possible.

Verb endings are also almost totally unproblematic. Three noteworthy feminine line endings in MS L are the inflected infinitive *to done* (216; P omits)[158] and the single instance of a <bb> form of the verb

[155] See above, p. 51.
[156] See above, p. 65.
[157] At 107 the construction is dative: *saue* [PAUC *bot*, D *but of*, E *but be*] *þe Holy Goste*. At 115 *Holy Goste* [P *hegh halygast*] is the subject. Barney, in 'Langland's Prosody', notes that 'Holy Gost' also appears anomalously at line ending at *PP* B 17.285b (= C 19.266), 'men offenden þe holy goost', where MS F reads 'þe holy goost offende'.
[158] The only other possible example of an inflected inf. in L is *to seyn* (868; P *say*).

'to have' in infinitive *habben* (820; P *hab*), emended by Hanna and Lawton to *habiden*, the reading of AUDEC.

The only certain case of a line ending in a singular strong past tense is *knewe* (797; P *knewen* is metrical but not comprehensible); the typical avoidance strategy is to switch to the historic present, as happens in the following line (*byddis*, miscopied in A as *badde*). The only other example of a strong singular preterite, *stode* (1287), is doubtful, since in AUE the subject (and therefore the verb) is plural (*walllis* not *walle*).

Past participles of irregular weak verbs do, however, occasionally present anomalies: *hytte* (829), *broȝt* (933; P *broght*, also1056), *bouȝte* (1214), and *souȝte* (1281). For *wroȝte* (331, 897; P *wroght*), *ywroȝt* (466; P *wroght*) and *laft* (185, P *lefte*),[159] forms in *–ed* are possible. At 934, L's *made* is refuted by P's *maked* and confirmed by participial *maked* at end of 1026 (the only example of this form in L). *Sette* at 401 is emended by Hanna and Lawton to *assised*, the reading — confirmed by the source (*assis*) — of MSS UDC. On the other occasions when *sette* occurs at line ending (474, 957; P *sett*), the context requires the sense 'seated': *sette* may be the p.p. of the strong verb *sitten*. Hanna and Lawton construe *sette* at 957 accordingly, and the MSS variants at 474 (E *saat*, pret.sg.; A *solde sytt*) suggest some of the scribes also did so.[160]

It is clear from these data that the poet of *SJ* avoided masculine line endings. That being the case, line endings (and their variants in extant MSS) deserve more editorial attention than they have yet received. Of particular concern are various emendations by Hanna and Lawton that give rise to strong sg. preterites at line ending. There are three examples. The first concerns the members of the Trinity:

> Alle ben þey endeles and eu[en] of o myȝt [L *euer*]
> And weren [inwardly] endeles o[r] þe [erþe] byg[a]n (117–8)
> [L *and weren endeles euer byfor þe world was bygonne*;
> P omits; UDEC *And weren or þe world was euer bygonne*;[161]
> A *Alle inwardly endeles was never nane*]

[159] Possibly also *lefte* at 599 (P *walden*), construed as pret. sg. by Hanna and Lawton but as p.p. by Kölbing and Day.

[160] As has already been pointed out (see above, pp. 28, n. 35), the ME p.p. of 'set' *sete* (securely attested by rhyme in Gower's *Confessio Amantis*) may point to some confusion between the verbs 'sit' and 'set'.

[161] Spellings of *world* differ in UEDC: UD *world*; E *wurld*; C *worlde*. We simplify for the sake of clarity.

L 118b is suspect on grounds of alliteration and b-verse metre, but Hanna and Lawton's solution is tortuously unsatisfactory (in view both of the MSS and of the avoidance of singular strong preterites). Sense and metre would be better served by

And euer weren endeles or erd was bygonne

At 212b 'þat to Nero come' [*sic* UD; L 'þat to Nero was come'; P 'þat Nero to come'; A 'þat was to Nero come'; E 'as y to yow tolde'], the past tense produces an irregular line ending, where the past participle does not. The Hanna and Lawton reading removes L's unmetrical two long dips in the b-verse, but some solution to that problem (e.g. the A reading) that does not sacrifice regular line-ending metre to regular b-verse metre is called for.

The third instance is 943–4 (following a textual lacuna):

Þat [a]s naked as an nedul þe newe emperour
[L *Þat is*; P omits *þat*; E *and they*; C *They made hym*]
For sire Sabyns sake alle þe cite drowe
[L *drowe hym*; P *was drawen*; C *drawen*]

Hanna and Lawton argue that 'All openings to this line are probably scribal smoothings to construct a narative sequence following losses, and are simply beyond our repair'. This may be true; but in the source text, Higden's *Polychronicon*, the new emperor (Vitellius) is not the *object* but the *subject* in a passive construction: 'deinde ... a ducibus Vespasiani inde protractus, per urbem nudus palam est ductus'[162] ('then he was led away by Vespasian's leaders, and led naked for all to see though the city'). And some emendation based on *is* ... *drawen* rather than preterite *drowe* would be more in accord with the source and the metre of the poem.

Metrical considerations also have a bearing on some other editorial decisions. At l. 1100, MS L reads as follows:

Þan þus in langur to lyue and lengþen our fyne
[AVUD *pyne*; EC *peyne*; P illegible]

Hanna and Lawton consider L's reading 'the *durior*, in fact almost too good a, reading'. But the final *–e* in *fyne* < OF *fin* is not organic, and emendation to either *pyne* < OE feminine n. *pin* (disyllabic in Orm and

162 We cite *Polychronicon* from the edition by Hanna and Lawton in their appendix to *SJ*.

Chaucer) or *peyne* < OF *peine* (the reading adopted by Kölbing-Day) is therefore preferable.

At 675, grammar and metre favour a plural noun in the b-verse:

> Brenn[and]e leed and brynston [many] barel fulle
> [*sic* UD; C *many a barel*; LPA *barels*]

Hanna and Lawton note that they might 'equally have read trisyllabic *barel[e]s*, as we do *kirnel[e]s* 686'. And since adjectives without grammatical or etymological –*e* are not found at line ending, and *fulle* therefore presupposes a plural antecedent, *bareles* (adopted by Turville-Petre and Kölbing-Day) is indeed to be preferred to *barel*. The same applies to 1279, 'Clene cloþes of selke, many carte fulle' [UC *cartes*; V *cartes to*].

On the other hand, metre would support Hanna and Lawton's emendation of 844:

> Was mychel leuere a leche þan layke myd his to[les]
> [L *ton*; P *toles*; A *toose*; CUDE *any thing / layk / pley / body elles*]

The plural *ton* (or *toose*), normally monsyllabic, would be difficult at line ending, so metre would support Hanna and Lawton's emendation to *toles* (weapons) or *toiles* (slings), as suggested in their note.

*Destruction of Troy (14,044 lines)*

It is instructive to compare the alliterative poems we have examined thus far with *DT*, which, as Luick observed, was written by a poet who observed no metrical constraint at line ending. What do we find in such a poem that we do not find in other alliterative poems?

Firstly, there is an abundance of strong singular preterites, e.g. *felle* (25, 73, 76, *etc.*); *sprong(e)* (295, 1079, 4814, *etc.*); *toke* (140, 844, 885 *etc.*); *blew* (1057, 4588, 6991, *etc.*); *lay* (1788, 4523, 5233, *etc.*). Second, we encounter many strong adjectives without organic –*e* at line ending, e.g. *olde* (99, 1114, 1841, *etc.*); *stronge* (2120, 7729, 9759 *etc.*); *fell* (909, 5099, 5936, *etc.*); *full* (5064); *soche* (786); *hegh* (1702); *negh* (928). Non-dative nouns without organic or analogical –*e* occur freely at line ending, e.g. *kyng* (141, 1130, 1786, *etc.*); *lond* (721, 2324, 12922, *etc.*); *gold* (459, 997, 2900, *etc.*); *god* (163, 697, *etc.*); *wif* (3160, 4483, 8714, *etc.*). Other irregular nouns that occur frequently at line ending are *se(e)* 'sea' (269, 1315, 2548, *etc.*); *men* (818, 2211, 2411, *etc.*); *(f)fo(o)* (4989, 7230, 7950, *etc.*). Having observed the avoidance of monosyllabic verb forms in other alliterative poems, one is struck by *DT*'s tolerance of such words as *has* (718, 1864, 2404, *etc.*); *be* (2587, 3361, 4244, *etc.*); *is* (2425, 11664; *was*, 28, 852, 1387); *went* sg. (avoided at line ending in other alliterative poems by means of *ȝede/ȝode*) (679, 5788, 7907 *etc.*); *shall* sg. (153, 266, 601, *etc.*); *may* sg. (572, 2127, 2197, *etc.*); *se* inf. (318, 334, 356 *etc.*); *do* inf. (230, 2442, 2873); *go* inf. (2491, 6658, 9233, *etc.*); *lis/lys* 'lies' (4992, 5369); *tas* 'takes' (661, 2070, 8313); and irregular weak past participles such as *broght* (869, 1442, 1456, *etc.*); *wroght* (41, 1548, 1634, *etc.*); *set* (265, 1610, 3053, *etc.*). Notable adverbs and prepositions that are elsewhere avoided at line endings but favoured by the poet of *DT* are *to(o)* 'to' (360, 628, 761, *etc.*); *with* (44, 62, 364, etc.); *now(e)* (43, 240, 3151, etc.); *well/wele* (101, 233, 1121, etc.); *so* (1318, 2817, 3324, etc.); *forth(e)/furth(e)* (2440, 2467, 2983, etc.); *why* (359, 556, 2487, *etc.*). A monosyllabic personal pronoun (*him*, *hit*, *her*, etc.) is occasionally used by other alliterative poets as the final unstressed syllable; in *DT*, by contrast, it frequently provides a stressed ending (as the rule requiring one long-dip in the b-verse indicates), e.g.:

| | |
|---|---|
| for lernyng of vs (32b) | & safly to hym (4997b) |
| blessid were I (473b) | ne chosyn by hym (7202b) |

*DT* is, however, atypical. As we have suggested in the Introduction, *DT* is later than the other poems we have examined, and changes in the language (such as the recession of final *–e*) are likely to have led the poet to a different understanding of alliterative metre. In the fourteenth century, however, it was plainly a rule of alliterative metre, as it was commonly understood and practised, that the line should end in an unstressed syllable. It is therefore incumbent upon editors of these poems to signal as problematic or corrupt any apparent exceptions to this rule, and to attempt to explain or emend the text by such ways as we have suggested.

There are various other implications for future research. Our analysis casts serious doubt on the consensus view that final *–e* had more or less disappeared in all but southern dialects. It was clearly still available in literary usage to alliterative poets, whose grammar of final *–e* (at least at line ending) agrees broadly with that of Chaucer's. It also agrees with Chaucer's in some finer points (*soþ* is monosyllabic, but takes final *–e* when it is preceded by article or preposition). The use of dative *–e* by alliterative poets is, if anything, slightly more liberal than Chaucer's, whose use of it is restricted to a closed class of set phrases. The fact that alliterative poets avoided masculine line endings means that their verse presents new opportunities for advancing our understanding of how final *–e* was used in verse. Nouns pose particular problems here. Many, but by no means all, feminine nouns acquired analogical *–e*, and, for reasons that are none too clear, so did a few neuter and masculine nouns. How can we know whether or not a noun had acquired a non-etymological final *–e*? No-one has systematically pursued that question since 1942, when Ruth McJimsey published *Chaucer's Irregular Final –E*, so we have had to rely on our own research into the practices of careful metrists such as Orm, Chaucer, and Gower. However, many uncertainties remain in the data and in our interpretation of them. It is to be hoped that informed analysis of the poems we have studied and those we have not will clarify some of these uncertainties and lead others to improve upon our suggestions.

# 2. FINAL –*E*. THE EVIDENCE OF INFINITIVES AND ADVERBIAL AND ADJECTIVAL SUFFIXES

In the previous chapter we have argued that historical final –*e* was pronounced at line ending. In this chapter we propose to examine the status of final –*e* within the alliterative long line. This status is a matter of serious importance to metrists, historical linguists and editors. In the study of metre, the status of final –*e* is a determining factor in the syllable count, since there are few lines in any Middle English poem where –*e* does not affect scansion. Janet Cowen and George Kane found just nine unambiguous lines in the whole of Chaucer's *Legend of Good Women*, though admittedly that number also excludes lines with scansion uncertainties other than final –*e* (such as the possibility of syncope).[1] To editors, judgements about the poet's grammar of final –*e* and his metrical norms and rules can inform choices between textual variants and the decision as to whether or not to emend. Historical linguists have always taken an interest in the fortunes of final –*e*,[2] not least because its mutescence is part of the process that slowly transformed English from an inflected language into a predominantly analytical one. Whether the issue is also of interest to literary critics depends a good deal on the nature of their engagement with poetry. To anyone who thinks that the achievement of poets rests on their ability to communicate within, and by virtue of, constraints of rhyme and metre, linguistic questions such as why and whether poets wrote –*e* or –*en*, –*ly* or –*lyche*, may mean rather more than to those whose interests are socio-historical.

Thanks to the combined efforts of many scholars (from Kittredge to Cowen and Kane) we now know a great deal about Chaucer's grammar of final –*e*, enough to realise that its value depends on many variables

[1] Geoffrey Chaucer, *The Legend of Good Women*, ed. Janet Cowen and George Kane (East Lansing, Mich., 1995), p. 114. It would be beyond the scope of this chapter to provide an overview or bibliography of the scholarship on the question. Cowen and Kane's section on 'The Grammar of Final *e* in Relation to Editorial Problems of Metre' provides an excellent treatment of the topic in relation to Chaucer.

[2] See especially Donka Minkova, *The History of Final Vowels in English: the Sound of Muting*, Topics in English Linguistics 4 (Berlin, 1991).

such as syntax, historical grammar, rhyme position, eliding context, and so on. In the case of alliterative poetry, such clarity is still a distant prospect. Whereas we know, for example, that Chaucer *always* pronounced inflectional *–e* in his infinitives at line ending and *usually* did so mid-line,[3] we remain largely ignorant about what major alliterative poets, such as the *Gawain* poet, did. It is a symptom of this uncertainty that the two scholars who have tried hardest to advance learning in this area arrived, at least initially, at radically different conclusions: Thomas Cable arguing, on the one hand, that historically justified *-e* was *invariably* pronounced by alliterative poets;[4] and Hoyt Duggan arguing, by contrast, that final *–e* was more or less defunct.[5] Although the rhyme evidence of *Sir Gawain and the Green Knight* shows that on a couple of occasions final *–e must* be sounded for the sake of rhyme (*to þe* : *forsoþe* 'in truth' (413–5) and *waþe* ('danger' < ON *vaði*): *ta þe* (2355–57), more extensive study of the rhymes in *G* has itself led to radically different conclusions. While Karl Luick concluded that the rhymes show that final *–e* was normally pronounced (with apocope as a permissible licence),[6] Marie Borroff has argued the very opposite.[7] Whoever may be right, it would be hazardous in any case to infer regular linguistic practice from rhyme usage: poets (and Chaucer is a case in point)[8] do things in rhyme that they do not do anywhere else.

In this chapter we hope to clear up a small area in the minefield of final *–e* by examining in detail the use of *–ly* and *–lyche* in adjectives and adverbs and of inflectional *–e* and *–(e)n* in infinitives within a selected

[3] For infinitives at line end see Stephen Barney, *Studies in Troilus: Chaucer's Text, Meter, and Diction* (East Lansing, 1993), and see Cowen and Kane, 'Grammar of Final *e*', for some infinitives with optional *–e* mid-line.

[4] Cable, *Alliterative Tradition*, p. 78.

[5] Duggan, 'Final *–e*'. Duggan may be changing his mind about the value of final *–e*. In 'Aspects of A-Verse Rhythms', p. 485, he writes that there is some evidence that alliterative poets 'occasionally made use of … inflectional and etymological *–e*'s on stressed stems for metrical convenience'. Although Duggan does not explicitly say it, this position contradicts his previous views on the subject.

[6] Luick, 'Stabreimzeile', and see also Joseph Fischer, *Die stabende Langzeile in den Werken des Gawaindichters*, Bonner Beiträge zur Anglistik, 11 (1901), 1–64.

[7] Borroff, *'Sir Gawain'*, pp. 155–8.

[8] For example, dative *–e* in *yere* is only ever attested in rhyme position in Chaucer; the same is true for analogical *–e* in *there*. See Wild, *Eigentümlichkeiten*, pp. 9, 11, and McJimsey, *Chaucer's Irregular –E*, p. 104.

corpus of alliterative poetry. Our corpus consists of the Cotton Nero poems,[9] *Alexander and Dindimus* (*B*), *The Siege of Jerusalem* (*SJ*) and *William of Palerne* (*WP*). In a final concluding section we shall look briefly at some other alliterative poems — *Death and Liffe*, *Saint Erkenwald*, *Destruction of Troy*, *Wars of Alexander* and *Morte Arthure* — in order to frame our findings in a larger context.

We restrict our study to infinitive endings and adverbial and adjectival *–ly* and *–lyche* for the following reasons.[10] First, it seemed preferable to us to deal as comprehensively and transparently as possible with a restricted body of material rather than to deal with a larger corpus impressionistically and without being able to make full disclosure of the evidence. Second, as will become evident later, the existing scholarship, as reflected in treatments of accidence in the editions of alliterative poems and in specialised studies, offers unsatisfactory treatments of these topics, which would therefore benefit from further consideration. Third, it cannot be assumed that the situation of infinitives and *–lych* suffixes is comparable with that of other verb forms or other adjectives and adverbs. In infinitives, *–n* disappeared more rapidly than in other verb forms. This is reflected in the alliterative poems under investigations, where *–en* is much more frequent in present and preterite plurals than in

[9] We do not intend to re-open the question of the authorship of the four Cotton Nero poems; however, for the sake of transparency, we should say that we assume common authorship, and we include *Pearl*, even though it is not an alliterative poem, on that basis. References will normally be to the following editions: *Cleanness* [*C*], ed. J. J. Anderson (Manchester, 1977), *Patience* [*P*], ed. J. J. Anderson (Manchester, 1969); *Pearl*, ed. E. V. Gordon (Oxford, 1953), *Sir Gawain and the Green Knight* [*G*], ed. J. R. R. Tolkien and E. V. Gordon, rev. Norman Davis (Oxford, 1967).

[10] Other aspects of the infinitive which are of linguistic and metrical interest are the choice between *to* and *for to* and the use of the plain infinitive. These aspects have received attention from other scholars. See, for example, Henk Aertsen, 'The Infinitive in *Sir Gawain and the Green Knight*', in *This Noble Craft: Proceedings of the Xth Research Symposium of Dutch and Belgian University Teachers*, ed. Erik Kooper (Amsterdam, 1991), pp. 3–28; Tsuneo Sakai, 'On Some Aspects of the Infinitive in ME *Sir Gawain and the Green Knight*', *Bulletin of Kochi Women's University* 11 (1962), 1–15; Olga Fischer, 'Infinitive Marking in Late Middle English: Transitivity and Changes in the English System of Case', in Jacek Fisiak (ed.), *Studies in Middle English Linguistics* (Berlin, 1997), pp. 109–34; Duggan, 'Aspects of A-Verse Rhythms'; Noriko Inoue, 'The A-Verse', pp. 134–143. See also below, pp. 247–8.

infinitives; and in the past participles of strong verbs *–en* is in fact the default form. Since the distribution of *–e* and *–en* varies from one grammatical context to another, each case requires individual attention. In the case of *–lych*, too, we need to be prepared to make distinctions. For example, we should not assume that an adjective like *godlych* will be inflected like all other disyllabic adjectives. *Uncouth*, *godlych* and *bitter* are all disyllabic, but they provide (in the order as listed) increasingly unfavourable conditions for the survival of *–e*. In oxytonic adjectives *–e* follows a syllable with primary stress; in adjectives ending in *–lych* final *–e* follows a syllable with secondary stress; in *bitter* a syllable with weak stress. The traditional position was that inflectional *-e* was retained both in oxytonic adjectives (though not necessarily French-derived ones) and in adjectives terminating in suffixes ending in consonants (e.g. *–lych*, *–les*, *–ful*), but not normally retained in disyllabic adjectives with suffixes ending in vowels (e.g. *–ly*) or disyllabic adjectives in unaccented *–er*, *–en*, *–el*, or vowels.[11] Although this position has been abandoned by modern metrists, including Duggan and Cable, we believe it to be soundly based.

Our choice of corpus may likewise require some explanation. With the exception of *SJ* we focus on poems in single manuscripts. For reasons we have already made clear, we do not share Duggan's distrust of evidence derived from single-manuscript poems. Moreover, in order to determine the finer points of linguistic usage in a period of rapid change, it makes sense to concentrate on witnesses temporally close to the period of original composition. As the earliest extant manuscripts of alliterative poetry, King's College Cambridge, MS 13 (c1375, containing *WP*), British Library, MS Cotton Nero A.x (c1400), Bodleian Library, MS Bodley 264 (c1400, containing *B*), Bodleian Library, MS Laud Misc. 656 (late fourteenth-century, containing *SJ*) and Princeton University Library, MS Taylor Medieval 11 (late fourteenth-century, also containing *SJ*) are of special interest, though close dialectal proximity between the language of the scribe and that of the poet is assured only for the poems of MS Cotton Nero A.x.[12] By contrast, with the exception of *SJ*, substantial alliterative poems extant in multiple copies (*WA*, *The Parliament of the Three Ages*) survive only in manuscripts dating from around the middle of the fifteenth century and later, and the insight into the linguistic habits of

[11] For statements of this position see for example, Karl Luick, *Historische Grammatik*, p. 509, Fernand Mossé, *Handbook of Middle English*, trans. James A. Walker (Baltimore, 1952), p. 64, and ten Brink, *Language*, p. 156.
[12] See our discussion above, p. 11.

fourteenth-century poets given by such late witnesses is likely to be limited and obscured by the passage of time.

By examining the distribution of *–e* and *–en* infinitives and suffixes in *–ly* and *–lych* in this corpus, we hope to shed light on a number of broader problems, including the following:

1) To what extent was infinitive *–n* and *–lych* retained by later Middle English poets, and in what circumstances?
2) What metrical constraints are operative in the alliterative long line?
3) Did alliterative poets still assume historically justified final *–e*?

Because the variation between *–e* and *–en* in infinitives and between the *–ly* and *–lych* termination is closely bound up with these larger questions, we begin our discussion of both issues by summarizing briefly the assumptions guiding current thinking about them.

## Part I. Infinitives in *–e* and *–en*

*Background*

As regards the retention of *–en* in infinitives, much depends on date and dialect, as well as on the grammatical situation, the phonological environment and the metrical constraints. Inflectional *–n* in verbs was lost earliest in Northern dialects (where, however, it was systematically retained in the past participle of strong verbs); in verbs it was lost first in infinitives (apocopated forms of which are already attested in OE) and only later in plurals, perhaps because here final *–n* continued to be functional as the marker distinguishing plurality from singularity, as Karl Luick has suggested.[13] Karl Brunner writes of infinitives that in 'the South *–en*, *–n* remains until the end of the fourteenth century, and somewhat longer in monosyllabic forms (*ben* 'to be', *sen* 'to see', *etc.*). In the Midlands *–en*, *–n* disappears rather earlier.'[14] Although this needs qualifying — the date of c. 1400 for the disappearance of *–n* in infinitives is at least a century too early, and an exception should be made for the South East Midland dialect, which 'seems inclined toward a greater retention of *–n* than the other areas'[15]—,it is nevertheless clear that by the fourteenth century *–n*

[13] Luick, *Historische Grammatik*, p. 956. Luick's hypothesis does not explain, however, why final *–n* was more tenacious in preterite than in present plurals.
[14] Brunner, *Outline*, p. 71.
[15] David Reed, *The History of Inflectional N in English Verbs Before 1500* (Berkeley, 1950), p. 259. A complementary treatment of loss of *–n* in nouns may be found

was distinctly recessive. In Chaucer's language, which has attracted the most thorough study, infinitives in *–n* are outnumbered by forms with *–e*/Ø, the former occuring especially (though by no means systematically) before a vowel or unaspirated *h–* to prevent hiatus.[16] This practice is sometimes in conflict with the demands of metre. G. V. Smithers has argued that Chaucer *never* used *–en* in eliding contexts where this would result in a sequence of two unstressed syllables,[17] and editors often emend *–en* to *–e* where this would be the result.[18] Yet the latest thinking is that Chaucer tolerated *–en* infinitives before an unstressed syllable in eliding position.[19] In Chaucer's language, then, the distribution of *–e* and *–en* infinitives is not entirely conditioned by metre.

In the Midland dialects of alliterative poetry inflectional *–n* is rarer than it is in Chaucer's language. Scholars have generally assumed that infinitives with and without *–n* occur in free variation in alliterative verse. In the case of the Cotton Nero poems and other alliterative poems, the sections on accidence in the standard editions treat forms with *–en* as a minority form that could be used, occasionally and apparently *ad libitum*, alongside forms with *–e* (and zero ending). The editors of alliterative poetry have thus tended to treat infinitives in *–e* and *–en* as interchangeable forms, occasionally emending the former to the latter where they believe the metre requires it. To take an example from *WA*, Thorlac Turville-Petre and Hoyt Duggan emend 'to kepe þa landis' (73b) to 'to kepe[n] þa landis', in order to secure the double dip required by the rules governing b-verse metre. The assumption seems to be that the poet

in Samuel Moore, 'Loss of Final *n* in Inflectional Syllables of Middle English', *Language*, 3 (1927), 232-59.

16 Wild, *Eigentümlichkeiten*, p. 296.

17 G. V. Smithers, 'The Scansion of *Havelok* and the Use of ME *–en* and *–e* in *Havelok* and Chaucer', in *Middle English Studies Presented to Norman Davis*, ed. Douglas Gray and E. G. Stanley (Oxford, 1983), 195–234.

18 For example, Stephen Barney emends his copy-text of *Troilus* (Cambridge, Corpus Christi 61), l. 1.189, 'But gan to *preisen* and lakken whom hym leste', to 'But gan to *preise* and lakken ...'.

19 Stephen Barney, *Studies in 'Troilus'*, p. 98. Chaucer's disciple Hoccleve, on the other hand, uses *–en* forms almost exclusively where they are necessary for the syllable count: there is only one example in the Hoccleve holographs of the use of *–en* before a consonant. See Judith A. Jefferson, 'The Hoccleve Holographs and Hoccleve's Metrical Practice', in *Manuscripts and Texts: Editorial Problems in Middle English Literature*, ed. Derek Pearsall (Cambridge, 1987), pp. 95–109 (pp. 102–3).

was free to replace –*e* with –*en* if he needed the extra syllable. (The emendation also depends on the further assumption that *kepe* is monosyllabic; we shall come to this issue shortly).

With regard to the metrical constraints of the alliterative long line, since these constraints are of fundamental importance to the understanding of grammatical choices made by alliterative poets, we need to recall that the alliterative long line has two (or more, according to both Duggan and Cable) alliterating beats in the a-verse and two beats in the b-verse, only the first of which must alliterate, and that the b-verse should contain one, and only one, long dip (a long dip being a sequence of two or more unstressed syllables).[20] This syllabic rule was first discovered by Karl Luick, who also believed that a further metrical constraint on the b-verse is that the line should end in one and only one unstressed syllable.[21] Further evidence for the avoidance of masculine line endings has been advanced in our first chapter. Thomas Cable also argues that a-verses must contain two long dips, but the evidence for this is tenuous. We believe that alliterative poets normally wrote a-verses with a long initial dip and a long medial dip, and only departed from this norm:

(1) in a-verses containing an extra-long dip (four or more unstressed syllables);

(2) in a-verses containing a long or heavy final dip (a heavy dip being a syllable or one-syllable word with secondary stress).

Evidence for this rule will be provided in the final chapter. Finally, with regard to final -*e*, we recall that most scholars assume that it had ceased to be pronounced in alliterative poetry. (Thomas Cable, however, argues that final –*e* was *always* pronounced in a wide range of grammatical categories.) For example, in their recent edition of *SJ*, Ralph Hanna and David Lawton talk of the 'certain absence of –*e* from the author's dialect' (p. xxix). It appears from their editorial practice that this generalisation should not to be taken at face value, for in fact Hanna and Lawton assume that final –*e* could still be sounded in weak and plural adjectives with a monosyllabic stem and also in present participles on –*ande*.[22] Thus

[20] See especially Duggan, 'The Shape of the B-Verse'.

[21] Luick, 'Die englische Stabreimzeile', especially §24.

[22] In one respect, Hanna and Lawton go further than Duggan in the majority of his articles, since they also permit the sounding of final –*e* in adverbs. Thus they refrain from emending 477b, 'þat loude couþe singe', because, as they suggest in a note, *loude* might be disyllabic.

— though they emend all metrically irregular b-verses — they do not emend 396b 'with foure kene bladdys' (alliterating on *f*), presumably because *kene* is taken to be disyllabic. Nor do they emend 230b, 'and rennande teris', because they think that, after present participial *–and*, *–e* could also retain its syllabic value. In treating these two grammatical categories as 'exceptions', Lawton and Hanna follow in the footsteps of Duggan, who, as we have seen, has until recently argued very strongly that final *–e* had no syllabic value in alliterative poetry, and that allowances should be made only for a few exceptional grammatical categories and for one exceptional poet, Langland, who *did* sound final *–es*, his language being in this and other respects 'a good bit more conservative than that of any of the other alliterative poets.'[23] Accordingly, both Duggan and Turville-Petre and Hanna and Lawton emend, or reject as scribal, b-verses in which the long dip would depend on the sounding of final *–e* in other, non-exceptional, categories. For example, they do not consider final *–e* to be syllabic in nouns even where it is historically justified:

a *fote* thik yse (*WA* 3009)
(ME *fot* as measure is frequently disyllabic in ME)[24]
new *note* ryses (*WA* 3152) (< OE *notu*)
hem *grace* [for]to sende (*SJ* 1023) (OF *grace*)

Apropos of *WA* 3009 and 3152, Duggan and Turville-Petre note: 'The b-verse is unmetrical in both manuscripts, and we have no convincing emendation'. Similarly, *SJ* 1023 has been emended by Hanna and Lawton on the assumption that the pronunciation of organic and grammatical *–e* was no longer an option for the poet (though note that the line would be perfectly metrical if it had been read by Chaucer or Langland).

[23] Hoyt Duggan, 'Langland's Dialect and Final *–e*', *Studies in the Age of Chaucer*, 12 (1990), 157–91. See also Duggan's article, 'Final *–e* and the Rhythmic Structure of the B-Verse in Middle English Alliterative Poetry', *Modern Philology*, 86 (1988), 119–45. For Duggan's more recent views, see note 7 above. M. L. Samuels also argues that 'Langland must have made at least some use of grammatical final *–e*': 'Langland's Dialect', *Medium Aevum*, 54 (1985), 232–47, repr. in *The English of Chaucer and His Contemporaries*, ed. J. J. Smith (Aberdeen, 1988), pp. 70–85 (p. 80).
[24] Cf. Chaucer: 'And er they ferther any *foote* wente' (*CT* V.1177), 'Was plated half a *foote* thikke' (*HF* 3.1345), and *MA* 801b, 'tene fote large', *MA* 1855b, 'sex fotte large'. According to McJimsey, *Irregular –E*, p. 72, the final *–e* may be traceable to an earlier dative case; more probably, the usage is generalised from the partitive genitive *fote* (<OE *fota*) after numerals. See Eugen Einenkel, *Geschichte der englischen Sprache* (Strasbourg, 1916), p. 51.

Consequently, they routinely emend infinitives in –*e*, following the precedent set by Duggan and Turville-Petre. For example:

to *serche[n]* ȝour wille (*SJ* 343) to *pyne[n]* foreuere (*SJ* 1327)

In all the emendations we have cited, Hanna and Lawton over-rule the evidence of the manuscript tradition, which stubbornly supports the reading which they assume to be spurious.[25] What is more, the belief that final –*e* is insignificant is so firmly held by both pairs of editors that they omit from the apparatus any systematic record of final –*e*. This means, of course, that their editions are of limited use to scholars who do not share this belief, or who wish to test it, since the apparatus edits out 'insignificant' final –*e*s in much the same way as the edited text does, except that in the apparatus the editorial omissions are undetectable.[26]

The present study of infinitive endings challenges some of the assumptions we have described above while strengthening others. To anticipate our conclusions, we hope to show that the variation between infinitives in –*e and* –*en* in this corpus is patterned, and that the use of –*en* infinitives (which are rarer than scholars generally suppose) provides strong support for the long-dip requirement in the b-verse and for our a-verse rules. We also hope to show that the emendations of infinitive –*e* to –*en* in non-eliding position are highly improbable in view of the specialised use of –*en* infinitives. The corollary of this is that b-verses in which inflectional –*e* contributes to the long-dip requirement are probably authorial, and hence that inflectional –*e* in infinitives could still be syllabic in the alliterative poems of our corpus.

*The Cotton Nero Poems*

MS Cotton Nero A.x contains remarkably few infinitives in –*en*. We begin with *Pearl*, which is not in alliterative metre but in rhymed stanzaic verse, with four-stress lines in loose iambic metre. This means that we

[25] Duggan and Turville-Petre's emendations are conjectural; Hanna and Lawton emend to a minority reading.

[26] Hanna and Lawton are clear on this point: 'We attempt no record of –*e*, which was almost certainly silent for our poet' (*Siege*, p. lxxxix). Duggan and Turville-Petre state (*Wars*, p. xlv) that they 'record all variants that we regard as substantive or possibly so', but their practice patently does not extent to variants such as *laythely* A and *lothlyche* D (*WA* 3358), *grysely* (A) and *gryslyche* (D) (*WA* 3366). Some potentially significant variation of this kind is listed by Steffens, *Versbau und Sprache*, pp. 56–64.

can approach the question of infinitive inflections without any *a priori* assumptions about the syllabic constraints of alliterative metre. The situation in *Pearl* is that infinitives end in *–e* (also occasionally Ø, or *–y*). E. V. Gordon claims in his edition (p. 110) that the ending *–n* is found only in the following four cases:

Where rych rokkeȝ wer to *dyscreuen* (68)
Þe lyȝt of hem myȝt no mon *leuen* (69)
When Jesus con to hym warde *gon* (820)
For *meten* hit syȝ þe apostel John (1032)

He omits one further instance:

Þen moȝte by ryȝt vpon hem *clyuen* (1196)

The infinitive *gon* is, as Gordon observes, a special case: as we have already noted, *–n* was lost more slowly in monosyllabic verbs with a vocalic stem (and was, as is well known,[27] lost more slowly in monosyllables in general). Gordon also suggests that *to dyscreuen* may be an inflected infinitive, comparable to *to sene* (45) and *to done* (914), but this is doubtful. As in Chaucerian usage, relics of the OE inflected infinitive are restricted to the most common verbs (*to sene*, *to done*, *to sayne*, and, in alliterative verse, also *to bene*).[28] Historically this *–n(e)* inflection represents OE dative *–enne*, and it is important not to confuse it with infinitive *–en* (< OE *–(i)an*). The key to understanding the continued usefulness of the OE inflected infinitive to the *Gawain* poet is that the dative ending *–ne* brings historically justified final *–e* into play. Thus *to sene* at *Pearl* 45 is used to rhyme with words with historical final *–e*, namely *grene* (adj. < OE *grene*), *kene* (adj. < OE *cene*), *bytwene* (adv. < OE *betweonan*), *wene* (vb. 1st pers. pres.) and *schene* (adv. < OE *schene*), whilst *to done* at *Pearl* 914 rhymes with *bone* (n. < ON fem. *bón*, with analogical *–e* from EME, hence disyllabic *bone* in Chaucer[29]), *won* (inf.; the omission of final *–e* is presumably scribal),[30] *trone* (n. < OF *trone*), *hone* (inf.), and *mone* (n. < OE *mona*). Gordon's premise that 'when all the rhyme words in a group have final *–e* that is organic … it may be assumed with some probability that it was sounded' would lead to the conclusion that *sene* and *done* were disyllabic.

[27] Reed, *History*, p. 236.

[28] See Ten Brink, *Language*, p. 135 and Luick, 'Stabreimzeile', p. 553.

[29] Ten Brink, *Language*, p. 147.

[30] Cf. Gordon (ed.): 'it seems reasonable to suppose that in some cases where there is no final *–e* in the MS. its omission is scribal and not original' (p. 107).

What Gordon fails to note is that, with a single exception, final –*en* in infinitives is used for the purposes of rhyme. *Dyscreuen* (68) and *leuen* (69) rhyme with *sweuen* (n.), *meuen*, *cleuen*, *weuen* (all three present plurals); *gon* (820) with *Jon*, *ston*, *vpon*, *non*, *con*; *clyuen* (1196) with *gyuen* (p.p.), *þryuen* (p.p. adj.), *dryuen* (p.p.), *toriuen* (p.p.), *stryuen* (pres. pl). This suggests that the –*n* infinitive was not part of the *Gawain* poet's normal repertoire but a specialised form used *metri causa.* This hypothesis casts a spotlight on the single anomaly, *Pearl* 1032: 'For meten hit syȝ þe apostel John'. *Meten* can be construed not only as an infinitive (with verb of perception, here *syȝ*), as by Gordon, but also as a past participial complement, as by Andrew and Waldron.[31] The latter interpretation avoids the need to construe *meten* as a passive infinitive and brings *Pearl* closer to the Vulgate, in which John sees the heavenly city being measured (Rev. 21.15-17). The fact that infinitives in –*en* are otherwise found only in rhyme increases the likelihood that *meten* is not an infinitive but a past participle.

Turning to the question of the syllabic value of the poet's normal infinitive ending in –*e*, we may observe that in *Pearl* only the pronunciation of –*e* can avoid clashing stress in such lines as:

By þe way of ryȝt to *aske* dom (580)
Of motes two to *carpe* clene (949)

Duggan, who has argued forcefully that *Pearl* is in iambic metre, accepts the pronunciation of final –*e* in such infinitives and in fact proposes the emendation of infinitive *carp* to *carpe* (381) and infinitive *ask* to *aske* (564) in order to make these verses metrical.[32] It is odd, therefore, that he has been reluctant to accept the value of inflectional –*e* in the alliterative works by the same poet or in other alliterative poems such as the *SJ* and *WA*, where, as we have seen, –*e* is emended to –*en* in a number of b-verses on the assumption that the former cannot be syllabic.

[31] *The Poems of the 'Pearl' Manuscript*, 4th edn. (Exeter, 2002). Parallels for the use of a past participle after a verb of seeing are offered by *Pearl* 385 and 790–91. See also Herbert Koziol, *Grundzüge der Syntax der mittelenglischen Stabreimdichtungen*, Wiener Beiträge zur Englischen Philologie (Vienna, 1932), p. 119.

[32] Hoyt N. Duggan, 'Libertine Scribes and Maidenly Editors: Meditations on Textual Criticism and Metrics', in C. B. McCully and J. J. Anderson (eds), *English Historical Metrics* (Cambridge, 1996), pp. 219–37 (p. 232). Further evidence for this position has been adduced in Putter and Stokes, 'Spelling'.

When we look at infinitives in the *Gawain* poet's alliterative works, we find a comparable pattern of distribution. In *Patience* (*P*), the *–en* inflexion occurs only four times:

> Suffraunce may *aswagen* hem  and þe swelme leþe (3)
> Hef and hale vpon hyȝt  to *helpen* hym seluen (219)
> Þat he gef hem þe grace  to *greuen* hym neuer (226)
> For he þat is to rakel  to *renden* his cloþeȝ (526)

In these instances, final *–n* is found only in situations where a final *–e* would be subject to elision. At *P* 219, 226 and 526 the poet's normal form in *–e* would produce unmetrical b-verses. The poet's recourse to *–en* thus provides strong confirmation of the long-dip requirement in the b-verse. At *P* 3, the final *–n* creates a long final dip in the absence of an initial long dip. By our theory of a-verse metre (see ch. 5 and our summary above, p. 79) the *–n* in *P* 3 is therefore also metrically required.

The specialist use of *–en* in eliding position should be contrasted with the normal use in the same poem of infinitives in *–e* in b-verses where elision is not an issue, but where final *–e* would have to be pronounced to satisfy the long-dip requirement:

> to *holde* for euer (14)
> þenne *suppe* bihoued (151)
> to *slepe* so faste (192)
> þat *kenne* myȝt alle (357)
> schal *tylte* to grounde (361)
> þat *wale* ne couþe (511)
> *disserne* noȝt cunen (513)

What are we to make of these b-verses? The position consistent with Duggan and Turville-Petre's and Hanna and Lawton's editorial practices would be to regard these b-verses as unmetrical, and to assume that the infinitives originally ended in *–en*. However, such emendations would introduce infinitive *–en* into non-eliding contexts, where they do not appear to belong. If, on the other hand, we assume that the poet did sound final *–e* in these infinitives (as in those of *Pearl*), no emendation *metri causa* would be required. The only infinitive in *P* that must be emended to secure the long dip is in line 491b, 'to wax so sone', but on the evidence presented thus far, the correct emendation is 'wax[e]'.

Finally, we should emphasise that a final *–en* in infinitives may be part of the stem (followed by the zero inflection common after an unstressed syllable) rather than an inflection. Editors sometimes list such infinitives with zero ending (e.g. *waken*, *reken*, *herken*) as examples of infinitives with inflectional –*en*,[33] but they should be kept separate.

In *Cleanness* (*C*), infinitives in –*en* are in even shorter supply.[34] We find only four examples:

To dryȝ her delful deystene and *dyȝen* alle samen (400)
Where þe wynde and þe weder *warpen* hit wolde (444)
And he *conueyen* hym con with cast of his yȝe (768)
And if þay gruchen him his grace, to *gremen* his hert (1347)

It is again striking that this marked form occurs exclusively in contexts where final –*e* would be subject to elision. In the b-verses of 400, 444 and 1347, final –*e* would produce unmetrical b-verses. In the a-verse of 768, the final –*n* may be used to guard against ecthlipsis[35] (we assume first-syllable stress in *conueyen*).[36] It appears, then, that in both *C* and *P* final –*n* is used to protect the inflectional ending against elision; it never occurs before a consonant.

The exclusion of –*en* before consonants should be contrasted with the ready use of –*e* infinitives in b-verses where the inflectional syllable is metrically required. Here are some examples from *C*:

he *scape* by moȝt (62)
and *þole* much payne (190)
bot *loke* to kynde (264)
þat *rayne* schal swyþe (354)
to *wasche* þe fayly (548)
may *spede* to mysse (551)

[33] For example, in her recent edition of the *Alliterative John Baptist Hymn*, part of her edition of *Three Alliterative Saints' Hymns: Late Middle English Stanzaic Poems*, EETS, OS 321 (Oxford 2003), Ruth Kennedy lists the forms *neuen* and *listen* as 'fully inflected infinitives' (p. lxii). In fact, the only instance of a fully inflected infinitive in this poem is *gone* (l. 19) — in rhyme position — which Kennedy glosses as a past participle. In *P* 160a, 'And al to lyȝten þat lome', *lyȝten* probably represents ME *lightnen* (thus MED) rather than *lighten*, yet Anderson lists it as his one example of an infinitive on –*en* (p. 78). In the comparable case of *waken* (469), the issue is settled by the poet's past tense form (*wakened*, *wakned*).

[34] The infinitives *waken* (323), *herken* (458), *samen* (870), and *neuen* (1376) do not belong here, nor does *wakan* (948), which Anderson lists among infinitives in –*n*.

[35] Ecthlipsis is the elision of the unstressed vocalic ending before vowel or weak *h*–: see Ten Brink, *Language*, pp. 182–4.

[36] The possibility that prefixes like *con*–, *dis*–, *per*– can take stress has been demonstrated by Hoyt N. Duggan, 'Stress Assignment in Middle English Alliterative Poetry', *Journal of English and Germanic Philology*, 89 (1990), 309–29.

Emendation of *–e* to *–en* cannot be justified in these circumstances. If the long dip requirement is indeed a metrical rule (as we believe it is), it is reasonable to conclude that the poet met this requirement by pronouncing final *–e* in infinitives. The few unmetrical b-verses in which the requisite inflectional ending is absent, such as 225b ('*stynt* ne myȝt') and 332b ('and *swelt* þose oþer'), should be emended by the addition of final *–e*, not *–en*.

Let us finally turn to *G*. The distribution of *–e* and *–en* in this poem is not as clear-cut. (We suspect that this poem had a longer scribal tradition than the others in the same codex.)[37] Leaving to one side infinitives with stems in *–en*, such as *lysten* (30), *samen* (1372) *lassen* (1800),[38] infinitives in *–n* are found five times in non-eliding contexts:

And I schal *bayþen* þy bone    þat þou boden habbes (327)
Þat þou schal *byden* þe bur    þat he schal bede after (374)
For to hent hit at his honde,    þe hende to *seruen* (827)
Thenne watz hit list vpon lif    to *lyþen* þe houndez (1719)
Þat yow *lausen* ne lyst –    and þat I leue nouþe (1784)

Since the use of *–en* rather than *–e* has no metrical effect in such contexts, some such examples are probably only to be expected. However, the fact that infinitives in *–en* are so rare in non-eliding position in this manuscript does make the above examples suspect, and there are, in fact, other grounds for suspicion. *Seruen* is the only infinitive in *–en* at line ending in this MS, and the form may have been prompted by the fact that the opening word of the next line (*His*) begins with weak *h–*. *Lyþen*

[37] Possible differences in scribal transmission were suggested some time ago by J. P. Oakden, ('The Scribal Errors of the MS Cotton Nero A.x', *The Library*, 4th series, 14 (1932), 353–8). For further differences see Putter and Stokes, 'The Linguistic Atlas'.

[38] *MED* lists this s.v. *lessen*, rather than *lessenen* where it belongs: the poet's past tense form *lasned* (*Cleanness* 438, 441) suggests that *–n* is part of the uninflected verb. The same is true for *lysten* (cf. *lystened* at *G* 2006). This bears on the emendation (due to J. A. Burrow, *A Reading of Sir Gawain and the Green Knight* (London, 1965), p. 105) of *G* 1878: 'Þat he wold lyste [MS *lyfte*] his lyf    and lern hym better'. The proposed emendation of *lyfte* to a verb meaning 'to listen' is convincing, but, since the poet only ever uses the later formation *list(e)nen*, the correct emendation should perhaps be *lysten*, which also restores a-verse metre. The b-verse, 'and lern hym better', also requires emendation (to *and leren hym better*). Note that the emendation restores the distinction, observed elsewhere in the MS, between ME *leren* (< OE *læran* 'teach') and *lernen* (< OE *lēornian* 'learn').

misses the opportunity of a pun (*lysten*).[39] *Lausen* could represent ME *losnen*, but the ending is more likely to have been scribally produced under the influence of following *ne*.

In all other cases (5x), infinitives in –*en* are found in eliding contexts:

> Keuer hem comfort and *colen* her carez (1254)
> And I schulde *chepen* and chose to cheue me a lorde (1271)
> Alle þe haþeles þat on horse schulde *helden* hym after (1692)
> Bot for to *sauen* himself, when suffer hym byhoued (2040)
> For mon may *hyden* his harm, bot vnhap ne may hit (2511)

The authenticity of these forms is confirmed by the metre. In the b-verses (1254, 1692) it protects the long dip against elision; in the a-verses it secures the two long dips that are metrically required unless the a-verse contains either an extra-long dip, of four or more syllables, or a long or heavy final dip (see above, p. 79). Since these conditions do not apply at 1271, 2040, 2511, the final –*n* is metrically required.

Finally, there are two instances of –*ne* after a stressed vowel, the first at the end of the alliterative long-line, the second in rhyming position in the bob-and-wheel:

> Bot mon most I algate mynn hym to *bene* (121)
> Þat chapel er he myȝt *sene* (712, rhyming with *grene* and *vnbene*)

The first of these is an ingenious use of the inflected infinitive (< OE *bēonne*). The point is that the poet's normal form *be* (the only other form of the infinitive in Cotton Nero A.x) cannot be used at line ending (which is always feminine).[40] Tolkien and Gordon also construe *sene* as a relic of OE *sēonne*. Historically speaking, the inflected infinitive is incorrect without preceding *to*, but perhaps such licences became acceptable once the grammatical distinction between the inflected and uninflected infinitives was lost.

[39] That puns were lost in scribal transmission is suggested by *G* 2191–2: 'Wel bisemez þe wyȝe wruxled in grene / *Dele* here his deuocioun on þe *deuelez* wyse'. Here *deuelez* should probably be emended to *delez*, the shortened form for 'devil', also used *metri causa* at 2188. The emendation restores the wordplay and the b-verse metre.

[40] This point was well understood by other alliterative poets. Cf. *WP*, which also only ever uses the inflected *bene* at line ending (1473, 1738, 1930). See the observations by Bunt (ed.), *William of Palerne*, pp. 47–49, 63; and also Magoun (ed.), *Gests*, where *be(e)ne* is also reserved for line endings (281, 523, 404, 736, 865).

Editors who believe that inflectional final *–e* is not sounded are faced with a large numbers of b-verses which would be unmetrical by Duggan's b-verse rules. For instance:

| | |
|---|---|
| myȝt voyde þis table (345) | to fonge þe knyȝt (816) |
| to wynne me þeder (402) | to deȝe watz borne (996) |
| and dele no more (560) | |

See also 1396, 1457, 1839, 1896, 2121, 2194, 2213, 2303, 2438. (The requisite inflectional syllable is missing in the zero infinitives at 411, 522, 1878, 2286). It does not seem to us that the few examples of *–en* infinitives in non-eliding contexts (unique to *G*) inspire confidence in the belief that final *–e* in such b-verses as the above was a scribal corruption for original *–en*. It may well be that the sounding of final *–e* (on which the metricality of these b-verses depends) would be archaic in the poet's spoken language, but, of course, so was the use of *–en* in infinitives. Emending *–e* to *–en* is wrong because it conflicts with the discernible pattern that governs the distribution of inflectional endings, and illogical because it removes one archaism only to replace it with another.

*Alexander and Dindimus*

This poem (*B*) survives in a manuscript (Oxford, Bodley 264) from around 1400. The scribe wrote in a South East Midland dialect,[41] but the original was probably composed in or near Gloucestershire.[42] In this poem, final *–e* is definitely the unmarked form for infinitives. It predominates over infinitives on *–en* in a rough proportion of 5:1. Infinitives in *–en* occur much more frequently, however, than in Cotton Nero A.x. Presumably this is due, first, to the more southerly language of the poet, and second to the influence of the scribal SE Midland dialect, where final *–n* was lost more slowly. We can nevertheless discern a pattern in the distribution of *–e* and *–en* endings. As in Cotton Nero A.x, *–en* is used almost exclusively in eliding contexts. The following categories can be distinguished:

(1) a-verses where *–en* is metrically required, either because it safeguards the long initial and medial dip (in the absence of any form of metrical compensation) or because it provides a long final dip to compensate for a short initial dip (19x):

[41] Skeat (ed.), *Alexander*, p. xxvi.

[42] Magoun (ed.), *Gests*, pp. 78 and 112.

To *bi-holden* her hom (46)
Scholde *talken* hem til (148)
Whan mihte *lakken* oure limus (328)
Þat likeþ vs to loken on (473)

See also 229, 235, 323, 329, 406, 427, 572, 637, 751, 761, 853, 937, 995, 1047, 1070.

(2) a-verses where final *–en* avoids hiatus, but where the inflectional syllable is not metrically constrained (10x):

Þat Y may witen of ȝour werk (208)
To witen of þe wisdam (242)
Ne to faren in þe feld (301)

See also 316, 338, 407, 411, 502, 757, 1089.

(3) b-verses in which *–en* is metrically required (22x):

*maken* us tine (36)
to *worchen* on erþe (99)
to *carpen* him tille (166)

See also 10, 184, 232, 320, 328, 435, 455, 457, 549, 549, 594, 601, 854, 858, 861, 874, 899, 1031, 1134.

(4) b-verses in which *–en* avoids hiatus but is not metrically constrained (7x):

to *lacchen* upon erþe (70)
to *witen* of here fare (150)
*forgiuen* us þe sinne (386)

See also 404, 551, 757, 852.

In categories 1 and 3, the ending on *–en* can be shown to be authorial on grounds of metre. In categories 2 and 4, the manuscript readings cannot be corroborated in this way: we may be dealing with a scribal tendency to use *–en* before vowels and unaspirated *h–*. Progressive scribal translation could explain why there are fewer examples of this in the first half of the poem, although the tendency is in any case sporadic, for final *–e* is frequently used in eliding position where the metre allows it, for example: 'to kenne of hure fare' (48b), 'Me to lere of ȝour lif' (66a).

The use of *–n* in non-eliding position is rare. We find only eight instances:

*reden* þe sonde (21b)
*Aspien* ful spedliche (172a)
*maken* to sclepe (535b)
to *gien* ȝou here (561b)
þan ȝe mow *forþen* (570b)
*offren* to venus (720b)
to *gyen* þe peple (815b)
*wenden* ȝe schulle (1106b)

*Forþen* at 570 is the only infinitive in *–en* at line ending; it could have been used purposefully to avoid confusion with the adverb *forth.* The infinitives *aspien*, *gien*, and *gyen* present special cases: inflectional *–e* is vulnerable to assimilation after a vocalic stem,[43] and final *–n* may be used here to accentuate the inflection and so protect it against assimilation.

Finally, there are a few *–n* infinitives in monosyllabic verb stems ending in a vowel or diphthong:

> We sen selkouþe þing, þat is ta *sain*, heuene (475)
> And alle þat seggeus mowe *sen* siþen on þe skiuus (478)
> Þe side se we mowe *sen* set vpon erþe (481)

In the idiomatic phrase 'that is to say' (475), *sain* is probably a relic of the OE inflected infinitive; infinitive *se* does not occur in this poem, in which *sen* is the only form used: we recall that *–n* was lost more slowly in monosyllabic verb forms.

Compared with the number of *–en* infinitives before a vowel or unstressed *h–* (55x) the use of *–en* in non-eliding contexts (8x) is rare. It is also rare when we compare it with the number of infinitives in b-verses in which the inflection in *–e* contributes to the regular long dip. Since instances are too numerous to list (37x), we cite a short passage to illustrate the pervasiveness of metrically required *–e* infinitives in the b-verse:

> Hit is no leue in oure lawe þat we land erie
> Wiþ no scharpede schar to *schape* þe forwes;
> Ne sette solowe on þe feld ne *sowe* none erþe,
> In ony place of þe plow to *plokke* wiþ oxen,
> Ne in no side of þe se to *saile* wiþ nettus,
> Of þe finnede fihcs our fode to lacche.[44]
> For to hauke ne hunte haue we no leue,
> Ne foure-fotede best *ferke* to kille;
> Ne to faren in þe feld & *fonde* wiþ slyhþe
> For to refe[45] þe brod of briddus of heuene. (292–302)

[43] Cf. the variable pronunciation *espyed*/*espyde* in Chaucer, and see Ten Brink, *Language*, pp. 129–30, and Barney, *Studies in Troilus*, p. 96. Barney uses the possibility of assimilation to explain the variable pronunciation in Chaucer of infinitives such as *sey(e)* and *dy(e)*, but also notes that in Chaucer *–e* is retained after *–y* in French words. The same appears to be true for *aspie* (343) and *gye* (263) at line ending in *B*.

[44] B-verse metre also demands the voicing of *–e* in the noun *fode* (< OE *foda*).

If final *–e* is regarded as inconsequential, the long-dip requirement in the b-verse would force an editor into many emendations. The easiest emendation, of *e* to *en*, is unlikely, because the distribution of *–e* and *–en* infinitives suggests that the latter is only regular in eliding position (note *faren* at 301).

*The Siege of Jerusalem*

We turn now to *SJ*, which is preserved in nine manuscripts and manuscript fragments. Of these the oldest are Bodleian Library, MS Laud Misc. 656 (L, copied in Oxfordshire) and Princeton University Library, MS Taylor Medieval 11 (P, copied in Yorkshire). The dialect of the original poem was probably North-West Midland.[46] P omits some lines and ends at line 1143; in addition to these lacunae, the vellum is worn and has suffered water damage, so that not all the text is legible. Both manuscripts are late fourteenth-century. Before presenting the evidence, we should mention a stylistic peculiarity that is particularly pronounced in manuscript L: it often fails to express the subject pronoun, even when there is a change of grammatical subject (see e.g. 841–49, 1151–3). This peculiarity sometimes makes it difficult to interpret the grammatical status of the verb. All cases of such ambiguity will be signalled.

Citations from L are taken from Hanna and Lawton's edition. Variants from P are cited from the manuscript.[47] In L infinitives in *–en* are the minority form, though again they are rather more common before vowels and unaspirated *h–*. In the a-verse, there are eight examples of such infinitives in eliding position:

> Þe kyng lete *drawen* hem adoun (717; P *draw þaim doune*)
> Assaylen on eche a side (802; P *Assayles*; *Assailen* may be pres. pl.[48])
> For we wol *hunten* at þe hart (889; P *hunte*)
> To *voiden* alle by vile deþ (1102; P illegible)
> To *worchyn* under þe wal (1109; P illegible)
> Lest fomen *fongen* hem schold (1168; P ends at 1143)
> My3t no man *stoken* on þe stret (1246; editors emend to *styken*)

[45] 'Alliteration imperfect ... The right word is *bruten*, to destroy' (*Alexander*, ed. Skeat, p. 48, note to this line). Emendation to *berefe* should also be considered.
[46] See above, pp. 11–12.
[47] This is a necessary measure, since Hanna and Lawton regard variation involving final *–e* as meaningless and not worth recording, which limits the usefulness of their edition for metrical studies such as ours.
[48] It is so construed by Kölbing and Day in their edition of *SJ*.

And forto *paren* his pere (1331)

By our understanding, the final –*n* is metrically required at 1102, 1109, 1331, and possibly 717 (if the poet wrote *doun* as in P, rather than *adoun*).

In the b-verse, –*en* appears in eliding position in eleven cases:

and *newen* his sorowe (186; P *new him*)
þou may *seken* euer (297; P *sygh*)
and *walten* alle ouere (355; P *walt*)
schal *iuggen* alle þinges (431; P *juggen*)
to *fiȝten* at þe walles (654; P *faght on*)
to *angren* hym more (705; P *anger hym more*)
to *cacchen* hem reste (737; P *take*)
to *vengen* his broþer (941; P *venge*)
may no man *demen* elles (988; P *deme*)
and *lengþen* oure fyne (1100; P illegible)[49]
*lengen* hem were (1139; P *longer*)

In most of these cases (186, 355, 705, 737, 941, 1100, 1139 and possibly 431, if *alle* is monosyllabic), the ending in –*e* (or the zero ending common in P) would lead to unmetrical b-verses.

Infinitives in –*en* do, however, occur in non-eliding position. We find, for instance, four at line ending:

alle folke to *byholden* (701; P *be holedyn*)
and on þe walle *hengen* (792; P *hungen*)
oþer wo *habben* (820; P *hab*)
to no grace *taken* (1180)

It is possible, however, that at least some of these are scribal. The phrase 'to behold', found in 701, is a favourite of the poet's, also occurring at line ending at 338 ('briȝt to byholde'), 645 ('was deil to byholde') and 1247 ('was pite to byholde'), but there is only this one single instance of an –*n* infinitive. In 792, the variant readings for *hengen* (*hangeth* U, *hangede* AC, *hem hongyth* E) suggest the possibility that the original was a 3rd pers. sg. verb, as in the Latin source (Higden's *Polychronicon*), 'Josephus … commentum inuenit, quo vestes aquis infusas muris urbis *suspenderet* …'[50] Compare this with the L reading:

Iosophus ...
Hadde wroȝt a wonder whyle  whan hem water fayled

[49] On the evidence of *MED*, the newer formation *lengthenen* is not attested until 1450 (see *MED* s.v. *lengthenen.*

[50] We cite from Hanna and Lawton's edition, appendix to *SJ*, 166.71–72.

Made wedes of wolle    in water forto plunge,
Water-waschen as þey were,    and on þe walle hengen. (789–92)

At 820, the manuscripts AEUDC have *habide*; the editors emend to *habiden*. At line 1180 'Ne gome þat he gete may    to no grace taken', *taken* may be a past participle ('And that no man that he may capture (be) received into grace').

Within the b-verse, infinitives on –*en* before a consonant occur twice:

*carpyn* bygonn (361; P *to carpyn þus*)
to *brennen* þe corses (718; P *burne*)

At 361 a significant variant reading is the verbal noun (UE *carping*, C *spekynge*). Compare also 869b: 'and talkyng (P *talkyn*) bygynneþ'. The ending –*yn* is most unusual for infinitives in L. The only other examples are *worchyn* (1109) and possibly *betyn* at 718 (construed as imperative plural by Hanna and Lawton), which needs to be seen in the context of the difficult passage surrounding it (the punctuation is Hanna and Lawton's):

þe kyng lete drawen hem adoun    whan þey dede were,
Bade, 'a bole-fure betyn    to brennen þe corses, (P *bite*; *burne*)
Kesten Cayphas þeryn    and his clerkes [alle], (P *keste*)
And bren[n]en euereche bon    into browne askes. (L *brenten*; P *brynd þai*m[51])
Suþ wen[de] to þe walle    on þe wynde syde (PL *went*)
And alle abrod on þe burwe    bl[o]wen þe powdere. (P; L *blewen*)
"Þer is doust for ȝour drynke",    adoun to hem crieþ (P *a duke* for *adoun*)
And b[id]de hem bible of þat broþ    for þe bischop soule'. (L *bade*; P *bad*)
(717–24)

The editorial note to this passage reads as follows:

We perform extensive, though minimalist, surgery throughout this passage, in the belief that the original passage followed the extensive subordination and parallelism of BF [The French source: *La Vengeance de Nostre-Seigneur*] 484–86: '*Puis fist alumer … et fist geter… Et ilec fist ardoir … et puis fist la poudre venter et espandre*'. From *bade* until the end of 724 is all Vespasian's speech (including in 723 one bit of directed [*sic*] speech within speech). To convey this, we change a series of scribal efforts to depict simple action with past tense verbs into the series of imperatives which follow the command here.

[51] The final –*m* in *þai*m has been expanded by Hanna and Lawton from a tilde, which is sometimes otiose in P.

There are several reasons why we do not find this convincing. The shift to direct speech in 718 is clumsy and cannot be justified by appealing to the French source, which relates the emperor's orders indirectly throughout. Grammar poses another serious obstacle: the endings *–yn* and *–en* rule against the possibility that the verbs *betyn*, *kesten*, *etc.* are imperatives (which end in *–e* and *–eþ* in *SJ*, as one would expect in West Midland dialects). A sensible solution is to retain the MS readings and to construe *betyn* and *to brennen* (perhaps *to-brennen*) as infinitives, and *kesten*, *brenten*, *blewen*, and *wente* as preterite plurals. This is the solution adopted by Kölbing and Day and by Turville-Petre in their editions of *SJ*.[52] It further seems possible that the a-verse of 718 should be understood as, or emended to, 'Bade a bole-fur [be] betyn'. This would explain the MS variants of *betyn* (UD *to be fet*; E *be maad faste*) and regularise the *–yn* inflection (which is common in strong past participles but anomalous in infinitives).

Six infinitives in *–en* are found in non-eliding position in a-verses:

Cloudes clateren gon (58a; P *claterd on loude*)
Garde hit gayly agysen (262a, followed by *in*; P *gayly it gyse*)
Geten girdeles and gere (642a; P *getyn*)
Fourty to fyghten (779a, followed by *aȝens*; PE *defende*; AUD *fende off*)
Merken myd manglouns (803; P *marken*)
Þat wolden wrecken þe wounde (820; P *wreke*?)

Most of these instances are problematic for other reasons. *Gon* is unique to L, and Hanna and Lawton emend to *on lofte*. *Agysen* is not otherwise attested in Middle English. *Geten* at 642 may also be construed as a preterite plural, comparable with *Kesten* (645); this interpretation, adopted by Kölbing and Day and Turville-Petre, is supported by AC, which make the change of subject explicit (*thay gatt*). *Merken* at 803 may be a present plural.[53] At 779, the MS reading is unsatisfactory on grounds of sense: Hanna and Lawton emend to *defenden* after P, which actually reads *defende*, with no final *–n*. For reasons of a-verse metre, we think AUD *fende off* is more likely to be archetypal (see below, pp. 244).

Finally, a few infinitives have *–n(e)* after a stressed vowel:

þat erand to done (216b; P omits line)
Non oþer dede was to don (908a; P *es to do*)

[52] See Thorlac Turville-Petre (ed.), *Alliterative Poetry of the Later Middle Ages: an Anthology* (London, 1989).
[53] Thus Kölbing and Day.

to seyn for hem alle (868b; P *to say*)

At 216 and 908, we appear to be dealing with a relic of the OE inflected infinitive. (At 216 the final –*e* must be syllabic to produce the unstressed line ending[54]). The final –*n* in *seyn* is more likely to be a reduction of –*en* than a relic of OE –*enne*.

MS P can be dealt with more quickly. As we have seen, P often has –*e* or zero ending where L has –*en*, even where the latter is metrically required (P appears in this respect less reliable than L). Infinitives in –*n* peculiar to P are consequently infrequent and of dubious authenticity:

> To softyn þe grete sore (91a; L *softe*)
> his saghes to p*re*chyn (139b; L *preche*)
> his wordes to schewen (140b; L *til hy were atwynne*)
> þair hetes to kepyn (279b; L *here hestes to kepe*)
> whoso will lysten (462b); L *whoso wite lyste*)[55]
> So Criste his knyghtes kepyn (612a; L *gan kepe*)
> & boldely to kyssyn (1010b; L *and barouns hit kyssen*)

At 91a, *softyn* may represent ME *softenen* (cf. the variants *softyng* [L] and *softnyng* [E]), and ME *listenen* probably lies behind *lysten* at P 462b. At 139b, 140b, and 279b, final –*en*/–*yn* appear at line ending before vowel and weak *h* in the following lines. 612 is odd altogether. There seems to be some confusion both in this line and in 1010 between the infinitive and the present plural.

In conclusion, in the earliest manuscripts of *SJ* infinitives overwhelmingly end in –*e* (or zero). Infinitives in –*en* are found in eliding position and are much less securely attested in non-eliding position. Endings in –*en* occur sporadically at line ending in P and L, but they are not used within the b-verse except in eliding position. There are only two exceptions in L (361 and 718) and none in P. In this same position, however, the inflection with final –*e* is securely attested and well supported by the manuscripts:

> to serche ȝour wille (343; *sic* LPDC; *serchen* U; *wetyn* E)
> to rynge ful loude (411; *sic* LA; no other witnesses)
> to abide þis oþer (432: *byde* PDC, *abyden* U)
> spare scholde none (641; *sic* LPA; remaining MSS have a slightly

[54] The spelling with final –*e* occurs only here; cf. *WP*, where the inflected infinitive *done* is used only after *to* and to avoid masculine line endings (2546, 2581, *etc*).
[55] The reading in P is evidently a misunderstanding of the original reading 'whoso wite lyste' ('whoever would like to know'), preserved in L.

different or no reading)
to mynde foreuer (923; P *mene*; A *menyn*; U *mynne*, D *myn*)
to pyne foreuere (1327; *pyne* LVUDEC; *pynen* A)

In all these instances, Hanna and Lawton emend to *–en*, despite the weight of the evidence provided by the extant witnesses, and despite the fact that *–en* infinitives are abnormal within b-verses except to prevent elision of *e*. In this respect, *SJ* is no different from the other alliterative poems we have examined. It appears, therefore, that the final *–e* in these b-verses from *SJ* is authorial and that it was sounded to meet the metrical requirement of a long dip.

*William of Palerne*

*WP* is by far the longest poem in our corpus (5,540 lines). This poem is unusual in having a relatively high proportion of lines that do not conform to the *aa/ax* or *aa/aa* pattern.[56] Bunt assumes this pattern is normative only. He also notes that the poet favours long medial dips in both the a-verse and the b-verse, and a final unstressed syllable at line ending, though he again sees this as a matter of preference rather than a rule.

Whatever the truth of those matters, with regard to the distribution of *–e* and *–en* infinitives, *WP* is comparable with the other alliterative poems in our corpus. The first thing to note is that infinitives on *–en* are uncommon. Bunt counts 1292 infinitives, most of them ending in *–e* (rarely *–i/y*); 250 infinitives have no ending. Only 35 infinitives end in *–en*. Bunt provides no line references for these, but we also find 35 such infinitives. As we have come to expect, *–en* infinitives occur predominantly in eliding position (26x):

to *kepen* is bestes (8b)
to *buschen* on felde (173b)
forto *worchen* his wille (307a)
to *wirchen* his hest (468b)
*walken* aboute (2129b)
*leten* he nolde (2184b)
to *ȝelden* hem never (3019b)
and *wateren* ate wille (3234b)

[56] See above, p. 12.

| | |
|---|---|
| *knowen* hire sore (577b) | þat for to *liven* or deyen (3353a) |
| mow I *geten* a grece (636a) | *setten* al on fure (3759b) |
| *wissen* here ladi (640b) | to *hiden* in hem boþe (4697b) |
| gan *menden* here chere (647b) | to *saven* here lives (4703b) |
| forto *lissen* his langour (848a)[57] | and *leren* in ȝouþe (4770b) |
| *fulfillen* in haste (1451b) | *desiren* of eny deyntes (5065a) |
| to *lappen* inne hire frendes (1712b) | and *erden* in þat empire (5260a) |
| to *hiȝen* hire hastily (1969a) | to *lelen* here sawes (5284b) |
| so *meken* in his mercy (2118a) | to *saven* his reaume (5484b) |

The inflectional ending typically secures a long medial dip in the a-verse and the b-verse by protecting the inflection against elision.[58] In the b-verse only four instances (1712b, 3234b, 3759b, and 4697b) are not explicable as metrical expedients.

In non-eliding position, the *–en* ending is found nine times:[59]

| | |
|---|---|
| ande wolden *brusten* þe best (154a) | miȝte of *heren* (3227b) |
| forto *hardien* þe hertes (1156a) | þat for to liuen or *deyen* (3353a) |
| to *herien* God heiȝli (1875a) | þat men schold of *heren* (3419b) |
| seie him oute *lepen* (2753b) | wel to *liven* for ever (5394b) |
| schal þi dere douȝter *ȝiven* (2963b) | |

Verbs with a vocalic stem (*do*, *go*, *etc.*) are predominantly without inflection. Bunt counts only five examples of *–n*: all are in eliding position (1283, 3203, 3872, 4902), except for 1682b, 'to flen (= 'flay') wilde bestes' (read *flei*?). The ending *–ne* (*done*, *sene*, *bene*) is not uncommon (17x), but, with the single exception of *to done*, which occurs in

[57] The poet's form corresponds to ME *lissen*, not *lessen*.

[58] It should be pointed out that the text as we have it appears to show an unusual tolerance for hiatus if we assume that the poet avoided short b-verses. In b-verses such as 'to winne insiȝt' (94b), 'wende him fromme' (424b), 'to blame I were' (972), the expected final *–n* is not found. The fact that such instances become more frequent as the poem progresses, while, conversely, the number of infinitives in *–n* declines, might suggest that authorial pre-vowel/*h* *–en* infinitives were lost as a result of progressive scribal translation. Compare Bunt's comments on the gradual decline of *–lyche* and the concomitant rise of *–li* (p. 74).

[59] Most of these examples could readily be explained as scribal errors. For *brusten* read *brutten*; for *hardien* read *harden*; the *–en* infinitives at the end of lines 2753, 3227, and 3419 are followed (and arguably induced) by a word beginning with vowel or *h–* in the next line; at 3353 *deyen* imitates *liven*; since the b-verse at 5394 has two long dips, *for* is suspect.

mid-line, it is found only at line ending. We are presumably dealing with relics of the OE inflection (*–enne*) to produce a feminine line ending.

The evidence of *WP* thus indicates that infinitives in *–en* are used to meet metrical rules or preferences. In non-eliding position they are avoided. There is, on the other hand, no evidence to suggest that the poet avoided b-verses with medial dips consisting of infinitive *–e* plus a single unstressed syllable. On the contrary, such medial dips are frequent: for example,

to prove þe soþe (116b)
to deme þe soþe (151b)
to seie þe trewþe (454b)
to prove þe soþe (750b)
to serve min hert (463b)
and blame my hert (486b)
gan morne so strong (586b)

If we assume that these and many similar lines have normal or regular b-verse metre, the final *–e* must be syllabic. An editor who thought that final *–e* should be emended to *–en* in such b-verses would have much work to do, and would be imposing a pattern of usage (*–en* before consonants) that is not warranted by the manuscript evidence.

*Conclusion*

It is time now to summarise our findings concerning infinitives:

(1) Infinitives in *–en* are unusual in the alliterative poems of our corpus; with few exceptions they are restricted to eliding positions, where they are predominantly used to secure the long medial dip which is required in the b-verse and (in the absence of forms of metrical compensation) in the a-verse. It follows that infinitives with final *–e* before a consonant in b-verses can be considered to be authorial. We therefore disapprove of the practice, first suggested by Duggan in critical articles, and subsequently implemented in the most recent editions of the *WA* and *SJ*, of emending infinitive *–e* (or unmetrical zero infinitives) to *–en* in non-eliding position.

(2) Since infinitives in *–e* were the default form for alliterative poets, the use of *–en* is likely to represent a deliberate choice and thus to be revealing about the metrical norms and rules to which alliterative poets were writing. Within the b-verse, the striking use of *–en* before a single eliding off-beat confirms that alliterative poets felt obliged to write b-verses with one long dip. The use of OE inflected infinitives at line ending, furthermore, confirms the requirement that the line should end on one and only one unstressed syllable. Although we

still know much less about a-verses, it seems that here *–en* infinitives are prompted by the expectation that the initial and medial dip should be long. More tentatively, we would suggest that the use of *–en* infinitives in a-verses without both a long initial and medial dip points to an expectation that this shortage should be compensated for by adding another unstressed syllable to the final dip of the a-verse or by creating an extra-long initial or medial dip.

(3) Since in our corpus the infinitive inflection, represented by *–en* in eliding position and *–e* before consonants, is commonly found as the first of a sequence of two syllables, both of which must count to meet the long-dip requirement of the b-verse, the syllabic value of *–e* in infinitives is assured. This does not mean that final *–e* should *always* be pronounced in infinitives, as Cable has argued. For a variety of reasons, we hesitate to go this far. First, this assumption would lead to some very long dips in the a-verse and also to a number of b-verses with two long dips (e.g. *WP* 2945, *C* 1661, *B* 910). Our impression is that such unmetrical b-verses are rare and quite possibly scribal, but no-one, including Cable himself, has systematically dealt with the instances that contradict Cable's hypothesis.[60] Second, we do not think it likely that final *–e* was normally pronounced after paroxytonic verbs, and b-verses such as *C* 921b, 'þat þe warisch myȝt', bear this out.

The limits of our corpus raise one further question. Would our findings still hold up if we widened our corpus to include alliterative poems in later manuscripts? We think that this would not fundamentally alter the picture. As regards the use of infinitives in *–en*, this inflection generally becomes more unusual in such manuscripts (as we would expect of a recessive form). For example, *The Destruction of Troy*, probably dating from the early fifteenth century but extant in a sixteenth-century copy, normally has *–e* or zero inflection in infinitives, with *–yn* inflection on only a

[60] *B* contains only a couple of examples: *B* 910b, 'to a-corde in trowþe', and *B* 982b, 'to abide þer-inne'. Although elision between *to* + vowel (*t'abide*, *t'acorde*) might suggest itself as the obvious solution to these lines, our evidence indicates that scribes expanded original aphetic forms (*bide*, *corde*): see, e.g., *B* 675b, *D* 180b, *SJ* 432b. The only b-verse in the Cotton Nero poems rendered unmetrical by the pronunciation of infinitive *–e* in oxytonic infinitives is suspect: 'Þenne blynnes he not of blasfemy on to blame þe Dryȝtyn' (*C* 1661). The preposition *on* is odd, despite Anderson's attempt to explain it in his editorial note.

very few occasions.[61] The two examples given by Hiroyuki Matsumoto in his recent edition and the only other example we managed to find in the first eight books of the poem (ll. 1–3530) all occur in eliding position in a-verses:

Forto *fillyn* our fare (1108a)
Ffor to *heuyn* on þi harme ( 2082a)
And *hewyn* vppon hom (10608a)

In *Death and Liffe* (*D*), a fourteenth-century poem surviving only in the seventeenth-century Percy Folio, we find only two infinitives in *–en*, both in eliding context where the inflectional syllable is required for b-verse metre: 'to *greaten* our workes' (17b),[62] and 'to *kithen* his strenght' (392). Again, since infinitives with *–en* do not occur before consonants, b-verses such as 'and latche full well' (434) are regular, because the poet pronounced inflectional *–e*. The situation is similar in *WA*, extant in two northern mid-fifteenth-century manuscripts: A (Oxford, Bodleian Library, Ashmole 22) and D (Dublin, Trinity College, MS 213). The editors claim that the metre shows that *–en* endings 'were more common in the poet's language' than the extant MSS suggest,[63] but their treatment of this point is imprecise. Their list of examples of infinitives with inflectional *–n* in A includes infinitives that do not belong here: *–n* in *rekyn* is not an inflection but part of the stem, and *sene* at 1185b, 'was meruale to sene', represents the OE inflected infinitive (used conventionally at line ending: see above, pp. 87, 94–5, 97–8). The few genuine examples again tend to occur in metrically-constrained position:

to *welden* a spere (651b)
Þai gone *agrayþen* vp þaire gods (3584a)
& *lachen* his esee (3989b)
Thurghis to *thrawyn* in (4581a)

(D is defective at these points and offers no comparisons.) The only anomalous infinitive is in 2423b, '& of himselfe *halden*' (D *hald*); here *halden* may have been influenced by the past participle *hatten* in the next line. To judge by the examples listed by the editors, D also tends to use –*en* in eliding position:

to *craue* him þaire dettis (1010b, D *crauen*)

[61] John Clerk of Whalley, *The Destruction of Troy: a Diplomatic and Color Facsimile Edition*, ed. Hiroyuki Mastumoto, Society for Early English and Norse Electronic Texts (Ann Arbor, 2002), section VI, 2.4.1. In the older edition by Panton and Donaldson, these are lines 1109, 2083, 10607.

[62] *Greaten* = ME *greithen* (set in order), which Donatelli emends to 'greithen'.

[63] Duggan and Turville-Petre (eds), *Wars*, p. xxix.

to *reche* him his sweuyn (1477b, D *rachen*)

Since the extra syllable created by *-en* is not metrically required, these readings may of course be scribal. This pattern of distribution, confirmed by other alliterative poems, would support Duggan and Turville-Petre's conjectural emendations of *–e* to *–en* before vowels in verses such as 334b, 'to proue[n] his sleȝtis'.[64] The distributional evidence also supports similar emendations of infinitives based on A, such as 1902b, 'to sese[n] oure landis'. What it does not support, however, is the conjectural emendation 'to kepe[n] þa landis (73) and the emendation (based on D) 'to leue[n] þaire frynde' (1381). For in *Wars*, too, the *–en* inflection appears to be out of place before consonants. Likewise, *Saint Erkenwald* (from MS BL Harley 2250, dated to 1477) contains not a single infinitive in *–en*,[65] and editors would, in our view, be ill-advised to emend b-verses such as these:

for nourne non couþe (101)
& sike ful colde (305)
þat lethe schal neuer (347)

There is every reason to regard these b-verses as authorial and the final *–e*s as syllabic.

## Part II. The syllabic value of *–ly* and *–lych* adverbs and adjectives

*Background*

Just as the distribution of infinitives in *–e* and *–en* shows that final *–e* was retained in infinitives, so the distribution of adjectives and adverbs in *–ly* and *–lych* indicates the retention of inflectional *–e* after *–lych*. Here, too, final *–e* is historically justified in adverbs (< OE *lice*) and in weak and plural adjectives; but whereas in infinitives final *–e* normally follows directly after a strongly stressed syllable, *–lych* only has secondary stress — though in Chaucerian verse that secondary stress can take the beat if an unstressed syllable precedes: 'He félt a cóold swerd sódeynlíchë glýde'

[64] Also correct is their emendation of 4828b, 'And als ȝe fonde may no forþire to [*felsen*] ȝoure name' [MS *hyȝen*], where the need for emendation is indicated not only by alliteration but also by the consideration that organic *–en* (in *felsen*) before consonants is regular while grammatical *–en* (in *hyȝ*en) is not.

[65] Henry Savage (ed.), *St. Erkenwald* (New Haven, 1926), erroneously claims that the 'infinitive ends in *–e*, more rarely in *–en*'; but he gives no examples and may have had in mind verbs such as *fulsen* (124) and *herken* (134, 307) where *–n* is in fact part of the stem.

(*CT* I.1575), 'It ís imprópreliché séid (*CA* 5.51). As these lines show, final *–e* was evidently capable of surviving even in conditions less conducive to the retention of the inflectional vowel than in the case of infinitives (at least in Chaucer's and Gower's language). There are, however, many scholars who believe that it did not survive in contemporary dialects further north, such as Langland's Worcestershire dialect.[66] We think there is compelling evidence to show that it did.

In the case of adverbs, the suffix *–ly* slowly replaced *–lych*, and became the norm in the fourteenth century in all but southern dialects;[67] *–lyche* forms are found as far north as Lancashire but not further north.[68] In most alliterative poems both endings are found, *–lych* being spelt with and without final *–e*, and *–ly* without. If the variation is not scribal or random, then the criterion governing the selection of *–ly* and *–lych(e)* must be explained. Recent scholarship on this question is to our minds unsatisfactory. According to Cable, adverbs in *–ly* and *–lyche* do not differ in terms of the syllable count: 'both retain the disyllabic structure of the sources of that ending (OE *–lice* and ON *–liga*)'.[69] This would mean that *–ly* always takes final *–e* (*lyë*), regardless of the fact that final *–e* never appears in the spelling. In support of his view, Cable notes that *–ly* is strictly avoided at line ending, where a single offbeat is required, but where *–ly*, according to Cable, would yield a double off-beat. According to Duggan, who argues that final *–e* was retained only for the weak form of monosyllabic adjectives, *–ly* and *–lych* cannot take final *–e*, which is merely graphical where it appears in spelling (as it frequently does after *–lych*).[70] Duggan agrees with Cable that *–ly* was not permitted at line ending by any alliterative poet except Langland (who seems to have played by a different set of rules). But, for this 'surprising fact' Duggan proposes a different explanation, which fits his theory of why alliterative

[66] Duggan, 'Langland's Dialect and Final *–e*', 177–81.

[67] Brunner, *Outline*, p. 54.

[68] See Oakden, *Alliterative Poetry*, I, pp. 32–3.

[69] Cable, *Alliterative Tradition*, pp. 78–9.

[70] Duggan, 'The Role and Distribution of *–ly* Adverbs in Middle English Alliterative Verse', in *Loyal Letters: Studies on Mediaeval Alliterative Poetry and Prose*, ed. L. A. R. J. Houwen and A. A. MacDonald (Groningen, 1994), 131–154. See also 'Langland's Dialect and Final *–e*', 177–181. Both articles are unfortunately flawed by Duggan's failure to discriminate between *–ly* and *–lych* forms: he does not, for example, notice that all sixteen cases of apparently disyllabic adverbial suffixes in Langland's b-verses are forms in *–lych*.

poets seem to have tolerated disyllabic adjectives (which cannot take sounded *–e*, according to Duggan) in b-verses where the metre requires a stave followed by a long dip (/xx), as in *WA* 1202b, 'fyftene burghes'.[71] Duggan argues that, though final *–e* was no longer pronounced in these disyllabic adjectives, alliterative poets continued to admit them in this position in deference to the practices of earlier poets; similarly, the exclusion of *–ly* at line ending remained present 'as a fossil long after the phonology which created the original requirement had changed'.[72] In other words, *–ly* was unmetrical for these poets at line ending because it had once been disyllabic, and *vice versa* disyllabic adjectives were deemed to provide a long dip in the b-verse because they had once upon a time taken final *–e*.

However, it should be noted that the exclusion of *–ly* adverbs from line endings is part of a much larger ban. The surprising fact is not that alliterative poets avoid *–ly* at line ending but that they outlaw a whole range of suffixes there, such as *–ful*, *–ship*, *–dom*, *etc*.[73] As we observe in Chapter Five, these suffixes create 'heavy' dips and are especially common at the end of a-verses whose syllabic structure is not otherwise distinguishable from that of b-verses. The obvious explanation for the avoidance at *–ly* at line ending is, therefore, not that *–ly* was disyllabic or was still counted as such by archaising poets, but that alliterative poets wrote lines in which both primary and secondary stress were impermissible at line ending.[74]

In this part of the chapter we hope to show that *–ly* and *–lych* adverbs are prosodic variants rather than equivalently disyllabic (as Cable claims) or monosyllabic (as Duggan claims). It is important to bear in mind that the two suffixes offered different phonological environments for final *–e*, and that many Middle English poets (in various dialects) made motivated choices between *–ly* and *–lyche* forms. To take the phonology first: it is well known that inflectional *–e* was not normally added after vowels.

[71] Duggan, 'Final *–e*', pp. 132–3.

[72] We quote Karl Hagen's summary of Duggan's position (which Hagen endorses): 'Adverbial Distribution in Middle English Alliterative Verse', *Modern Philology*, 90 (1992), 159–71.

[73] We owe this important insight to Nicolay Yakovlev (personal communication).

[74] Langland, as Duggan notes, is an exception, but what makes him exceptional is not just his tolerance of *–ly*, but his overall tolerance of secondary stress, at line ending, e.g. *–yng* (*PP* B 5.293, 5.420), *is* (B 6.11, C 8.10).

Thus *–e* was not retained in ME after adjectives ending in vowels (e.g. *many*, *wily)*.[75] Since ON *–liga* followed the development of OE *ig* > *i*, final *–e* was lost after *–ly* in EME. However, palatals and velars offered final *–e* protection from preceding vowels, so in these contexts (e.g. after *–ing*, *–lich*, *–ish*) *–e* survived into LME.[76] Even in the fifteenth century we find disyllabic *–liche*, as the following lines by Hoccleve demonstrate:

> So largeliche opned is thy syde (*Complaint of the Virgin*, 88)[77]
> Thou hast of hem so largeliche said (*Dialogue*, 755)[78]

The resulting variation between monosyllabic *–ly* and disyllabic *–lyche* gave poets options. For example, in the metrical grammar of Orm (*c.* 1190, Lincolnshire) the two forms constitute a minimal prosodic pair: the adverbial suffix *–liȝ* is always monosyllabic, whereas the ending on *–like* is disyllabic except before vowels, where Orm uses *-like* to prevent hiatus. The system is illustrated in the following lines:

> Oxe gangeþþ haȝheliȝ / & aldelike lateþþ (1228)
> (An ox goes quietly and bears himself solemnly)
>
> ȝif þu þe ladest all wiþ skil / and haȝhelike & faȝȝre (1247)

*Aldelike* has four syllables; *haȝheli* has three; and *haȝhelike* is used to prevent hiatus. This also explains the selection of *gastlike* (e.g. 13168, 13171, 14496) as opposed to *gastliȝ* (e.g. 14869, 14501).

Chaucer's usage of *–ly* and *–lych* is comparable. To judge by the best manuscripts, Chaucer tended to write *–liche* rather than *–ly* before a preceding vowel.[79] Moreover, whereas *–ly* is invariably monosyllabic, adverbial *–lych* is disyllabic (in non-eliding contexts). Thus Chaucer wrote 'tendrely' (adv.), except on two occasions in *Troilus*, where the best

[75] Mossé, *Handbook*, p. 64.

[76] Richard Jordan, *Handbuch der Mittelenglischen Grammatik: Lautlehre* (2nd edn, Heidelberg, 1934), p. 128.

[77] Quoted from *Hoccleve's Minor Works*, ed. F. J. Furnivall and I. Gollancz, rev. J. Mitchell and I. Doyle, EETS OS 61, 73 (London, 1892–1925, repr. 1970). It is worth noting *en passant* that this line again suggests that elision was not inevitable before accented vowels. This point bears on b-verses such as *WP* 5039b, 'godliche ouȝt', and *PP* B 19.87, 'sooþliche offrede', of which Duggan writes, 'Elision would ... make sounding of *–e* on *–liche* impossible' ('Langland's Dialect', p. 179).

[78] Thomas Hoccleve, *Thomas Hoccleve's Complaint and Dialogue*, ed. J. A. Burrow, EETS OS 313 (Oxford, 1999).

[79] Wild, *Eigentümlichkeiten*, p. 258.

manuscripts (Cambridge, Corpus Christi 61 and Pierpont Library MS 817) read:

And Pandare, that ful tendreliche wepte (4.353)
Gan for to wepe as tendreliche as he (4.369)

In the first instance Chaucer selected *–liche* because he needed the extra unstressed syllable for the metre; in the second, to avoid hiatus.

The same considerations apply to adjectival *–ly* and *–lych* forms. Duggan uses Chaucerian practice to argue against the possibility that final *–e* may have been pronounced in adjectives other than monosyllabic ones: 'By the end of the fourteenth century, in even so conservative and southerly a dialect as Chaucer's, we do not find disyllabic adjectives with inflectional *–e*' ('Final *–e*', 136). Yet, of course, Chaucer writes in iambic metre and so has no use for the pattern /xx. And his treatment of inflectional *–e* is altogether different when adjectives are trisyllabic, for in this environment the metre supports the inflection:

Thus much as now, O wommanliche wif (*T&C* 3.106)
Shal ben your fresshe wommanliche face (*T&C* 5.244)

Final *–e* is justified in both contexts (in vocative and weak adjective). Again the *–liche* ending (disyllabic) should be contrasted with *–ly*, which is invariably monosyllabic:

Lat se now of youre wommanly pitee (*CT* I.3083)

Chaucer's verse clearly demonstrates that *–e* was still operative in literary language after adverbial and adjectival *–lych* and that the distribution of *–ly* and *–lyche* forms follows prosodic and syllabic needs.

If we look now at the distribution of adverbial *–ly* and *–lyche* in alliterative verse, we find the choice between the two forms to be similarly motivated. Because the rhythmical rules of the a-verse are controversial, we shall focus exclusively on b-verses, where the syllabic value of *–ly* and *–lych* is easier to deduce.[80]

### *The Cotton Nero poems*

[80] For a study that also examines the distribution of *–ly* and *–lych* in a-verses we would cite to Noriko Inoue, 'The Metre of Middle English Alliterative Verse: *–ly* and *–lych(e* Adverbs and Adjectives', forthcoming in *Modern Philology*. We agree with her conclusion that one of the main functions of *–lych* in the a-verse is to secure a long medial dip and (at least in the *Gawain* poems) to prevent hiatus before polysyllabic words beginning with schwa.

The most telling piece of evidence that *–ly* was monosyllabic for this poet and *–lyche* disyllabic is the conspicuous absence of the *–lych* suffix from the iambics of *Pearl*, whereas in *G*, by contrast, *–lych* (rarely *–lich*) occurs thirty times, in *C* 20 times, in *P* eight times. Since the metre of *Pearl* tends to exclude double offbeats, the *–ly* suffix (monosyllabic) is naturally preferred to *–lyche* (disyllabic) in lines such as 'To clanly close in golde so clere' (*Pearl* 2). The remarkable absence of *–lych* in *Pearl* strongly militates against the standard emendation of line 1086: 'For ferly of that frelich [MS *freuch*] fygure'. The emendation (due to E. V. Gordon) imports a form that is utterly alien to this poem,[81] for *frelich* would be trisyllabic if the poet's grammar of final *–e* were historically correct (as we shall argue it was). The emendation *fresch* (in the sense of 'vivid') gives better sense and metre. In the iambic bob-and-wheel lines of *G*, *–lych* suffixes are also conspicuous by their absence. As in *Pearl*, double offbeats are unusual in the bob-and-wheel, and the poet evidently avoided them where possible.[82] It follows that *–ly* is monosyllabic in such verses as 'Ful lúfly cón ho léte' (*G* 1206; cf. 388, 415, 441, 1101, 1598, 1689, 1716, 1789), and in 'I am dérely to yów bihólde' (1842), where disyllabic *–ly* would create a highly anomalous triple offbeat.[83]

The distribution of *–ly* and *–lych* adverbs and adjectives in the alliterative poems confirms that the two are metrical variants. Some examples will illustrate the pattern.

(1) Both *gostly* and *gostlych* are found in the *Gawain* poems. The former is the unmarked form:

[81] The spelling *–lich* is also anomalous and peculiar to *G* (136, 183); as we have argued elsewhere, *G* shows signs of having had a scribal history different from that of the other poems: see Putter and Stokes, 'The Linguistic Atlas'.

[82] Note, for example, the selection of the marked form *mas* at *G* 106, 'Much mirthe he mas withalle', and of the shortened *dele* (for *devil*) at *G* 2188, 'Þe dele his matynnes telle'.

[83] Yasuyo Moriya, in 'The Meter of the Verse Line of the Middle English *Pearl*', *Studies in Medieval English Language and Literature*, 11 (1996), 49–79, provides some useful statistics on the occurrence of double and triple offbeats in *Pearl*: 'In *Pearl*, however, the single offbeat is dominant, with the double offbeat occupying less than ten percent of all the offbeat positions. The triple offbeat ... is found in only two lines' (p. 63). The lines adduced by Moriya are 'And to þe gentyl Lomb hit arn anjoynt' (895), and 'Þe apostel in Apocalyppce in theme con take' (944). The syllable count of 944 is uncertain since elision could well yield 'Þ'apost'l in Apoc'lyppce'.

I hoped þat gostly was þat porpose (*Pearl* 185)
Þe apostel hem segh in gostly drem (*Pearl* 790)

The –*lych* variant is used just once, 'With glopnyng of þat ilke gome þat gostlych speked' (*G* 2461), where pronounced final –*e* is necessitated by the long dip required in the b-verse.

(2) A very common word in this MS is *clanly* (adjective and adverb), e.g. *G* 393, *Pearl* 2, *C* 264, *etc.* The –*lyche* variant is found only once, at *C* 310 — 'A cofer closed of tres clanlych planed' — where b-verse metre again requires voiced final –*e*.

(3) The adverb *brem(e)ly* is also common in this corpus (e.g. *C* 509, *G* 779, 2233), the –*lyche* variant occurring only once, 'Bryddez busken to bylde, and bremlych syngen' (*G* 509), where a sequence of two unstressed syllables is again metrically required to meet the long-dip requirement. It is true that adverbial –*lych* has not been spelt with final –*e* in these instances, but in a couple of cases the spelling accurately reflects the syllabic requirements:

At this cause þe knyght comlyche hade (*G* 648)
Þo wern Loth and his lef, his luflyche deȝter (*C* 939)

Although final –*e* is not otherwise retained in the manuscript orthography, we believe that the spelling at *G* 648 and *C* 939 faithfully reflects the syllabic status of –*lyche* in adverbs and weak and plural adjectives.

The picture suggested by these examples is confirmed by a more systematic analysis of the distribution patterns. Apart from the examples cited above, –*lych* is used only in the following b-verses:

an aghlich mayster (*G* 136)
and comlych ladies (*G* 539)
with luflych greueȝ (*G* 575)
þat coyntlych closed (*G* 578)
with comlych panez (*G* 855)
semlych ryche (*G* 882)
your comlych fere (*G* 2411)
and hagherlych serued (*C* 18)
to a worþlych prynce (*C* 49)
in fleschlych dedeȝ (*C* 265)
wern derelych fayre (*C* 270)
wyth lyflych wordeȝ (*C* 809)
þose broþelych wordeȝ (*C* 848)
semlych burdes (*C* 1247)
and loþelych werkes (*C* 1350)
a worþelych queen (*C* 1351)
saf onelych twcyne (*C* 1749)
and serelych deled (*P* 193)
of frelych dryȝtyn (*P* 214)
ferslych biddeȝ (*P* 337)
þe worþelych leues (*P* 475)

In most of these verses, the long-dip requirement demands a trisyllabic pronunciation of the adjective or adverb. This pronunciation can, in a few cases, be achieved by the sounding of a medial *–e* rather than a final one. Such a medial vowel is possible but not etymological in the case of *hagherlych* (< ON *hagr*; *hagliga*; cf. German *behaglich*);[84]*semly* has etymological *–e* (< ON *sœmiligr*), and Chaucer on occasion pronounced it, but Gower and the *Gawain* poet apparently did not;[85] *worþlych*, also *worþelych*, can be one of two words, ME *worthly* < OE *weorðlic* (disyllabic) or ME w*orthily* < *worthy* + *ly* (trisyllabic in Chaucer);[86] *aghlich* has organic medial *e* if the etymology suggested by Tolkien and Gordon is correct (ON < *agi* + *lic*; OE *egeslic*; cf. *aȝhefull* in *Ormulum*), but the word may be related to ME *egleche* < OE *aglaeca*, with organic final vowel.[87] There are no other cases where etymology or discernable usage[88] makes medial *e*s very likely. In the majority of b-verses, then, final *–e* must be pronounced to create regular b-verse metre. And, also in the majority of b-verses, that final *–e* is grammatically justified. This is also true of *P* 214, 'of frelych dryȝtyn', since adjectives modifying proper names (including words for 'God') were normally treated as weak, the referent being definite.[89] The only exceptions are *C* 49,[90] where the long dip is already in place and final *–e* would actually be unmetrical, and *C* 1351 and (depending on choice of

[84] *Ormulum* has the forms *haȝherlikke* and *haȝhelig*.

[85] On the *Gawain* poet's pronunciation of *semly* see below, p. 109.

[86] The co-existence of the two lexical items may have give poets a useful option. Cf. Chaucer's use of *worth* and *worthy*, on which see Bihl, *Wirkungen*, p. 134.

[87] As argued by Mark C. Amodio, *Writing the Oral Tradition: Oral Poetics and Literate Culture in Medieval England* (Notre Dame, Ind., 2004), p. 142, OE *aglaeca* 'awesome opponent', 'ferocious fighter', typically applied to 'an unusually powerful, threatening, liminal human figure' fits the context (a description of the Green Knight) remarkably well.

[88] Scribes' spelling should not, in our view, be relied upon as a guide to pronunciation.

[89] See Burnley, 'Inflexion'. Naturally, this fact also applies to alliterative verse: see e.g. *SJ* 199 (Hanna and Lawton's note is beside the point), *P* 166, *C* 1730.

[90] At *C* 49 *worþlych* is suspect on grounds of sense. The contrast with *in heuen* (MS *in her euen*) in the following line suggests that the poet wrote a word meaning 'wordly', and Gollancz emended to *werldlych*: see I. Gollancz (ed.), *Cleanness* (London, 1921), note to lines 49–50 ('I suggest that "worþlych" is due to an earlier "wordlych" [i.e. worldly] being misunderstood'). Gollancz makes the further assumption (unwarranted in our view) that the poet's form was 'werdly'.

etymologies) *G* 136, both containing strong adjectives with a possible medial vowel that would satisfy the long-dip requirement.

The typical use of *–lych* in long-dip position makes it clear that the suffix was disyllabic. Conversely, the fact that the poems do not select *–ly* in this position suggests that Cable is wrong to think *–ly* was disyllabic. In over 90 percent of cases, the *–ly* suffix occurs when the long dip is already in place. Instances are too numerous to list, but a few examples will illustrate the usual pattern:

| | |
|---|---|
| hym loȝly to serue (*G* 851) | prestly þat tyme (*G* 911) |

Particularly interesting is the use of the double *–lyly* suffix for adverbs (and once for an adjective), a speciality of the *Gawain* poet. In b-verses, the double suffix occurs only in the following positions:

| | |
|---|---|
| of ferlyle schappes (*C* 1460) | sellyly ofte (*G* 1803) |
| semlyly fayre (*G* 622) | and luflyly sayde (*G* 2389) |
| and ferlyly long (*G* 796) | and ferlyly he telles (*G* 2494) |
| and sellyly blered (*G* 963) | and luflyly acorden (*G* 2514) |

As with *–lych*, the reduplication occurs when b-verse metre requires two unstressed syllables (*G* 2494 and *G* 2514 are the two exceptions, both occurring to compensate for elisions before a following unstressed syllable with *h–* or vowel). As Duggan has observed, the key factor in the selection of these unusual forms is the poet's wish to avoid disyllabic 'ferly', 'semly', 'selly', and 'lufly', and this in turn suggests that the medial vowel that occasionally appears in manuscript spellings (e.g. *semely*, *C* 1442, *louely*, *C* 1486) is graphical and does not reflect the poet's phonology.

Only rarely does the *–ly* suffix occur in positions where metre requires a long dip. We would not include amongst such cases the following b-verses, where a medial vowel is likely:

| | |
|---|---|
| kyndely serued (*G* 135) | kyndely sware (*C* 319) |
| were worthily smale (*G* 144) | þe worþely peple (*C* 651) |
| craftyly sleye (*G* 797) | oddely dere (*C* 698) |
| metely come (*G* 1004) | and rychely hwed (*C* 1045) |
| is hendely praysed (*G* 1228) | and hastyly sone (*C* 1150) |

In some of these words the medial vowel derives from original *i* ('worthily', 'craftyly', 'hastyly');[91] in others the medial vowel is justified by etymology and/or paralleled by the usages of other poets.[92]

This leaves us with the following anomalies:

| | |
|---|---|
| fersly brenned (*G* 832) | and derely serued (*G* 1559) |
| and stylly speken (*G* 1117) | and pertly halden (*C* 244) |
| and derfly vpon (*G* 1183; *vpon* = open vb.) | and kenely flowen (*C* 945) |

At *C* 945, a medial *e* in *kenely* is perhaps possible (cf. *E* 63b, 'so kenely mony'). *Pertly* could be an error for *apertly*. *G* 832 is suspect on other grounds: *fersly* is a correction by the second scribe of *ferfly*, and emendation to accord with *P* 337, 'ferslych[e] bidde3', should be considered. *G* 1183 is also suspect:

> And as in slomeryng he slode, sle3ly he herde
> A littel dyn at his dor and derfly vpon.

Tolkien and Gordon emend to *dernly* ('and heard it stealthily open') for good reasons: the error (presumably due to confusion of *u* and *n*) would be an easy one to make and *dernly* makes better sense in the context, which emphasises the Lady's furtiveness.[93] (Cf. the lady's departure: 'Þat drof þe dor after hir ful *dernly* and stille' (1188). Since ME *derne* has etymological –*e* (cf. *dærnelike* in *Ormulum*), Tolkien and Gordon's emendation should in turn be corrected to *dernely* to restore b-verse metre.

All in all, there are very few exceptions to the general pattern that governs the distribution of –*ly* and –*lych*. The latter is used in long-dip position and the former where a short dip is needed. We conclude from this that in this manuscript –*ly* is monosyllabic and –*lyche* disyllabic.

[91] The possibility of a medial vowel in these cases is confirmed by *Pearl* 695, 'Bot hárdÿlý with-oúte perýle'. Here the medial vowel corresponds with *i* (<OF *hardi*) rather than weak *e*.

[92] *Rychely* and *kyndely* are trisyllabic in Chaucer and Gower; *metely* (< OE *gemete*, but *gemetlice*) is *metelike* in Orm; trisyllabic *oddely* is also indicated by *WA* 275b, 'odly fourmed'. Duggan and Turville-Petre suggest that 'a svarabhakti vowel appeared in *od[de]ly* in the poet's dialect'; in fact *e* is organic (ON *odda* + ly).

[93] This point has been emphasized by Jeremy Smith, 'Semantics and Metrical Form in *Sir Gawain and the Green Knight*', in *New Perspectives on Middle English Texts: a Festschrift for* R. *A. Waldron*, ed. S. Powell and J. J. Smith (Cambridge, 2000), pp. 87–103.

*Alexander and Dindimus*

The more southerly dialect of *B* is reflected in the preponderance of –*lych* in adjectives (where it is the unmarked form). We find the following instances in the b-verse:

here wordliche makus (58)
þe semliche prynce (111)
flechliche lustus (334)
of ert[h]liche werkus (442)
wordliche fode (450)
lordliche holdeus (576)
þat lodlich is founde (592)
wiþ worldiche godus (604)
helplich of grace (673)
comeliche flourus (730)
worldiche godus (804)
of worldiche craftus (837)
of wordliche peple (924)
for wordliche glose (1016)
erþliche werkus (1053)

It is striking that the spelling generally reflects historical grammar: plurals and weak adjectives are spelt with –*e*, while strong adjectives (*B* 592, 673) are not. There are three exceptions (450, 924, 1016). Explanations for these could be found: *peple* and *fode* could be notionally plural,[94] and *glose*, too, may be plural (following the pattern of OF nouns ending in a sibilant).[95] But it is curious that they all involve the adjective *wordliche*, and more curious still that this same adjective and its synonym *erthlich* also give rise to irregularities in *B*'s a-verses, as we shall see below (see p. 236). We cannot confidently explain the anomaly, but have observed something similar in *Ormulum*, where *eorþlice* happens to be to the only adjective with ungrammatical final –*e*.[96] Significantly, the spelling –*liche* occurs in all positions where final –*e* is essential for the metre. The only adjective in –*ly* to occur in the b-verse is 'heartily' (with medial vowel derived from *i*): 'wiþ herteli þouhtus' (95).

In adverbs, by contrast, the –*ly* ending is more common than –*lych* (3:2). The distributional pattern we observed in the Cotton Nero poems emerges here, too, with startling precision: –*ly* adverbs occur if and only

[94] See Mustanoja, *Middle English Syntax*, p. 62.

[95] Mossé, *Handbook*, p. 52. Cf. *MA* 808, 'In the seven scyence the sutelest fondene'.

[96] Martin Lehnert lists *eorþlic* as one of three adjectives (also 'heathen', 'English') to which Orm takes the liberty of adding –*e* without apparent grammatical justification (e.g. 'onn Ennglissche spæche', 17596), 'an hæþene king' (9457), 'an erþlike mann' (18322). See Martin Lehnert, *Sprachform und Sprachfunktion im 'Orrmulum'* (Berlin, 1953), pp. 36–38. 'English' and 'heathen' could perhaps be analysed as nouns (with justified –*e* of genitive plural), but 'earthly' seems genuinely anomalous.

if the long dip does not require a disyllabic suffix, as in 'soþli þei ne hadde' (9), 'cofli to feche' (125), *etc.* It is not found in eliding position, with two exceptions both involving accented *h*/vowel (648, 1062). By contrast, the marked forms in *–lyche* or *–liche* occur exclusively in the following b-verses:

| | |
|---|---|
| cofliche saide (64) | soþliche echone (646) |
| tidliche enquere (148) | hollyche segge (657) |
| hastiliche aftur (167) | & folliche seggen (740) |
| goodliche he sente (246) | & onliche of bestes (743) |
| mekliche endure (269) | holliche i-like (792) |
| soþliche i telle (286) | menskliche hit radde (1073) |
| & wordliche serue (427) | |

It is clear that the poet chose the suffix either to create a mandatory long dip (64, 427, 657, 740) or to avoid hiatus (148, 167, 246, 286, 646, 743, 792, 1073). The historically justified *–e* is again consistently reflected in the spelling.

*B* thus clearly indicates that justified final *–e* was pronounced after *–lych* and not after *–ly*.

*Conclusion*

It is obvious from our analysis that *–ly* and *–lyche* were used as metrical doublets as much by alliterative poets as by rhyming poets such as Orm, Chaucer and Hoccleve. For poets of both these types of verse, suffixes in *–ly* and *–lych* were not different 'spellings',[97] but variants with potentially different syllable counts: the former is monosyllabic, the second takes inflectional or adverbial *–e* or wards off hiatus. Editors of alliterative verse should be aware that these suffixes may well have been similarly exploited for metrical reasons in their poems. Of course, the distributional pattern may not be as clear as it is in *B*, *C*, *P* and *G* in poems that are preserved in later manuscripts or texts with a longer or more complicated scribal history. The evidence provided by *Siege of Jerusalem*, for instance, is sparse, though not contradictory.[98] The only

[97] This unfortunate terminology is used by Hagen, 'Adverbial Distribution'.

[98] The *–lych* suffix is rare in the earliest manuscripts L (Hanna and Lawton's copy-text) and P. In L the suffix *–ly* is normal, and it is not used in long-dip position; *–lych* occurs only in the b-verses of 141 (P *semely*), 453 (P *deuely*), 458 (P *ferly*), 653 (P *wonderly*), 915 (P *baldely he*), 985 (P *semelych*), 1334 (P omits). Variants from the other MSS cannot reliably be recovered from Hanna and Lawton's apparatus, but the following data is supplied by Kellog, 'The Language', pp. 50–

case where manuscripts L and P agree on a *–lych* suffix (L985b, 'semelich lord', PAV, 'semelyche lord') is suggestive: in this position final *–e* is metrically required and grammatically correct in the vocative; it is also the form selected in comparable b-verses in other poems (*B* 111, *C* 1247, *G* 882, *WP* 49, 1454, 2594, 5472, 5509).[99]

Metrical exploitation of the doublets may, of course, vary in degree and kind across different texts. In *William of Palerne*, for instance, there is good evidence to suggest that here, too, the alternation between *–ly* and *–lyche* was guided by syllabic and prosodic considerations, but such considerations do not tell the whole story. With regard to adverbs in the b-verse, we find that *–ly* (much the more common form) is clearly monosyllabic (see 17, 37, 554, *etc*) and that *–liche* (66 occurrences) is usually found before vowels or *h* (30x) or where a disyllabic form is required by b-verse metre (15x).[100] As we would expect, cases in which a disyllabic pronunciation of *–liche* would lead to unmetrical b-verses are statistically negligible (2x).[101] There are, however, many attestations of *–liche* (19x) in b-verses where the metre allows, but does not require, a disyllable. The same situation obtains with regard to adjectives in *WP*: *–ly* is plainly monosyllabic (see 20, 50, 138, *etc*) and *liche* (16 occurrences) presumably disyllabic in all cases (10x) where metre requires the sounding of final *–e*.[102] But the form also occurs in cases where it is not metrically required to be a disyllable (4x),[103] though only rarely (2x) where pronounced final

60: C only has forms in *–ly* except for *deuylych* (453); U has only three *–lych* forms (*semeliche* 141, *deueliche* 453, and *komeliche* 1014); D has only four *–lych* forms (*semelich*, 141, *deflich*, 458, *comelich*, 1014, and *comlich*, 1216). In L, pronounced final *–e* is metrically necessary at 141 and possibly at 453 (assuming syncopation of *deuylych*, as suggested by D, *deflich*). In the other examples disyllabic *–lych* is possible but not necessary. 458b, 'a ferlich nonbre' is the only example of a b-verse where disyllabic *–liche* would regularise the metre but is not historically justified. MS C (which reads *and a*) offers a basis for emendation.

[99] As argued above (p. 109), medial *e* is unlikely.

[100] See 126, 199, 225, 393, 408, 711, 819, 844, 1195, 1329, 1898, 2074, 2532, 3238, 5039. It could be argued that a medial *–e* is possible in some of these cases (e.g. *blyþeliche*, 199; *mildeliche*, 1898).

[101] See 2591b and 1030b. The reading of the latter, 'þat I yow geynliche hiȝt', should be contrasted with 636b, 'þat I gaynli knowe'.

[102] 49, 355, 1454, 1814, 2058, 2232, 2594, 2700, 5742, 5509. Final *–e* is grammatically justified in all b-verses except 2232.

[103] 2245, 2579, 2704, 4849.

*–e* in *–liche* would lead to an unmetrical b-verse with two long dips.[104] In *WP*, therefore, *–liche* does not *only* occur where metre *demands* a disyllable.

Provenance and date will also affect whether and to what degree metrical exploitation of the doublets is visible in manuscripts. As might be expected, texts copied by Northern scribes and later poems contain fewer examples of *–lych*. There are none in *Saint Erkenwald*, and only two in *Death and Liffe*, where *lodly* varies with *lothelich*:

> and lodly to see (162b)
> a lothelich name (303b)
> lotheliche hands (374b)

*Lothelich(e)* is the form used in long-dip position, but final *–e* is justified only at 374. *WA* also yields little data, and it is hard to get at it, because potentially significant manuscript variation as between *–ly* and *–lych* is not recorded in the editorial apparatus. Our research suggests that in manuscripts A and D the adverbial ending is *–ly*, with one exception (A 228: 'he maistirlike said') which sheds no light on the syllable count of the ending. Adjectives in A end on *–ly* (also *–li* and *–le*), again with a single unrevealing exception (*dedelike*, 4186). It is only in D that we find adjectives in *–lych*, once in an a-verse ('Als with a dedly [D *dedlich*] duke', 2005), but otherwise only in the long-dip position of the b-verse:

> Erell*e* or ony Empero*ur* or erthlich prince (1735)
> [A: *Erle or emperour or any erldly prince*]
> a sellich nounbre (1856) [A *selly*]
> my awne semelych modir (2143) [A *my semely modir*]
> a semlich nonn (2306) [A *a semely summe*]
> þat frelich lady (2853) [A *frely*]
> semelyche kniȝtis (3170) [A *selkuth*]
> with lothlyche woundes (3358) [A *lathely*]
> & gryslyche teris (3366) [A *grysely*]

Final *–e* is not justified in 1735,[105] 1856, and 2306; however, it is correct and would regularise the metre in all other cases (with the omission of *awne* at 2143).[106] *Selkuth[e]* is to be preferred at 3170. In the light of the evidence from other alliterative poems that final *–e* was retained after *–lich*, future editors might consider the possibility of emending A 2853,

[104] 568, 2637. At 568 the alliteration is suspect and at 2637 the final *–e* is ungrammatical.

[105] But on *eorþlic*, see n. 96, above.

[106] The medial vowels in the A variants *lathely* and *grysely* are not etymological.

3358, and 3366, after D. The alternative is to assume (as the editors do) that the poet pronounced the medial *e*s that appear occasionally in the spelling of manuscript A (*semely*, *lathely*, *grysely*, also *rodely*, 784, *dedeli*, 2003, *loueli*, 5139, and others) and twice in editorial additions (*ster[y]nly*, 841, *[whiste]ly*, 1977).

But how safe is that assumption? The case of the *Alliterative Morte Arthure* is instructive here. Like *WA*, *MA* was copied by a Northern scribe (in this case Thornton), and neither he nor the A- and D-scribes of *WA* are likely to have introduced –*lych* forms, which were alien to their dialects. In *MA* the ending in –*lych* does occur commonly in both adverbs and adjectives, and the distribution of the form shows that the poet chose it when he needed a disyllable or wished to avoid hiatus. For example, the adverb 'highly' is *heyly* (464, 2663, 2920), but once *helych* is found, 'fulle helych blawen' (1286), to create the long dip. The usual forms for 'lovely' are *lufly* and *louely*, but the alternative suffix is selected once, at 2674, 'þat lufflyche songen'. The adverb 'rudely' usually appears in this manuscript as *ruydly* (785, 794, 1124), except at 1877b, 'ruydlyche wondyde', where final –*e* is required. In these cases, as in others,[107] the alternation between –*ly* and –*lyche* is so consistent that we can only see it as a motivated choice by the original poet. This has interesting implications for the way we think about problematic b-verses, such as

louely coruyn (426)
and ruydly wondyde (1415)
louely clethid (5003)

The fact that –*lyche* forms were used deliberately in long-dip positions unsettles the assumption that the poet pronounced a medial *e* to meet the demands of the metre. It is much more likely that we are looking at cases of scribal translation resulting in the partial replacement of archetypal –*lyche* suffixes by the scribe's indigenous –*ly* forms.

[107] Compare also 'appertly' (1478) with 'appertlyche graythed' (589); 'clenly' (673, 850, 851, *etc.*) with 'clenlyche' or 'clenliche' occurring in b-verses only before vowels (628, 654, 919, 1849, 1895, 2182, 2559, 3258, *etc.*) or where final –*e* is needed: 'fulle clenlyche burneschte' (2123); 'semly' (1949, 2457) with 'semliche bowndene (3316b), 'semlyly arrayede' (3787b) and 'semliche arrayede' (4064). There are no b-verses where disyllabic adverbial –*liche* would create two long dips, and only four cases where adverbial –*lich* cannot be explained as due to the avoidance of hiatus or the long-dip requirement: 1357, 3270, 3279, 3377.

The picture for adjectives in *MA* is crystal clear: in b-verses adjectival *–lych* and *–lich* terminations occur exclusively in long-dip position, and on each and every occasion (25x) final *–e* is justified (plural and once vocative at 3371). There is a single anomaly, 'Thane they buscches and bawmede thaire honourliche kyngis' (2298), but here the breakdown of alliteration confirms scribal error. Mary Hamel emends to *bourliche* (cf. 586, 730, 1002, 3662); this emendation tallies exactly with what we now know about the poet's use of adjectival *–lich* in alliterative verse.

The specialised use of adjectives and adverbs in *–lych* in the long-dip position of the b-verse undermines Duggan's hypothesis that uninflected disyllabic adjectives (producing only a short dip) were a throwback to a bygone age when *–e* was more extensively used. First, adjectives cannot be an isolated case, since adverbs in *–lych* are preferred in the same position. Second, it is a mistake to think that *–e* had vanished from fourteenth-century English in all but monosyllabic adjectives. Chaucer's verse clearly shows that inflectional *–e* survived in polysyllabic adjectives and should be pronounced where metre requires it. Examples of sounded *–e* in polysyllabic adjectives are easy to find: 'And dremen of the dredfulleste thinges' (*T&C* 5.248), 'Al the Troianysshe blood' (*HF* 201), 'Hath his kyndelyche stede' (*HF* 829). That we do not find disyllabic adjectives with final *–e* in Chaucer's verse is the natural outcome of its being iambic and therefore hostile to double offbeats. In alliterative metre, a double offbeat is, by contrast, a metrical requirement in the b-verse, and it is therefore no more remarkable to see alliterative poets using final *–e* after disyllabic adjectives than to see Chaucer doing so after trisyllabic ones.

Our conclusion that final *–e* could still be pronounced in infinitives and adjectives and adverbs in *–lych* raises the question of whether historically justified final *–e* was also alive and well in other grammatical categories. As we have shown in Chapter One, it certainly was at line ending; and the evidence provided by the poems in our corpus is that final *–e* could also be syllabic within the long line in many different grammatical categories, including nouns with etymological or analogical final *–e*, petrified datives, genitive plurals in *–ene*, weak or plural adjectives,[108]

[108] With the exception of disyllabic adjectives ending in *–y*, *–er*, *–el*, and *–en* (but not when *–en* is a suffix as in 'golden'). That such adjectives follow the strong flexion in alliterative verse is shown by such b-verses as 'and ful siker kniȝtes' (*G* 111), 'for þy reken wordeȝ' (*C* 756), 'and þe reken fyþel' (*C* 1082). Disyllabic

adverbs, subjunctives, imperatives, 1st person present, plural verb endings, 1st and 3rd person singular preterites of weak verbs in *–te*, *–de*, past participial adjectives in *–ede* and *–ene* and perhaps even in preterites in *–ede*.[109] In other words, the sounding of inflectional *–e* in infinitives and after *–lych* should not be thought of merely as an additional exception to the rule that final *–e* was insignificant but as an indication that no such rule ever existed in alliterative verse.

It must be emphasised, however, that the positive evidence for the pronunciation of final *–e* is not uniform across the entire corpus of alliterative poetry. In the alliterative poems extant in the earliest manuscripts, the syllabic value of final *–e* is easier to demonstrate, for in these MSS the metricality of a substantial number of lines depends on the sounding of final *–e*. However, in the later manuscripts the situation is different. Some poems, such as *E* and *Alexander A*, also show a strong metrical dependency on syllabic final *–e*. But there are also other poems, such as *WA*, *WW*, *P3A* and *MA*, whose dependency on final *–e* is minimal. The most plausible explanation for this fact is that the fifteenth-century northern scribes of these poems were still familiar with the rhythm of alliterative verse but could no longer hear or trust their readers to hear the sound of final *–e*, compensating with syllables of their own making.

If this explanation is right, the modern editors of *WA* and *SJ* belong to a long tradition of scribal interference. By editing out of their texts and apparatus instances of metrically required final *–e* in these poems, they are at last completing the work that medieval scribes left undone.

adjectives ending in suffixes are avoided in this grammetrical position. See below, pp. 234–6.

109 Chaucer seems occasionally to have taken advantage of this option: see e.g. *CT* I.756 (*lakkedë*), 868 (*weddedë*), 2561 (*touchedë*), *LGW* 1119 (*shynedë*). Although the final *–e* is not represented in some of the better MSS, alternative manuscript readings produce metrically irregular lines. The same option was available to Gower: see *CA* 2.4553 (*Supplantedë*) and 5.1678 (*percedë*). There are various verses in alliterative poetry (e.g. *C* 131, 668, *P* 447) that might suggest the same was true for alliterative poets, as indeed Luick argued apropos of *B*: see *Historische Grammatik*, p. 511.

# 3. ALLITERATIVE PATTERNING IN THE *MORTE ARTHURE* AND THE COTTON NERO POEMS

Most alliterative poems are extant in only one manuscript, and the use of single witnesses to provide evidence for the poetic practices of alliterative poets presents obvious difficulties. Thorlac Turville-Petre observes that any statement about the alliterative patterns in the existing manuscript of the *Morte Arthure* is true only of the text as it stands in this unique manuscript and is likely to misrepresent the practices of the poet himself.[1] One of the things we would like to do in this chapter is to explore the types of evidence which might nevertheless enable us to make judgements about poets' metrical practices. Such judgements can be arrived at not only by careful study of the poems themselves, but also in some cases by the use of such extraneous evidence as material drawn from sources or independent information about the scribe's habits. The poems we shall mainly be concerned with are the *Alliterative Morte Arthure* (*MA*), *Sir Gawain and the Green Knight* (*G*), *Patience* (*P*), and *Cleanness* (*C*).

The task of distinguishing authorial from scribal usage in these poems presents varying degrees of difficulty. In the case of *MA*, the single extant manuscript (Lincoln Cathedral MS 91, the Thornton MS) stands at some considerable distance from the poet's original. The stemma suggested by Mary Hamel in her 1984 edition, for instance, postulates four stages between the Thornton copy and what she terms the author's prototype;[2] and a complicated textual history is confirmed by the

[1] Thorlac Turville-Petre, 'Emendation on the Grounds of Alliteration in *The Wars of Alexander*', *English Studies*, 61 (1980), 302–17 (302). See also Hoyt N. Duggan, 'The Evidential Basis for Old English Metrics', *Studies in Philology*, 85 (1988), 145–63 (147).

[2] Hamel (ed.), *Morte Arthure*, p. 13. Some aspects of Hamel's stemma, in particular those related to Malory's *Morte Darthur*, may require modification in the light of the findings of P. J. C. Field. See the discussion in his *Malory: Texts and Sources* (Cambridge, 1998), especially pp. 9–13, which suggests that the evidence for an intermediate stage between the Caxton version and the shared archetype of the Caxton version and the Winchester manuscript is slight. However, it should be noted that Field himself observes (p. 13) that the Roman war section of the *Morte Darthur* was a special case and that an intermediate stage

language of the extant poem, which is dialectally mixed, containing both Midland and Northern features.[3] The text has plainly been vulnerable to scribal corruption, and it would therefore be naive to suppose that the metrical patterns found in the Thornton MS are accurate reflections of the author's original.

The Cotton Nero poems seem to offer fewer obstacles: the language of the poems is 'reasonably homogeneous',[4] yet there is some evidence to suggest that *G* had a different and more complicated scribal transmission, since it contains forms that are anomalous or absent in its manuscript companions (e.g. *scho* for 'she', *hor* for 'their', *worche* for 'work').[5] Yet we cannot be certain that the manuscript precisely reflects the poet's metrical system even in the case of *P* and *C*, which there is reason to suppose are not far removed from the poet's original. Statistics should be able to tell us which rhythmical or alliterative patterns are rare, but they cannot tell us whether the responsibility for these patterns lies with the poet or with the scribe. In texts that are not autographs, such distinctions must depend on other types of evidence. Multiple witnesses, if available, are obviously very valuable, but they are not the only resource. Careful study of the text may show that a significant proportion of statistically abnormal lines are deviant in other respects or are closely paralleled by lines that offer metrically correct readings. External evidence may also be brought to bear. In the case of *MA*, we know that the scribe, Robert Thornton, also copied the *Siege of Jerusalem* (*SJ*), and because that poem does survive in multiple manuscripts we can learn something about Thornton's scribal habits. We also have the benefit of an additional witness to the archetype, namely Malory's *Morte Darthur*, which contains sections corresponding so closely with *MA* that Malory's intensive use of the alliterative poem (in whatever version) cannot be in

between the Caxton version and the archetype in this particular section is a possibility (see p. 148). Nevertheless, his discussion as a whole still seems to imply a single revision of the archetype.

[3] See S. O. Andrew, 'The Dialect of *Morte Arthure*', *Review of English Studies*, 4 (1928), 418–23, and A. I. McIntosh, 'The Textual Transmission of the Alliterative *Morte Arthure*', in *English and Medieval Studies Presented to J. R. R. Tolkien*, ed. Norman Davis and C. L. Wrenn (London, 1962), pp. 231–40.

[4] A. I. McIntosh, 'A New Approach to Middle English Dialectology', *English Studies*, 44 (1963), 1–11 (4–5). But see the qualifications by Putter and Stokes, 'The Linguistic Atlas'.

[5] See also above, p. 10–11.

doubt. In the case of *C* and *P* we also know the main source, the Vulgate Bible, which, though the *Gawain* poet's translation is often very free, does provide some check on the lexical possibilities of specific lines.

Drawing on such potentially useful supplementary evidence, we wish to address the much-debated question of the appropriateness of emendation *metri causa* in *MA*, *C*, *P* and *G*. Since there has been very little discussion until recently about the syllabics of the alliterative long line, scholarly debate has often focused on alliterative patterning, and this is the aspect of the metre on which we too intend to focus: to what extent do non-*aa*/*ax* lines represent a legitimate variation introduced by the poet himself, and to what extent are they scribal? There is much disagreement about this question. A brief look at the different editions of *MA* and their reception by various scholars will show the nature of that disagreement. O'Loughlin, writing in 1935, observes that up to and including Mary Banks's 1900 edition the handling of the text was conservative, but that a new attitude became evident with the publication in the same year of Mennicken's essay on the versification of *MA*.[6] Mennicken in his essay, Holthausen writing in *Englische Studien* in 1902, and Bjorkmann in his 1915 edition, which draws on both, all emend heavily for the sake of alliteration.[7] The following examples show the reading of the MS, with emendations from Bjorkmann's edition in parentheses.[8]

| | | | |
|---|---|---|---|
| Schelde vs fro schamesdede | and *syn*full werkes | (3) | (schend- *Hh*) |
| Sweys in-to Swaldye | with his *snell* houndes | (57) | (swifte *Me*) |
| This ilke kyde conquerour | and *helde* hym for lorde | (65) | (kende *Me*) |
| Þou sall be feched with force | and *ouersette* fore euer | (111) | (forfette *Me*) |
| His scoulders ware schalyde | all in *clene* syluere | (766) | (schire *Me*) |
| So may þe wynde weile turnne | I *quytte* hym or ewyn | (1788) | (rewarde*Hh*) |

[6] J. L. N. O'Loughlin, 'The Middle English Alliterative *Morte Arthure*', *Medium Aevum*, 4 (1935), 153–68.

[7] Franz Mennicken, *Versbau und Sprache in Huchowns'Morte Arthure'*, Bonner Beiträge zur Anglistik, 5 (1900), 33–144; F. Holthausen, Review of Mennicken's 'Versbau und Sprache', in *Englische Studien*, 30 (1902), 271–5; Eric Björkman (ed.), *Morte Arthure* (Heidelberg, 1915).

[8] *Hh* indicates an emendation proposed by Holthausen, *Me* one proposed by Mennicken. In order to avoid privileging one particular editorial approach, quotations have been transcribed from the facsimile: *The Thornton Manuscript (Lincoln Cathedral 91)*, ed. D. S. Brewer and A. E. B. Owen (London, 1977). Abbreviations have been silently expanded.

O'Loughlin strongly disapproves of this practice, which he describes as assuming that a text which hitherto had been regarded as fairly representative of its original is 'nothing more than a product of minstrel tradition of the sort that bequeathed to us the Cambridge fragments of *Havelok*'. 'If there is one thing,' he says, 'of which we can be certain in the mysteries of Middle English prosody, it is that at no time was *aa/ax* the exclusively correct mode of alliteration.'[9] He believes, on the contrary, that he has discovered a rule which will account for much of the *Morte*'s alliterative variation: that where two lines are linked by the same alliterating letter only one of them need have perfect alliteration.[10] The consequences of this disagreement for the text of the *Morte* are illustrated by the two lines below: 716, where Mennicken emends *Twys* to *Sweys*, but O'Loughlin would retain *Twys*; and 1653, where Mennicken and Brock emend *lythe* to *kythe* but O'Loughlin would retain *lythe*, in each case justifying this retention by the presence of alliterative linkage.

And then cho swounes fulle swythe when he hys swerde aschede
*Twys* in a swounyng swelte as cho walde (715–16; Sweyes *Me*)

Will kyth for his kynges lufe craftes of armes
We are comen fro þe kyng of þis *lythe* ryche (kythe *Me*, *Brock*)
That knawen es for conquerour corownde in erthe (1652–4)

Recent editors and critics (not only of the *Morte*) have, basically, accepted O'Loughlin's argument.[11] Although Hamel does in fact emend both the lines just cited, her reasons for doing so have nothing to do with the metre.[12] She generally accepts and even extends O'Loughlin's view. Thus she accepts as metrically regular variations such as the following:

[9] O'Loughlin, '*Morte Arthure*', pp. 153 and 155.

[10] This would not account for all the examples cited above, but it would be relevant to 65, 111 and 766.

[11] See Valerie Krishna (ed.), *The Alliterative Morte Arthure* (New York, 1976), pp. 24–5; Hamel (ed.), *Morte Arthure*, p. 18ff., and Yasuyo Moriya, 'The Role of the Sound *r* in *The Alliterative Morte Arthure*', *Poetica*, 53 (2000), 1–13. A slightly more restricted use of O'Loughlin's argument is made by Trigg (ed.), *Wynnere and Wastoure*, p. xxxiv.

[12] See Hamel's notes to the lines in question. Noriko Inoue, 'The A-Verse', mounts a similar argument that the *Gawain* poet permitted non *aa/ax* patterns (at least in *G*), since many of them occur in lines with interlinear alliteration or in lines where a final stave alliterates with the first staves of a the following or

The flour of þe faire folke of *Amazonnes* landes
All thate faillez on þe felde be forfette fore euere (584–5)

Indeed, she also accepts lines with even less regular alliteration, such as 305, which she considers to be metrically satisfactory because of its alliterative linkage with both the previous and the following lines (304 alliterates on /b/ and the final stave of 305 (*besekes*) echoes this;[13] 306 alliterates on /a/ and the second stave of 305 (*Arthure*) anticipates this):

Thane the *b*urelyche *b*eryn of *B*retayne þe lyttyll
Counsayles Sir *A*rthure and of hym *b*esekys
To *a*nsuere þe *a*lyenes wyth *a*usteren wordes (304–6)

Or take, for example, the couplet found at 4151–2:

He es *e*ldare than *I* and *e*nde sall we bothen
He sall *f*erkke be-*f*ore and I sall *c*ome *a*ftyre

Hamel's note to this couplet reads: 'The alliterative pattern of these two lines is aa:ax/bb:xa; no emendation is necessary'. Or consider the couplet at 827–8:

And *þ*ow sall hafe þe *v*ictorye thurghe *h*elpe of oure Lorde
As *þ*ow in thy *v*isione was *o*pynly schewede

Hamel believes this to be acceptable because the two lines have parallel alliteration (*þow* twice; *victorye* and *visione,* both alliterating on /v/; *helpe* and *opynly*, alliterating on vowel and /h/). 'The pattern here', she says, 'might be called ab:cx'.

Now there is something quite appealing about this tolerance of abnormal patterns of alliteration. It suggests a degree of authorial flexibility and subtlety and it privileges freedom over discipline in a way that is perhaps particularly attractive to modern editors (though, for reasons we explain in the conclusion to this chapter, we do not ourselves favour it). There may be something quite appealing, too, about Hamel's comment that variation from the standard pattern can be introduced to give relief from boredom in places where a whole string of lines alliterates on

preceding lines. She considers these alliterative linkages to be a deliberate 'compensatory' device.

13 Hamel's scansion here is problematic. For the beat to fall on *be–* it would have to be permissible for the line to end in two weak syllables. This is not the usual practice in the alliterative *Morte*, which normally ends on one and only one unstressed syllable, nor in alliterative poetry in general. See Chapter One, above.

the same sound. Nevertheless, it is also true that such an approach provides a neat justification for what may be in fact an *a priori* editorial reluctance to emend for metrical reasons. Hamel's view of what is metrically regular is so inclusive that the question of whether or not to emend *metri causa* seldom arises, but even where she clearly suspects metrical irregularity she is reluctant to make emendations. Her approach can be illustrated from her comments on 2872–4:

> Who so meles of þat mayde myſkaries he *n*euer
> Be þese wordes ware *ſ*aide they ware *n*oghte ferre be-hynd
> Bot the lenghe of a launde and Lorayne aſkryes

'The only linkages here,' says Hamel, 'are between *neuer* and *noghte* and perhaps *myskaries*, *saide* and *askryes*. But there is no reason to suspect the line of corruption except its lack of alliteration; W's summary … offers no evidence that Malory's immediate source read any differently. Without a stronger reason, to emend is to run the risk of rewriting the poet's work.' Or consider Hamel's analysis of the line 'Twa thosande in tale *horsede one* stedys' (335). Hamel rejects the emendation proposed by Mennicken (*on trappede stedys*)[14] and that proposed by Gordon and Vinaver (*attyred on stedes*)[15] on the grounds that both imply (inappropriately in context) 'smaller and less valuable horses'. It is not clear to us that 'trappede stedys' would carry such an implication here — or at, e.g. 713, where 'trappede stedys' form a category amongst other horses (*blonkez*, *haknays*, *horsez of armez*) in a list of items loaded onto ships. But, for the moment, we are more interested in what Hamel goes on to say next. 'The line', she concedes, 'occurring in isolation, *is* defective in alliteration, but the context suggests that a /w/ word would be as valid an addition as a /t/ word; 334 and 336 alliterate on /w/. But any emendation would be the merest guess'. That is, Hamel is willing to allow what she regards as a corrupt line to stand rather than to risk emending erroneously.

The linkage explanation for irregular lines, then, may well serve as a convenient justification for a general editorial inclination toward non-interventionism in metrical matters. But this is not, we think, its only problem. O'Loughlin makes two further important statements. He says that the frequent occurrence of pairs of lines, one of which has regular alliteration and one of which does not, is 'ample proof' of his assertion

[14] Mennicken, 'Versbau und Sprache', p. 137.

[15] E. V. Gordon and Eugène Vinaver, 'New Light on the Text of the Alliterative *Morte Arthure*', *Medium Aevum*, 6 (1937), 81–98 (94).

of the flexibility associated with linkage; and he points out in support of his argument that many of these couplets are linked not only by alliteration but also by syntax.[16] One of the problems with O'Loughlin's proposition is, however, that it is hard to see how it can be proved or disproved. *MA* contains a very high proportion of lines with alliterative linkage: around 75 percent.[17] In some portions of the poem the percentage is much higher. Between 1200 and 1300, for instance, there are only 13 lines which are not linked by their main alliterating sound to the previous or following line, and the proportion rises if one is prepared to include all the types of linkage which Hamel is happy to recognise. This being the case, even if the irregular lines were the result of scribal corruption one would nevertheless expect that they would frequently occur in positions of linkage.[18] Nor is it particularly surprising that such pairs of lines are often also linked syntactically. This is simply the normal pattern of the poem, even in passages with perfectly regular alliteration.[19] It *is* true that there is very little irregular alliteration in the early lines of the poem, where there is also comparatively little linkage, but it is difficult to be certain of a causal relationship here: presumably one might well expect just such a pattern of early regularity if the non-*aa/ax* lines were scribal.

[16] O'Loughlin, '*Morte Arthure*', p. 155.

[17] We take the statistics from Yasuyo Moriya, 'Identical Alliteration in the *Alliterative Morte Arthure*', *English Language Notes*, 38 (2000), 1–16 (1).

[18] This is, of course, not always the case. The following are examples of lines with defective alliteration where linkage is not a factor (non-alliterating staves in the body of the line are in italics ):

In the regestre of Rome   who so ryghte lukez
With-*owt*tyn more trouflyng   the trebute we aske
That Iulius Cesar wan   wyth his ientill knyghttes. (113–5)

Thare [is] some segge in this sale   and he ware sare greuede
Thow *durste* noghte for all Lumberdye   luke one hym ones
Sir sais the senatour   so Crist mott me helpe. (134–136)

In grete goblettez ouergylte   glorious of hewe
There was a cheeffe *buttlere*   a cheualere noble
Sir Cayous the curtaise   þat of the cowpe seruede (207–9).

[19] As, for example, in 52–53, 68–69, 104–5, 106–7, 110–11, 116–7, 124–5, 132–3, 138–9, 150–51, 166–7, 173–5, 194–5, 225–6, 239–40, 251–4, 263–4, 278–9, 284–5.

We would like to argue that there is evidence to suggest that the original alliterative patterns of *MA* and the *Gawain* poems were considerably more regular than the readings found in the manuscripts. At a later stage in the discussion, when we come to consider evidence external to the poems themselves, we will return briefly to the question of linkage. First, however, we shall look at evidence drawn from the poems themselves and consider what this suggests about lines with non-*aa/ax* alliteration.

To begin with *MA*, it is noticeable that certain words are over-represented in the non-*aa/ax* lines. Such lines seem to cluster round particular lexical items. One of these is 'man' or its plural 'men'. In only 18 cases does this word bear both beat and alliteration, as in:

> The *m*yghtyeste of *M*acedone   with *m*en of þa *m*arches (603)[20]

Most commonly, however, 'men' is used as the second part of an adjective-noun combination with the adjective forming the alliterating stave as, for example, in

> Kynde *men* and courtays   and couthe of courte thewes (21)[21]

Where the beat falls on the word 'man' itself, the line is twice as likely to have non-*aa/ax* alliteration as regular alliteration:

> With þe *men* of þe walle   they weyde vp þeire ankyrs (493)
> And al to-ruscheez oure *men*   withe theire ryste horsez (1428)
> Wyth fyue hundrethe *men*   appon faire stedes (1440) [22]

Now such lines frequently have at least one alliterating stave in the a-verse and one in the b-verse and they also frequently have alliterative linkage, so a number of editors would doubtless consider them acceptable. But the pattern can, we think, usefully be contrasted with that of the synonyms *freke(s)*, *gome(s)*, *lede(s)*, *renke(s)*, *schalke(s)*, *segge(s)* and *wye(s)* (150 examples in all), the use of which never causes a non-*aa/ax* line, even though the vast majority of examples (18 out of 22 in the case of

[20] And see also 129, 260, 1314, 1315, 1382, 1533, 2015, 2207, 2670, 2683, 2951, 3569, 3767, 3875, 4220. It should be noted that in two of these examples (1314 and 3875), 'man' is a term of address.
[21] There are 110 examples. See, for instance, 19, 157, 167, 178, 273, 279, 303, 362, 364, 366, 641, 1213, 1895, 2978, 3429, 3581.
[22] There are 36 cases. See also 299, 301, 1329, 1399, 1405, 1421, 1492, 1523, 1540, 1624, 1658, 1684, 1878, 1880, 2235, 2268, 2341, 2473, 2496, 2717, 2723, 2818, 2944, 2989, 3027, 3341, 3717, 3756, 3785, 3787, 3928, 4065, 4083.

*freke(s)*, 28 out of 36 in the case of *renke(s)*) occur in lines with linkage.[23] It is perhaps possible that 'men' is the author's chosen form when he decides to introduce variation from the regular alliterative pattern, but, since 'men' is invariably an easier reading than any of the possible alternatives, it seems much more likely that this particular cluster is the result of scribal error and that, instead of *men*, the reading in 493 should be *wyes*, in 1428 *renkes* and in 1440 *frekes*. The same may be true of some comparable words of low alliterative rank, such as *knyght* and *lord*, which occur in a few lines with irregular alliteration:

> That euer owre soueraygne *Lorde* sufferes hyme in heuene (1167)
> Of the Sowdanes *knyghtes* owt of sere londes (2816)
> Alle thaa laddes are *knyghttes* that lange to the mowntes (3535)

Did the poet write *syre* at 1167, *segges* at 2816, and *ledes* at 3535? Admittedly, these lines show interlinear alliteration, but so do most others in the poem, so it may be more relevant to bear in mind that substitutions of specialised alliterative vocabulary are routine in scribal transmission. The manuscript tradition of *SJ* shows this fact very dramatically: every *gome*, *wyȝe*, *renk*, *segge*, and *lede* written by the poet seems to have been replaced with something simpler (e.g. *man*, *knight*, *lord*, or pronoun) in at least one of the manuscripts of the poem.[24]

[23] For examples of *freke* (sg. and pl.), see 557, 742, 873, 1061, 1174, 1360, 1364, 1735, 1966, 2260, 2709, 2775, 2782, 2822, 2899, 3343, 3394, 3472, 3677, 4239, 4249; for *gome*, 85, 1209, 1353, 1372, 1461, 1731, 1773, 2525, 2538, 2562, 2748, 2943, 3419, 3476, 3620, 3683, 3684, 3709, 3758, 3850, 3868, 3877; for *lede*, 138, 430, 473, 854, 997, 1035, 1102, 1313, 1721, 1820, 2326, 2399, 2431, 2532, 2801, 3284, 3285, 3584, 3381, 3585, 3624, 3697, 4092, 4097, 4149, 4166, 4270; for *renke*, 17, 147, 391, 466, 1057, 1206, 1410, 1473, 1524, 1675, 1882, 1994, 2035, 2041, 2135, 2278, 2402, 2453, 2665, 2784, 2790, 2794, 2902, 2912, 3217, 3470, 3612, 3753, 3825, 3859, 3892, 3940, 4048, 4098, 4229, 4291; for *schalke*, 1098, 1857, 2170, 2211, 2333, 2456, 3398, 3747, 3628, 3842, 4116, 4232; for *segge*, 134, 1043, 1420, 1422, 1951, 3271, 4035; for *wy(e)*, 56, 164 , 336, 533, 695, 891, 1616, 1807, 2547, 2826, 3495, 3553, 3839, 4025, 4204, 4331, 699, 2515, 2669, 2967, 2968, 2980, 3479. The alliterative pattern may occasionally be disrupted by the presence of other non-alliterating staves, as in the case of 854, where *lede* is regular, but where the major-category word which occupies the second stave begins with the letter *m*.

[24] For line references see Hanna and Lawton's glossary. See also Eiichi Suzuki, 'Notes on Lexical Substitution in *The Siege of Jerusalem*', in *Philologia Anglica: Essays Presented to Professor Yoshio Terasawa*, ed. Kinshiro Oshitari (Tokyo, 1988), pp.

In addition, a number of words which do more frequently supply an alliterating stave nevertheless seem to be at least possible candidates for emendation in positions where they disturb the normal alliterative pattern, once again on the ground that they are easier readings. There is quite a cluster of non-*aa/ax* lines containing the word 'come', for instance. This verb does quite commonly provide the alliterating stave, as in:

> *Come* at his commandmente clenly at ones (518)
> When I to contre *come* if Cryste will it thole (676)[25]

Nevertheless, it is true to say that the presence of 'come' in a line frequently results in non-*aa/ax* alliteration, as in, for instance,

> Thane *come* of þe Oryente ewyn hym agaynez (774)
> *Comen* of þe rycheste that rengnez in erthe (865)
> Þare *comez* two messangers of tha fere marchez (1232)[26]

Out of 33 examples where the verb 'to come' appears in a position where it affects the alliterative pattern,[27] there are 13 cases where its use results in non-*aa/ax* alliteration. Once again, the fact that these lines without full alliteration involve a word that appears to be a possible if not a probable easier reading suggests scribal corruption. Unusual verbs of motion do not produce these non-*aa/ax* lines. The verb *enter*, for example, never disrupts the alliterative pattern, and neither do *cayre*, *raike* and *ayre*; *ferke* results in a non-*aa/ax* pattern only once (in 19 occurrences).[28] As far as 'come' in particular is concerned, it will be

184–94. Thornton's copy of *SJ* compares well with other manuscript versions but he (or a preceding scribe) was responsible for some such substitutions (e.g. *wight* for *wyȝe*, at *SJ* 273, 632).

[25] See also 131, 176, 987, 1198, 1274, 1512, 1579, 1581, 1653, 1828, 2119, 2126, 2193, 2242, 3149, 3490, 3503, 3867, 4022, 4222.

[26] See also 80, 1439, 1532, 1752, 1818, 1971, 2307, 2448, 3973, 4152.

[27] I.e., not in the final stave or in extended verses where 'come' appears without ictus and where the alliteration is carried by another major-category word.

[28] For *enter*, see 565, 1239, 1499, 1691, 1967, 2007, 2387, 2805, 3120, 3448, 4069, 4162, 4309; for *cayre*, 6, 243, 444, 480, 627, 641, 877, 1192, 1195, 1272, 1319, 1531, 1707, 1787, 2282, 2304, 2342, 2882, 3094, 3634, 3897, 3916, 3996; for *ayre* see 1329 (where *men* causes a non-*aa/ax* line) and 3596; for *raike*, 237, 889, 1057, 1762, 2179, 2352, 2920, 2983, 3362, 3469; for *ferke* see 933, 949, 984, 1037, 1188, 1452, 1811, 2071, 2257, 2420, 2501, 2806, 2900, 3002, 3597, 3907, 3927,

remembered that we have already considered 4152 (p. 123 above) and that Hamel justifies retention of the manuscript reading on the grounds of alliterative linkage (between *aftyre* in 4152 and the vowel alliteration of 4151):

He es *e*ldare than *I* and *e*nde sall we bothen
He sall *f*erkke be-*f*ore and I sall *c*ome *a*ftyre (4151–2)

It is, however, interesting to compare these lines with the couplet at 2733–4:

Whethire he fyghte or he flee we sall *folowe* aftyre
Fore all þe fere of ȝone folke forsake sall I neuer.

Here the linkage is even closer, but the verb is the alliterating 'follow' rather than the non-alliterating 'come'. Of course, this example cannot *prove* that 4152 should be emended — authorial variation is always possible — but it is at the very least easy to imagine scribal substitution of 'come' for 'follow' and subsequent editorial justification of this reading on the grounds of linkage.

In the Cotton Nero poems, non-*aa*/*ax* are much rarer than they are in *MA* (where they account for around 15 percent of all lines[29]). In *P* and *C* just under two percent of lines have non-*aa*/*ax* patterns.[30] In *G* the proportion is significantly higher, closer to eight percent,[31] and it is not surprising that editors and critics of that poem in particular have defended such patterns as being authentic.[32] However, in the Cotton Nero manuscript, too, low-ranking words for 'man' and common verbs

4152 and 2452 (this last a non-*aa*/*ax* line, which should possibly begin with 'Raikande' rather than 'Ferkande'; compare 1762, 2179 and 3469).

[29] J. P. Oakden's statistics in *Alliterative Poetry*, I, pp. 187–8, cannot be relied on since they do not recognize alliteration of vowel and *h*–. Our estimate is based on an analysis of a sample (1738–2238).

[30] The statistics for *C* are discussed above, pp. 9–10. The statistics for *P* are given as 2.07% by Noriko Inoue ('The A-Verse', p. 202), but she includes a few lines that we think are acceptable (*P* 212, 300, 495). We accept as unmetrical *P* 78, 144, 238, 305, 332, 364, 462, 526.

[31] Inoue, in 'A-Verse', p. 46, counts 9.19 percent of lines, but again she includes some lines that seem acceptable to us (e.g. 25, 111, 350, 1495, 1922, 2191, 2321).

[32] See e.g. Joan Turville-Petre, 'The Metre of *Sir Gawain and the Green Knight*', *English Studies*, 57 (1976), 310–28. Noriko Inoue argues, rather like Mary Hamel and O'Loughlin, that non-*aa*/*ax* patterns are compensated for by metrical devices such as interlinear alliteration ('A-Verse', pp. 20–47).

of motion are implicated in numerous metrical irregularities. Here are some examples:[33]

> For I se hit wel þat hit is soþe    þat alle *manneȝ* wytteȝ (*C* 515)
> And of my þreuenest *lordeȝ*    þe þrydde he schal (*C* 1571)
> Of þat wynnelych *lorde*    þat wonyes in heuen (*C* 1807)
> Þen comaunded þe *lorde* in þat sale    to samen alle þe meyny (*G* 1372)
> And euer our luflych *knyȝt*    þe lady bisyde (*G* 1657)
> I *com* wyth þose tyþynges,    þay ta me bylyue (*P* 74)
> As hit *com* glydande adoun    on glode hym to schende (*G* 2266)
> Þerfore I eþe þe, haþel,    to *com* to þy naunt (*G* 2467)

*C* 515 is doubly suspect, since the preceding b-verse reads 'for no *manneȝ* synneȝ'. The repetition appears to be scribal and all sensible editors emend *manneȝ* to *seggeȝ* at 515. But a good case can also be made for the emendation of some of the other lines. The scribe who wrote *C* 1807 had just copied 'to loke on oure lofly lord' (1804); conceivably the poet repeated the word 'lord', but it is more likely that the scribe miscopied *wyȝe*, which is used in similar periphrases for God at *C* 5, 'For wonder wroth is þe wyȝ    þat wroȝt alle þinges' and *P* 111, 'He wende wel þat þat wyȝ    þat al þe world planted'. The word *syre* would regularise *G* 1372, and Gollancz made the emendation in his 1940 edition.[34] *Lede* for *knyȝt*, and *payneȝ* for *lordeȝ*, are plausible emendations for *G* 1657 and *C* 1571. *P* 74 cries out for the verb *tee* (cf. *P* 87, 416): the inevitable link that Jonah sees between going to Nineveh and being captured can then be heard in the pun on *tee* and *ta*. At *G* 2266, where 'hit' refers to the Green Knight's axe, *glent* would fit well, since that verb of motion was used especially of weapons (see *MED* s.v. *glenten* v(2)). Finally, at *G* 2467, *helde* for *com* is possible.

Both in the *Gawain* poems and in *MA* we may discern other suggestive, if slightly different, types of cluster. Many non-*aa/ax* lines, for instance, have what might be described as light a-verses, that is a-verses which have less than the usual number of major-category words.

[33] We have already, in a different context (see above, p. 19), drawn attention to two lines in *G*: 'Þe *knyȝt* wel þat tyde' (*G* 736*rh*), and 'And folk frely hym wyth, to fonge þe *knyȝt* (*G* 816). The first of these lines is the only example of a rhyming line in *G* with unavoidable clashing stress, and also one of only a few such lines that contain no alliteration. Borroff's suggested emendation to *wyȝe* (with historical –*e*) seems to us reasonable. The second line has no feminine ending, and the same emendation might be considered.

[34] *Sir Gawain and the Green Knight*, ed. I. Gollancz, EETS OS 210 (Oxford, 1940).

The following examples, which are not exhaustive, occur within the first 500 lines of the *MA*:

> When he and his senatours    bez sette as them lykes (97)
> Withowttyn more trouflyng   the trebute we aske (114)
> Sen we are in thy manrede   and mercy þe besekes (127)
> Might I with wirchipe   wyn awaye ones (468)
> Wythowttyn more scownntyng   þey schippide þeire horsez (491)
> (And see also 372, 389, 415)

It is, of course, quite acceptable in alliterative poetry for a beat to fall on a minor-category word in the absence of a major-category candidate,[35] but the coincidence of an a-verse which is both light *and* which also lacks one alliterating stave, i.e. which has two odd things about it, must surely arouse suspicion. Moreover, if we look more closely at some of these lines, we will, we believe, find additional reasons to be doubtful about them. *MA* 97 might usefully be compared with *SJ* 1042a, where MS E reads, 'How *he* so sodeynly', for 'How *þe segge* so sodeynly'. Both lines involve a scribal error of a recognizable and straightforward kind: lexical substitution involving a specialised 'man'-word.[36] At *MA* 468, the beat might perhaps be taken to fall on either 'might' or 'I'. However, examination of the practice in the rest of the poem suggests that, where lines alliterate on /w/, the promotion of a non-alliterating closed class word to take a beat is normally avoided by adding something like 'iwysse' before the caesura, as in

> For all oure wirchipe i-wysse    awaye es in erthe (2685)
> ȝe are owre wardayne i-wysse    wyrke as ȝowe lykes (2740)[37]

Now, of course, the poet may have decided not to take this course of action in one particular line, but adverbs which are peripheral to the meaning of the sentence are easy to lose — and Judith Jefferson's work

[35] See Duggan and Turville–Petre (eds), *Wars*, p. xx.
[36] For a different view see Helen Cooper, 'Textual Variation and the Alliterative Tradition: *Canterbury Tales* I.2602–19, the D Group and Takamiaya MS 32', in *The Medieval Book and a Modern Collector: Essays in Honour of Toshiyuki Takamiya*, ed. Takami Mastuda, Richard A. Linenthal, and John Scahill (Cambridge, 2004), pp. 71–81 (p. 75). Cooper cites *MA* 97 in support of her view that *aa/ax* patterns were really only an optimal norm. The other example she cites, *G* 2512, 'For þer hit onez is tacched twynne wil hit neuer', is in fact regular ('hit onez' alliterates on /t/).
[37] And see also 546, 2020, 2332, 2828, 3339, 3392, 3769, 3770, 3977.

on the scribal copies of the Hoccleve holographs suggests that they often *were* lost[38] — and it therefore seems possible that this line, as it now appears in the Thornton manuscript, is the result of scribal error.[39] Or take 114 and 491, the two lines with 'withouten'. These two lines would probably seem somewhat less acceptable to us (in that the a-verse would give the impression of being somewhat too short) if the preposition were simply 'without', i.e. lacking the final *–en*. And there is some evidence to suggest that in some (though not all)[40] cases 'withouten' was a scribal form and may even have been introduced by Thornton. It certainly appears to have been Thornton's preferred form: it is the form always used, for example, in the Thornton version of *SJ*, even where other manuscripts have 'without'.[41] In *MA*, the form is probably scribal in 'withowttyn þe wode hemmes' (2825b; contrast 'withoute þe flod merkes', 461b), because four-syllable dips in b-verses are highly anomalous and probably unmetrical in *MA* and other alliterative poems.[42] 'If 'withouten' was indeed the form with which Thornton was happiest, then the original reading of 114 may well have been 'Withowt tene of more trouflyng', Thornton subsequently misreading 'without tene' as his preferred, longer form of the preposition.

In the Cotton Nero poems, too, a suspiciously high proportion of non-*aa/ax* lines are also light. Here are a few examples:[43]

[38] Note, e.g., scribal omission of the adverb *al* in Hoccleve's *Letter of Cupid*, 183.

[39] Hamel suggests that the omission of the second stave was characteristic of Thornton. See the note to 869 in her edition and see also her 'Scribal Self-Corrections in the Thornton *Morte Arthure*', *Studies in Bibliography*, 36 (1983), 119–37 (130).

[40] The long form of the preposition is found in a number of a-verses without a long opening dip, where it contributes to an extra-long dip (of four unstressed syllables), as in 'By lukyng withowttyn lesse a lyon the semys' (129, cf. 748, 911, 2043). By our a-verse rules, this extra-long dip is metrically required in such a-verses (for a summary of our a-verse rules, see above, p. 75 and for further discussion see ch. 5). The long form is also found at line ending (3017).

[41] See Kölbing and Day (eds), *Siege*, ll. 103, 175, 443. In Hanna and Lawton's edition these are lines 107, 179 and 447. Because Hanna and Lawton think the a-verse has no syllabic constraints, variation as between 'without' and 'withouten' is not recorded in their textual apparatus; in this and other respects Kölbing and Day's edition retains its usefulness.

[42] See Noriko Inoue, 'The A-Verse', p. 215.

[43] There are many others, such as *C* 1483, 1655, *G* 860, 1187, 1537, 1912, 2132.

Bi þe haspede he hentes hym þenne (*P* 189)
For he þat is to rakel to renden his cloþeȝ (*P* 526)[44]
Bot my forward with þe I festen on þis wyse (*C* 327)
Bot, for I haf þis talk, tatȝ to non ille (*C* 735)
Þe þre ledes þerin, Loth and his deȝter (*C* 993)
And þenne arn dressed dukeȝ and prynces (*C* 1518)
He sayd, ȝe are welcum to welde as yow lykez (*G* 835)
Þat watz not forward, quoþ he, frayst me no more (*G* 1395)

In most of these a-verses there is only one obvious candidate for the beat. It has been observed apropos of *G* that many non-*aa/ax* lines occur in the dialogue scenes of that poem, as if the poet were trying to catch the 'looseness' of ordinary conversation.[45] To this argument, it might be objected that much lively dialogue in *G* and the other Cotton Nero poems is perfectly regular, thanks (amongst other things) to the wide range of vocatives available to alliterative poets. Because of their inherent redundancy, parenthetical words of address were easily omitted by scribes (as anyone familiar with multiple-manuscript poems will know).[46] This kind of scenario has conceivably left some of the above-cited a-verses short:

Bot my forward wiþ þe, [frende] (*C* 327; cf. *C* 139)
He sayd, ȝe are welcum, [wyȝe] (*G* 835)

Other kinds of omissions are more than likely in the other lines. For example, at *P* 526 'þe renk' may have been replaced by 'he', and at *G* 1395 'þe freke' by 'he'. At *C* 993 a missing word is indicated by the loose logic of the lines:

Þat noȝt saued watȝ bot Segor þat sat on a lawe
Þe þre ledes þerin, Loth and his deȝter,
*For* his make was myst, þat on þe mount lenged ... (*C* 992–4)

Gollancz's emended to 'Þe þre ledes [lent] þerin' (*lent* in the sense 'waited, 'tarried'), and it seems very likely that some 'l-verb' (*lent* or *longed*) was originally present, regularising the metre and clarifying the otherwise puzzling *For*: Loth not being in Zoar *because* his wife was lost.

[44] It might be argued that *P* 526 has linking alliteration on /r/ ('For he'), but the a-verse is suspect on syllabic grounds also (see below, ch. 5).
[45] Inoue, 'A-Verse', p. 21.
[46] It is instructive to examine the MS variants for vocative *wye* in *Piers Plowman* (see e.g. A 10.89, B 3.106).

The criterion of discursive cohesion also supports the following emendation of 1518:

> Þen þe dotel on dece drank þat he myȝt,
> & þenne [þat] arn dressed [derrest],[47] dukeȝ & prynces ...
> As vchon hade hym in helde he haled of þe cuppe. (1517–20)

Belshazzar drinks first, followed by those who are have been placed in the seats of honour (lit. 'and then those that are arranged most nobly...'). No satisfactory sense can be made of *P* 189. Jonah is being pulled up by something so a noun is required. At *C* 735, Abraham in the poet's source says, 'Quia semel *coepi*, loquar ad Dominum meum' ('I have taken upon me to speak unto the Lord', King James Version). We would emend to 'For I haf [tan vp] þis talk', taȝ to non ille'. For a similar alliterative pattern, see *G* 1811: 'Iche tolke mon do as he is *tan*, *tas* to none ille'.

In our discussion of *C* 735 and *MA* 114, 491, we have already invoked external evidence, and we would now like to look in a little more detail at the ways in which this type of evidence can sometimes throw light on the author's metrical practice. For instance, although there is only one manuscript of *MA,* some of the advantages of having an additional witness can be obtained from Malory's prose version.[48] Though the *MA* material found in the Winchester Malory has been much reduced and revised, it often follows *MA* quite closely, with passages of word-for-word correspondence.[49] Such evidence is complicated by Hamel's suggestion that the first scribe on the Malory branch of the stemma (referred to in her edition as 'scribe E') may have been inclined to indulge in a little emendation of his own for the sake of alliteration,[50]

[47] For reasons of a-verse metre we have adapted Gollancz's emendation '& þenne þat derrest arn dressed'.

[48] For the relationship between the alliterative *Morte* and Malory's *Morte Darthur* see Hamel (ed.), *Morte Arthure*, pp. 3–14. The general view is that one of Malory's sources was a version of the alliterative *Morte* which is no longer extant. William Matthews is alone in arguing that Malory made use of the Thornton MS (see Matthews, *The Ill-Framed Knight* (Berkeley, Cal., 1966), p. 99, and the comment by Field, *Malory*, p. 142). For more detailed discussion of the ways in which evidence drawn from Malory can provide useful evidence for possible readings in the alliterative *Morte*, see Gordon and Vinaver, 'New Light'.

[49] This is less the case with the Caxton Malory because of its extreme compression of the material on the Roman wars (see Hamel's edition, pp. 4–5), and its associated tendency to use less alliteration (see Field, *Malory*, p. 148).

[50] Hamel (ed.), *Morte Arthure*, pp. 9–13.

but, nevertheless, Malory's version does sometimes suggest possible emendations. To be sure, there are also examples where Malory's wording confirms irregularly alliterating lines, but in this respect the situation is no different from that of other alliterative poems extant in multiple witnesses: non-*aa*/*ax* readings in one manuscript are sometimes contradicted by another witness (or witnesses) but are sometimes shared, presumably because of a common ancestor that was not the poet's original. In such a line of descent, shared errors are to be expected, and Hamel adduces sound evidence (based on the names of characters known from the chronicle tradition) that *MA* and the version of the poem known to Malory share errors that point to a common ancestor.[51]

The first example of a case where Malory and *MA* disagree on an irregularly alliterating verse is another light a-verse:

Tyll þat I haue venquiste þe Vicounte of Rome (325)

Malory's reading here is 'and þer to vynquyshe with victory þe vyscounte of Roome'[52] It is possible that the regular alliteration found in Malory results from scribal emendation but, given that Hamel herself notes that Thornton's self-corrections suggest a tendency to omit the second stave,[53] it seems equally possible that 'with victory' has been lost as the result of eye skip. We would also like to suggest that the use of pleonastic 'that' here may be scribal, an attempt to compensate for what was felt to be a somewhat inadequate a-verse, and that the original probably read ' Tyll I haue venquiste with victorye'.[54] Pleonastic 'that' is unusual in this poem and in the a-verse is found only in half-lines lacking alliteration and lacking the normal minimum of two major-category words. Compare, for instance, the following:

*With-thy þat* thowe suffre me for sake of thy Cryste (2587)
*With-thy* thowe say me sothe what thowe here sekes (2591)[55]

[51] Hamel (ed.), *Morte Arthure*, pp. 6–9.
[52] BL Additional MS 59678 (Winchester MS), fol. 72.
[53] See note 39 above.
[54] See discussion above, p. 132.
[55] See also *Qwene that* (26) and *Lesse that* (2439). It is worth noting that there is something odd about the syntax of the passage which begins at 26; see Hamel (ed.), *Morte Arthure*, pp. 22–3 and Krishna's note to this line. As Krishna observes, it is difficult to be certain where the subordinate clause which begins with 'when' actually ends. Krishna suggests that this is because the poet has

Another instance of a line where the reading in Malory confirms scribal error is *MA* 144, which reads 'Bot I sall *tak* concell at kynges enoyntede', whereas Malory reads 'and shall calle vnto me my counceyle'.[56] In this and other cases,[57] it is again possible to argue that the reading in Malory reflects a scribal attempt to emend for the sake of alliteration, but misreading of 'call' as 'take' is surely very likely. Thornton's own forms of /c/ and /t/ are easy to confuse, and confusion of letters with looped ascenders (<b>, <h>, <k>, <l> ) is common.[58] Moreover, 'take' is another of those words around which irregular lines seem to cluster;[59] and there is evidence from other poems copied by Thornton to

difficulty managing hypotactic syntax, but the first 11 lines of the poem do not suggest that this was a particular problem for him, and it therefore seems possible that 'when' may be an error. Unease about the length or weight of the a-verse may also be the reason for the use of *for to* rather than the far more usual *to* in 2349: 'Efte *for to* brawlle theme for my brode landez'.

56 BL Additional MS 59678 (Winchester MS), fol. 71v.

57 For some further examples see *MA* 1889a, 'Bytoke theym the Proueste', where Winchester MS, fol. 83v, reads 'beleffte þe prisoners þer with the Pure proveste'; and *MA* 2111a, 'And all theis geauntez before', where Winchester MS, fol. 85r reads 'And þe grete gyauntes of Gene'.

58 Hamel, 'Scribal Self-Corrections', p. 125, and see also George Kane (ed.), *Piers Plowman: the A Version*, rev. edn. (London, 1988), pp. 120–1. Simple misreadings of *h*, *l*, and *b* provide explanations for various irregular *aa/ax* patterns in the Cotton Nero poems, e.g. 'Baltaȝar vmbebrayde hym, and "Leue sir" he sayde' (*C* 1622; read *Beau sir*, and cf. *G* 1622); 'Þen Abraham obeched hym and loȝly him þonkkeȝ' (*C* 745; read *hiȝly* 'devoutly', as in *G* 773, 'and heȝly he þonkez'); 'For my hyeȝ hem boȝt to bow haf I mester' (*C* 67; perhaps read Northern *byeȝ* 'farms'; *hyeȝ* is not attested as a spelling of either ME *hine* or *heue*); in one instance editors may be making the same mistake as the scribe. 'For he schal loke on our Lorde with a loue chere' (*C* 28) is read by some editors (e.g. Richard Morris (ed.), *Sir Gawayne and the Green Knight*, EETS OS 4 (Oxford, 1864) and Andrew and Waldron (eds.), *Poems*) as 'with a bone chere'. The poet must have written the former: the expression *with a low chere* is idiomatic. Cf. *Destruction of Troy*, ed. Panton and Donaldson, 1778 and 3106, where the spelling *loue* is also found: 'So be lokyng of length with a loue chere'.

59 The verb 'to take' appears most frequently in verses where other words provide the alliterating staves, as in 156, 349, 421, 1359, 1682, 1746, 2242, 2262, 2651, 3049, 3151, 3401, 3406, 3586, 3588, 4154. Where it appears in beat position, it does sometimes form a regular alliterating stave as in 73, 275, 328, 668, 840, 1015, 1190, 3568, 4094, but more frequently its presence results in irregular alliteration, as in 144, 148, 659, 693, 713, 807, 1264, 2282, 2700, 2843, 4288.

suggest that Thornton himself had a tendency to use 'take' as a simplifying replacement for other major-category words. The following two examples are taken from *SJ*; variants from Thornton's copy (A) appear in brackets:

At Vi[enn]e, þer he [v]eniaunce & vile deþ *þoled* (*SJ* 1328; A *tuke*)
Whan alle was demed & d[on] þei *drow*[*en*] vp tentis (*SJ* 1335; A *tuke*)

In 328 scribal error is confirmed by A's masculine line ending; in 1335, by the irregular alliteration.

Very occasionally, a reading with more regular alliteration can be suggested by sources or analogues. We have seen one example of this in *C* 735, where the addition of a verb, 'For I haf [tan vp] þis talk', is supported by *coepi* in the source. Another possible example is *P* 238, 'To oure mercyable *God*, on Moyses wyse'. Here the Vulgate reads not *Deus* but *dominus*, of which *mayster* would be a literal translation. The same collocation occurs at *C* 1113: 'ȝis, þat mayster is mercyable'. The following couplet from *MA* provides a further example:

Þou sees þat þe emperour es angerde a lyttill
Yt semes be his sandismen þat he es sore greuede (265–6)

The first of these lines, as it appears in the Thornton manuscript, is an *xa*/*ax* line, the sort of line that Hamel describes as the type of traditional variant which it is hardly necessary to defend.[60] Nevertheless, it seems likely that the original reading was 'hear' rather than 'see'. In the corresponding speech made by Arthur in Laȝamon, for example, he says:

Nu ȝe habbeoð *iherd*, haeȝe mine þeines
what Romanisce men redeð heom bitwenen
and wulc word heo sendeð us here into ure londe.[61]

This pattern can be compared with that of the verb *lachen*, the use of which never disrupts the alliteration: see 750, 874, 1515, 1817, 1826, 1902, 2226, 2292, 2541, 2693, 2702, 2998, 4183.

[60] Hamel (ed.), *Morte,* p. 19.

[61] Laȝamon, *Brut*, ed. W. R. J. Barron and S. C. Weinberg (Harlow, 1995), 12476–8.

Wace also uses the word 'hear'.[62] The change from 'hear' to 'see' is surely a likely scribal error. At *SJ* 129, for instance, Thornton has 'tell' for 'hear'. 'See' rather than 'hear' at *MA* 265 similarly replaces a more specific form ('hear with your ears') with a more general one ('perceive', by whatever means). Moreover, the reading may well have been influenced by 'seems', which occurs in exactly the same place in the following line. This last possibility is especially important because this type of eye skip from one line to another can result, as it does in this case, in what some editors would classify as linkage and can thus suggest one of the ways in which such linkage may sometimes have arisen. The following examples from *SJ* suggest that errors due to the eye being caught by staves found either in the preceding or in the following line, i.e. errors which would naturally tend to result in some sort of alliterative linkage, may well have been characteristic of Thornton (variants found in A appear in brackets):[63]

& þermyd baptemed be in blessed water.
Forþ þey fetten a font & *foulled hym þer* (*SJ* 192–3; A *baptizede þat beryn*)

Of þis kerchef & my *cors* þe kepyng Y þe take'. (A *body*)
Þan bygan þe burne biterly to wepe (*SJ* 224–5)

Þroȝ kernels cacchen her deþ many *kene* burnes. (A *bolde*)
Brenten & beten doun b[e]ldes wel þycke. (*SJ* 660–1)

And *issed* out of þe ost with eȝte hundred speres, (A *faste hyes*)
Fel on þe fals folke, vmbe-feldes hem sone (*SJ* 1130–1)

*Criour[s]* callen hem forþ as hy þat Crist slowen, (A *and bedells*)
And beden Pilat apere þ*at* p*ro*uost was þa*n*ne (*SJ* 1299–1300)

So was he bargayned & bouȝt & as a beste quelled
Now corsed be he quoþ þe kyng þat þe *[a]cate* made (*SJ* 1307–8; A *bargan*)

[62] '*Oï* avez le mandement / E des lettres l'entendement / E le surfet e la fierté / Que li Romain nus unt mandé' (Wace, *Roman de Brut*, ed. and trans. Judith Weiss, rev. edn. (Exeter, 2002), 10799–802). Geoffrey of Monmouth has no corresponding clause.

[63] This type of error, i.e. 'cross-alliteration', is common in the scribal tradition of *Piers Plowman*. George Kane in his edition of *Piers Plowman: The A Version* (p. 141) suggests that it arises from a deliberate attempt to produce something particularly elegant, but it is difficult to judge, certainly in Thornton's case, whether such changes were deliberate or unconscious.

Evidence drawn from *MA* itself can sometimes suggest the possibility of lexically more difficult but alliteratively more satisfactory readings. Compare the following:

And Sir Gawayne hym gyrd    with a grym launce
That þe grounden *spere*    glade to his herte (2971–2)

He gyrdes hym in at þe gorge    with his grym launce
Þat þe grownden *glayfe*    graythes in sondyre (3760–61)

Alliterative linkage occurs in both these examples, so that cannot explain the different readings. Authorial variation is, once again, a possibility, but the fact that *spere* occurs not only in 2972 but also in 2976 and in exactly the same place in the line ('That the slydande spere    of his hande sleppes') rather tends to discount this explanation and to suggest instead that 'spear' is a scribal error resulting from eye skip or a *facilior lectio.* Hamel suggests in her discussion of Thornton's scribal practice that he copied difficult words quite carefully even where those words in fact were errors and therefore did not make any sense,[64] but evidence from *SJ* suggests that Thornton (or the scribe of his exemplar) quite often did replace more difficult with easier non-alliterating alternatives. Thus *forbesyn* ('example') in *SJ* 399 is replaced in A by *schewyng*; *byes* in 643 by *rynges*; *taysen* ('aim') in 659 by *thay shotte*; *etnes* in 789 by *gyauntes*; *eure* ('destiny') in 998 by *tym*; *eued* ('gave birth to') in 1228 by *had.*

Or consider the parallel constructions found in *MA* 1369–70 and 3757–8:[65]

He gryppes hym a *grete spere*    and graythely hyme hittez
Thurghe þe guttez in-to þe gorre    he gyrdes hym ewyn

Bot *Sir* Gawayne for grefe    myghte noghte agayne-stande
Vmbegrippys a *spere*    and to a gome rynnys

The most likely explanation for this variation is surely that in the second example an adjective has been lost. The standard a-verse, after all, normally has two major-category words, not three, and an extended a-verse (with three open-classed words) is therefore by definition a more difficult reading.

[64] Hamel, 'Scribal Self-Corrections', p. 122.
[65] Quoted by John Finlayson, 'Formulaic Technique in "Morte Arthure"', *Anglia*, 81 (1963), 372–93 (377).

In the Cotton Nero poems, too, parallel constructions may suggest emendation. Compare, for example, the following couples of lines:

> *Ledes* hym to his awen *chambre*, þe [c]hymne bysyde (*G* 1030)
> Þe lorde hym *charred* to a *chamber*, and chefly cumaundeȝ (*G* 850)
>
> And þere in *longyng* al *nyȝt* he *lengeȝ* in wones (*C* 779)
> Þay wolde *lenge* þe *long naȝt*, and logge þeroute (*C* 807)

The verb *charren* 'go, lead, direct', is one of this poet's alliterating specialities. Lexical substitution of *charres* by *ledes* plausibly explains the defective patterning at *G* 1030. At *C* 779 it is easy to imagine a scribe who had already written 'longyng' omitting the adjective 'long'.

To see just how easily such omissions occurred, it is instructive to look at Thornton's copy of *SJ*, where one or other of the major category words in extended verses is routinely missed out, sometimes with alliterative effect, sometimes without; in the following examples, the items omitted in A are in italics:

> To softe þe *grete* sore þat sitteþ on my cheke (*SJ* 91)
> Þan xij barouns bolde þe emperour *bade* wende
> (*SJ* 233; Thornton also alters *wende* to *went*)
>
> & monye *der* daies worke dongen to grounde (*SJ* 680)
> Neuer *suþ* o[n] þat syde cam segge of hem after (*SJ* 1322)

We would like to end by looking briefly at lines in the Thornton version of *MA* which have one particular alliterative pattern, i.e. *aa/xa*, as in

> Rynnande on rede blode as my stede ruschez (392)

Once again, deliberate variation is an appealing hypothesis. The a- and b-verses are still linked by alliteration and, although the regular alliterative pattern is disrupted, compensation for this disruption occurs within the same line. Nevertheless, there is a certain amount of evidence for the avoidance of such lines by the poet. For instance, the impersonal verb 'likes' normally appears in final position in the b-verse, and the result is an *aa/ax* line:

> ȝa I haue broghte þe berd quod he the bettyr me lykez (1033)[66]

[66] It is possible that 'quod he' in the a-verse is extra-metrical. See, e.g., Hoyt N. Duggan, 'Some Unrevolutionary Aspects of Computer Editing', in *The Literary Text in the Digital Age*, ed. Richard J. Finneran (Ann Arbor, 1996), pp. 77–98 (p. 98, n. 38).

However, where regular alliteration demands it, this pattern is reversed, as in

ȝone lorde es lyghttede  me lykes the bettyre (1781)

Likewise, it is normally the case that the verb *lengen* ('to remain', 'to stay' etc.) appears as the final element of the b-verse, usually preceded by a prepositional phrase, as in the following examples:

I was so hawtayne of herte  whills I at home lengede  (2612)
The konyngeste cardynall  that to the courte lengede  (3177)
Of Arthure þe auenant  qwhylls he in erthe lengede  (3651)
Off all þat Alexandere aughte  qwhills he in erthe lengede
(4160; see also 2960)

But this pattern is reversed in 3285, in order to maintain the *aa/ax* pattern:

And all ledis me lowttede  that lengede in erthe

The clause 'he casts in fewter' (i.e. 'he places (his weapon) in a rest') normally appears in the b-verse in the order verb+prepositional phrase, and is therefore most frequently used in lines alliterating on /k/, as in the following:

Thane this cruell kyng  castis in fewtire (1769)
Cryez A Cornewale  and castez in fewtere (1791)
Lythes vn-to þe crye  and castez in fewtire (1810)
Þane Sir Cador þe kene  castez in fewtire (1830)
Thane the comlyche kyng  castez in fewtyre (2058; see also 2165, 4112)

The expression can, however, also be used in lines alliterating on /f/, and in these cases the usual word order is reversed so that the verb is final:

A faire floreschte spere  in fewtyre he castes (1366)
Thane Sir Florent was fayne  and in fewter castys (2764)

In addition, evidence drawn from elsewhere in the alliterative *MA* can sometimes suggest that particular *aa/xa* lines may well be corrupt. Consider, for example,

Thow arte þe lordlyeste lede  þat euer I one lukyde (138)

which has an *aa/xa* pattern, and compare it with

For the vnlordlyeste lede  þat I on lukede euer' (1313)

This is basically the same b-verse, but at 1313 the word order gives instead a regular *aa/ax* line. And this latter b-verse surely has the more difficult reading from the point of view of word order.

Once again, evidence drawn from *SJ* suggests that restoration of a more regular word order with resultant *aa/xa* alliteration is quite characteristic of Thornton (variations present in A appear in brackets):

Whan Pharao and his ferde were *in þe floode drouned* (SJ 483;
A *dronkynede in the flode*)

Þe kyng lete drawen hem a-doun *whan þey dede wer* (*SJ* 717;
A *for þay were sone dede*)

Leyþ a ladder to þe wal *& alofte clymyþ* (*SJ* 1194;
A *and clymbys one lofte*)

Þat euer so precious a place scholde *per[i]sche for her synne* (*SJ* 1262;
A *for thaire syn perische*)

To conclude, although the existence of only a single manuscript for both the alliterative *Morte Arthure* and the *Gawain* poems undeniably causes difficulties, the type of evidence which is nevertheless available shows that a study of metrical usage is by no means beyond the bounds of possibility. At the very least it is feasible to investigate the characteristic strategies adopted by the author in support of his metre as well as the characteristic scribal errors which disrupt it. Particularly useful are patterns of usage of words and phrases within the poems themselves and external evidence from sources and related poems, and in the case of *MA* from another alliterative poem copied by the same scribe.

On the basis of this kind of evidence we also believe that the *aa/ax* pattern was a condition of metricality in the alliterative *Morte Arthure*, *Cleanness* and *Patience*. The case of *Sir Gawain and the Green Knight* is harder to judge. The metrically peculiar context of unrhymed alliterative lines rounded off with a rhyming bob-and-wheel could possibly be taken as indicating a greater metrical freedom and adventurousness than in *Cleanness* and *Patience*, and the non-*aa/ax* patterns in *Gawain* are certainly both more numerous, and harder to emend, than those in *C* and *P*. However, since there is independent evidence that the transmission of *G* was more complicated than that of *C* and *P*, the greater proportion and plausibility of non-*aa/ax* patterns may just as well be due to the intrusion of new scribal errors and the bedding down of old ones in the process of secondary revision — due, that is, to the natural consequences of intensive manual copying.

We end with a word about poetic freedom, since it is sometimes thought that metrical rules, such as the *aa/ax* rule in alliterative verse, constitute an affront to that freedom. We think the opposite: what prevents metrical rules from being felt as an imposition is the poet's readiness and ability to meet them; and what prevents them from seeming artificial is their adoption as the categorical condition of poetic expression. From that perspective, the steady production of *aa/ax* lines in poems such as *Cleanness* and *Patience* becomes artificial precisely when we do *not* think there was a constraint to be overcome. For would it not be artificial, to say the least, for a poet to write *aa/ax* (or *aa/aa*) lines in around 98 percent of all cases if he was at liberty to write all kinds of other patterns? Emendation of metrical irregularities, such as the ones we have suggested in this chapter, therefore seems to us a logical response and tribute to the trouble alliterative poets took to achieve metrical regularity elsewhere in their poems.

# 4. SENTENCE STRESS AND BEAT IN ALLITERATIVE METRE

## Introduction

A fundamental problem that bedevils the study of alliterative metre concerns the number of beats in the alliterative long line. In over a century of modern scholarship, views on the subject have varied considerably. One view, which is now no more than a historical curiosity, was that the alliterative long line is a septenary, with four beats in the a-verse and three in the b-verse.[1] Another view, held by Karl Luick, Marie Borroff, Joan Turville-Petre, and others is that alliterative metre is a four-beat rhythm, with two beats in the a-verse and two in the b-verse.[2] More recently, however, scholars (including Thomas Cable[3] and Hoyt Duggan[4]) have proposed a different theory, namely that the alliterative long line has a normal (four-beat) form, and an 'extended' one: the a-verse may contain not just two beats but three and perhaps even more. Our own view is that the alliterative long line has four beats. It would be quite impossible to argue our position with reference to all so-called extended a-verses; what we can do is muster some linguistic evidence coupled with empirical evidence from the poems themselves that calls into question Duggan and Cable's general rules of stress-assignment and some specific instances of their scansion.

Both Duggan and Cable are clear about the criteria by which 'stresses' (coterminous with 'beats' in their usage) can be identified and distinguished from 'unstressed' syllables. Both claim that these criteria are lexical, that is, based on word class, with open-class words generally being stressed and closed-class words being unstressed. Both seem to think that these same criteria govern stress assignment in ordinary language. According to Cable, the 'rules of stress' in Middle English alliterative verse are as follows:

[1] See e.g. Mennicken, *Versbau und Sprache*, and Steffens, *Versbau und Sprache*.

[2] Luick, 'Stabreimzeile'; Borroff, *'Sir Gawain'*, pp. 190–210; Turville-Petre, 'Metre'.

[3] Cable, *Alliterative Tradition*, p. 92.

[4] See especially Hoyt N. Duggan, 'Extended A-Verses in Middle English Alliterative Poetry', in *Medieval English Measures: Studies in Metre and Versification*, ed. Ruth Kennedy, special issue of *Parergon*, 18 (2000), 53–76.

> Nouns, adjectives (except indefinite and interrogative pronominal adjectives: *alle*, *many*, *fele*, *oþer*, *on*, *no*, *uche*, *ilk*, *what*), infinitives, and participles always receive metrical stress.
>
> Finite verbs and adverbs might or might not receive metrical stress. (The determining factors are complex, involving the rhythmical structures of the verse, the pattern of alliteration, semantic considerations, etc.)
>
> Articles, prepositions, conjunctions, linking verbs, the verb *have*, pronominal adjectives and pronouns (personal, demonstrative, indefinite, relative, and interrogative) do not receive metrical stress unless they occur at the end of the half-line.[5]

Duggan's approach is essentially similar. His rules state that:

> Alliteration always falls on a stressed syllable. Metrical stress usually coincides with normal prose phrase stress.
>
> A hierarchy of word classes generally determines which words may appear in ictus. Words from open classes (virtually all nouns and adjectives, most verb forms, adverbs ending in *–ly* or consisting of two syllables, pronouns ending in *self*) take precedence over words from closed classes (prepositions, conjunctions, some verbs, auxiliaries, pronouns, monosyllabic adverbs). Alliteration falls on the latter only when there is syntactic inversion or in the absence of a word from the open classes.[6]

We want to leave aside for the moment some of the small differences between these sets of rules and the minor errors in both, to concentrate on an underlying assumption that we think is seriously flawed: it is the assumption that the rhythms of alliterative verse or ordinary language ('normal prose phrase stress') can be worked out on the basis of word classes. Cable briefly alludes to the things that would seem *prima facie* crucial to the prosody of verse, namely such 'complex factors' as semantics and rhythm, but he says nothing more about them, and, surprisingly, thinks that they come into play only in the context of 'finite verbs and adverbs'. Duggan manages not to mention such factors at all. Word-class, he claims, determines stress with the proviso that with regard to adverbs only polysyllabic ones bear stress and the further proviso that closed-class words are accentable in the case of inversion or 'in the absence of a word from the open classes'. By that subsidiary 'promotion rule' (as we shall call it), Duggan must mean that a closed-

[5] Cable, *Alliterative Tradition*, p. 80.

[6] Duggan, 'Stress Assignment', p. 311.

class word cannot be accented unless there is only *one* other open-class word in the a- or b-verse.

Our purpose in this chapter is to shed some further light on the 'complex factors' of semantics and rhythm, and to show they play a larger part in alliterative verse than either Duggan or Cable supposes. Lexical category is, in our view, an unreliable indicator of 'sentence stress' (or 'accent'), i.e. the stress given to words in connected speech. For instance, the word 'jacket' will often be strongly stressed on the first syllable, but 'sentence stress' depends on the communicative situation and context. In the imaginary dialogue — 'Look at that cólourful jácket'; 'It looks like a fláshy jacket to mé'[7] — the sentence stress of the reply is at odds with predictions based on lexical category: 'jacket' is weakly stressed because it is given; and the pronoun 'me' is accented because of an implied contrast (it looks colourful to *you*, but not to *me*).

Rhythmical factors in the language, too, can affect the degree of stress that is given to open- and closed-class words. Thus English speakers tend to avoid strong stresses in adjacent syllables or words. This 'rhythm rule', as it is known, would therefore predict that, when three strongly stressed words come together, the second tends to receive weak sentence stress: Énglish plum púdding, a héavy round stóne'.[8]

There is plenty of evidence to show that speakers of Middle English also tended to avoid clashing stress[9] and shared other of our speech habits, such as our inclination to put the main stress on the right-most lexical item in a tone unit, in accordance with the 'nuclear stress rule',[10]

[7] We adapt an example given by Dwight Bolinger, *Intonation and Its Parts* (London, 1986), p. 119.

[8] The rule was first identified by Henry Sweet, *A New English Grammar, Logical and Historical*, 2 vols (Oxford, 1892–8), II, pp. 28–34; his discussion of sentence stress remains relevant. The examples are his. Sweet's rule is termed the 'rhythm rule' in Susan F. Schmerling, *Aspects of English Sentence Stress* (Austin, Texas, 1976), p. 98. See also Elizabeth Selkirk, *Phonology and Syntax: the Relation Between Sound and Structure* (Cambridge, Mass., 1984), pp. 170–91.

[9] See Donka Minkova, who shows that avoidance of clashing stress played a part in the retention of final *–e* in Middle English prose and verse: *The History of Final Vowels in English: the Sound of Muting*, Topics in English Linguistics 4 (Berlin, 1991), pp. 301–35.

[10] Donka Minkova and Robert Stockwell, 'Against the Emergence of the Nuclear Stress Rule in Middle English', in J. Fisiak and W. Winter (eds), *Studies in Middle English Linguistics* (Berlin, 1997), pp. 301–35.

to raise our voice at the end of yes/no questions but to lower it at the end of open ones.[11] It is reasonable therefore to assume continuity in the language unless we find clear indications to the contrary. There is inevitably much disagreement amongst the various linguists who have studied intonation (e.g. Roger Kingdon,[12] Noam Chomsky and Morris Halle,[13] Dwight Bolinger,[14] Carlos Gussenhoven,[15] Susan Schmerling,[16] D. J. Allerton and A. Cruttenden,[17] David Crystal[18]), and no-one would claim that the complexities of accentuation have been fully understood; but equally no-one with a faint acquaintance of the scholarship in this area would claim that any rules of stress based on the lexical categories of words give an adequate explanation of why in connected speech we give prominence to certain words and not to others. In Susan Schmerling's words, 'any theory which claims such correlations between stressability and category membership is forced to make either false or empirically vacuous claims'.[19] So if we are to take seriously Duggan's proposition that the stress patterns of alliterative verse are based on those of spoken language, we shall need to pay more attention to sentence stress as it actually works. This chapter attempts to do this for alliterative verse. Undoubtedly, much of what we shall say will need revision and refinement, but we think that the kinds of considerations that we bring to the problem are the right ones and leave us in a better

[11] See J. A. Burrow, 'Hoccleve's Questions: Intonation and Punctuation', *Notes and Queries*, n.s. 49 (2002), 184–8.

[12] Roger Kingdon, *The Groundwork of English Intonation* (London, 1958).

[13] Noam Chomsky and Morris Halle, *The Sound Pattern of English* (New York, 1968).

[14] We have made use of the following studies by Dwight Bolinger: *The Phrasal Verb in English* (Harvard, Mass., 1971); 'Accent is Predictable (if you're a mind reader)', *Language*, 48 (1972), 633–44; *Intonation and Its Parts*; 'Two Views of Accent', in Carlos Gussenhoven, Dwight Bolinger, and Cornelia E. Keijsper, *On Accent* (Bloomington, Ind., 1987), pp. 51–107; and *Intonation and Its Uses* (London, 1989).

[15] *On the Grammar and Semantics of Sentence Accents* (Dordrecht, 1984). The first chapter in this book is reprinted in Gussenhoven, Bolinger, and Keijsper, *On Accent*, pp. 1–50.

[16] Susan F. Schmerling, *Aspects of English Sentence Stress* (Austin, Texas, 1976)

[17] D. J. Allerton and A. Cruttenden, 'Three Reasons for Accenting a Definite Subject', *Linguistics*, 5 (1979), 49–53.

[18] *The English Tone of Voice* (London, 1975).

[19] Schmerling, *Aspects*, p. 57.

position to grasp both the regularity of the rhythms of alliterative poetry and the nuances of its meanings.

We appreciate, of course, that verse is a stylised form of language. The economic principle of effective communication, which works to keep the number of acoustic 'highlights' in any unit of intonation to a minimum,[20] does not apply in, say, an iambic pentameter. For that reason, open-class words have a higher probability of being perceived as accented in verse than in normal speech, though in verse, too, the distribution of beats is influenced (in determinate ways) by tendencies of speech rhythm.[21] Another appreciable difference between verse and speech is that verse rhythm is influenced not only by linguistic factors but also by the poem's 'metrical set', that is, the expectancy created by the rhythmic pattern established by the poem and/or its metrical tradition. So in Chaucer's *Troilus*, we have no difficulty in perceiving a regular five-beat line in 'It fálleth náught to púrpos mé to télle' (1.142). But there are several reasons why we hear a beat on *me*, and not all of them are metrical. One is that the pronoun *me*, which would normally bear weak stress, is nevertheless more salient than the unstressed syllables that surround it (for in connected speech *acoustic prominence is always relative*);[22] another is that, as psychological experiments have

[20] Bolinger, 'Two Views of Accent', p. 85.

[21] The point is made by Marina Tarlinskaja, *Shakespeare's Verse: Iambic Pentameter and the Poet's Idiosyncrasies* (New York, 1987), p. 33.

[22] The crude dichotomy between 'stressed' and 'unstressed' words misses the point that some 'unstressed words' are more 'unstressed' than others: in ordinary language there are degrees of stress and this is reflected in poetry. Research on English verse in iambic pentameter and counting-out rhymes has shown that there is scale of probability for the likelihood of words occurring in stressed position (in the abstract metrical pattern WSWSWSWS(WS): nouns (94% in formal verse; 88% in counting-out verse), verbs (76%; 80%), adverbs (71%; 79%), adjectives (61%; 61%), modal auxiliaries (41%; 45%), auxiliaries/copulas (40%; 37%); pronouns (34%; 30%), prepositions (32%; 41%), conjunctions (14%; 19%); articles (11%; 9%). We take the percentages from Michael Kelly and David C. Rubin, 'Natural Rhythmic Patterns in English Verse: Evidence from Child Counting-Out Rhymes', *Journal of Memory and Language*, 27 (1988), 718–40 (733). This means, for example, that closed-class words with higher stress-probability offer poets options. The most intelligent discussion of this point is by Derek Attridge, who writes: 'semantic and metrical demands are constantly in operation together, moulding the neutral contours of stress provided by syntax and phonology, and ... the particular prosodic usefulness of lexical

shown, the second syllable in a series of three unaccented syllables tends naturally to be perceived with 'a lesser secondary accent';[23] and last but not least there is the fact that a rhythmical pattern, once it is established, will not cease to impose itself on the ear unless the mismatch between what we expect and what we get is so great that the perception of equivalence becomes quite impossible. The ictus on 'me' is therefore partly, but not exclusively, the product of the poem's metrical set. Our approach to beats in alliterative verse is based on the assumption that Chaucer's line vindicates: to meet metrical requirements competent poets make use of natural linguistic tendencies.

This chapter is divided into two parts. In the first part we discuss some general tendencies that influence sentence stress, and hope to show the relevance of these tendencies in the scansion of alliterative verse. First, we deal with contrastive stress and its opposite, namely the de-accenting of 'background' information; then we discuss set phrases and idioms; and finally we consider the effects of the 'rhythm rule' in alliterative verse. Having described some of the broader semantic and rhythmical factors that influence stress in the first part of the chapter, we proceed in the second part to an examination of the stress patterns of specific word-classes, with the aim of refining the crude and inaccurate rules of stress-assignment that currently hold sway. We discuss respectively 1) compounds and complex words; 2) adverbs, pronouns and prepositions; 3) verbs; 4) adjectives and nouns. In a conclusion we test the explanatory power of our hypotheses on a number of verses that have given rise to scansion problems.

Our observations about sentence stress are informed by linguistic work on the subject. In demonstrating the relevance of that work to the

categories like the pronoun lies in the degree to which they are able to bend according to these demands': *Rhythms of English Poetry* (New York, 1982), p. 227.

23 Herbert Woodrow, 'Time Perception', in *Handbook of Experimental Psychology*, ed. S. S. Stevens (New York, 1951), pp. 1223–36. The tendency to perceive as accented the second in a series of three unstressed syllables is related to the rhythmical tendency to de-accent the second in a series of three stressed syllables. In both cases a dipodic pattern is created, with regular alternation of weak and unstressed syllables. The metre of the bob-and-wheel everywhere depends on this dipodic principle. Take, for example, G 759–60: 'He róde in hís prayére / And crýed for hís mysdéde.' Our accents marks are not intended to indicate that 'his' is strongly stressed: if the three syllables after the first beat are given weak stress the beat will naturally fall on 'hís'.

metrical analysis of alliterative verse we have chosen to start with b-verses, and then to apply the insights they yield to a-verse problems. The procedural advantage of this is that b-verse metre is better understood, for there is broad agreement that the b-verse only ever has two beats.[24] The major alliterative poems contain, however, a substantial number of 'extended' b-verses, that is, b-verses with three open-class words. As Noriko Inoue has recently argued,[25] such extended b-verses pose serious problems for Duggan and Cable; according to their stress rules, such verses must contain three beats; but according to the rules of b-verse metre, metrical b-verses should contain two beats and one and only one long dip. Both Cable and Duggan go some way towards recognizing the problem. Cable speculates that possibly 'nouns and adjectives [may] occasionally (though very rarely) be demoted', but does not permit 'demotion' in practice. Having ruled it out in the a-verse, he does the same in the b-verse, and simply counts extended b-verses 'among the exceptions'. [26] Since, as we shall see, extended b-verses are evidently authentic and numerous, and involve *all* kinds of open-class words (not just 'nouns and adjectives', as Cable writes) we do not think that calling them 'exceptions' is adequate: a metrical theory cannot be fully functional if the numerous verses that contradict its postulates have to be categorised as 'exceptions'. Duggan, on the other hand, has entertained the 'possibility of three potential lifts in the b-verse', two or three of which might be filled in any given instance.[27] This speculation seems to us even more unhelpful: it cannot be maintained that b-verses obey strict metrical rules, as Duggan has argued elsewhere, when the conditions of metricality (two beats and one long dip) do not apply in various b-verses. At best, Duggan imports to the b-verse the same implausible argument that Cable makes for the a-verse: the metre there, Cable claims, is rhythmically regular (based on two beats and two long dips) except when there are three beats, in which case '*any* pattern of dips' (our italics) will do.[28] It is hard to believe that alliterative poets

[24] We note some hesitations expressed by Duggan below.

[25] Noriko Inoue, 'A New Theory of Alliterative A-Verses', *Yearbook of Langland Studies*, 18 (2005), 107–32. A fuller discussion of the matter may be found in Inoue's dissertation, 'The A-Verse'.

[26] Cable, *Alliterative Tradition*, p. 103.

[27] Duggan, 'The Authenticity', p. 36.

[28] Cable, *Alliterative Tradition*, p. 92.

aimed at rhythmical regularity in one set of lines but were indifferent to it in another.

Extended b-verses and hyper-extended a-verses, i.e. a-verses with four open-class words, can be used negatively, as illustrating the failure of the current stress rules to generate the rhythmical regularity they are supposed to reveal; but we try to show in this chapter that they can also be used constructively, as a body of evidence that sheds light on the conditions that make it possible for open-class words to be weakly stressed and, conversely, for closed-class words (especially prepositions and pronouns) to take the beat, even in the presence of two other open-class words in the same verse (i.e. in contravention of Duggan's 'promotion rule'). We shall illustrate these patterns on the basis of an extensive coverage of extended b-verses in *Cleanness* [*C*], *Sir Gawain and the Green Knight* [*G*], *Patience* [*P*], *Saint Erkenwald* [*E*], *Alexander and Dindimus* [*B*], *Morte Arthure* [*MA*], *Siege of Jerusalem* [*SJ*] and *Wars of Alexander* [*WA*], with a few additional examples taken from other alliterative poems, namely *Piers Plowman* [*PP*] and *Winnner and Waster* [*WW*].[29] We show that in practice the b-verse cannot be scanned as a regular two-beat hemistich unless we are sensitive to sentence stress, and consequently to meaning and rhythm and not just word-class, and that this same kind of scansion will naturally reveal two-beat a-verses where Duggan and Cable perceive three or even four beats. Although we do not cite every extended b-verse from our corpus in this chapter, we discuss most of them and are reasonably confident that the kinds of extended b-verses that occur in our corpus are fully represented. We shall also draw occasionally on the rhyming iambic lines of *G* and occasionally on those of *Pearl* by way of confirming that particular open-class words do not necessarily take the beat. The explanations we propose for this are based on well-documented tendencies of English sentence stress, and we would like to suggest that these explanations also work for extended a-verses.

As the brief outline of this chapter will have indicated, the data we have gathered will be presented under different explanatory principles and headings. We are conscious that the explanatory order we impose on

[29] References are to the editions specified at p. 5, n. 13, above. References to *PP* are to the editions by George Kane, *Piers Plowman: the A Version* (London, 1960), George Kane and E. Talbot Donaldson, *Piers Plowman: the B Version* (London, 1975), and by George Russell and George Kane, *Piers Plowman: the C Version* (London, 1997).

our data may involve some simplification of a complex situation. In reality, the forces that influence and affect accentuation are multiple and tend to operate simultaneously, sometimes collaboratively, sometimes antagonistically. The interaction of semantic and rhythmical tendencies makes it difficult to discuss them consecutively without some cross-referencing, and difficult also to base an explanation on any one of these tendencies when others are likely to be implicated. But since we have to start from a position where the rhythmical and semantic factors that influence the stress patterns of alliterative verse have been largely neglected,[30] isolating such factors (even if they interact with others) may at least serve the purpose of identifying them and of demonstrating their existence.

We deliberately leave aside the issue of the possible disjunction of stress and alliteration.[31] It would be premature to address this question if (as we think we can show) the principles of accentuation have not been properly understood. In all the examples of b-verses cited below, the reader can therefore assume that the first b-verse beat is borne by the alliterating syllable.

## Part I

*Contrastive Stress and Lexical Presupposition*

Students of alliterative metre have had little to say about contrastive stress and its effect on the accentuation of alliterative verse. George Kane has made the case for its relevance to *PP*, but Duggan has denied its existence in other alliterative poems, claiming that the use of 'rhetorical stress ... is yet another way in which Langland differs from other alliterative poets'.[32] In ordinary language, contrastive stress and its opposite, the unstressing of 'given' information, operate as a matter of course, and account for many uncommon stress patterns (e.g. 'Lóok in the cúpboard. No, not ón the cupboard'). Research has found no evidence that the acoustic correlatives of 'contrastive stress' differ in any way from those of 'normal stress', and although we follow other linguists in treating it as a 'special case' we emphasise that contrastive stressing is

[30] Joan Turville-Petre (see n. 2 above) is a notable exception.

[31] George Kane, in 'Music', has made the case for disjunction of stress and alliteration in Piers Plowman; disjunction has also been posited by e.g. Andrew and Waldron (eds), *Poems*, pp. 47–50, and Noriko Inoue, 'A New Theory'.

[32] Duggan, 'Authenticity', p. 37.

really only a more pronounced instance of what we usually do when we accent a word (which is to single it out, to focus on it). The difference between 'contrastive stress' and 'normal stress' is therefore 'merely one of degree'.[33]

Since contrastive stress is deeply embedded in our language, Duggan's claim that it has no role to play in alliterative verse (outside Langland) seems inherently implausible, and we do not find his supporting arguments very convincing. The first of his arguments is that interjections and exclamations (such as *lo*, *ye*) do not normally take the beat in alliterative verse, but since the semantic load of such words is light they do not appear in ictus in other poets either. So in Chaucer[34] and Shakespeare[35] common exclamations typically appear in arsis, and no one would think that a reason for doubting that they use rhetorical stress. Duggan's second argument rests on a misreading of *P* 493, where Jonah contradicts God with 'Hit is not lýttel, quoþ þe léde,  bot lýkker to rýȝt'. If rhetorical stress operated, Dugan argues, we would expect *not* to take stress. This misses Jonah's point: he says that his grounds for complaint are not 'little' but 'to right', i.e 'in accordance with right, justified'). The contrast is between one adjectival complement (*lyttel*) and another (*to ryȝt*) and the beats therefore fit the rhetorical needs perfectly.

To show that alliterative poets do make use of contrastive and rhetorical stress, we would like to discuss ten examples:

1) Þaȝ Í be not now hé  þat ye óf spéken (*G* 1242)

2) 'Bi Máry', quoþ þe ménskful,  mé þynk hit an óþer (*G* 1268b)

3) Lét hym lýȝe þer stílle,
He hátz nere þát he sóȝt,
And ȝé wyl a whýle be stýlle
I schal télle yow hów þay wróȝt. (*G* 1994–7*rh*)[36]

[33] Schmerling, *Aspects*, p. 65. She continues: 'There is a sense in which anything meaningful is contrastive (in fact, one traditional definition of "meaningfulness" involves lack of total predictability in context) and the either/or kind of contrast with which we usually associate "contrastive stress" is but the limiting case'.
[34] See e.g. *CT* I.3719, 3445, 3906, 3907 4098, etc.
[35] Marina Tarlinskaja, 'General and Particular Aspects of Meter', in *Rhythms and Metre*, ed. Paul Kiparsky and Gilbert Youmans, special issue of *Phonetics and Phonology*, 1 (1989), 121–54 (136).
[36] We use *rh* to designate lines from the bob-and-wheel of *G*. As Borroff has shown, the metre of the wheel is a tetrameter with iambic alternation of accen-

4) Át þe soper and áfter, mony áþel sóngez (*G* 1654)

5) And whýn ert þou & whó and whát makys þou hére? (*WA* 835) [37]

6) With alle méschef þat þou máy neuer þou mé spáreȝ (*P* 484)

7) Now Nóe néuer stynteȝ – þat nýȝt he begýnneȝ (*C* 359)

8) God schýlde, quoþ þe schálk, þat schál not befálle (*G* 1776)

9) Lo, þe wýtles wréchche, for he wólde noȝt súffer (*P* 113)

10) In táillours craft and týnkeris craft, what trúþe kan deuýse (*PP* B 5.547)

These lines pose varying degrees of difficulty for Cable and Duggan. In the first six examples the beat falls on a word that should be unstressed according to their stress rules. Duggan's 'promotion' rule could be invoked to explain some (but not all) of these lines, but it seems quite unnecessary to posit an additional rule if, as we believe, the stress patterns are simply the ones that are normal in the language. In the first example, 'Þaȝ *I* be not now *he*', the pronouns are explicitly contrasted: Gawain insists on the difference between the way he sees himself (*I*) and his image as constructed in the words of the lady (*he*); the accentuation of the pronouns is an essential exponent of the sense. In the second example, the Lady of the Castle contradicts Gawain's view: '*I* think otherwise'. Contrastive emphasis is also at work in the third and fourth examples. In the rhyming lines of *G*, the hero lies still, and then *we* are asked to be 'still'. At *G* 1654, we know already that the company are enjoying supper (so *sopper* is not the word that requires emphasis); what

ted and unaccented syllables. The only licences the poet takes are inversions of the first foot (i.e. /x for /x/), headless lines (i.e. / for x/) and double offbeats. Clashing stress is systematically avoided (though the avoidance is sometimes obscured by scribal loss of final *–e*), with one exception, *G* 736, which like Borroff we take to be scribal. See Borroff, *Stylistic and Metrical Study*, p. 160.

[37] Duggan, 'Authenticity', p. 37, argues that his 'promotion rule' can be stretched to deal with the b-verse, since the open-class word *makys* 'happens to be one most commonly subject to stress-subordination', but his choice of words shows the persistence of a muddled theory of stress: his idea is that *make*, because it is an 'open-class' word, automatically comes with stress into an utterance, so that when we find it unaccented we must conclude that this stress has somehow been 'subordinated'. The fact of the matter is that high-frequency verbs (make, do, come, go, etc.) tend to be more weakly stressed than others.

matters here is the abundant entertainment, in this case the songs that are sung both *during* and *after* dinner. In the fifth example, the insistence of the interrogative pronouns (*whyne*, *who* and *what*) invites the accent. The pattern is as common in alliterative verse[38] as it is in our own speech,[39] and rules of stress assignment ought to be able to deal with it. In our sixth example, Jonah complains that God pesters him more than anyone else: 'fórbi alle óþer' (483). The pronoun *me* is accented because Jonah claims God has it in for him. The adverb *neuer*, on the other hand, is weakly stressed in this instance). *Pace* Duggan, this is pretty normal for common adverbs of time and place, including disyllabic ones, as in 'cóm neuer móre' (*C* 191b) — but poets can emphasize the adverb as in example seven, 'Now Nóe néuer stynteȝ': 'Noah did not stop once'. In example eight, *schal* is of course the only obvious candidate for stress in this b-verse, but what makes the choice inevitable is that *schal* has full modal force and is not just a future auxiliary: *schal* expresses the hero's resolution.[40] As speakers of English, we should have no difficulty with this stress pattern, for we stress 'such auxiliaries as *can*, *may*, and *will* ... if

[38] For example, *PP* B 14.40, 'Whérof or whérfore  or whérby to líbbe', *WA* 4321, 'Quáse þai were, quéthin þai were,  & of quát kínd', *WA* 5342, 'Quá þai were, & of quéþen,  & quát was þaire érrande', and *G* 398, 'Whére schulde I wále þe', quoþ Gauan, 'whére is þy pláce'. In the last example the interrogative *Where* bears stress in preference to the name 'Gawain', because the inquit formula ('quoþ Gauan') is expounded as the nuclear tail (i.e. the sequence of unstressed syllables after the tonic, in *wale*). This option is again normal in the English language.

[39] An example from John Le Carré, *Our Game* (London, 1995), p. 162: 'Find out *why* and find out *where* and find out *who*'. The italics showing where the stresses should go are the author's.

[40] Cf. also the rhyming lines in which the Lady begins her campaign to make Gawain accept a gift (the green girdle):

Þaȝ Í had nóȝt of yóurez,
ȝet shúlde ȝe háue of mýne. (1815–6)

The accentuation satisfies the requirements of rhythm, metre, and rhetoric all at once. In 1815 the beat (*Í*) is not only secured by the metrical set and the dipodic principle but also by an implied contrast: 'even if *I* don't get anything, *you* should.' The accenting of *schulde* rather than the pronoun *ye* in the subsequent line responds to the thematic fronting of the auxiliary, which brings out its full modal force (obligation). Sense and accentuation are thus inseparable: we hear the lady prosecuting her case not only with logic (though I am disappointed, you won't be) but also with emotional pressure: 'you *must* have a gift'.

we want to accent ability, possibility or will.'[41] The foregrounding of volitional modality (as distinct from futurity) also plays a part in the accentuation of *P* 113,

> Lo, þe wýtles wréchche, for he wólde noȝt súffer (*P* 113),

describing Jonah's obstinate refusal to obey: *wolde noȝt* has the emphatic sense of 'refused to'.

Our final example needs more extensive discussion because it introduces us to the problem of hyper-extended a-verses. We owe it to a list of examples given by Duggan, who thinks they show that some a-verses may have not just *three* but *four* beats. If one thinks that beats are determined by lexical category, this conclusion is inescapable. Duggan cites some more examples (we take the liberty of indicating a possible two-beat scansion):

> Bot as smýlt mele vnder smál siue   smókes for þíkke (*C* 226)
> Of brýȝt golde vpon silke bórdes   bárred ful rýche (*G* 159)
> With thre búlles of blé white   bróuden withín (*WW* 144)
> My plówpot schal be my pýk-staf   and pícche atwo the rótes (*PP* B 6.103).[42]

By Cable and Duggan's stress rules, these a-verses have *four* beats (and *PP* B 6.103 could have seven beats: 'My plówpót schal be my pýk-stáf and píchhe atwó the rótes'.[43] Duggan raises the possibility that lines with four open-class words are scribal, but has 'come to think that only their rarity leads us to suspect their authenticity'.[44] To our minds, too, the possibility is not a credible one, not least because the notion of their 'rarity' blatantly contradicts Duggan's earlier assertion (in the same article) that '[m]any more lines might easily have been cited'.[45] Below are some more examples of our own that persuade us there are indeed many such verses:

> Ful gráyþely gos þis gódman   and dos Gódeȝ héstes (*C* 341)

[41] A. Western, *On Sentence Rhythm and Word Order in Modern English*, Videnskabs-Selskabet Skrifter 2 (Christiania, 1908), p. 48.
[42] Duggan cites the edition by J. A. W. Bennett, *Piers Plowman, B-Text* (Oxford, 1972).
[43] Duggan, 'Extended A-Verses', p. 55.
[44] *Ibid.*, p. 74.
[45] *Ibid.*, p. 55.

And fýue wont of fýfty, quoth God, I schal fórȝete álle (*C* 739)[46]
Þré dayes and þ[r]é nyȝt, ay þénkande on Drýȝtyn (*P* 294)
Bed me bílyue my bále stour and brýng me on énde (*P* 426)
Þe godman glýft wyth þat glám and glóped for nóyse (*C* 849)
In gód fayþ, quoþ þe góode knyȝt, Gáwan I hátte (*G* 381)
And cum to þat mérk at mýdmorn, to máke quat yow lýkez (*G* 1073)
Gef hym gód and góud day, þat Gáwayn he sáue (*G* 2073)
The chief séed þat Piers séw, ysáued worstow néuere (*PP* B 19.406)[47]
Send prékers to þe príce toun, and pláunt there my ségge (*MA* 355)

Duggan deserves credit for seeing the difficulties that his stress rules produces, but, instead of drawing the obvious conclusion that they need rethinking, he concedes the possibility that a-verses may have as many as *four* beats, and is happy, on that basis, to conclude that a-verses have no metre at all if by that we understand 'a regular and recurrent pattern'.[48]

We shall give the reasoning and evidence for our two-beat scansions of these hyper-extended a-verses in the appropriate sections below, but the two-beat a-verse, 'In táillours craft and týnkeris craft...' (*PP* B 5.547a),

[46] The scansion of words such as 'fóryete' raises problems that require further attention. Our scansion follows Duggan's argument, in 'Stress Assignment', that stress can fall on a range of prefixes. Cf. C 203, 'For as I fynde þer he forȝet alle his fre þeweȝ' (203). The inquit formula ('quoth God') is unlikely to be scribal in view of the biblical source: 'Et ait' (Gen. 18:28), but as in ordinary language these tags can be unstressed. The 'extra-metricality' of inquit formulas is thus not a 'poetic licence' but a linguistic fact. See below, p. 181.
[47] George Kane, in 'Music', p. 82, scans the a-verse with disjunction of stress and alliteration: 'The chíef seed þat Piers séw'. We are not persuaded by this example. When one looks at the behaviour of *chief* in ME verse ('As hé which ís chief lórd abóve', *CA* 7.469, cf. *CA* 5.1112, 'Is chief sóvereign ouer hymsélf his sóule to ȝéme', *PP* A 10.72, and when one considers the variable accentuation in alliterative verse of the broader class of 'limiter adjectives', to which *chief* may be said to belong, Kane's intuitive scansion becomes rather less convincing. On 'limiter adjectives', which 'particularize the reference of the noun' (e.g. main, own, same, only) see Randolph Quirk and Sidney Greenbaum, *A University Grammar of English* (London, 1973), §5.5. Unlike most other adjectives, 'limiter adjectives' cannot be compared or intensified; they constitute (in Carl Bache's words) a 'function class of adjectives', and are consequently often weakly stressed like closed-class words. See Carl Bache, *The Order of Pre-Modifying Adjectives in Present-day English* (Odense, 1978), pp. 32–33.
[48] Duggan, 'Extended A-Verses', p. 75.

belongs in this section on contrastive stress. The prosodic rule that determines the accentuation, as given by David Crystal, is that in

> lexical sets in coordinate structure ...the tonic is placed on the items belonging to the same set, e.g.
> /this book costs FIVE dollars/ and this one THREE dollars/[49]

The open-class words 'dollars' (in Crystal's example) and 'craft' (in *PP*) are weakly stressed, and the words that precede them carry the tonic and receive much greater emphasis; they are rhetorically contrasted.

The opposite of contrastive stress is the de-accenting of information that can be taken for granted from the preceding discourse. This tendency not to give stress to familiar items is often referred to as the effect of 'lexical presupposition'. The influence of lexical presupposition on intonation has been widely recognised by linguists. David Crystal gives the example:

X /that was some ACCIDENT/ WASN'T it/
Y /a TERRIBLE accident/[50]

Amongst scholars of alliterative metre, however, there is no agreement (and often no recognition) that the discursive context matters in scansion.

We would like to provide some arguments and evidence for the influence of lexical presupposition on stress in alliterative verse by analysing a few examples of unaccented nouns in extended b-verses. In the following examples, nouns and proper names bear no accent because they are predictable from the preceding discourse:

| | |
|---|---|
| sáyde þe burde þénne (*G* 1846b) | as Nathan tóld hádde (*SJ* 266b) |
| and léteȝ my gestes óne (*C* 872b) | Sé! so Sare láȝes (*C* 661b) |

At *G* 1846, 'þe burde' is obviously the Lady of the Castle, but she has not been speaking for a while and therefore needs to be re-introduced by a noun rather than a pronoun. At *SJ* 266 the poet reminds us of Nathan's prediction: but if we can remember *that* we surely remember his name, which has been mentioned repeatedly (e.g. 191, 212), and so does not need to be stressed. At *C* 872, the 'gestes' of which Lot speaks are the angels; he could not have said 'létes hem one', because he has just been talking of his attractive daughters. In addition, 'gestes' quietly

[49] Crystal, *English Tone of Voice*, p. 25.
[50] Crystal, *English Tone of Voice*, p. 26.

reminds the Sodomites why they should show respect. At *C* 661, Sarah again does duty for the pronoun, but (as the invitation to *see* makes clear in a different way) she had gone 'byhynde þe dor' (653) and has briefly disappeared from view. The nouns function more or less like pronouns, but offer the advantage of referring back beyond the immediate antecedents to preceding ones.

We can solve the problem of the hyper-extended a-verse, 'Þe godman glýft wyth þat glám' (*C* 849a) in the same way. The change of subject, from the Sodomites to Lot, requires the use of something more substantive than a pronoun, but, like the pronoun, 'godman' basically functions to refer us back to a familiar character. Applying this insight to the opening lines from *G* —

Siþen þe ség‍e and þe assáut    watz sésed at Tróye
Þe borȝ bríttened and brént    to bróndez and áskez

— we notice that *borȝ* refers back to *Tróye.* Since the noun is anaphoric it does not take the 'accent of interest' (in Bolinger's words).

We shall discuss in the second part of this chapter some other nouns that appear regularly without a beat in a- and b-verses (*king*, *knight*, *lord*, *etc*); this may have something to do with their commonness in alliterative verse, but another reason for their low accentual rank is that they tend to be used anaphorically, to refer back to named personages that are lexically presupposed. The noun 'king' in *G* is used in this way, to refer back to Arthur. It appears regularly after an alliterating adjective, and is apparently itself unaccented (as our examples will show). It is always tempting to explain this enclitic pattern by positing some universal rule, such as the compound stress rule, which Yasuyo Moriya uses to make sense of such contours,[51] but the anaphoric use of the noun often offers a simpler and more convincing explanation. The first two times the *Gawain* poet refers to Arthur as king, the noun is accented: 'Þis kýng lay at Cámylot' (37a), and 'And he þe cómlokest kýng' (53a). From then on 'king' refers to a known quantity and can function as a semi-pronoun, as in its next appearance in the wheel, 'Kyng hýȝest món of wýlle' (57*rh*),[52]

[51] Yasuyo Moriya, 'Alliteration Versus Natural Speech Rhythm in Determining the Meter of ME Alliterative Verse', *English Studies*, 6 (2004), 498–507 (503).

[52] This is the only noun in initial position of the wheel that does not take the beat. This makes it unlikely that the accentuation is determined by the blanket operation of a 'demotion rule': 'a stressed syllable may realise an offbeat when it occurs between two stressed syllables, or after a line-boundary and before a

and in the b-verses, 'þe stíf kyng hisséluen' (107b) and 'cóm þe kyng nérre' (*G* 556). Both b-verses have three beats by Duggan and Cable's stress rules, but two if we attend to the nuances of meaning.

We would like to end this section with three fine passages from *E*. To bring out the creative intelligence behind the prosody it is essential that we see the passages in their immediate context and the larger context of the poem.

In the historical prologue of *E*, the poet tells us that the churches of old were once temples 'þat témyd to the déuell' (15). St Paul's, one of the three most important temples, was devoted to the top idol: 'For he was drýghtyn dérrest  of ydóls práysid' (*E* 29). It makes sense, therefore, for the poet to adopt the following accentuation when he describes what devil inhabited the cathedral:

> Þe mécul mýnster þerinne[53]  a máȝty deuell áght (*E* 27)

What matters to the poet is not that the cathedral belonged to the devil (for that was true of all churches in pagan times) but that it belonged to a powerful one. Sense and accentuation are perfectly attuned.

In the next example, the dead pagan judge speaks and explains why God has allowed his body to remain intact:

> And móst he (= God) ménsknes men  for mýnnyng of *ríȝtes*
> Þen for al þe méritorie médes  þat men on mólde úsen.
> And if rénkes for *ríȝt*  þus me aráyed hás,
> He has lánt me to lást  þat lóues *ryȝt* bést. (*E* 269–72)

The word *right* runs through these lines, and righteousness provides the logical connections to which the conjunctions point. God honours righteousness, and *if* the people honoured the righteous judge by arraying him in splendour when he died, *then* God, who is right's greatest champion, has done something more remarkable still by permitting the judge to 'last'. It will be remembered that by a divine miracle the judge's dead body and clothes has stayed immaculate, even though his soul is in

stressed syllable' (Attridge, Rhythms, p. 160). The terminology of 'demotion' may be misleading in this instance: in the discursive context 'king' does not have much sentence stress; if the 'demotion rule' has a role to play in the poet's prosody of *G* 57, it is so because the poet uses words that are already inclined to do what the rule would command.

[53] Or (some might argue) with disjunction: 'þe mecul mýnster þerínne'. But note our comments on adverbials of time and space.

Limbo, and that St Erkenwald's sympathy for the judge (which is *his* tribute to the judge's *riȝt*) will in due course elicit from God another miracle: the body is re-animated for a moment that is brief but long enough for the saint to enact the rite of baptism. Line 272 is very carefully worded and accented. The a-verse alliteration *lant* and *last* gains added point because it studiously avoids the usual alliterative collocation of *lenen* with *life* or *live*: the judge *lasts* but does not *live*. The striking failure of *ryȝt* to take the beat in *E* 272b is due to the discursive connection with the preceding line (*ryȝt* is anaphoric). When we read the verse with unaccented *ryȝt* (as the alliteration asks us to do) we become conscious of the connection and consequently of the logical difference between God and his *renkes*: if they love *right*, God loves right *more*.

Our final example makes it clear that lexical presupposition occurs not only when the same lexical item is repeated but also when a particular concept is understood. In the following lines the judge tells us he served

> Vnder a prínce of párage   of páynymes lághe
> & vche ségge þat him séwed   þe sáme fayth trówid. (203–4)

The 'same faith' refers back to the pagan religion ('paynymes laghe'): 'fayth' is given, as 'same' makes clear.

*Idioms*

Another weakness of the current rules of stress assignment is their misguided focus on the word as the unit of assessment, their purpose being the determination of 'which *words* may appear in ictus' (Duggan; our italics). However, sometimes the word is too large a unit, for words can take more than one beat; and sometimes it is too small a unit, for words can unite into predictable formulas which are treated prosodically like single words. We shall deal with the first problem in our section on compounds and complex words, and with the second one in this section.

To see the difficulties that idioms pose, we begin with a revealing example:

> And in þe mýry mórnyng   ȝe máy your waye táke (*C* 804).

Here the modal auxiliary 'may' takes the beat, but the open-class word 'way' does not. How can this be? Neither the stress rules nor the promotion rule can tell us why. The obvious explanation is that words readily combine into lexical units. For this reason linguists who discuss stress prefer to speak not of words but of lexical items. As David Crystal explains 'lexical item' is chosen, rather than (say) 'open-class word', in order to avoid the misleading implication of the term 'word': lexical items include many kinds of multi-word units with an invariable or unpredictable internal structure, and which have their prosody dealt with in the same way as simple words. Included under this heading, therefore, are: idioms (e.g. at ANY rate, ANY old thing) compound names (e.g. the WINSLOW boy), compounds (e.g. TOY factory), and phrasal verbs (e.g. look UP to).[54]

It is instructive to compare the placement of the accent in Crystal's examples with the one that Cable and Duggan's rules would predict. In *C* 804b, 'ȝe máy your waye táke', the idiom 'take your way' behaves like a single lexical item, with one accent on the verb. The same applies to the a-verse of *P* 66, 'Ným þe way to Nýnyue', which is a three-beat a verse if it scanned according to word-class but a two-beat one if 'Nym þe way' is considered as an idiomatic unit. Another example of such a unit is 'Shút the door' (the noun usually following predictably from the verb and the situation), and the accentuation of *E* 116b follows that pattern: 'dítte þe durre áfter'.

There are various types of 'lexical units' that require attention. Two obvious types already mentioned by Crystal are compound names and phrasal verbs. Examples of the former type are found in

Forþy þe dérk déde see (*C* 1020a)
And fér ouer þe Frénch flod (*G* 13a)

'Dead Sea' and 'French flood' (i.e. the Channel) take compound stress on the adjective. Phrasal verbs, or verbs with set prepositions or adverbs, are instanced in the following verses:

and stonde bý yow þére (*G* 344b)
Þay let dóun þe grete dráȝt (*G* 817a)
We liggen dóun in our dén (*B* 446a)
He did him fórþ to flód' (*B* 138a)[55]
On óure byfóre þe sónne go dóun (*Pearl* 530, cf. 230)

In the first example 'stand by' is a lexical unit with the incipient sense of 'support' (see *OED* s.v. *stand* v. 70). The accentuation of such units in Modern English presents numerous complications and depends on many

[54] Crystal, *English Tone of Voice*, pp. 22–3.
[55] According to Duggan, 'Extended A-Verses', pp. 61–62, these are three-beat a-verses. Needless to say, this kind of scansion would have the effect of turning *G* 344b and comparable verses into three-beat b-verses.

variables,[56] including the relative specificity of the verb and the particle. Bolinger revealingly contrasts 'He went áfter it' with 'He wént for it', where 'after' is concrete and spatial and 'for' abstract and relational.[57] In alliterative verse the verb is more likely to take the beat than the preposition or adverb (which does not usually carry the alliteration),[58] but, as our examples show, the pattern of 'stand bý' is a legitimate possibility, particularly, it would seem, when the verb is semantically weak, as is the case with 'go', 'lie', 'do', 'let', and 'stand' (which means little more than 'be'). Phrasal verbs may also take two beats in the absence of suitable competition for the beat, as in *G* 2263a, 'Hade hit drýuen adóun'.

Closely related to phrasal verbs are verbs that occur idiomatically with particular nominal or adjectival complements. As Carlos Gussenhoven has pointed out, in normal pronunciation expressions such as 'make háppy', 'pay áttention', catch cóld', 'leave alóne' are expounded in much the same way as phrasal verbs, that is, as a single lexical item. Here are some b-verses that establish this point for alliterative verse:

| | |
|---|---|
| take héde to ȝour énd (*WA* 3221) | take képe to ȝour sélfen (*MA* 1682b) |
| letten þe rínk óne (*P* 216b)[59] | and dráw no lytte lángere (*MA* 550b) |

In the expressions 'draw lytte' (= delay), the first element appears to take the stronger stress. The a-verse 'He may not drýȝe to dráw allyt' (*C* 599a) has two beats on this analysis.

Some modifiers and nouns are so frequently collocated that they become a single lexical item in pronunciation. Examples from Modern English are 'trúe love',[60] 'líon's share', both with quasi-compound stress on the first word. In Middle English the formulae 'good faith', 'good day' are good examples. In both Chaucer and Gower's verse these phrases are single-accented, with accent on the first word (*CT* I.1649, *T&C* 2.162, *CA* 4.966) or the second (*CT* I.2740, *Former Age,* 55, *CA* 1.727 ), as

[56] See H. Eitrem, 'Stress in English Verb + Adverb Groups', *Englische Studien*, 32 (1903), 69–77, and Dwight Bolinger, *The Phrasal Verb in English* (Harvard, Mass., 1971).

[57] *Intonation and Its Uses*, p. 106.

[58] Luick, 'Stabreime', pp. 397–9.

[59] The rarified poeticism for 'man', *rink*, invariably attracts the beat in alliterative verse.

[60] As in *G* 1540b, 'to trúluf expoún'.

metre requires.[61] The same is true in alliterative verse. The extended b-verse 'in gód fayth hit is yówrez' (*G* 1037b) is entirely regular, as are a-verses such as *G* 1241, 'In gód fayth, quoþ Gáwayn'; *G* 1264a, 'For I haf fóunden, in god fáyþ'; and *E* 230a, 'And euer in fóurme of god fáithe'. Another example is 'graunt mercy' ('great thanks') which takes *one* beat because it is *one* lexical item (as reflected in the spelling 'gramercy'). Usually, the adjective is stressed,[62] as in

gráunt mercy þat óþer (*C* 765b) gránt mercy þerfóre (*G* 1392b)

Problems of hyper-extended a-verses also disappear with scansions that pick out lexical items rather than words in isolation: 'Gef hym gód and góud day' (*G* 2073a) has two beats, as does 'In gód fayth, quoþ þe góode knyȝt' (*G* 381a).[63] 'Gráunt mercy quod þe gréte clerk' (*WA* 370a), which Duggan cites as an a-verse with four possible ictus positions,[64] has two beats on our reading of the evidence.

We have so far mentioned two-word units, whether few adjective-noun combinations (good faith, good day) or phrasal or quasi-phrasal verbs (let down, stand by) but the point that has a much wider application. Below are some more b-verses with unaccented nouns or complements:

þat lif bére mówe (*B* 619b)
þe lórde hit tayt mákez (*G* 988b)
þe búrde in mynde háde (*G* 1283b)
só Crist mott me hélpe (*MA* 136b)
só me God hélpe (*MA* 1443b; cf. *PP* B 5.369)
ás þe buke téllis (*WA* 17b)
ás the storye télles (*P3A* 306b, cf. 423b)

[61] Metre is not the only conditioning factor. The stress is more likely to fall on the second word at the end of tone units. See below, p. 176.

[62] In the Cotton Nero poems one rhymed line could indicate stress on the noun, 'Graunt mercy, quoþ Gawayn' (*G* 838rh), but initial inversion is possible.

[63] 'Give' and 'knight' are words of low accentual rank, as b-verses show (see pp. 191, 203).

[64] Duggan, 'Extended A-Verses', p. 55. Generic *clerk* does not alliterate in extended a-verses when preceded by an adjective. An indication of its low accentual status is given by *WA* 398a, 'Þan Ánectanebus hire áwyn clerk', for the limiter adjective 'awyn' does not usually take the beat, and will only take precedence over nouns of low accentual rank (such as 'body', 'God'). Cf. *CT* VI.1173, 'A yóng clerk rómynge bý hymsélf they métte'.

The rhythm rule may have a role to play in the examples from *G*, but so, we suggest, does the idiomatic and hence predictable nature of the verb phrases 'bear life', 'have in mind', and 'make it tait'. In the unmarked order, it is not the verb but the complement that would attract the accent, so poets use inversion to counteract this stress pattern. Duggan and Turville-Petre suggest the possibility that *WA* 17, 'ás þe buke téllis', is scribal (and emendable after 'as I am enfourmed', *WA* 306) but retain the manuscript reading because of the parallel in *P3A*. As Turville-Petre has argued, 'It is possible to argue that *as* may alliterate in such circumstances' (i.e. in authority tags').[65] This authenticity of the line need not be in question. The reason why the nouns are unaccented is that a number of other ones can be slotted into this formula (book, story, tale). Because the meaning does not depend on the particular noun that is chosen, we should not expect it to be strongly stressed. As the verses from *MA* show, the same principle applies to pious formulae and exclamations. Various nouns (God, Christ, Lord) can be put into the grammetrical frame without changing the basic meaning. The closed-class word *so* therefore becomes a candidate for the beat.[66]

*The Rhythm Rule*

Having looked at some of the semantic factors (contrast, anaphoric and idiomatic predictability) that influence the stress patterns of alliterative verse, we shall now discuss a rhythmical influence, namely the rhythm rule. Stated simply, the rule predicts that weaker stress is given to the second of series of three adjacent content words. 'Rule' is not here used to imply that this will always happen: we have already seen cases *a contrario* (e.g. 'as Nathan tóld hádde, *SJ* 266b). We are dealing rather with a rhythmical tendency, which needs the right metrical and semantic conditions to prevail.

As Sweet's examples of the rhythm rule suggest ('Énglish plum púdding', 'a héavy round stóne'), a context that is especially favourable to the rhythm rule is that of the noun phrase with two lexical premodifiers. The reason for this is that multiple premodification introduces an element of predictability based on the fact that premodifers tend to come in a set order. To simplify a complex problem, the preferred sequence is determiner (the, some, my), quantifier (e.g. three),

[65] Turville-Petre, 'Emendation', pp. 307–8.

[66] See n. 79 at p. 170 below, for further discussion.

intensifier/limiter adjective (e.g. very, own), followed by (in this order) general adjective of subjective impression, size, shape, age, colour, participles, provenance, nouns, denominals, and then finally the head.[67] When the order is coordinated in this usual way, adjectives are not individually accented but the accent will fall on the first of two adjectives and the noun (excepting nouns of wide denomination, which tend to take weak sentence stress when preceded by an adjective[68]), as in a 'gréat red cóat. Only multiple adjectives that do not display order-restrictions tend to be accented separately, with each new modifying phrase constituting a new tone unit, as in the following example (from Crystal):

that very táll/ prétty/ but rather áwkward girl/[69]

These tendencies illuminate a number of things about alliterative metre. They account, we suggest, for the following accentual patterns in alliterative verse:

| | |
|---|---|
| with brýȝt golde léttres (*E* 51b) | and swýþe rych máydenes (*C* 1299b) |
| in brýȝt brode chéldez (*G* 1611b) | twénty spere lénþe (*C* 1383b) |
| of réd golde wérkeȝ (*G* 1817b) | fíf berly lóues (*SJ* 134b) |
| of móny þro þóȝtes (*G* 1751b) | with fóure kene bláddys (*SJ* 396b) |
| bóþe two his hándeȝ (*C* 155b) | a wónder stronge póle (*SJ* 681b) |
| þo þré þerue kákeȝ (*C* 635b)[70] | a líttil tyne égg (*WA* 507a; *tyne* = 'tiny') |

Words that do not usually take the beat in alliterative verse (intensifiers such as *wonder* and *swyþe*, quantifiers such as *mony*, *swyþe*, *little* and numerals) are strengthened by virtue of being the first of two premodifiers and so become accentable, while other open-class words, both ones with low accentual rank (*gold*, *rych*, *spere* as measure of length) and ones with good credentials (*berly*, *kene*, *þro*, *tyne*) receive weak sentence stress.

The alternative pattern, with the first adjective unstressed and the second stressed, is also found,[71] but only when the first premodifier is anyway weakly stressed, as in the case of quantifiers:[72]

[67] See Quirk and Greenbaum, *University Grammar*, §13.40–41, and Bache, *Order of Premodifying Adjectives*.
[68] For further discussion see below, pp. 197–98.
[69] Crystal, *English Tone of Voice*, p. 20.
[70] Anderson punctuates the noun phrase as a compound ('þerue-kakeȝ').
[71] We do not include under this head double adjectives in postposition, as in 'of cíties aþel fýue' (*C* 940b), where the rhythm rule operates as expected.

in mony bréme hórne (*G* 1601b) wyth mony gólde fréNges (*G* 598b)
many gréte cáuys (*B* 7b) mony áþel sóngez (*G* 1654b)

What we do not find are b-verses of the type *'red gólde wérkes', which suggests to us that the needs of alliteration will not normally coerce adjectives into unaccented position unless semantic factors (in the case of quantifiers) or rhythmical tendencies (such as the rhythm rule) cooperate. The rhythm rule also has a role to play in explaining variations in prosodic contours. In the following b-verse 'eight hundred' takes one beat, because 'hundred' has reduced stress between two stressed words:

with éȝte hundred spéres (*SJ* 1130b)[73]

but 'five hundred' *naturally* takes on a different shape when no strong stress follows:

aȝens fýue húndred (*SJ* 779b)

The demands of metre are aided and abetted by the lack of content words in *SJ* 779b. Such variation is good poetic practice. Thus in Chaucer 'snow-white' is *naturally* accented on the first element in attributive position ('Whít was this crówe as ís a snów-whit swán', *CT* IX.133), where it is subject to the rhythm rule, but on the second in predicative position ('Upón an hórs snow-whít and wél amblýng, *CT* IV.388).

Alliterative poets show their sensitivity to the intonational consequences of adjectival sequences by taking advantage of the rhythm rule to meet the demands of alliteration. However, the best poets do so even more tellingly by deliberately infringing order restrictions. In *E* 155, '& we haue oure líbrarie láited þes lóng seuen dáyes', the normal order — first quantity, then size or duration, as in 'with séuen gret wáteres' (*C* 1380b) and 'móny longe dáy (*P* 329b) — is inverted in order to foreground *long* and to steer us toward the required accentuation. 'His léfly two déȝter' (*C* 977b) is another example of a breach in order-restriction: 'lefly' is put before 'two' to emphasize the attractiveness of Loth's daughters, and the desired accentuation cannot fail to fall into place. The same technique takes care of the caesura at *P* 453, 'Þe gome glýȝt on þe gréne, grácIouse léues'. Joseph Fischer found the division

[72] For further examples see below, p. 209.

[73] The pattern is confirmed by alliteration. Alliteration on vowels and *h*–, though possible in some alliterative poems, seems not to be permitted in *SJ* (or at least is very rare: exceptions being 5, 671, 998). See Schumacher, *Studien*, pp. 81–94.

awkward,[74] and it certainly would have been if the adjectives had come in the normal order, but the inversion naturally leads to the separation of the adjectives into two different tone units. The caesura therefore coincides naturally with a pause in the intonation.

Perhaps the most subtle example of the poet's intuitive grasp of this prosodic operation is the description of the old hag at Castle Hautdesert: 'Þe ólde áuncian wif   héȝest ho syttez' (*G* 1001). The poet has avoided the obvious, but feebler 'ancient old wife' for good reason. The point is partly that 'old' would not have had quite the same force in the normal order, for in their familiar positions the adjectives 'old' and 'little' tend to be terms of endearment, as in 'góod old Jóhn'. In 'old, ancient wife', however, the hypocoristic sense is rudely removed from the realm of possibilities, so that we are left with a most unflattering picture of the crone's old age. 'Ancient' reinforces the primary sense of 'old', though it adds venerability and so sets up the b-verse (which shows her in the seat of honour). In the context of our discussion, we draw particular attention to the prosodic benefits of the poet's breach of order-restrictions. 'Old, ancient wife' gives us *two* tone units, not one (as in 'ancient old wife'), and consequently both adjectives become fit for alliterating duty. Out of order, *old* and *ancient* are separately stressed, while the generic noun *wif* cedes the accent to the preceding adjective.[75]

The rhythm rule affects the scansion of a considerable number of other a-verses, of a type that is common:

> & wyth a schrýlle scharp schóut (*C* 840a)
> Stúrne trumpen stráke (*C* 1402a)[76]
> Alle þe góude golden góddes (*C* 1525a)

In our view these are two-beat a-verses. At *C* 1402 our scansion points up the long dip, which we believe to be a metrical rule in *all* a-verses. Although Duggan has noted that this long dip is present in all but a tiny minority of a-verses, neither he nor Cable have been able to draw the

[74] Fischer lists the line amongst his examples of weak caesuras in *Die stabende Langzeile in den Werken des Gawaindichters*, Bonner Beiträge zur Anglistik, 11 (1901), pp. 1–64.

[75] We do not assume disjunction of stress and alliteration since *wif* is a generic noun. Cf. 'and háf þi wif wíth þe' (*C* 349b), *PP* B 5.223b, 'þis cráft my wif úsed', and 'Ne bé no búrgesse wyffe' (*MA* 3126a, *olim* 3082a), where the linking verb 'be' takes the beat because 'wyffe' is of low accentual rank.

[76] *trumpen* is genitive plural (with *–en* reflecting OE *–ena*).

obvious conclusion that a long dip is a metrical requirement in the a-verse (as it is in the b-verse), because they are prone to see beats in open-class words that may in reality have reduced stress (as b-verse evidence confirms). Theories about stress thus affect our ability to discern the syllabic rules of the a-verse; and one of the virtues of our scansion of verses such as *C* 1402a is that it reveals in them the operation of a rhythmical rule that three-beat scansions are unable to demonstrate.[77]

The rhythm rule could also provide an explanation for the failure of nouns to take the beat. Duggan and Cable's stress rules state clearly that nouns are accented, but a number of b-verses cast doubt on their claim. Since we deal with single adjective+noun combinations in a later section, we deliberately exclude them from our examples:

to márie his here dére (*C* 52b)
forférde a kyth rýche (*C* 571b)
on fólde no flesch stýryed (*C* 403b)[78]
grésse ne wod náwþer (*C* 1028b)
for Dríghtyns loue in héuen (*WW* 244b)
in kýngez hous Árthor (*G* 2275b)
kéne corres twéye (*SJ* 711b)
Néymes sone of Grécys (*SJ* 45b)
sáf for merk óne (*P* 291b)[79]
and góst of lyf hábbeȝ (*C* 325b)
and hólwe diches únder (*SJ* 666b)

[77] *C* 1402 is one of a number cited by Duggan as evidence for the existence of 'less common but probably authentic lines [he means a-verses] in which there are no long dips' (p. 73). In fact, the a-verse probably had four unstressed syllables in the poet's pronunciation (Stúrnë trumpen[ë] stráke). See below, pp. 234–5.
[78] Duggan erroneously takes 'on folde' with the a-verse, thereby creating an hyper-extended a-verse and an unmetrical b-verse ('Extended A-Verses, p. 55).
[79] The promotion rule breaks down in this case: *saf* is a preposition, though it is not always distinguishable from the adjective. Word-classes have fuzzy boundaries and a number of words that are on the periphery of the prepositional category ('maugré', 'sauf') may take advantage of the situation by behaving as if they were open-class words. Cf. *G* 1565, 'And máde hym máwgref his hed forto mwé útter', where 'mawgref' takes the beat, and 'hed' does not, since it is one of many nouns ('chekes', 'hert', etc.) that can be slotted into this position. The 'promotion rule' gets us nowhere. Cf. *PP* B 19.190b, 'sáue of dette óne', and *PP* B 18.81, 'Máugree his mánye teeþ'. Hanna and Lawton are therefore on insecure grounds when they rely on 1039a, 'Sáue þe sélf Iosophus', as evidence that 'Iosophus' can alliterate on /s/. The principle of lexical presupposition means that names do not have to take a beat, as is shown by *SJ* 266b and *SJ* 805a, 'Þerof wás Iosophus wáre'; and where the name Josephus *does* alliterate the poet accepts the difficulty of having to find a companion that will alliterate on /dj/. The only clear exception is 1057a, 'Þan sayþ Iosophus', where AVC read

The rhythm rule can explain all these cases, though it is noticeable that a couple of these unaccented nouns (*sone*, *hous*) are of low alliterative rank and also occur in dips without being flanked by open-class words. It is possible that the rhythm rule may be interacting with semantic factors (and obviously with the metrical set). And since the same patterns (with nouns in arsis) are securely attested in the *Gawain* poet's rhymed verse and in poetry at large —

Þe bórȝ was ál of brénde gold brýȝt (*Pearl* 998)
Þe quýte snaw láy besýde (*G* 2088*rh*)

— we reject the suggestion that the extended b-verses we cite above are 'exceptional' or contain three-beats.

## Part II

*Compounds and Complex Words*

In this second part of the chapter we look in more detail at specific classes of words, in order to correct and refine some of the imprecise generalisations about stress in recent scholarship. We begin with compounds and complex words.

Compounds give rise to interesting scansion problems in alliterative verse, and not all such problems have been adequately discussed. In samples of their scansion, Duggan and Cable treat compounds as containing two lexical stresses and consequently two beats, so that extended a-verses with compounds are analysed as follows:

Húrled into hélle-hóle (*C* 223a)[80]
And róue þe wyth no róf-sóre (*G* 2346a)[81]

It is easy, however, to demonstrate that compounds can take two beats or one, and, to complicate matters further, that this single beat can fall on either the first word or the second. A more difficult issue is whether there is anything (apart from metrical expedience) that explains the variability.

Complex words (prefix+noun, or noun+suffix) raise similar issues. One problem (which also affects compounds) is that modern pronun-

'sir Iosophus'. It is not at all evident to us that 'sir' is an 'intruder', as Hanna and Lawton argue.

[80] Cable, *Alliterative Tradition*, p. 58.

[81] Duggan, 'Extended A-Verses', p. 72.

ciation may not always be a reliable guide to medieval word stress. This problem has been well discussed by Duggan, who notes numerous examples of complex words that alliterate on the prefix (where modern pronunciation puts stress on the stem). We are persuaded by his argument that prefixes have historically 'demonstrated a tendency to retain strong secondary stress which in appropriate prosodic contexts can be elevated to primary stress',[82] but would like to remark upon a possibility that he does not discuss, namely that complex words can carry more that one beat. As we shall see, one and the same complex word (and one and the same compound) can assume different metrical shapes. This flexibility suggests to us that lexical stress, i.e. the stress pattern of words and compounds in their 'citation forms', does not necessarily tally with the stress patterns in the verse line. One possible conclusion would be that poets could do more or less what they liked with compounds and complex words. We would like to argue, however, that the variation is governed by tendencies of normal speech rhythm as well as metrical convenience.

It is clear from b-verse metre that alliterative poets normally realised compounds in the same way we do today, with single compound stress on the first word. Here are some examples:

st[á]r[k]e-blynde wéxen (*SJ* 580b; MS *storte*)
thre gráyhondes of sáble (*MA* 2521b)[83]
of chálk-whytte sýluer (*MA* 2522b)
a scháftmonde lárge (*MA* 2546b)
flóke-mowthede schréwe (*MA* 2779b)
þat héuen-kyng mýntes (*C* 1628b)
by lýnde-wodez éuez (*G* 1178b)
til báwemen hit bréken (*G* 1564b)
and dáy-belle rónge (*E* 117b)
stón-dede þay lýgge (*MA* 3823b)

If we were to scan these compounds in the same way as Duggan and Cable scan compounds in extended a-verses, these verses would have to be either 'exceptions' or verses with three ictus positions. The simple alternative is to assume, as we do, that normal compound stress operates in extended verses. This also avoids the need to invent another metrical type, namely the four-beat a-verse, which Duggan and Cable would need to cope with a-verses such as 'Gódfader and gódmoder' (*PP* B 9.97a), 'Ful gráyþely gos þis gódman' (*C* 341a), and 'Bed me bilýue my bále stour and brýng me on énde (*P* 426).

[82] Duggan, 'Stress Assignment', p. 325.

[83] Quantifiers (here 'three') are weakly stressed. See below, pp. 199, 208–9.

The double-accenting of compounds is very much the exception rather than the rule, and occurs when the second beat has nowhere suitable to go, as in the following cases:

withinne a hónde-whýle (*C* 1786b)
vpon Krýstmásse (*G* 37b; cf. 471b)
Boþe þe kynges síster-súnes (*G* 111a)
þat seen hire gódchíldren (*PP* B 9.77b)
alle þe wóke týme (*SJ* 1285b)
vpon wódcráftez (*G* 1605b)
vnder wódbýnde (*P* 446b, cf. 497b)

*G* 111a and *PP* B 9.97b may seem anomalous, since there are other open-class words in contention for the beat ('king' and 'see'), but 'king' has become a semi-pronoun in *G*,[84] and 'see' is a stative verb, and these often take weak stress.[85]

Complex words show similar patterns. Alliterative poets are at liberty to bestow the beat on the secondary stress of a polysyllabic word, but only when the surrounding words provide no competition for accent. So we have

And crýed for hís mysdéde' (*G* 760*rh*)
and schéwed hys mysdédez' (*G* 1880b)
ȝour séggez are supprýsside (*MA* 1420b)
mýskaries he néuer' (*MA* 2872b)
fórfete his blýsse (*C* 177b)

but in the absence of strongly stressed words we get:

that thus are mýskáryede' (*MA* 1237b)
As þou hadeȝ neuer fórféted (*G* 2394a)
and his mýsdédes' (*P* 287b)
þat þus was súpprísede (*MA* 1845b)

Other examples are words like 'prophecy' and 'courtesy', which can *either* be double-accented, in

Bot súm for córtaysýe' (*G* 247*rh*)
bi his cóurtaysýe' (*G* 1300b)
in his prófecíes (*C* 1158b)[86]
of ídolatrýe (*C* 1173b)

*or* single-accented, in

þat córtaysy úses (*G* 1491b)
His clánnes & his córtaysye (*G* 653a)
And þe prýce of þe prófetie (*C* 1308a)
With ýmages of ȝoure ýdolatry (*WA* 4588a)

Depending on the contexts in which compounds or complex words are embedded, the secondary stresses (on prefixes, suffixes and compound

[84] See above, p. 160.
[85] See below, p. 189.
[86] Cf. *Pearl* 821, 'He sáyde of hým þys prófessýe'.

elements) — which may have been closer to even stresses in Middle English than in modern pronunciation[87] — may or may not be heard as beats. Although the variations between single- and double-accented words may seem to complicate metrical analysis, hearing the verses correctly is simply a matter of perceiving the two most prominent syllables in the verse as the beats (as we naturally do). Syllables with primary or secondary stress are thus no more than *potential* beats.[88]

The variable treatment of compounds and complex nouns is not a peculiarity of the metrical grammar of alliterative poets but a fact of linguistic competence, and as such it is reflected in medieval and later verse at large. Thus in *Pearl*, too, single-accented compounds (*strópe-men*, 115, *dáy-glem*, 1094) are found alongside double-accented ones (*áldermén*, 1119, *lómpe-lýȝt*, 1046). We find the same flexibility in Chaucer, who can stress either (or both) elements in compounds and even complex words. Ten Brink usefully observes that this flexibility has its source in 'two antagonistic tendencies' in the language: on the one hand, a tendency to treat the two words as one lexical item (usually, but not always, with initial stress) and, on the other hand, 'a tendency to accentuate the second element of a compound felt as such, and consequently to emphasise a living derivative suffix by the accent'.[89] These antagonistic tendencies are reflected in conflicting metrical patterns: compounds and complex words can be double-stressed or single-stressed, and so have one or two beats, and on occasion the second element may take the beat instead of the first. So in Chaucer even well established words such as 'household', 'friendship' and 'forhead' are occasionally accented on the suffix (see respectively *CT* III.99, *HF* 307, *CT* I.154).

A further complication is that compounds are not always easy to distinguish from other word groups (such as adjectives+nouns). The convention of writing compounds as one word did not exist, and, conversely, combinations of adjective+noun and preposition+noun frequently appear in medieval manuscripts without word division.[90] Much therefore depends on the interpretation of editors. For example, in *C* 50,

[87] There is evidence to suggest that the secondary stress was rather more prominent in Middle and Early Modern English. See E. J. Dobson, *English Pronunciation 1500–1700*, 2 vols, 2nd edn. (Oxford, 1968), I, 445.

[88] See Tarlinskaja, *Studies*, pp. 32–3.

[89] Ten Brink, *Language*, p. 197.

[90] Hans Sauer, *Nominalkomposita im Frühmittelenglischen mit Ausblicken auf die Geschichte der englischen Nominalkomposition* (Tübingen, 1992), p. 71.

'ȝet hým is þe hýȝe kyng hárder in héuen', 'high king' may not look like a compound (and is not glossed as such by the editor), but the frequent and historic collocation of *high* and *king* surely gives the poet the option of treating the noun phrase as one lexical unit, a compound (after OE *heahcyning*), with normal compound stress on the first word.[91] *Kyng* is therefore weakly stressed and the pronoun *hym* naturally takes the beat, not because of any 'promotion rule' but because the intonation responds to the 'thematic fronting'[92] of the pronoun: the indirect object (the unclean man) is the poet's 'theme' and is accordingly placed before the subject and verb. The treatment of 'high king' as a compound also explains the iambic verse of *Pearl* 596, 'Þou hȝe kyng áy pretérminábl e', *G* 1038b, þe héȝe Kyng yow yélde', and *G* 1963, 'Your hónour at þis hýȝe fest þe hýȝe kyng yow yélde', where 'hye fest' may also be considered as a compound with initial stress (cf. *heyday*, OE *heohfreols*, Dutch *hoogfeest*). We emphasise that this is an option, not an inevitability: the noun may perfectly well be accented also (as we have seen), and we see this flexibility not as a sign of indifference to ordinary language but as a recognition of its multiple possibilities: some noun phrases can justly be analysed and articulated either as one lexical item (with compound stress) or as an adjective followed by a noun (with even stress). Compounds consisting of two nouns give rise to similar ambiguities. The first nouns in such phrases as *helle hole* and *heuene kyng* can legitimately be analysed either as compound elements or as genitives in a complex noun phrase,[93] and in that grey area different accentual possibilities can thrive.

One accentual possibility that needs further attention is the phenomenon of stress-shift (whereby the second rather than the first element in a compound or the affix in a complex word is stressed).

[91] There is further evidence that alliterative poets poets did so in certain b-verses where metre (e.g. the restriction of the long b-verse dip to three unstressed syllables) indicates that 'high' was not treated as an adjective (see *Death and Liffe*, 212, 264, where 'high' is uninflected despite preceding 'the').

[92] The terms 'thematic fronting' and the definition of 'theme' as the 'communicative point of departure' are due to Quirk and Greenbaum, *University Grammar*, §14.10.

[93] Cf. Tauno F. Mustanoja, *A Middle English Grammar* (Helsinki, 1960), p. 72: 'The interesting question whether the first member of combinations like *chirche dore*, *dore bem*, *helle houndes*, and *sterre lyht* is to be understood simply as an *s*-less genitive or whether the attributive use of the nominative must also be taken into consideration … has not been elucidated in a fully satisfactory way so far'.

Although stress-shift is often thought to be a metrical licence, it is apt to occur also in spoken language. In some compounds and complex words fluctuating stress is normal. We tend to say, for example, 'mánkind', 'wéekend', 'thírteen', when they come before strongly stressed words, but 'mankínd, weekénd, thirtéen' at the end of tone units. Even apparently 'stable' compounds are liable to shift stress at the end of tone units. Here are some examples (the first two based on recorded speech):

> My secretary takes very good *shorthánd*
> The road is below *sea lével*[94]
> The solution seemed *fool-próof*[95]

As Bolinger notes, such stress-shifts are conditioned by our habit of 'putting the main accent as far to the right as [we] dare ... and frequently ... on a syllable ... farther to the right than the recognized lexical stress.'[96] James Bailey draws attention to this aspect of our linguistic competence in order to explain why his amateur readers had no difficulty executing the apparently 'artificial' stress shifts demanded in Yeats's poem 'Cap and Bells', where rhyme and the strict alternation of masculine and feminine line endings require:

> It had grówn wise-tóngued by thínking
> Of a qúiet and líght footfáll;
>
> But the yóung queen wóuld not lísten
> She róse in her pále night-gówn. (7–10)

Bailey notes that 'Yeats has skillfully rigged the rhythm by positioning the compound nouns so that they come before a marked break at the end of the line, where a terminal intonation contour is most likely to produce the desired shift.'[97] If comparable stress-shifts in Middle English verse were *not* connected with speech rhythms, it would be hard to explain why here, too, they occur predominantly at the end of a tone units, not just at line ending (where rhyme might be said to dictate it) but also before a caesura (as in *House of Fame*, 307).

[94] The two examples are given in Tarlinskaja, *English Verse*, p. 61.
[95] The example is due to James Bailey, 'Linguistic Givens and their Metrical Realization in a Poem by Yeats', *Language and Style*, 8 (1975), 21–33.
[96] Bolinger, 'Accent is Predictable', p. 644.
[97] Bailey, 'Linguistic Givens', p. 26.

Although cases of compounds or complex words with oxytonic stress are rare in alliterative verse (as in rhymed verse), it is significant that they occur typically at line ending or before the caesura:

> Lýftande vp his eghelýddes (*E* 178a)
> to réche hondesélle (*G* 66b)[98]
> And hit lýfte vp þe yȝelýddez (*G* 446a)[99]
> Láykyng of enterlúdeȝ (*G* 472a)
> He métez me þis godmón (*G* 1932a)
> at bóþ noseþrýlles (*SJ* 1203b)
> and lépen þiderwárdes (*E* 61b)
> Þe þéeffe at þe dede-thráwe (*MA* 1150a)
> býnne þe schippe búrde (*MA* 804b)
> hur hóle lif-tíme (*B* 565b)
> & bríngen hur a niht-bríd (*B* 723a)
> oþer mýry baw-lýne (*C* 417b)[100]
> Parfórmed þe hyye fáder (*C* 542a)[101]
> and ráȝt hem lyflóde (*C* 561b)
> in hárd iisse-íkkles (*G* 732b)[102]
> and sétte on þe walle síde (*SJ* 806a)
> Léches by torche-líȝt (*SJ* 850a)

As might be expected, oxytonic stress on the compound becomes likelier if the first element is semantically weak. In the following examples, the first element of the compound remains recognisable as an adjectival or adverbial premodifier (*mid-*, *ay-*, *half-*, *wel-*, *alder-*, *clen-*) or is a

[98] In this example, the poet deserves credit for making visible the word's etymological status as compound. ME *hanselle* 'gift' appears in the familiar spelling and accentuation at *G* 491a, 'This hánselle hatȝ Árthur', where it is barely recognisable as a compound at all, but in the form 'hondesélle' (< OE *hand-selen* 'pledge by hand') the word's origin as compound has been made new, in order that the accent can naturally settle on the head word *selen.*

[99] We should not discount the possibility that this stress pattern is in fact the normal one. Cf. *G* 1201a, 'And vnlóuked his yȝe-líddez', and *MA* 3953a, 'Lókes on his eye-líddis'.

[100] Cf. *P* 104b, 'þe spáre bawe-lýne'. Influence from French *boeline* may be a factor here.

[101] The word was a compound in OE (*heahfader*); whether the poet conceptualised it as such is doubtful.

[102] B-verse metre requires emendation to 'hard[e]'; the alternative would be to suppose subordination of the adjective 'hard', but alliterative poets do not double-accent compounds at line ending in the presence of content words.

noun of broad semantics and low accentual rank (*man*, *day*, *way*).[103] Examples are not restricted to pre-caesural or line-terminal position:

> Þe wayférande fréke3 (*C* 79a)[104]
> inmónge3 mankýnde (*C* 278b)[105]
> wyth monkýnde þére (*C* 564b)
> A wel-lángaged lúd (*B* 171a)
> Clene-míndede mén (*B* 626a)
> til mydmórn páste (*G* 1280b)
> By alder-trúest tóken (*G* 1486a)
> Here mý3t abóute mydný3t (*G* 2187*rh*)
> Árþurez half-súster (*G* 2464b)
> and halfe-déd hym léuys (*WA* 3330b)
> Qwen þe day-ráw róse (*WA* 392a; cf. 5181a and *C* 893a)
> For þe ay-lástande lífe (*E* 347a)

It would be false to speak of stress-shift here, for the contours here are not abnormal.

The use of oxytonic compounds thus appears to be patterned: they either come before a strong syntactic break or have as their first compound item a word that semantically weak. Toshio Nakao lists various additional examples of oxytonic compounds in alliterative verse,[106] which

[103] As we demonstrate below, pp. 197–8.

[104] The modern pronunciation, with primary stress on *way* may be a misleading guide to early English pronunciation in which the compound is unstable. Poets such as Robert Manning and Henry Lovelich, who write in alternating rhythm, may have put the main stress on *faring*, for both open lines with 'wey-farende men' (*Chronicle*, ed. F. J. Furnivall, 2 vols, Rolls Series (London, 1887), I, 3659), 'weyfaryng men' (*History of the Holy Grail*, ed. F. J. Furnivall, EETS ES 20, 24, 28, 30, 95 (London, 1874–1905), 45.758.45.758). Cf. Spenser, *Fairy Queene*, V.xi.330, 'An aged wight wayfaring all alone'. *MA* has the noun 'wayfare' (1797), alliterating on /w/, but that is the only attestation of the noun in Middle English, so there is no telling what the 'regular' pronunciation of this compound was (if indeed there was one).

[105] The beat is likely to fall on the preposition 'inmonge3'. The poet's normal form is 'among', 'inmonges' being a metrical speciality used to manipulate the syllable count. See above, p. 54.

[106] Toshio Nakao, *The Prosodic Phonology of Late Middle English* (Tokyo, 1978), p. 123. Nakao's book is useful for the material it gathers, but the data need checking and re-interpreting now that the metrical constraints of the alliterative long line are becoming clearer. A third exception, not discussed by Nakao, is *B* 258a, which appears in Skeat's edition as 'Þe rihte-wisnesse wite'. As the definite

allow us to test the reliability of our 'rules' further. We find that all cases fall within the rules, with two possible exceptions:

For almus-déde dó ȝe non as ȝe démen álle (*B* 870)
Þat most mýrþe myȝt méue þat Crystenmás whýle (*G* 985)

Neither of these exceptions is inexplicable. At *B* 870, the inversion of subject, verb and object seems designed not only to ease the stress on 'dó' but also to create a grammatical break that assists the required stress-shift in 'almus-déde'. At *G* 985, the curious stress pattern 'Crystenmás' coincides with an unusual spelling (the normal spelling being 'Krystmasse' or 'Cristmasse', as in *G* 37, 471, 1655, *etc.*),[107] which may well be deliberate. For in the spelling 'Crystenmas', 'Crysten' (< OE *cristen*) is the *adjective* (see OED s.v. *Christenmas*), and compounds in which the first element can be recognized as an adjective or adverb are more naturally oxytonic.

One final consideration, which is particularly important because we are dealing with poetry, is that freshly coined compounds, in Attridge's words, 'function more easily in metrical environments which permit the first stress to be demoted.' Without a pre-existing 'citation form', the stress can go where it likes. Attridge's example is:

The háir soft-lífted bý the wínnowing fíeld (Keats, 'To Autumn')

The above-cited passage from Yeats's 'Cap and Bells' contains another fine ilustration:

It had grówn wise-tóngued by thínking

(In both cases, the adjectival status of the first compound element may be a contibutory factor.)

The *Gawain* poet's verse contains a finely worked example of a compound with second-word stress:

Vch hílle hade a hátte, a myst-hákel húge (*G* 2081)

'Mist-hakel' in *G* 2081 is the poet's own coinage, ingeniously calqued, we suggest, on the familar word 'mass-hakel' ('mass cope'). In this new-

inflexion on 'right' shows, however, this is an adjective + noun combination (*wisnesse* = wisdom, judgement).

[107] The only other exception is *G* 502a, 'After Crýstenmas cóm', where the longer form is needed for the long medial dip.

minted compound, the lexical stress is bound to be indeterminate, and so the requirements of alliteration can settle the matter.

A final illustration of the Gawain poet's inventiveness is the contour he creates for his periphrasis of Christ as 'both God and man':

> So cléne watȝ his hóndelyng    vche órdure hit schónied,
> And þe grópyng so góud    of Gód and man bóþe ...(*C* 1101–2)

'Man' tends to be weakly stressed when preceded by an adjective or where it stands for the indefinite pronoun 'one', but in this context it is not semantically weak, for the poet says that Christ is both human and divine, 'God and man'. Later writers conveyed the consubstantiality of Father and Son by means of the compound 'godman' (see *OED* for examples); the *Gawain* poet does it by treating of God-and-man as a prosodic unit, with compound stress on the first element.

To sum up, the stress patterns of compounds and complex words cannot be predicted according to a simple rule. A variety of factors (semantics, context, poetic design) need to be taken into account.

*Adverbs, Pronouns and Prepositions*

With regard to the stressing of adverbs, Cable's position (that the issue is 'complex, involving the rhythmical structures of the verse, the pattern of alliteration, semantic considerations, *etc.*') seems to us the correct one. We hope in this section to elucidate some of these factors, and to show that the syllable-count is not the decisive factor that Duggan claims it to be. While it is true that many monosyllabic adverbs (e.g. *now*, *then*, *there*, *aye*, *here*, *so*, *thus*) tend to be weakly stressed,[108] this is not just a matter of the syllable count. Marina Tarlinskaja treats these adjectives as 'adverbs of broad semantics' that tend to be unstressed in English, but it may be possible to characterise the situation more carefully. Based on an analysis of recorded speech, Gussenhoven distinguished five kinds of words or phrases that appear frequently as the nuclear tail of intonation units:

(1) time-space markers (e.g. 'today', 'from time to time');

[108] A good source of evidence for the unstressed nature of these adverbs is Richard Spalding's *Alliterative Katherine Hymn*, ed. Ruth Kennedy, in *Three Alliterative Saints' Hymns: Late Middle English Stanzaic Poems*, EETS, OS 321 (Oxford, 2003). Spalding uses these adverbs to secure feminine line endings. See Ad Putter, 'Weak *e* and the Metre of Richard Spalding's *Alliterative Katherine Hymn*', *Notes and Queries*, n.s. 52 (2005), 288–92.

(2) cohesion markers which express logical or discursive connections (e.g. 'then', 'so', 'though', 'on the other hand');

(3) hearer-appeal markers (e.g. final vocatives and comment phrases, such as 'sir', 'you know');

(4) report phrases, e.g. 'he said';

(5) approximatives, that is, expressions that indicate the approximate nature of a proposition (e.g. 'more or less').

It is useful to approach adverbs in alliterative verse with Gussenhoven's categories in mind. In the following b-verses, adverbs belonging to the first two of Gussenhoven's categories do not alliterate and so appear to be weakly stressed. B-verse metre shows that some of these adverbs must be polysyllabic:

but súch neuer áre (*G* 239b)
þer dóel euer dwéllez (*C* 158b)
and sere fýue sýþez ('and in each case five times', *G* 632b)
that heghe in héuen síttez (*MA* 1261b)[109]
gós theder sóne (*G* 935b)
wýnne hider fást (*G* 2215b)
bóȝed hider fýrst (*G* 2524b)
whereso þe báre schéwed (*C* 791b)
how-se-euer þe déde túrned (*G* 1662b)
máy þereof wýnne (*B* 1038b)
and þerto ȝé trýst (*G* 2325b)

Semantic considerations evidently outweigh syllabic ones in these instances. For example, *þer* is unstressed but so is *þider*; and we see no reason why the principle should cease to be relevant if the word were expanded further, as in 'And búskyd thiderward býtime (*E* 112a).

For our purposes, it is convenient to take 'approximatives' as a subspecies of a larger category, namely adverbs of degree, which are the adverbial equivalent of quantitative adjectives. As Kingdon has noted, quantitatives are frequently weakly stressed, and so are adverbs of degree (scarcely, very much, nearly, *etc*) — which 'often lose their stress when

[109] Our accentuation is guided by the consideration that 'high' is an adverb of place and of low alliterative rank while 'heaven' is high-ranking. See the statistics and discussion in Borroff, '*Sir Gawain*', pp. 75–6, 78, 83–5. Note also *Pearl* 207: 'Hiȝe pýnakléd of clér quyt pérle'.

they precede strongly stressed words'.[110] Below are some b-verse examples:

clécde euen óuer ('completely covered over') (*MA* 3241b)
and sumquat chíldgéred (*G* 86b)
hit fáyre innoghe thóȝt (*G* 803b)
and mychel Chríst lóued (*SJ* 277b, cf. 897b)
cóuþe aluendel rékene (*SJ* 132b; *aluendel* = 'the half part')
þat fayn scápe wólde (*P* 155b; *fayn* = 'very much')
wýȝe half so blýþe (*G* 2321b)

Intensifiers also belong here. Cable and Duggan make allowances for *ful*, but fail to recognize that many other words can function as intensifiers and are stressed in exactly the same way as *ful*:

a wonder bréme nóyse (*G* 2200b)
a ferly fáire tóumbe (*E* 46b)
& ferly fáire schápen (*WA* 5049b)
to swyþe grét nóumbre (*C* 1283b)
he wépt swiþe sóre (*PP* B 5.462)

It is only logical to assume that the same pattern obtains in a-verses such as the following from *C*:

For wonder wróth is þe wýȝ (*C* 5a)
And distrésted him wonder stráyt (*C* 880a)
So ferly fówled her flésch (*C* 269a)
And ferly fláyed þat fólk (*C* 960a)
Ferly férd watȝ her flésch (*C* 975a)

Or in these a-verses, with adverbs of degree, from *C* and *G*:

Lénge a lyttel with þy léde (*C* 614a)
Þenne lóke a littil on þe láunde (*G* 2146a)
And schránke a lytel with þe schúlderes (*G* 2267a)

Our suggestion that certain adverbs of degree, cohesion, and time-space, are of low accentual rank may also clarify the stress patterns of verses that infringe rules based on lexical categories. In the following examples from *G*, words that should be unstressed take the beat:

nót a whyle sésed (*G* 134b; *a whyle* = adv. 'for a moment')
Neuer-þe-lece to mý méte (*G* 474a)
Welneȝ to úche háþel (*G* 867a)

[110] Kingdon, *Groundwork*, p. 197.

for hít was nieȝ nýȝt (*G* 1922b)

'Nevertheless' is a cohesive marker, 'a whyle' an adverbial phrase of time, while 'welneȝ' and 'nieȝ' are adverbs of degree.[111] Our hypothesis that the words are weakly stressed explains why the beat can fall on words that should be unstressed by Duggan and Cable's rules.

Whether or not pronouns take the beat depends also on semantic factors, and the notion that pronouns (except ones in *–self*) are unstressed is simply wrong. Quite apart from the issue of contrastive stress, a distinction must be made between *anaphoric* pronouns that refer back to an antecedent that is 'lexically presupposed' and deictic pronouns, which pick out a person (or class of persons) that has not yet been specified. The former are naturally unstressed in the language, but the latter are stressed more strongly (e.g. 'Give it to *her*', '*He* who speaks will die').

This fact is the obvious explanation for the following stress patterns in alliterative verse:

He es éldare than Í and énde sall we bóthen (*MA* 4151)
Nor Í, quod an Ápeward, by áuȝt þat I knówe (*PP* B 5.631)
Bot let hým þat ál shulde lóute' (*G* 248*rh*)
And syþen I háue in þis hóus hým þat al lýkez (*G* 1234)
He hátes hélle no more þen hém þat are sówle (*C* 168)
A God hólde ȝe hým hélplich of gráce (*B* 673)
Þen húmmed hé þat þer lay and his hédde wággyd (*E* 281)
And suþ hónsched on hém þat þis hóld képyn (*SJ* 980)

These pronouns single out a person or type of person that has not yet been specified in the discourse (in many examples the specification follows in the restrictive relative clause). The promotion rule cannot cope with *PP* B 5.631a (since compounds such as 'Apeward' have two possible ictus positions); nor can it cope with *B* 673a or *E* 281a, where 'God' and 'lie' are open-class words but of of low accentual rank, as we shall see. And while the 'promotion rule' does seem to work for the other lines, its usefulness is illusory. For the problem is that the rule gives us no guidance about *which* of the various minor-category words are to be elevated. In the examples before us, how would such a rule prevent us from stressing *He* (or *is*) instead of *I* in the first example; *an* rather than *I* in the second; and so on? The answer is of course that we naturally stress the pronouns in 'Nor me!' and 'He is older than me', because

[111] 'Nieȝ' could conceivably be the preposition.

*me* is in both cases deictic and the rightmost word in an independent intonation unit. And if normal intonation patterns apply, then why do we need the promotion rule in the first place?

The failure to discriminate between deictic and anaphoric pronouns leads to another error in the orthodox stress rules. According to Duggan, pronouns in *–self* are accented, but again we need to distinguish between *deictic* reflexive pronouns (which single out the person involved) and *anaphoric* ones. The contrast still applies in our language. Contrast: 'he dréssed himself and went óut' with 'I wóuld not say so mysélf'. As in Modern English, pronouns in *–self* are often unstressed in alliterative verse when they are not isolative (barring inversion):

> þat sáue hemself tráwed (*C* 388b)
> Þaȝ þou bére þyself bábel (*C* 582a)
> Þe kérchef clánsed hitself (*SJ* 245a)

Prepositions are also more complicated than Duggan or Cable allow for. We have already drawn attention to some prepositions derived from nouns and adjectives (*maugré*, *sauf*), which stand on their pedigree and take the beat ahead of open-class words. But these are not the only troublemakers. Prepositions with unstressed objects that come at the end of tone units usually attract strong stress in spoken English.[112] An example from recorded speech is the following utterance (transcribed by David Crystal, who uses capital letters to indicate the main sentence stress):

> /the second deplorable thing ABOUT it/

Such contours are also found in alliterative verse:

> I kéuered me a cómfort   þat now is cáȝt fró me (*P* 485)
> Enter ín þenn, quoþ hé,   and háf þi wif wíth þe (*C* 349)

Cable's rules cannot cope at all with these verses. With his promotion rule Duggan at least goes some way towards recognizing that acoustic prominence is relative, but he misses the point by thinking that such relativity is entirely a matter of the presence or absence of open-class words. *C* 349, 'and háf þi wif wíth þe', shows it is not so, for 'wíth' takes the beat regardless of open-class 'wif'.

The other examples we found of accented prepositions that take the beat in preference to open-class words have a number of things in

[112] See Kingdon, *Groundwork*, p. 200.

common, all of which may be relevant. Consider the following extended verses:

> býnne þe schippe búrde (*MA* 804b)
> and únder campe hóres (*C* 1695b)[113]
> bifóre her boþe ýȝen (*C* 978b)
> bífore þe halle ȝátez (*G* 1694b)
> amóng þe fre ládyes (*G* 1885b)
> abóute þe hals késtes (*G* 621b)
> abóute foure mýle (*SJ* 292b' aboute' is all around')
> He máde inmýddi[s þe] ost (*SJ* 1317a; 'ost' = crowd)

The metrical set and the rhythm rule may be helping out the prepositions, and so may the fact that some of the noun phrases ('four miles', 'noble ladies', 'ship board' and 'hall gate') form recognizable units that tend to take only a single stress. Although this stress would normally fall on the modifier,[114] at line ending the contour is subject to stress-shift, as we have seen. It is important to realize, however, that the prepositions in question have a significant degree of stress to begin with. The semantic distinction between concrete and abstract prepositions can tell us why. As Bolinger notes, the stressing of 'It is únder the táble' differs from 'He is under an obligátion' because *under* is spatial in the former example but abstract in the latter.[115] When we look at the preposition+ noun combinations in which the preposition takes the beat, it is striking that such prepositions are usually spatial.[116] As such they bear out Sweet's insight that 'prepositions of definite and marked meaning may have full stress ... those of indefinite and abstract meaning are generally subordinated'.[117] A final consideration to be factored in is the syllable count. The longer a word, the greater the likelihood that one of its syllables will be strongly stressed. So, although an alliterating preposition such as 'inmýddis' looks anomalous from the perspective of Duggan's or Cable's stress rules, the fact that it has three syllables makes it a plausible accent-bearer. Cf. 'inmýddez þe flóre' (*G* 1932b), 'Now inmýddez þe méte' (*C* 125a). As has already been observed, 'among' never takes the

[113] We suspect scribal error here (read *anunder*).
[114] Cf. 'séxty mile fórthir' (*MA* 478b), 'The góude ladyeȝ were géten' (*G* 1625a), Þer háles in at þe hálle dor' (*G* 136a).
[115] *Intonation and Its Uses*, p. 106.
[116] We find only one anomaly, *WA* 572b, 'was óf hir son líȝtir', which we discuss below, pp. 202–3.
[117] Sweet, *Grammar*, p. 35.

beat in *B*, but 'amongus' always does; the same is true of the Cotton Nero poems and *MA*.[118]

To conclude this section: prepositions, pronouns and adverbs in alliterative verse display stress patterns which are not accounted for by the current rules of stress assignment but, rather, correspond to patterns in the language. Duggan's principle that accentuation is based on 'normal prose phrase stress' is therefore worth more than the rules he actually proposes.

*Verbs*

It is widely believed that verbs qualify as staves unless they belong to the restricted categories of modals, auxiliaries, and copulas or exceptions ('to be', 'to have'). We hope to show in this section that many other verbs can be unaccented, mainly depending on meaning, register and rhythm. Our evidence is based on a survey of non-alliterating lexical verbs in extended b-verses and in the rhyming lines of *G*. When we examined our data, the non-alliterating verbs seemed to fall into one of five categories: (1) stative verbs; (2) verbs of speech; (3) common verbs of motion; (4) verbs with verbal complements; and (5) high-frequency verbs. In this section we have tried to present all the data in the form of an argument that aims to make sense of the family resemblances they display. Our general conclusion is that one cannot tell whether a verb is stressed or not without taking meaning and register into account.

Meaning deserves to come first. As Cable's stress rules recognise, 'have' is a regular problem case, and a few examples will show he is right:

þat han in hért ráuþe (*P* 21b) haue of héȝþe þrétté (*C* 317b)
to haue hóle sýdes (*G* 1338b) þe déuel haue þat récche! (*SJ* 786b)

His solution is to set 'have' apart as an exceptional verb that is always unaccented. However, this simplifies not only the behaviour of the verb 'to have' but also that of verbs with a similar sense (e.g. *hold*, *bear*, *get*), which turn out to behave in similar ways.

To deal with 'have' first, readers may already have noticed that 'have' takes the beat in 'and háf þi wyf wíth þe' (*C* 349b). Of course, the specific sense of *haf* in this verse is not 'have' but 'take', but that merely goes to show that semantic considerations come into play at every stage: *have* in the sense of 'bring, take' readily takes the beat because in that

[118] See above, p. 54.

sense it is a *dynamic* verb, not a *stative* verb that expresses abstract relationships.[119] It is also accentable in the sense of 'have' when it is a main verb (e.g. *G* 496, 1806, 2218), but not, it seems, in preference to other open-class items, unless it comes at the end of the line (see *G* 210, 1283), for there *all* words (excepting only enclitic pronouns) take the beat as a matter of course. The *form* taken by the verb also matters. It is instructive in this regard to compare *G* 1962 with *G* 1252. At *G* 1962, Gawain thanks his host for the hospitality he has received:

> Of such a sélly sóiorne as Í haf had hére
> Your hónour at þis hýȝe fest, þe hýȝe kyng yow ȝélde ... (1962–3)

The alliterative patterning is a fine example of linking alliteration: 'as' and 'I' merge in natural pronunciation to provide the alliterating syllable /s/. The accents on 'I' and 'here' imply a contrastive focus: Gawain has received hospitality on many occasions but his stay in Hautdesert has been extra special. Now contrast 1962–3 with the superficially similar line 1252, where the Lady of the Castle tries to flatter Gawain:

> Bot hit are ládyes innóȝe þat léuer wer nówþe
> Haf þe, hénde, in hor hólde, as I þe hábbe hére ... (1251–2)

It seems to us likely that *habbe* takes the beat. In terms of semantic weight only 'I' (the focus of the ladies' envy) and 'habbe' (I've *got* you) would be in contention, but what swings the balance of probability in favour of the latter is the poet's striking use of the marked form *habbe* instead of his normal form *haf* or *haue*. The form is otherwise only ever used at line ending to avoid the masculine ending and is highly anomalous in the poet's dialect.[120] By choosing a highly distinctive form, the poet has made the verb remarkable, and 'remarkableness' and sentence stress go hand in hand.

The verb 'to have' is not alone in defying current rules of stress, for other verbs in the same semantic field also cause trouble. Thus the verbs

[119] Cf. *C* 1443, 'Þe áþel áuter of brasse watȝ háde into pláce'. (For the scansion of the a-verse see our discussion of non-count nouns below, pp. 203–4.)

[120] Apart from the Cotton Nero poems, *LALME* records no other uses of 'habbe' forms in the whole of the North-West Midlands. The poet seems to have borrowed this and a number of other forms (e.g. *segge* for 'say') from an adjacent Central-West Midland dialect. See Ad Putter and Myra Stokes, 'The Linguistic Atlas'.

'bear', 'hold' and 'get' also occur in extended verses, without apparently attracting the beat:

> Ér gete ȝe no hápe, I hópe forsóþe (*P* 212)
> and helde þe Róunde Táble (*MA* 53b)
> þat bare his brände rýche (*MA* 893b)
> and holde my Róunde Táble (*MA* 3214b)
> þat Crýst bare Hym sélfen (*MA* 3426b)
> þat haldez fýue póyntez (*G* 627b)
> Cowþ wél hald láyk alófte (*G* 1125*rb*)
> helde séuen mýle (*C* 1387b)
> and cróune bar of þórnes (*PP* B 19.49b)

At *P* 212 the alliteration falls on *er*. *Er* does not seem to alliterate anywhere else in this corpus except in the absence of strong competition, and that exceptional situation arises with *gete* in *P* 212. 'Hold' and 'bear' also occur in non-alliterating position. It appears that it is the semantic properties (and not the lexical category) of these verbs that accounts for the lack of accent.

What we have said about verbs that share the same basic meaning as 'have' applies also to verb with senses synonymous with 'to be'. That the main verb 'to be' is normally unaccented (even when not a copula) should not be contentious (see *C* 1000b, *C* 1034b, *P* 23b, *etc*),[121] but, as in the case of 'have', the same is true of verbs with a similar sense. In the following b-verses, the verbs are practically synonymous with 'to be':

> in mýnde stod lónge (*E* 97b)[122]
> and qúyck go hymséluen (*G* 2109b)
> þer cóstese lay drýe (*C* 460b)

Given the 'contentlessness' of the verbs it is hardly surprising that poets should treat them in the same way as 'to be', i.e. as verbs of low accentual rank.

We think that the undynamic sense of these verbs (coupled with their commonness) may have something to do with this. Some interesting linguistic research on the stress patterns of simple sentence structures containing subject and verb suggests that the dynamism of the verb is also a factor in speech rhythm. Generally, in clauses with a single

[121] But see Duggan, who (in 'Extended A-Verses', p. 72) scans 'Þat ár in Árþurez hóus' (*G* 2102a).

[122] Cf. *G* 344b, 'and stonde bý yow þére', discussed above, p. 164.

argument (subject or object) and predicate (verb), the verb carries the main accent, as in the following examples (from Allerton and Cruttenden, who indicate the sentence stress by means of capitals):

John PROTESTED My cousin's CELEBRATING

But the pattern is different in utterances like the following:

The KETTLE's boiling The PROFESSOR appeared
The CAR broke down The SUN is shining[123]

In these and in other examples adduced by Allerton and Cruttenden, verbs are often predictable (the sun *will* shine, kettles *will* boil) and may denote a state rather than a process. 'The verb may involve a minimum of verbal activity'.[124] Related to this is the tendency of grammatical subjects to be in an affected role rather than an agentive one.

Allerton and Cruttenden's observation could account for the failure of many so-called 'stative verbs' to take the beat in alliterative verse. Quirk and Greenbaum distinguish two kinds of statives: (a) relational verbs expressing abstract or possessive relations between nouns, e.g. *belong to*, *contain*, *possess*, *have*, *contain*, *lack*, *remain*, *be*, *exist*; and (b) verbs of inert perception and cognition, e.g. *believe*, *intend*, *know*, *love*, *dislike*, *see*, *hear*, *regard*, *think*.[125] The 'stativeness' of these verbs is reflected in the facts that many disallow the progressive (or change meaning in the progressive), and that the subjects tend to be non-agentive, which is why a number of such verbs (e.g. 'think' and 'love') were historically impersonal. Having said that, it should always be borne in mind that the choice of an unusual verb can override any tendency to de-accent stative verbs. Bolinger contrasts:

Tómmy saw a béar Tommy spótted a béar[126]

The force of a word is not merely an aspect of its meaning but also of its register.

[123] Allerton and Cruttenden, 'Three Reasons', call 'shine' an 'empty verb' (p. 51). Hence also the stress patterns in *Pearl* 1056, 'Súnne ne móne schon néuer so swéte' and Gower, *CA* 5.6128, 'The flées of góld schon fórth withál'.

[124] Alllerton and Cruttenden, 'Three Reasons', p. 52.

[125] Quirk and Greenbaum, *University Grammar*, §3.35.

[126] Bolinger, *Intonation and Its Uses*, p. 115.

Examining extended b-verses with verbs in our corpus, we observe that many are prosaic stative verbs. We have already dealt with 'have', 'be', and synonymous verbs, but there are many others:

and wende gréf þólie (*B* 50b)
Iwýsse I wot néuer (*G* 1487b)
láte hym wiet sóne (*MA* 420b)
whát-so scho þoȝt élles (*G* 1550b)
me thynke þe dáy hýes (*WW* 453b)
byhelde þe báre érþe (*C* 452b)
þat seen hire gódchíldren (*PP* B 9.77b)
þat féȝt loued bést (*C* 275b)
to gayn here grým sóres (*SJ* 42b)
and warre knáues tácches (*warre* = 'be aware of', *ABC* 19b)[127]
and couthe of cóurte théwes (*MA* 21b)
ech [líf] to know his ówene (*PP* B pr.122)

At *G* 1487b the indefinite pronoun 'what-so' alliterates while the verb 'think' misses out on the beat. This 'irregularity' again occurs with the impersonal 'forþynk'. In *C* 285, 'Mé forþynkes ful múch', the pronoun takes the beat. The most natural explanation is that 'think' and 'forthink' are weakly stressed.

In the wheel, stative verbs also occur without attracting the beat:

Now hýȝe and lét se týte (*G* 299*rh*)
And lét se hów þou cnókez (*G* 414*rh*)
Til hé seȝ Sír Gawáyne (*G* 1619*rh*)
Ech twó had dísches twélue (*G* 128*rh*)
Þaȝ Í hade nóȝt of yóurez (*G* 1815*rh*)

Of course, the rhythm rule and the metrical set work towards the same end, but that they do not tell us the whole story appears from the striking fact that in the rhymed lines of *Gawain* we find no verb in arsis that does not also occur without accent in our sample of extended b-verses. The single exception is 'wield', in 'Weldez nón so hýȝe hawtésse (*G* 2454*rh*). The most obvious factor here is the inversion of subject and verb; but it may be relevant to note that 'weldez', too, is a stative verb (meaning 'has').

Another group of non-alliterating verbs that crop up in extended b-verses are commonplace verbs of movement. Such verbs are generally weakly stressed in Modern English, particularly when they are used together with 'destination adjuncts':

[127] We cite the version in MS Harley 5086, ed. F. J. Furnivall, *The Babees Book: Early English Meals and Manners*, EETS OS 32 (London, 1868), pp. 9–10.

He went to MANCHESTER He's cycled to TOWN[128]

In alliterative verse, too, verbs of movement occur in b-verses without attracting alliteration. For example:

swíþe comeþ jóie (*B* 921b)
and fýrst commes áftyr (*MA* 393b)
came óut [vpon] l[óf]te (*SJ* 465b)
cam ségge of hem áfter (*SJ* 1322b)
& bíddis him ga swýþe (*WA* 1841b)

The wheels of *G* show these same verbs to be unaccented:

Com tó hym tó salúe (*G* 1472*rh*)[129]
He cálde, and hé com gáyn (*G* 1621*rh*)
Syn hé com híder er þís (*G* 1892*rh*)

The choice of register is a contributing factor: 'go' and 'come' are common in the discourse, and unremarkable verbs are more at home in unstressed position than uncommon ones.

This would explain why a number of high-frequency words (*do*, *make*, *give*, *take*) fail to take a beat when followed (or preceded) by a stressed object or adverb. For example:

lí3t 3af abóute (*B* 122b)
and yaf yow fýue wíttes (*PP* B 1.15b)
and dos Gódes héste (*C* 341b)
ménge and ma kákeȝ (*C* 625b)
quat báde makis þou hére (*WA* 3034b)
3euen dépe wóundis (*SJ* 842b)
oure Lórd 3yue vs ióye (*SJ* 896b)
3af hym fále wóundes (*SJ* 930b)
þat made grét nówmbre (*MA* 2884b)
take tént alls I býde (*MA* 3598b)

The idiomatic nature of verb and object collocations ('take tent, give light, make cheer') no doubt has a role to play in some of these verses, but that issue cannot be separated from that of high-frequency verbs, since such verbs are precisely the ones that are likely enter into idiomatic unions in the first place. The stress pattern of 'oure Lórd 3yue vs ióye (*SJ*

[128] The examples are adapted from Gussenhoven, *Grammar and Semantics*, p. 39. Gussenhoven's rule that destination adjuncts rather than verbs will take the accent is subject to the further proviso that the 'register' of the verb matters. We are unlikely to say 'He slithered to TOWN'.

[129] It is possible, but not necessary, to posit initial inversion (cf. Yeats, *Cap and Bells*, 'He báde his héart go tó her') or scribal error. Andrew and Waldron (eds), *Poems*, emend to 'To com hym to salue'.

896b, cf. *PP* A 5.88, *B* 5.108) is especially noteworthy, for it sheds light on the poet's intentions at *SJ* 1112, 'Gróbben faste on þe gróunde, and Gód ȝyue us ióye'. Hanna and Lawton emend *SJ* 1112 to 'and God [g]yue vs ioye' for the sake of metre.[130] However, the parallel case of *SJ* 896 suggests that the verb is unaccented and that the alliterating stave is *God*. The emendation is unnecessary.

Again the wheels of *G* show the same kinds of verbs in arsis:

And ȝét gif hým respíte (*G* 297*rh*) Dréde dotz mé no lóte (*G* 2211*rh*)
Þe knýȝt mad áy god chér (*G* 562*rh*) Þe knýȝt tok gátes stráunge (*G* 709*rh*)

Two further categories of verbs call for special attention. The first consists of verbs of speech, whose special status is demonstrated by b-verses such as these:

sayd þat gáy lády (*G* 1207b)
he sayd bý his tráwþe (*C* 63b)
sayde he nón cóuþe (*SJ* 93b)
quod þe kýnge thán (*MA* 3502b)
quoþ þe háþel þénne (*G* 309b)
ȝe call þe líttil wérde (*WA* 4623b)
and bade góde mórwen (*MA* 3476b)

*C* 63b, with ictus on the preposition, is irregular by the stress rules and the promotion rule, but the stress pattern is exactly paralleled in the wheel: 'Þe lórd said bí saynt Gíle' (*G* 1644*rh*).

The second category consists of verbs that take another verb as their complement. As has long been known, such verbs are likely to lose stress in connected speech:

go and lóok
come to stáy[131]
heard him gó

When 'open-class' verbs are used to introduce another verb, they take on some of the properties of 'closed class' auxiliaries. Again, the tendencies of sentence stress prove their relevance in b-verses that resist scansion on the basis of lexical categories. In the following examples, verbs are prosodically subordinate to the infinitives they introduce:

saien fólk róme (*B* 146b)
sai his prés stínte (*B* 162b)
don ȝou ílle wírche (*B* 754b)
doþ ȝou fúl ófte (followed by inf. *holde*, *B* 880b)

[130] Hanna and Lawton (eds), *Siege*, p. xciii.
[131] The first two examples are from Sweet, *New English Grammar*, II, 32.

bed týrue of þe hýde (*C* 630b)
and beden hym pásse fáste (*C* 942b)
& [biddis] hum gá swýthe (*WA* 1841b)[132]
and seȝes hi bréth fáile (*WA* 5709b)
and bede hem férk úp (*P* 187b)
téris lete he fálle (*MA* 3886b)
ne góssehawke latt flýe (*MA* 4001b)

In the wheel, the same patterns are found:

Bot let hým that ál schulde lóute (*G* 248*rh*)
Dos téchez me óf your wýtte (*G* 1533*rh*)[133]
Þe búrne bed brýng his blónk (*G* 2024*rh*)

The implications for the scansion of extended a-verses are obvious. If the same rules of stress apply to the a-verse, we should not necessarily expect the following verbs to bear sentence stress: (1) speaking verbs; (2) stative verbs, i.e. verbs of perception and cognition, and relational verbs including ones synonymous with 'do' and 'be'; (3) verbs of motion; (4) verbs followed by verbal complements; (5) high frequency verbs, sometimes in idiomatic expressions. We give some examples below; they include some of the hyper-extended a-verses that could have as many as four beats in Duggan and Cable's stress rules:

(1) *speaking verbs*

'Say me, frénde', quoþ þe fréke (*C* 139a)
Þenne sayde oure sýre þer he séte (*C* 661a)
& sayde sóftely to hirsélf (*C* 822a)
Túlkes tolden hym þe tále (*E* 109a)
Praieþ Gód as he góoþ (*SJ* 1023a)
Bed me bílyue my bále stour (*P* 426a)

132 The co-existence of a different prosodic pattern in *WA* 3128, '& [bíddis] þam ga swýth', leads Duggan in 'Authenticity' first to accuse alliterative poets of 'indifference in the assignment of alliteration' (36) and then to conclude that b-verses may have three lifts. As we see it, alliterative poets make intelligent use of the alternative possibilities: since both 'bid' and 'go' are both of low accentual rank, the metrical set will guide us in making the appropriate selection.
133 Tolkien and Gordon punctuate 'Dos, techez', and gloss 'dos' as *Come!* It is more likely that 'do' goes with, and intensifies, the infinitive. See Mustanoja, *Middle English Syntax*, p. 607.

(2) *stative verbs*

(a) *verbs of inert cognition and perception*:

Loueȝ no sált in her sáuce (*C* 823a)
To se þat sémly in séte (*C* 1055a)
& lélly louy þy lórde (*C* 1066a)
& holden gódesse gód (*B* 561a)
Míchel holde ȝe of míht (*B* 653a)
For béter likede him a bál (*B* 934a)
& míche, þinkeþ us, a mán (*B* 1058a)

(b) *relational verbs (some synonymous with 'be' or 'have')*:

And fýue wont of fýfty, quoth god (*C* 739a)
To sytte in séruage & sýte (*C* 1257a)
ȝou wantis wórdliche wón (*B* 891a)
Þe lýppe lyþ on a lúmpe (*SJ* 31a)
Was nóȝt while þe nýȝt laste (*SJ* 425a)
Wéle wanteþ no wýȝe (*SJ* 1280a)
Þat haldez þe héuen vpon hýȝe (*G* 2057a)

(3) *verbs of motion*

Comeȝ cóf to my córt (*C* 60a)
That alle góudes come of Gód (*C* 1326a)
And cum to þat mérk at mýdmorn (*G* 1073a)
Ful gráyþely gos þis gód man (*C* 341a)
Wende wépande awáy (*SJ* 1022a)

(4) *verbs introducing a verbal complement*

ȝe maken stínte of his stréme (*B* 530a)
And loke ye stémme no stépe (*C* 905a)
And hure [= hear] ráches rénne (*SJ* 890a)
And beden Pílate apére (*SJ* 1300a)
To see hem púlle in þe plów (*C* 68a)

(5) *high-frequency verbs (some with idiomatic complements)*

No mércy don to no mán (*B* 901a)
And séggus for ȝe só don (*B* 760a)
And lette lýȝt bi þe láwe (*C* 1174a)
Lauȝte léue of þat lórd (*SJ* 283a)
Þay ȝelden gráce to Gód (*SJ* 258a)
Iche tólk mon do as he is tán (*G* 1811a)
Vch mále matȝ his mách (*C* 695a)
Made hym Crísten kýng (*SJ* 194a)
Settes hir sófly by his sýde (*G* 1479a)

ȝaf hym spáce þat hym spílide (*SJ* 22a)
Gef hym gód and góud day (*G* 2073a)

It should be noted that our scansion benefits the regularity of the metre not just in terms of the number of beats but also in terms of the syllabic structure. In the majority of cases the unaccented verb is swallowed up in the opening anacrusis, so that the expectation of long opening dip (which Cable goes as far as positing as a rule in non-extended a-verses) is also satisfied in most of these extended a-verses. Most a-verses without a long anacrusis have an extra-long medial dip or a long or heavy final dip (which we believe to be a metrical requirement in a-verses without a long initial and medial dip).[134] Most importantly, the scansion is consistent with that of extended b-verses, where verbs in these categories cannot be metrically prominent unless we also admit three beats into the b-verse. However, Occam's razor rule militates against this admission, for 'to wield Occam's razor metrically is to assume that the best analysis is the one which most effectively, efficiently, and reasonably accounts for the largest variety of verses with the fewest units, rules, and exceptions'.[135] If two-beat explanations of extended a-verse and b-verses are reasonable, they are therefore to be preferred.

We make no pretence that the explanations we have produced for the failure of some verbs to take the beat in extended b-verses will take care of all cases of unaccented verbs in the a-verse. The differences between the a-verse and the b-verse in terms of both length and syllabic structure make it more than likely that a-verses pose additional problems. For example, we have found no b-verses that would offer precedents for a-verses such as

Ris, apróche þen to préch (*P* 349a)
Wayteȝ górsteȝ and gréueȝ (*C* 99a)

[134] Noriko Inoue, who in 'A New Theory' and 'A-Verse' argues that extended a-verses can be resolved according to purely metrical subordination rules, recognises these normative tendencies in the rules that she posits. Stated simply, her rule is that, where there are three open-class words, the first will normally be 'subordinated', unless there is no long dip between the second and third open-class words, in which case the second open-class word is subordinated. Her rules generally produce the right results, but unless we take the position that the beats are the product of the poet's metrical set, her rules cannot be accepted as offering an explanation. Metre, as we see it, is a beneficiary and contributory factor in 'subordination', and not the sole efficient cause.
[135] Seymour Chatman, *A Theory of Meter* (The Hague, 1965), p. 118.

Nor is that surprising, for b-verse metre simply does not permit the same degree of expansiveness. This does not mean, however, that reasonable explanations cannot be found. For example, there may be some connection between these cases and the fact that in iambic pentameter imperatives and exclamations are the most common types of open-class word to occur in weak initial position.[136] However, with the isolated exception of *P* 348b, 'lo, þe pláce hére', with unaccented exclamation/ imperative, we do not find any empirical evidence from extended b-verses that can confirm this possibility.

*Adjectives and Nouns*

The study of the prosodic profiles of adjective-noun combinations is further advanced in the fields of linguistics and mainstream metrics than it is in the field of alliterative metre. Cable and Duggan predictably stress both adjective and noun, as their actual scansions show:

Þe déne of þe dére pláce (*E* 144a)[137]
Swéued at þe fýrst swáp (*C* 222)[138]

The proponents of the two-beat a-verses have argued, by contrast, that such combinations may have just one accent, either on the adjective or the noun, as metre requires.

Either of these views (that poets accent *both* open-class words or may accent *one*, whichever is metrically expedient), might seem surprising in the light of what is known about adjective-noun combinations in connected speech and the tradition of English rhymed verse. For in speech the general principles that govern the accentuation of adjective-noun combinations are quite different. The most basic principle is that the choice of sentence stress, where there is a choice, will depend on the relative weight of the two words. When both adjective and noun are of equal status or the noun carries the greater semantic load, the adjective tends to be less prominent. So in the phrase 'a yellow carnation', the second word tends to receive the stronger emphasis.[139] Here the general

[136] Tarlinskaja, 'General and Particular Aspects of Meter', p. 136. The case of *P* 348a 'Ris, approche' may be compared with *CT* VIII.1207, 'Gooth, wálketh fórth...': 'go' and 'ris' are not quite independent imperatives (cf. ModE 'get up and go' , 'go and take a walk').

[137] Duggan, 'Extended A-Verses', p. 72.

[138] Cable, *English Alliterative Tradition*, p. 158.

[139] The example is from Attridge, *Rhythms*, p. 69.

rule (to which there are many exceptions) is what Chomsky and Halle call the 'nuclear stress rule',[140] which holds that English stress patterns replicate the underlying syntactical structures, so that premodifiers are subordinate to the following nouns, verbs to the following objects, and so on. Since one of the functions of prosody is to divide discourse into component parts, grammatical units (whether adjective+noun, subject+ verb, or verb+object) are likely to be perceived and intoned as organised groupings with a weak and a strong member respectively.[141]

Yet the facts are quite different when the noun is indefinite or generic. As Kingdon observes, 'nouns that have such a wide denotation that by themselves they give very little precise information' and 'nouns that denote large classes of persons or things' take sentence stress when standing by themselves to name a member of a general class, but relinquish it very readily when they are preceded by an attributive word.[142] Kingdon's examples of weakly stressed nouns include *man*, *woman*, *fellow*, *nut*, *ship*, *time*, *thing*, and he compares the stressing of 'That's a *nice* thing' with 'That's a nice *picture*.'

To the ground-rule that sentence stress is influenced by the relative specificity of adjective and noun we shall add some further refinements later, but before we complicate the picture let us consider whether it is at all relevant to poetry. Marina Tarlinskaja's study of Shakespeare's verse suggests to us that it is.[143] For in Shakespeare, most 'enclitic' nouns (i.e. nouns found in arsis after a preceding modifier) are ones of broad semantics (such as *thing*, *body*, *man*, *way*, *turn*) and abstract notions of time and space (*hour*, *time*, *year*, *world*, *day*). Thus Shakespeare writes: 'And éach doth góod turns nów untó the óther' (Sonnet 47) and 'what dárk days séen...' (Sonnet 97).

When we examine the practices of alliterative poets it soon becomes clear that they display the same linguistic tendencies. In extended a-verses the 'nuclear stress rule' (i.e. accent the noun and not the preceding adjective) applies in the majority of cases,[144] but alliterative poets are

140 Chomsky and Halle, *Sound Patterns*, p. 7.

141 Attridge, *Rhythms*, pp. 68–9.

142 Kingdon, Groundwork, p. 173.

143 Tarlinskaja, *Shakespeare's Verse*, pp. 220–23. See also her 'General and Particular Aspects of Meter', which give further examples from Fletcher's verse.

144 We discount *DT* (a late poem) as atypical. As shown by Inoue, 'A-Verse', p. 93, and Moriya, 'Alliteration', p. 504, in *DT* adjectives almost always attract the

likely to give weaker stress to the same kinds of words as Shakespeare. In the following b-verses notional words (*kind*, *half*, *thing*, *mile*, *man* and its synonyms) must be unaccented:

súmme men hit hólden (*G* 28b)
and féle kyn físchez (*G* 890b)
þat óþer half áls (*G* 1224b)
þe bólde burn sáyde (*G* 1631b)
þe chéf þyng alósed (*G* 1512b)
of wlónk wyȝeȝ þrýnne (*C* 606b)
with séx score hélmes (*MA* 380b)
séxty myle fórthire (*MA* 478b)
and wýse men of ármys (*MA* 19b)
þat Í haf men ȝárked (*C* 652b)
Þen stód þat stíf mon nére (*G* 322*rh*)

Adjective-noun combinations involving indeterminate nouns such as 'noise', 'tool', 'taste', which grant the adjective the power of specification, can be brought under the same rule. Consider the following verses:

and bréme noyse máked (*G* 1142b)
þat sált sauor hábbes (*C* 995b)
Ta nów þy grýmme tole tó þe (*G* 413*rh*)

The last line, *G* 413*rh*, is of course also subject to the rhythm rule (as is *G* 322*rh* above), but our belief that good poets ensure that the rule has the right material to work with is amply justified both by the fact that adjectives and nouns in the wheel behave in exactly the same way as they do in the alliterative long line,[145] and by the corresponding a-verse

accent. This confirms our suggestion (see pp. 22, 69–70) that this poet's metrical grammar had changed in fundamental ways from that of earlier alliterative poets.

[145] Our examples will illustrate this. All cases of enclitic nouns in the wheel are explained by the considerations that are spelt out in this section, except for a few nouns that are not accented because they are lexically presupposed. Lexical presupposition is the obvious explanation for 'Bot þaȝ mý hed fáll on þe stónes /I cón not hít restóre (*G* 2282–3*rh*), with contrastive stress on *my* ('you could put *your* head back' is understood); for 'Bot ón stroke hére me falleȝ' (*G* 2327*rh*), which follows 'I haf a stroke in þis sted without stryf hent' (*G* 2123); and it also explains the weak stress on the nouns 'spurs' and 'sayn' in *G* 586*rh* and 588*rh*:

With rýche cóte-armúre
His góld spores spénd with prýde
Gúrd wyth a brónt ful súre
With sílk sayn úmbe his syde.'

Géderez vp hys grýmme tole (*G* 2260).[146]

The good grasp of sentence stress displayed by alliterative poets might also explain the inversion of adjective and noun in the 'hyper-extended' a-verse of *WW* 144:

With thre búlles of blé white

The inversion neutralises the tendency to accent the adjective preceding a noun of broad semantics. Another point that bears on the accentuation of this verse is the tendency of quantifiers (here 'thre') to be weakly stressed.

Duggan's scansion of *E* 144a, 'Þe déne of þe dére pláce', seems to us improbable considering the vagueness of the noun and the affective charge of the adjective.[147] If the word 'place' did take the beat as a matter of course, one wonders why it hardly ever[148] alliterates in extended verses:

And pýled þat précious place (*C* 1282a)
The sóre of such a swéte place (*P* 507a)
To séke them a sýkyre place (*MA* 2423a)
Dame Próserpine in a préue place (*WA* 4545a)
a rýche place and a múrye (*PP* C 22.181b)

The noun 'house' sometimes misses out on the beat for the same reason as 'place'. The stress pattern that is likely in modern English (cf. let's go

The normal pattern is that words for material substances (whether nominal or adjectival) are weakly stressed. But this is a description of Gawain's arming, which follows a conventional pattern in life and literature, as shown by D. S. Brewer, 'The Arming of the Warrior in European Literature and Chaucer', in *Chaucerian Problems and Perspectives: Essays Presented to Paul E. Beichner, C.S.C.*, ed. E. Vasta and Z. P. Thundy (Notre Dame, Ind., 1979), pp. 221–43). 'Lexical presupposition' is therefore bound to exert an influence: since it is predictable that Gawain should wear spurs and a sash, it is their quality, as expressed by the adjectives, that takes the interest.

[146] Andrew and Waldron (eds), *Poems*, p. 46, use this line to illustrate their argument that the poet uncoupled stress from alliteration, which they scan as 'Géderez vp his grymme tóle'. But this scansion is questionable on linguistic and empirical grounds (see *G* 413*rh*).

[147] We take up this point later in our discussion of 'attitudinal' adjectives.

[148] The exception in our corpus is 'Þere faire plácus and pláin' (*B* 495), but 'fair' happens to be an adjective of low alliterative rank (see below, p. 208).

to mý house, *or* mý place), which would clearly infringe Cable and Duggan's stress rules, also occurs in alliterative verse:

> To umbe-lýȝe Lótheȝ hous, þe lédes to take (*C* 836)
> Þurȝ mýȝt of Mórgne la Faye, þat in mý hous lénges (*G* 2446)

At *G* 2446 the pronoun takes the beat and the open-class noun does not.[149] The 'promotion rule' cannot tell us why. Further research should be able to specify other nouns of low accentual rank. 'Work', 'good', 'body', 'thing' are obvious cases in point. Two other nouns are worth mentioning. As Kingdon has noted (see above, p. 197), 'ship' is a generic noun with a tendency to receive weak sentence stress when it is preceded by a strongly stressed adjective. Alliterative poets write a-verses that bear Kingdon out. In our corpus 'ship' occurs in the following extended a-verses:

> Gáles and gréte schipis (*WA* 65a)
> The schip schér vpon schóre (*SJ* 67a)
> Þat ón énd of the schip (*SJ* 71a)
> (with vowel alliteration on 'on', normally unstressed)
> Fýndes he a fáyr schyp (*P* 98a)
> He swénges me þis swéte schip (*P* 108a)
> The prýce schippez of þe pórte (*MA* 746a)

Andrew and Waldron scan *P* 97a as 'Fýndes he a fayr schýp', but, whatever one thinks of their argument that alliterative poets introduced variety by occasionally separating beat from alliteration, these verses show no variety: 'ship' never alliterates in extended a-verses from our corpus. Another noun worth mentioning is 'town', which is responsible for creating a potential four-beat a-verse in 'Send prékers to þe príce toun, and pláunte there my ségge' (*MA* 355). The hypothesis that *toun* takes weaker sentence stress in adjective-noun combinations is confirmed by the frequency of its occurrences after alliterating adjectives in extended a-verses (e.g. 'Jéwen toun' (*SJ* 1232a), 'próud toun' (*WA* 2237a), 'wále toun' (*WA* 2276a). If we took the view that accentuation was either a matter of metrical convenience or determined by word-class, it would be hard to explain why high-frequency words of wide denomination are favoured after alliterating adjectives, and why more colourful synonyms are not found in such environments. Phrases such as

[149] Cf. *PP* B 18.350, 'Thow fettest mýne in mý place [máugree] alle resoun.'

**Jewen cité* or **proud cité* simply do not occur in extended a-verses,[150] although they should be perfectly regular if poets stressed both words or could place the beat where they liked.

Other notions of space and time also appear to bear weak sentence stress, just as in Shakespeare's verse. *MA* illustrates the pattern:

| | |
|---|---|
| áught score wýnttyrs (278b) | on hálfe fote lárge (1079b) |
| with séx score hélmes (380b) | was fýfe fadom lárge (1103b) |
| séxty mile fórthir (478b) | this séx ȝere and móre (2925b) |
| thré hundreth at ónes (930b) | séuen hundrethe at ónes (3705b) |

To show that *MA* is not unusual in this regard, we give some more examples from other poems:

| | |
|---|---|
| and álle þe nyȝt résten (*SJ* 634b) | fówre fote lárge (*G* 2225b) |
| on þat óþer syde síttes (*G* 110b) | of t[wélfe] ȝer of áge (*WA* 649b; MS *ten*) |
| þat óþer half áls (*G* 1224b) | |

In the *Gawain* poet's rhymed verse, the same pattern is found:

Hit ís not twó myle hénne (*G* 1078*rh*)
On wýþer half wáter com dóun þe schóre (*Pearl* 230)

The scansion adopted here should be extended to the a-verse also, where numerous nouns of measurement and duration do not alliterate in extended verses. We scan 'týþe dol' (*C* 216), 'þíkke þousandes' (*C* 220), 'anóþer day' (*C* 481), 'sádde ȝer' (*C* 1286), 'séuen syþes' (*C* 1686), 'fórty dayes' (*P* 359, *C* 403), 'nórþ syde' (*P* 451), 'gódeȝ halue' (*C* 896), 'fáwre half' (*C* 950), to create regular two-beat a-verses. This principle also justifies our scansion of 'Þré dayes and þ[r]é nyȝt' (*P* 294a), which would have four beats by lexical stress rules. Scholars who would scan such adjective-noun combinations differently, either with two beats[151] or with a single beat on the noun, should take a look at the comparable b-verses and rhymed verses above and ask themselves why notional nouns steadily follow alliterating adjectives in extended verses and are common

[150] In the Cotton Nero poems and *SJ* (where *cité* is common) the word is never accompanied by an adjective in extended a-verses, with the exception of quantifiers.

[151] As do Duggan and Cable. The a-verse, 'Þíkke þowsandes þró', has three beats according to Duggan and Cable, while, according to Inoue, 'Þikke' would have to be 'subordinated'.

in arsis in rhymed verse.[152] And another question to ask is why alliterative poets frequently alliterate on words that are normally weakly stressed rather than on nouns of wide denomination. Here are some examples:

> To hólde on þat ón syde (*G* 771a)
> On úch syde of þe worlde [read *erde*?] áywhere ilýche (*C* 228)
> Sir Owghtréth on the tóther syde of Túry was lórde (*MA* 234)[153]
> And hítterly on ílk syde (*WA* 5448)[154]
> And Árthure on óure syde (*MA* 2802a)
> With áuntlers on áythere syde (*P3A* 28a)
> Ne non éuel on náwþer halue (*G* 1552a)
> (with linking alliteration in *non euel*)
> Þay hóndel þer his áune body (*C* 11a)

In all of these cases the alliteration falls on a word that does not usually alliterate,[155] in defiance of the promotion rule. The reason is that the nouns in question (*half, side, body*) are semantically vague and may be more weakly stressed than the premodifier.

It seems natural that unremarkable and unspecific nouns such as *man*, *child* and *son* should sometimes bear weak sentence stress (for they do so in our own language[156]). However, since the fictional worlds of alliterative verse are peopled with aristocrats rather than ordinary folk, our sense of which nouns are unremarkable should be adjusted in line

152 There are rare exceptions — *G* 697a, 'Alle þe íles of Ánglesay on lyft hálf he háldez' – but judging by the Cotton Nero poems, this stress pattern is a striking departure from the norm (contrast *C* 719, 896, 950, *G* 692, 1224, 1552, 2149, *P* 434).

153 The name *Owghtreth* is obscure. Hamel thinks it may be a corruption of *Witard.*

154 Duggan and Turville-Petre conjecturally emend to *ilk half.* Since vowels alliterate with /h/ in *WA* according to Duggan and Turville-Petre (p. xix), the emendation is unnecessary, and not supported by the 'fact that in l. 1511 *ilk syde* alliterates on /s/.' Such variation is to be expected (cf. ón syde, *G* 771a, and 'on sýde', *G* 1312a): since both words are weakly stressed, the metrical set will settle the choice.

155 As Cable's rules recognize. Adjectives bear stress, he writes, 'except indefinite and interrogative pronominal adjectives: ... *oþer*, *on*, *uche*.' The possessive pronoun *our* is of course also normally unstressed, as is the limiter adjective *own*, which is only accented when the noun offers no competition. Note, for example, to 'sée his awen fáce' (*C* 595b) and 'at Góddeȝ awen féste' (*G* 1036b).

156 Enclitic *–son* in surnames (e.g. 'Johnson') illustrates the tendency.

with cultural expectations. *King*, *queen*, *knight*, *lord*, *God* are frequently found in extended b-verses:

as áþel God lýkyd (*C* 411b)
God kýnned þerinne (*C* 1072b)
his wórþy God knáwe (*C* 231b)
he stóute goddes cállȝ (*C* 1343b)
þe dére kyng hymséluen (*MA* 1601b)
in óþer kyngys lándes (*MA* 400b)
were chéf lord to wórþe (*SJ* 963b)
þe mýlde Qwen of héuen (*MA* 4041b)
þe héie god alóne (*B* 641)
lét þe king sóne (*B* 171)
a sóþ god ipróued (*B* 685)
and léuez þe knyȝt þére (*G* 2154b)
men knówen me mony (*G* 454b)
& éldest childe báthe (*WA* 1964b)
was óf hir son líȝtir (*WA* 572b)
Wólde ȝe, wórþilyche lorde (*G* 343a)

In the last a-verse the modal auxiliary is accented, but *lord* is not: the noun is of low accentual rank. The *Gawain* poet's rhymed lines display the same pattern:

Þe óld lorde óf þat léude (*G* 1124*rh*)
To Goddeȝ wýlle I ám ful báyn (*G* 2158*rh*)[157]

The final category of nouns to appear regularly without alliteration after adjectives consists of nouns denoting a material or a substance (e.g. gold, steel, silk, silver, blood, water, wine). Such nouns are comparable to abstract nouns, having in common with the latter that they tend to be non-count nouns, while the preceding adjective tends to be a classifying adjective (cf. ModE 'spárkling water', 'réd wine', 'brówn bread').[158] We find these nouns well represented in extended verses:

with brýȝt golde bóunden (*G* 600b)
of brýȝt stel rýngeȝ (*G* 580b)
to ráw sylk lýke (*C* 790b)
þe fíne gold schéne (*B* 1027b)
þe féye blod rýnnys (*MA* 4121b; cf. 2144b)
st[úf]f[ed] steil únder (*SJ* 526b; L *stif*; P *stith*)
and féble ale drýnke (*PP* B 5.177)

[157] Presumably with elision of *e* in *Goddeȝ*: see Borroff, '*Sir Gawain*', p. 161.
[158] See Quirk and Greenbaum, *University Grammar*, §4.3.

Again the *Gawain* poet's rhymed verse confirms this usage:

> Good bér and brýȝt wyn bóþe (*G* 129*rh*)[159]
> Þe qúyte snaw láy bisýde (*G* 2088*rh*)
> Rýche blod rán on róde so róghe (*Pearl* 646*rh*)
> Wyth hórnez séuen of réd golde clér (*Pearl* 1111*rh*)

These patterns provide very reliable predictions about whether the adjective or the noun will take the alliteration in extended a-verses:

> Riȝt as a fláw of féll snaw (*WA* 1880a)
> Rýally with réd golde (*G* 663a)
> Of córtynes of cléne sylk (*G* 854a)
> Rýnisch wyne and Róchell (*MA* 203a)
> That all the hótt blod of hým (*MA* 1833a)
> (note that the 'promotion rule' fails)

They also provide good solutions to hyper-extended a-verses. In the apparent four-beat a verse 'Of brýȝt golde vpon silke bórdes' (*G* 159a), 'gold' and 'silk' are unaccented (as they are in the b-verses and rhymed lines above); in 'Bot as smýlt mele vnder smál siue' (*C* 226a) the material noun 'mele' is unaccented.[160]

It needs to be remembered, however, that at the end of tone units enclitic stress patterns are liable to shift stress. We have seen this happening with compounds, but it applies also to adjective-noun combinations.[161] We would expect the modifier to alliterate before nouns such as *lord*, *mile*, *wyntir* (for 'year'), *whyle* and *end*, as in

> séxty myle fórthire (*MA* 478b)
> And grémed þerwiþ þe gréte lorde (*C* 138a)

[159] One might object here that *ber* is also a substance but the adjective that precedes it (*good*) does not offer much counterbalast (see below, p. 208), unlike *bryȝt*.

[160] The adjective *smal* is accented because it specifies the type of sieve that produces the effect described in the b-verse, 'smokes for þikke'. Compare our comments on adjectives below, p. 207. Inoue makes the valid point that the unaccented element in adjective-noun combination does not necessarily lack semantic weight, and cites two examples —

> Þen gréne aumayl on gólde glówande bryȝter (*G* 236)
> Þat þe schéne blod ouer his schúlderes schót to þe érþe (*G* 2314)

— but the nouns in question happen to be non-count nouns denoting a material or substance.

[161] This applies also to 'empty verbs': lóng er þe sonne ríse (*G* 932b).

Gréte lordis of Gréke (*MA* 1463a)
féle wyntres wiþ álle (*PP* B 15.288b)
To méue in þe mórne-while (*MA* 2001a)
thurgh séuen wyntter ónes (*WW* 299b)
with góod end to déye (*PP* C 10.60b)

But at line ending we often get:

and óthire gret lórdes (*MA* 3973b, cf. 4075b)
had bén seuen wýnter (*G* 613b)
and sáyd þe later énde (*E* 136)[162]
stód a gret whýle (*G* 2369b)

The beat on 'ben' at *G* 613b, which contravenes the 'promotion rule', is not problematic if we conceive of the noun phrase (consisting of quantifier and time word) as a lexical unit. Of course, the pattern, with beat on the final noun, is insisted upon by the metre, but our instinct to place the main stress at the end of the tone unit means we can yield to the demands of metre without strain.

Another tendency we should mention is that nouns can be de-accented when preceded by a strongly emphatic adjective. David Crystal observes that content words may become part of the 'nuclear tail' (the unstressed syllables following the sentence accent) after 'attidudinally extreme lexical items', which 'display a strong tendency to attract the tonic', e.g.

/it's a TREMENDOUS result/ /that's a FANTASTIC idea/

In alliterative verse, a number of 'attitudinal' adjectives that express strong approval, admiration, disapprobation or repulsion, seem to be used to achieve this outcome. The adjectives *gay*, *wale*, *proud*, *dere*, *gentyl* and (on the negative side of the spectrum) *vile* and *hatel* are followed by non-alliterating nouns in extended b-verses:

in gáy bed lýgez (*G* 1179b)
víle deþ he þóled' (*SJ* 1328b)
þat dére Vter áfter (*G* 2465b)
þe wále kyng sáid (*WA* 2414b)
þat próude hors þénne (*G* 2048b)
a géntyl duc þénne (*C* 1235b)
þat hátel schor láste (*C* 227b)

Contributory factors involved here are the colourlessness and low alliterative rank of some of the nouns (king, horse[163]), the predictability

[162] The b-verse means 'and the last part [of the mass] was spoken' (and not sung, as at the beginning).

of some of the nouns in context ('lie in bed', 'thole death') and the rhythm rule.

In a-verses, too, these 'loud' adjectives function as conductors for beat and alliteration:

A gáy egle of góld (*SJ* 330a)
Gráthez on þis gáy gere
(*WA* 790a; cf. 4728a)
Þe gestes gáy and ful glád (*C* 830a)
Þe gáy coroun of gólde (*C* 1444a)
Wále wyn to þy wénches (C 1716a)[164]
Þy wále rengne is wált (*C* 1734a)

The corresponding b-verses provide empirical verification for the scansion we indicate here.

The emphasis on the adjective may be the product not only of its affective charge but also of its semantic force in context. A good example is the following passage from *SJ*, where an identical adjective-noun combination is used twice:

Also his fádere of flésche a férly bytíde;
A bíkere of waspene bées brédde in his nóse,
Hýued vp in his héd — he hádde hem of ȝóuþe —
And Wáspasian wás caled[165] þe wáspene bees áfter. (*SJ* 33–6)

Interestingly, 'waspish bees' has two different stress contours. The first instance 'waspene bées' shows Chomsky and Halle's 'nuclear stress rule' at work: the adjective is syntactically and prosodically subordinate to the following noun. This makes sense, too: if a man has bees growing up his nose, the fact that they are wasp-like is a minor detail. But when the poet explains how 'Waspasian' got his name the accent intelligently picks out the premodifier 'waspene', for it it is 'wasps' and not 'bees' that give Vespasian his name.

163 Cf. 'A gréne hors grét and þíkke' (*G* 175*rh*). As Borroff has observed ('*Sir Gawain*', p. 67), the poet has any number of more specific or more striking words for the animal if he wants the word to take the beat, but 'horse' is the quiet common denominator that lets the adjective do most of the talking.

164 Inoue would subordinate 'wyn', but the evidence from alliterative verse and the *Gawain* poet's rhymed verse is that non-count nouns denoting a substance tend to be enclitic.

165 Or with disjunction, 'And Wáspasian was cáled'. But 'call' is of low accentual rank and does not necessarily demand linguistic stress. Cf. *WA* 4623b, 'ȝe call þe líttil wérde'. 'Vespasian' in *SJ* can alliterate both on /v/ and /w/ (the latter reflecting Anglo-Latin pronunciation; cf. *PP* B 19.210: 'Welcome hym and worschipe hym with *veni creator spiritus*').

A fourth and final rhythmical tendency that is relevant to the stressing of adjective-noun combinations is that classifying (non-intensifiable) adjectives or adjectives that behave like them are more likely to take acoustic precedence over the noun than descriptive ones. Bolinger gives as his examples 'héat residue' and 'John is a crázy man (i.e. madman) and should be locked up'.[166] (Such combinations are closely related to compounds.) This rhythmical tendency is relevant to b-verses such as

þe gréte cloþ fálles (*P* 105b)
a þwárle knot alófte (*G* 194b)
at kýngez kort schíped (*G* 2340b)

The 'grete cloþ' is the mainsail,[167] and a 'þwarle knot' is an intricately coiled knot — the phrase survived as 'wharl-knot' in Lancashire dialects.[168] Describing a 'covenant' as having been made at the 'king's court', as the Green Knight does at 2340, tells us *which* court and by implication *which* agreement he is referring to (i.e. not the Exchange of Winnings but the Beheading Game). Our scansion is confirmed by the wheel that follows, which tells us that Gawain

To þe kýngez burȝ búskes bólde
And þe knýȝt in þe énker gréne
Whiderwárde-so-éuer he wólde. (*G* 2476–8*rb*).

Gawain is headed to the king's castle, i.e. Camelot, and the specificity conveyed by the premodifier gains added point by being contrasted with the mysterious vagueness of the Green Knight's destination. Extended a-verses offer many other examples of classifying adjectives that take the beat: a 'knáue child' (*SJ* 108a) is a baby boy,[169] the 'bálwe tree' (*SJ* 156a) is the gallows, the 'bróde sel' (*B* 968a) on Alexander's letter to the Brahmans is the great seal.

Our survey of enclitic nouns may have given the misleading impression that adjectives usually hold sway over nouns, but we have focused on them precisely because they are more unusual, both in alliterative verse and in English speech rhythm, and so call out for

[166] Bolinger, *Intonation and Its Parts*, p. 119.
[167] In *SJ* the mainsail is called the 'broad sail', again with accent on the adjective: 'þe bróde sail at o bráyd' (70a).
[168] As noted by Tolkien and Gordon in their glossary.
[169] But note again the familiar stress shift at line ending: 'with séuen knaue chíldre' (*MA* 1025b).

explanations. By our calculation about sixty-five percent of adjective-noun combinations in extended verses alliterate on the noun. Because proclitic structures are 'more in keeping with the general speech accentuation tendency in English than enclitic ones',[170] unaccented adjectives require less discussion; but since their existence is denied in the standard treatments of alliterative metre, we shall need to argue that they do exist.

The easiest way of doing so is to focus on some groups of adjectives that appear frequently without alliteration in extended b-verses. We begin with *good*, *fair*, and *clene* (in the sense 'fair'), which are commonly used in alliterative verse as descriptive epithets and metrical fillers. Their high frequency correlates with an apparent lack of strong stress in a significant number of verses:

watz clene vérdúre (*G* 161b)
and clene spúres únder (*G* 158b)
his fayre schélde únder (*G* 2318b)
that goud sáuor háde (*C* 1447b)
wiþ good chére bríngen (*B* 727b)
Þe knýȝt mad áy god chére (*G* 562*rh*)
he máde fayr bókes (*SJ* 1326b)

In our own language, 'good' (and adverbial 'wel') can also be weakly stressed, since their function is not to question background assumptions but to affirm them: 'good' (or 'fair') often means 'living up to expectation' (e.g. 'Why are you wearing it on your lapel? — Because it SMELLS good'; 'what are you using my pen for? Because it WRITES well').[171] 'Good' and 'well' are not 'attitudinally extreme' but (to use the linguistic jargon) 'adjectives/adverbs of proper functioning'.

In the interests of consistency, we would apply the same scansion to extended a-verses such as these:

Fayre fórmes myȝt he fýnde (*C* 3)
And if he lóuyes clene láyk (*C* 1053)
Þat gode cóunseyl at þe quéne (*C* 1619)

Quantifiers also behave in ways that conflict with Duggan and Cable's stress rules As Kingdon notes, in English intonation they often become 'unstressed in the vicinity of strong stresses', e.g.

There áren't many mistákes
I'd líke a little wáter

170 Tarlinskaja, *Shakespeare's Verse*, p. 204.
171 Bolinger, 'Two Views of Accent', p. 81.

This tallies with what happens in alliterative verse. Cable lists amongst his list of 'exceptions' a few adjectives that belong to the category of quantifiers (*on*, *fele*, *many*, *alle*) but seems quite unaware that many other words (adjectival and adverbial) are implicated, e.g. 'little', 'half', 'much', numerals ('two', 'three', etc.) and 'first',[172] as these examples show:

and litel hárm wírche (*SJ* 875b)
ful littyl jóye happyns (*MA* 3743b)
a litill dais éftir (*WA* 5273b)
an halfe fóte lárge (*MA* 1079b)
þat láid hire first égg (*WA* 1016b)
góuerne first hymsélue (*PP* B 5.51b)
ten wýse clérkis (*WA* 2556b)
tille two ȝéreȝ énde (*SJ* 1173b)
twa próude flúmes (*WA* 2720b)
and thre on lówe úndir (*WW* 80b)
to muche nýe were (*C* 1376b)
and two réde líppes (*E* 91b)
he ládde much jóye (*G* 1927b)

The assumption that quantifiers must be accented in alliterative verse[173] is contradicted by these b-verses, and leads to preposterous results in scansion. For example, 'For bóþe two here I þe béde bot two báre mýntes' (*G* 2352) would confront us with a three-beat b-verse and an a-verse in which the beat is inexplicably carried by a predeterminer (*boþe*) that does not normally bear stress. To understand the accentuation, one needs to know that *two* is not a 'normal' content word but a quantifier, with weak sentence stress.

The adjectives 'great' and 'high' are often used rather like quantifiers (meaning 'much, a lot of') or intensifiers (as in a 'great fool'), and may pay the price for doing so:

þat hyȝ hónour háldeȝ (*C* 35b)
þay cléche gret méde (*C* 12b)
and grete defénce máde (*SJ* 622b)
and grete píte hádde (*SJ* 1156b)

[172] The choice of the poetic synonym 'form' avoids the downgrading of the adjective: 'Þe fórme worde vpon fólde' (*G* 2373a).

[173] Duggan and Cable do. Duggan thinks that 'Ten fyne philosofours' (*WA* 2461) has three adjacent metrical stresses ('Extended A-Verses', p. 74) and Cable thinks that *C* 222, 'Swéued at þe fyrst swáp', is a three-beat a-verse (*Alliterative Tradition*, p. 158).

and gáfe [*read* ȝaf] me gret gýftes (*MA* 2628b)

Again the wheel confirms our scansion and reasoning:

Gret rúrd in þát forést (*G* 1149*rh*)
Much wéle þen wátz þerínne;
Gret périle bitwéne hem stód (*G* 1766–67*rh*)

The 'demotion rule' (allowing the first word of a line to be demoted before a stressed word) could be invoked to provide a different explanation, but semantics must play a leading role, for the only adjectives that are 'demoted' at the beginning of *G*'s rhymed lines are the quantifiers *great* and *much* and the 'adjective of proper functioning' *good*, in 'god bér and brýȝt wyn bóþe' (*G* 129*rh*).

Extended a-verses show the same patterns:

With gret bóbbance þat búrȝe (*G* 9a)
And práysed hit as a gret prýs (*G* 1630a)

However, grammar and rhythm can fortify weaker adjectives that tend not to attract the beat without special reasons. The rhythm rule and the metrical set work against the proclitic stress pattern in

and grét ioie hére (*B* 502b)
so fáire an end háues (*MA* 4253b)

Something similar happens to a weak adjective when it works in partnership with another adjective in postposition. A striking example of this phenomenon is provided by *SJ* 327–31:

With rópis of ríche silk ráysen vp swýþe
Gret téntis as a tóun or tórkeys clóþys,
Chóppyn ouer þe chéuentayns with chárboklis fóure[174]
A gáy egle of góld on a gílde áppul
With gréte dragouns and grým and al in gólde wróȝte ...

[174] We have repunctuated the line, which means, 'On top of the chieftain's (tent), they sculpted an elegant eagle of gold with four charbuncles'. *Choppyn* = MED *choppen* 'cut out'. Hanna and Lawton begin a new sentence and seem to think that *cheuentayns* is the plural subject. They argue that *choppyn* is a preterite verb, derived from ME *chape* 'metal plate', but in the only 'parallel use' of that verb in Chaucer (*CT* I.366–67) it is weak (as one would expect of new formations).

At *SJ* 327, 'silk' (a non-count noun) does not take the beat. In 'gret tentis', the adjective is weakly stressed, as is its wont (cf. *SJ* 91, 808, *B* 545, 557, *etc.*), but in the construction '*grete* dragouns *and grym*', it works in partnership with *grym*, which helps *grete* to become a stave. Although the partnership of a premodified and postmodified adjective does not bleach out the noun in all cases,[175] it does give poets the option of accenting adjectives that would not otherwise be fit for duty. So in *G* 583a, 'With góde cowters and gáy', the postpositive adjective again helps a weak partner ('good') to push aside the dominating noun.

**Conclusion**

The central argument in this chapter is that scholars working on alliterative metre have paid insufficient attention to sentence stress and to the variety of factors that influence intonation in spoken language. We have tried to demonstrate the relevance of these rhythmical and semantic factors by showing that they can explain the accentuation of extended verses, hyper-extended a-verses, and the *Gawain* poet's rhymed lines. Cable's treatment of extended b-verses as 'exceptions' is unsatisfactory. Since extended b-verses in particular form a sizable and authentic subspecies, we cannot brush aside the questions they pose. Duggan's response has been to concede the possibility that a-verses may have four ictus positions and the b-verse three. Yet there comes a point in the history of any theory when its effects become so implausible and irregular that it may be better to abandon the theory rather than to stick with it. In our view, the theory that stress is a matter of lexical categories is untenable; no linguist believes it; no-one working in the tradition of non-alliterating verse believes it; and extended verses can become regular two-beat verses if we abandon it in our scansion of alliterative metre.

That 'content words' (in the grammatical sense of that word) usually take the beat in verse is a consequence of the fact that the semantic content of an utterance tends to be concentrated in them rather than in grammatical function words; but the conclusion to be drawn from this is

[175] The only certain exceptions we find are 'With much réuel and rýche' (*G* 538a) and 'Bot hyȝe bónkkez and brént' (*G* 2165a) – which are, in their own way, quite regular. 'Much' (being a quantifier) does not normally take the beat, and in the second example 'high', qualifying 'hills', is pleonastic. Compare the stress contours in 'And bówed to þe hyȝe bónk' (*C* 379a) and 'And héterly to þe hyȝe hýlleȝ' (*C* 380a).

that the beats will fall on the words that do most of the semantic work in the context. Rhythmical factors (such as the tendency to place the tonic on the rightmost lexical item in a tone unit and the avoidance of clashing stresses in adjacent words) are also important, and explain some of the stress contours and variations in them that we have examined. Extended a-verses will require more attention than we have been able to give them. There are many of them and we do not claim to have given the answers for all of them. But we have made a start, and have provided empirical evidence to show that at least some of the scansions that underpin the three-beat theory are implausible on linguistic grounds and inconsistent with the patterns found in b-verse metre and in the *Gawain* poet's rhymed verse.

We would like to end this section by testing the explanatory power of our theory against some problematic b-verses. The solutions we shall provide conveniently recapitulate our main arguments. The main criticism that has been levelled against the theory of 'stress-subordination' is that it leaves us with no clear way of deciding which open-class word should be de-selected for stress. In support of this argument Duggan cites a number of verses where, he claims, deciding which word to 'subordinate' is such an 'arbitrary process' that it might be preferable to think of them as having *three* possible ictus positions. We cite his examples (with our accent marks):

þat sére sewes hálden (*G* 124b)
to lay a lél dáte (*C* 425b)
þe fálce fend wróȝt (*C* 205b)
néw note rýses (*WA* 3152b)
and stírre no fote férrere (*P3A* 47b)
bére-no-fals-wítnesse (*PP* B 5.589b, ed. Bennett)
and couthe of cóurte théwes (*Mum* 21b)
fóure & twenti thóusand (*WA* 3866b)
to tell of þa trées kínde (*WA* 4894b)
and shoke hir schíre léues (*WA* 5145b)
stode full of stíth réedis (*WA* 5587b)

Duggan writes that '[i]n my own dialect I should tend, I think, to read some of these verses most naturally with greater emphasis on the first and last element and thus to scan, e.g. *C*, 425 as x/xx/.[176] But I would not read *WA* [4894] so, and I should have nothing compelling to say to a reader whose intuitions were precisely the reverse.' Where intuitions conflict, however, it may be possible to educate our sensibilities, and research and reflection show that there is quite a lot to be said in favour of the accentuation that we have indicated. Let us consider the verses

[176] Duggan, 'Authenticity', 36. The scansion disregards etymological *–e* in *date* (< OF *date*).

one-by-one. At *G* 124, the poet is at pains to emphasise the lavishness of the dinner, even to the extent of putting the beat on *fele* in the preceding b-verse: 'and on so féle dísches' (122b);[177] it seems right that *sere* 'various' should also take the accent in *G* 124b, particularly since 'sewes' is non-specific. As ever, patterns of extension in the b-verse are matched in the a-verse, where the identical adjective-noun combination occurs at *G* 889a, 'Wyth sére sewes and séte', comparable with *WW* 339a, 'Róste with the ríche sewes'. At *C* 205 the subject is Lucifer, the perpetrator of the archetypal act of betrayal: 'For þe fýrste félonye þe fálce fende wróȝt'. *False* carries the poet's disapproval of the precise quality that Lucifer demonstrates. Duggan imagines that a reader of the line 'might choose at will between the alternatives, subordinating either noun or adjective as he pleased', but only a bad performer would not emphasise the attitudinally extreme adjective 'false'.

The new activity ('new note') announced by *WA* 3025 is the battle that is joined after the armies have got ready. *New* is accented: the poet has given us activity of one kind already (preparations) and is now promising us the beginning of another (war). The beat falls on what is *new*, not what is contextually given and notional. *Note* is a textbook example of a noun of 'wide denomination' that will usually be dominated by the adjective (cf. 'thing', 'gere', 'werk'). As such it naturally crops up in extended a-verses, as in *E* 38, 'A nóble note for þe nónes and néw werke hit hátte'. In this example, the abstract noun 'werk' is also weakly stressed after an alliterating adjective (cf. wýkked werk, *C* 1050a, 'stúrne werk', *G* 494a) and 'note' is even more indefinite: 'noble note' means 'something noble', and 'new note' 'something new'. Once we think in terms of sense rather than word class, the beats become easier to apprehend.

At *PP* B 5.589 Langland naturally treats 'false witness' as a lexical item, as he generally does:

To bákbite and to bósten and bére fals wítnesse (*PP* B 2.81)
And féffe fáls witness[e] wiþ flóryns ynówe (*PP* B.2.147)
Wiþ bákbyting and bísmere and bérynge of fals wítnesse (*PP* B 5.88)

177 Compare the description of Gawain's plentiful meal at Castle Hautdesert: 'Doubleféld, as hit fállez, and féle kyn físchez' (*G* 890). Although Cable lists *fele* as an 'unstressed adjective', the preceding a-verse ('served in double portions') emboldens the reader to accent the word, in appreciation of the sheer quantity of the food on the dinner-table.

[Thoruȝ] false mésures and mét   and wiþ fáls wítnesse (*PP* B 13.358)
For bráulynge and bákbitynge   and bérynge of false wítnesse (*PP* B 15.238)

The different prosodic contours here are of course metrically convenient, but they are not linguistically gratuitous. The double-accenting of the phrase is the exception rather than the rule, but inevitable in *PP* B 13.358b where no other word competes for accent. At *PP* B 2.147 'Fáls-witness' is a personification, and hence a compound name with stress on the first element. In the other cases the stress shifts to 'witness', because it is the last stressable word of the tone unit.

'Four and twenty' at *WA* 3866 obeys the rule that in attributive position the first element of a compound adjective tends to be more strongly accented than the second.[178] Compare 'she is twénty-fíve' (or in speedier delivery 'she is twenty-fíve') with 'twénty-five yéars'. The rhythm rule explains the pattern. The idiomatic 'stírre no fote férrere (*P3A* 47) should also cause Duggan no difficulty. As he has noted already, 'numerals, count words, and time terms like *day*, *month*, *year*, *terme*, *score*, *cubit(s)* ... show a marked tendency to lose expected stress'. In *P3A*, 'foot' is of course a measure of length (not a limb); moreover, in collocation with 'stir' the word 'foot' follows so predictably that its contribution to sense is negligible: the whole phrase might be regarded as a single lexical item.[179]

In *Mum* 21 and *WA* 5461 we encounter two familiar stative verbs ('couth') and 'stod' (in the weak sense of 'was'), while *WA* 4894 features a verb of speech, which is again entirely predictable from context:

It ware to tére any tóng   to tell of þa trées kínde. (4892–4)

Again, it is revealing that *tell* makes regular appearances in extended a-verses:

To tell him tákens of þe týmes (*WA* 283a)
To tell þaire tórfere entýre (*WA* 1384a)
And tell þe trúly all þe téxt (*WA* 5072a)
Túlkes tolden hym þe tále (*E* 109a)

And there is also a positive reason why *tre* must be stressed. While as a generic and prosaic noun, which repeats the poetic *lindes* (4892a), 'tree' is of usually of low alliterative rank, the demonstrative 'þa' lures the accent

[178] As in the nursery rhyme, 'Fóur and twenty bláckbirds ...'.
[179] The b-verse is thus an excellent example of the 'de-accenting of unnecessary information', on which see Crystal, 'Prosodic Features', p. 26.

to the noun that follows: 'þa' is always followed by an accented stave in *WA*.[180] Being 'focus-governing morphemes',[181] words like 'þa' and 'ful' have the advantage of signposting the place where the accent must go, and it is possible that poets used them for precisely that reason (cf. *C* 859a, 'Þenne he méled to þo mén', where *þo* confirms that the beat falls on a word of low accentual rank).

The case of 'lay a lel date' can be solved by giving further consideration to the kinds of words that we have to choose between. On the one hand, *lel* is a word of 'high alliterative rank':[182] it a poetic word that has a high probability of taking the alliterative beat. *Lay*, by contrast, is a high-frequency word with weak semantic force (comparable in this respect to verbs like *set* and *put*).[183] Significantly, it is frequently found in extended a- and b-verses, as these examples show:

I lóvue þat we lay lótes on lédes vchóne (*P* 173)[184]
To legge lým oþur stón lóþ is us álle (*B* 438)
All me lórdschipe láwe in lánde es layd úndyre (*MA* 4276)
And leiden fáutes vpon þe fáder þat fórmede vs álle (*PP* B 10.106)
Líf seiþ þat he líeþ and leieþ his líf to wédde (*PP* B 18.31; cf. C.8.289)
Layd wécche to þe wálle and wárned and in háste (*SJ* 386)

Outside alliterative verse too, the verb is sometimes found in arsis, as in 'Whan thát this knýght leyde hánd upón his réyne' (*CT* V.313). We therefore conclude that the beat and the alliteration fall on the adjective 'lel' rather the verb 'lay' in *C* 425b.

*WA* 5145b must also be seen in context. The whole line reads: 'Þan shógs hire þe són-tree & schoke hire schíre léues'. Here 'shake' is given, since it blandly repeats what the rare verb 'shog' has said much more

[180] We checked *WA* and the Cotton Nero poems and found no exceptions.
[181] The term is due to Gussenhoven, who gives the Modern English examples *even* and *only*. See *Grammar and Semantics of Accents*, ch. 1.
[182] See Borroff, '*Sir Gawain*', p. 78.
[183] These verbs tend to be unaccented in Modern English. Dwight Bolinger draws attention to the impossibly of accenting 'put' in 'How did he die? — They put him to déath', and compares 'They strángled him to death': stressing *put* is 'unacceptable because the relatively empty word *put* supplies no information' (*Intonation and Its Parts*, p. 119).
[184] But not 'For láy þeron a lump of léd, where *lump* is an indefinite partitive noun. Cf. Sweet's example, 'piece of bréad' and *C* 620a, 'And brýng a morsel of bréd'.

strikingly; by contrast 'schyre' belongs (with 'lel') to a group of distinctly poetic words of high alliterative rank.

In conclusion, none of the lines that Duggan thinks are problematic presents us with an 'arbitrary decision' in assigning the beat, and his examples are best taken as further evidence that open-class words and verbs of the kinds we have discussed are not always strongly stressed in alliterative verse.

# 5. THE STRUCTURE OF THE A-VERSE

## Introduction

As Hoyt Duggan has observed, 'we can with some confidence now claim to understand the metrical rules that account for the patterns of alliteration and the rhythmic structure of the b-verse in alliterative poetry'.[1] Work by both Duggan and Thomas Cable has confirmed Luick's orginal discovery that the b-verse operates on a principle of rhythmical dissimilation: it must have one and only one long dip.[2] If the first dip is short, then the second will be long and vice versa.[3] This rule is now considered so reliable that it has been used as a basis for emendation both by Duggan and Turville-Petre in their 1989 edition of *The Wars of Alexander* and by Hanna and Lawton in their recent edition of *The Siege of Jerusalem*.[4] There is so far, however, no similar agreement as to the pattern of the a-verse. Until very recently Duggan has provided only normative (as opposed to categorical) rules for the a-verse. Metrical rule 6 in his 'Meter, Stanza, Vocabulary, Dialect' is descriptive rather than prescriptive, although it does, admittedly, suggest that some a-verse patterns are commoner than others (there are normally three or fewer syllables for each dip, for instance):

> The a-verse consists of two or three lifts and from one to four dips. There are rarely more than six or seven syllables in an a-verse dip, and the most common rhythmical patterns involve three or fewer syllables in each dip. None to five unstressed syllables may occur before the first lift and from none to seven immediately follow it. None to three syllables may fall after the final stressed syllable. Though any two dips may have three syllables, the third dip in such lines tends to be light, and when any one dip contains

[1] Duggan, 'Some Aspects', p. 481.

[2] See Luick, 'Stabreimzeile', particularly §24.

[3] Duggan, 'Final –*e*', and 'The Shape of the B-Verse'; Cable, *Alliterative Tradition*, p. 92

[4] See Duggan and Turville-Petre (eds), *Wars*, pp. xvii–xxiv; Hanna and Lawton (eds), *Siege*, pp. xciv–xcv.

> four or more syllables, the other two dips tend to have two, one, or no syllables.[5]

Thomas Cable, on the other hand, has argued that there are categorical rules for the a-verse as well as for the b-verse, specifically that the a-verse must contain either two strong dips or three ictus positions.[6] In recent editions of alliterative verse Duggan's position has prevailed: while the syllabic structure of the b-verse is assumed to be metrically constrained (with irregular b-verses being emended accordingly), a-verses have not been emended *metri causa*. Moreover, the assumption that the a-verse obeys no rules other than one of alliterative patterning has important consequences for the textual apparatus in editions of alliterative poems. For example, in their edition of *SJ*, Hanna and Lawton record all variants affecting the syllable count in the case of b-verses; but for the a-verse, they make no such atttempt, since they think the syllable count there is immaterial. This inconsistency is undesirable, as it filters out some of the textual evidence that might enable other scholars to make further progress on the analysis of a-verse rhythms.

Duggan occasionally sounds as if he thinks that, as far as the syllable count is concerned, there simply are no categorical rules for the a-verse. Discussing the distribution of the monosyllabic and disyllabic forms of the noun 'crown', for instance, he observes that these forms are used systematically where necessary in support of the b-verse metre but that in the a-verse they are in free variation.[7] Given the poor state of our

[5] Hoyt Duggan, 'Meter, Stanza, Vocabulary, Dialect', in *A Companion to the Gawain Poet*, ed. Derek Brewer and Jonathan Gibson (Cambridge, 1997), pp. 221–42 (p. 232). This rule first appeared in the introduction to Duggan and Turville-Petre's edition of *Wars* (p. xx).

[6] Cable, *Alliterative Tradition*, p. 92.

[7] Duggan, 'Rhythmic Structure', p. 130 and n. 36. Not all the examples Duggan cites are convincing. The noun *crown* does not, for instance, appear in the a-verse of *E*, so no comparison between that and the b-verse is possible for this poem and, although it is true that the examples present in the b-verse do support the metre, there are only two of them, so it is difficult to argue that this pattern is statistically significant. *C*, likewise, has only two examples, one ('coroun') in an extended a-verse (1444), where the extra syllable is metrically required by our a-verse rules, and one 'crowne' in the b-verse (1275), so it is difficult here to be certain of any pattern. *SJ* only has examples of the monosyllabic form. There are no examples in *MA* where the form of 'crown' would make the difference between a metrical and an unmetrical b-verse: the difference is either between a

current knowledge about a-verse rules, the accuracy of this statement is difficult to judge (how do we tell if something is metrically determined or in free variation if we have no idea of the metrical requirements?), and it is worth noting that, in at least one of the poems cited by Duggan, these monosyllabic and disyllabic forms do appear to be in free variation in certain parts of the b-verse, i.e. in positions where the metrical effect is nil (see the use of long and short forms affecting the weak b-verse dip at *MA* 402, 673, 1244, 3352, 3962, 4206, 4316). It is true that the line ending might well be expected to be, in some respects, more strictly subject to rule than the beginning. As Bruce Hayes notes, it is a well-known and very general principle that 'Correspondence to a metrical pattern tends to be lax at the beginnings of units; strict at the ends'.[8] But it would nevertheless be surprising if no syllabic rules *at all* were to apply in the a-verse.[9] As David Lawton justly observes, 'it is inherently strange that in

short and a non-existent weak dip and the number of syllables in a long dip. The argument therefore really only applies to *WA*, where the disyllabic form is used three times in positions where the use of the monosyllabic form would make the b-verse unmetrical (at 1251, 2410, 5797). It is true that there is one example in *WA* where the A scribe writes the monosyllabic form in a position which makes the a-verse unmetrical in terms of the rules we outline below: see 3607, which, as it appears in A (D has no witness), has a weak medial dip with no compensation ('And was þe croune bekend'). It should be noted, however, that in *WA* the disyllabic form is the more unusual reading and that a similar line at *WA* 2925 ('And am þe coron be kynd') does have this more difficult reading, presumably selected in order to preserve the long medial dip.

8 Bruce Hayes, 'A Grid-based Theory of English Meter', *Linguistic Inquiry*, 14 (1983), 357–93 (p. 373). See also Roman Jakobson's account of the final downbeat in Russian binary verse forms, in *Language and Literature* (Cambridge, Mass., 1987), p. 75; Derek Attridge's discussion of the restrictions on the placement of trochaic inversion (*The Rhythms of English Poetry* (New York, 1982), p. 176); and similarly Attridge's account of demotion (where a stressed syllable realizes an off-beat: p. 169). Attridge does, however, point out that, in accentual-syllabic verse, the end of the line, like the beginning, is in one respect a point of relative metrical freedom: 'the metrical pattern may or may not have offbeats in these positions, or may have optional offbeats which permit variation from line to line' (pp. 186–7).

9 The end of an iambic pentameter line may have stricter rules regarding the arrangement of stressed and unstressed syllables than the beginning, but the arrangement of such syllables is nevertheless subject to certain constraints

[Duggan's] account a-verses and b-verses operate differently. According to Duggan, b-verses are syllable-counted and a-verses are not. This disparity requires to be analyzed and conceptualized further.'[10]

In undertaking this task, we can start by returning to earlier scholarship, which has in fact provided a-verse rules that do pay attention to the syllable count. Karl Luick, for instance, argued that what he called 'shortened verses' (i.e. verses without a long dip) occurred so rarely that their authenticity was questionable.[11] Duggan, too, has recently made the independent suggestion that a-verses without a long dip may be scribal, although he does not think this rule applies to extended a-verses,[12] and believes that hard evidence for any a-verse rules is impossible to find: 'In a number of minority a-verse patterns, I am confident that a few are unmetrical, but I am equally confident that in all but a few such cases we lack the evidence that would distinguish the unmetrical from the rare'.[13]

In this chapter we shall argue that a-verses without a long dip are indeed unmetrical, and shall propose some further rules governing the arrangement and number of weak syllables in the a-verse, concentrating on the practice of two particular poets, the author of *B* and the author of the *SJ*. In a conclusion we shall briefly look at *P*. All of these three poems, *B*, *SJ* and *P*, are extant in comparatively early manuscripts. As far as *SJ* is concerned, both manuscript L (Oxford, Bodleian Laud Miscellaneous 656, probably written in Oxfordshire, and the base manuscript for both EETS editions of this poem) and P (Princeton, Princeton University Library Manuscript Taylor Medieval 11, from Yorkshire) date from the fourteenth century. The same dating has been suggested for the section of MS Bodley 264 (probably copied in London) containing *B*, and for MS BL Cotton Nero A.x, containing *P*.[14] *SJ* and *P* were probably composed in a North West Midland dialect, and *B* further south in the Midlands, possibly in Gloucestershire.[15]

throughout the line, see e.g. most of the rules formulated by Attridge (the offbeat rule, p. 162; the promotion rule, p. 167; the demotion rule, p. 169).

[10] David Lawton, 'The Idea of Alliterative Poetry: Alliterative Meter and *Piers Plowman*', in *'Such Werkis to Werche': Essays on Piers Plowman in Honor of David C. Fowler*, ed. M. F. Vaughan (East Lansing, Mich., 1993), pp. 147–68 (p. 158).

[11] Luick, 'Stabreimzeile', especially pp. 424–5, 561–2.

[12] Duggan, 'Aspects of A-Verse Rhythms', p. 497, 'Extended A-Verses', p. 73.

[13] Duggan, 'Aspects of A-Verse Rhythms', p. 482.

[14] On the dating and localisation of these manuscripts see also pp. 10–13 above.

[15] See Magoun (ed.), *Gests*, p. 89.

In examining the evidence concerning the structure of the a-verse, we have excluded from consideration those a-verses where the placement or number of the beats is uncertain or likely to be the subject of argument, for instance a-verses which have only one alliterating syllable, extended a-verses, or a-verses where disjunction between beat and alliteration appears to be a possibility.[16] This exclusion should not be construed as a sign that we believe such lines to be exceptions to the a-verse rules we posit in this chapter. In our view, the poets of *B* and *SJ* only ever wrote a-verses with two beats, although such verses may have more than two alliterating syllables or more than two open-classed words. This view, which we have defended in the preceding chapter, is controversial, however, and it is procedurally sensible to disregard data that may be subject to different interpretations.

Our initial classification of dips as long or short did not take into account the possible syllabic value of final *–e*. We suspected that, in the process of making the classification, lines where pronounced final *–e* was necessary would reveal a distinctive typology which would give us clues about which final *–es* were in fact pronounced by our poets. A typology of this kind did indeed emerge, and is outlined below (pp. 233–44).

[16] For the purpose of determining which might be considered heavy a-verses, we have basically used Duggan's rules, i.e. that in general open class words bear stress, closed class words and monosyllabic adverbs do not (see Duggan, 'Stress Assignment'). We include, under closed-class words, predeterminers, ordinals and quantifiers such as 'all', 'each' and 'much', i.e. words such as those listed by Cable under item 1 of his stress classification (see Cable, *Alliterative Tradition*, p. 80, and cf. Randolph Quirk, Sidney Greenbaum *et al.*, *A Grammar of Contemporary English* (London, 1972), §4.17ff.). As our previous chapter outlines, we do not consider the rules outlined by Duggan and Cable to provide a reliable method of determining which words take a beat (or, indeed, how many beats there may be in a given a-verse), but that is a separate argument; in this particular discussion we shall admit as evidence only those lines where the placement of the beat is uncontroversial. Lines excluded from consideration on the above grounds include: *SJ* 2, 6, 12, 17, 23, 31, 34, 36, 37, 51, 55, 58, 59, 61, 62, 65, 67, 70, 71, 73, 75, 84, 90, 91, 93, 97, *etc.* and *B* 9, 10, 11, 12, 14, 34, 36, 41, 43, 47, 55, 58, 64, 69, 73, 83, 91, 94, 95, *etc.* On our two-beat scansion (without disjunction of beat and alliteration), virtually all extended a-verses are rhythmically regular by the rhythmical rules we propose in this chapter.

**The Long Dip Requirement**

Before we begin to consider which variations from the norm are permissible in the a-verse, it will be helpful to consider what that norm actually is. Of the three possible dips (the first dip before the first alliterating beat, the second dip between the first and second beats, and the third dip between the second beat and the caesura), the second dip is the one that is most consistently long. Of nearly 800 lines in *B* where the placement of the beats is clear, just over 80% have an uncontroversial long medial dip, i.e. a long medial dip which does not depend on final *–e* or an inflexion or other weak syllable which is not graphically present. A long medial dip is therefore at the very least an a-verse norm.[17] The opposite pattern applies in the final dip: just under 80% of the a-verses in *B* have a final dip consisting of zero or a weakly stressed syllable: either schwa, some sort of inflexional ending (*–es*, *–ed*, *–en*, infinitive *e*) or an enclitic pronoun, or words ending in *–el*, *–er*, *–en*, or vowels.[18] Over 75% of lines have long initial dips.[19] The proportions are slightly different in *SJ*, but they nevertheless suggest that the norm is the same: just under 80% of medial dips are long, nearly 70% of final dips consist of zero or a weakly stressed syllable and just over 50% of initial dips are long.[20] The norm, then, consists of a long initial dip, a long medial dip and a non-existent (or extremely weak) final dip, as in the following:

ȝif þou be prophete of pris (*SJ* 15)
Whan þis weith at his wil (*B* 1)[21]

[17] See e.g. *B* 1, 3, 5, 6, 7, 13, 15, 16, 17, 18, 21, 24, 25, 26, 27, 28, 29, 30, 33, 34, 35, 37, 40, 42, 43, 44, 45, 46, 49, 50, 51, 52, 53, 54, 55, 56, 58, 59, 60, 63, 66, 67, 68, 71, 73, 75, 76, 78, 79, 82, 83, 85.

[18] See e.g. *B* 1, 3–9, 11–16, 18–22, 25–35, 37–47, 49–54, 57–58, 60–62, 64–73, 75–76, 78, 80–85.

[19] See e.g. *B* 1, 5, 7, 8, 13, 16, 18, 20, 24, 25, 26, 27, 28, 29, 30, 31, 32, 33, 35, 37, 38, 40, 42, 44, 45, 46, 49, 50, 52, 54, 57, 59, 62, 65.

[20] For long medial dips in *SJ*, see, for example, 3, 5, 11, 14, 15, 18, 19, 20, 21, 25, 26, 30, 32, 33, 35, 38, 39, 40, 41, 45, 46; for final dips consisting of zero or a weakly stressed syllable, see 1, 15, 18, 19, 20, 21, 22, 25, 26, 30, 32, 33, 35, 38, 39, 40, 41, 46; for long initial dips, see 15, 18, 19, 20, 21, 25, 26, 30, 32, 33, 38, 39, 41, 42, 48.

[21] And see also *SJ* 18, 19, 20, 21, 22, 25, 26, 30, 32, 33, 38, 40, 41, 48, 49, 50, 55, 56, 63, 66, 68, 72, 75, 76, 77, 79, 82, 84, 86, 87, 88, 89, 90, 94, 96, 99, 100, 102, 107, 115, 116, 118, 122, 123, 130, 134, 135, 139, 140, 143, *etc*; *B* 5, 7, 13, 15 (assuming penultimate stress in *Alixandre*) 16, 24, 25, 26, 27, 28, 29, 30, 33, 35,

To what extent are variations from this statistical norm permitted? We think that Luick was right to believe that a-verses without a long dip were unacceptable to alliterative poets. Indeed, the evidence for this is consistently stronger than the evidence for a long-dip requirement in the b-verse. Thus in MS L of *SJ* there are 61 possible b-verses without a long dip; 58 of these have been emended by Hanna and Lawton.[22] In the a-verse, we find only 29 possible exceptions, some of which are regular if pronounced historical *–e* is assumed:

As clene as clef (106)
Tadde & Tomas (150)
A corteys Crist (181)
Of selke and sendel (418)
Hors and harnays (442 and 514)
Plate ne pesan (515)
As greued griffouns (556)
And mallen metel (560)
Made wide weyes (646)
And arwes arwely (658)
(assuming medial *–e* is not syllabic)
With deþ by dome (695)
Somme hent her heere (715)
(assuming final *–e* is not syllabic)
And somme for deil (716) (as above)
In tokne of tresoun (727)
(assuming elision)
Merked montayns (730)
Hanleþ harnays (758)
þan metles marre (782)
Fouȝt riȝt felly (822)
Marchals maser (886)
Se faucons fle (892)
Tornen trifflyn (895)
þan flowe þat freke (909)
And kayȝt þe cors (948)
þat fure out flowe (1126)
Bot Ion þe ienfulle (1137)
As glowande gled-fure (1256)
Doun bete þe bilde (1264)

Of these lines, nine have been emended by Hanna and Lawton on non-metrical grounds so that they do in fact have at least one long dip (646, 658, 715, 716, 822, 886, 895, 948, 1126). In a number of lines medial or historical *–e* (or an *–en* inflexion) is present or possible. At 181, 556, and 1137 we have disyllabic adjectives with justified inflectional *–e* in the vocative (*corteys*), after the definite article (*ienfulle*) and in the plural (*greued*).[23] The verbal ending *–ande*, present at 1256, is regularly disyllabic in the b-verse;[24] and at 1264 the verb *bete* is in the infinitive and would

37, 40, 42, 44, 45, 46, 49, 50, 52, 54, 58, 59, 66, 68, 71, 75, 76, 78, 82, 83, 85, 87, 89, 90, 92, 96, 98, 99, 100, 107, 108, 112, 113, 116, 117, 119, 122, 123 etc.

[22] See their list of emendations at *Siege*, p. xcv. Hanna and Lawton retain 199, 292, 477 (see their notes to these lines, and on 199 see below, p. 108 n. 89).

[23] As we have argued above (pp. 116 n. 108) our position is that inflectional final *–e* was retained in disyllabic adjectives excepting ones with stems in *–en*, *–er*, *–el*, or vowel.

[24] See Duggan, 'Rhythmic Structure', p. 143.

therefore normally be expected to have a pronounced inflexion in non-eliding position.[25] At 515 *Plate* has etymological –*e*. At 695 the noun (*deþ*) is in the dative. In the case of 560 the poet's form of the verb (glossed by Hanna and Lawton as 'hammered, pounded') may have been *malleden* rather than *mallen* (note that the –*eden* ending is regularly subject to scribal reduction, either to –*ed* or to –*en*),[26] and this might also suggest that *merked* in 730 should perhaps be read as *merkeden*. In the case of 727, *token* (rather than *tokne* with elision) is clearly a possibility. Medial *e* is possible in 782 (Hanna and Lawton, in fact, have *metles* in the text but *meteles* in the glossary; Kölbing and Day read L as *metles*). The scribal versions of 758 are many and various (and Kölbing and Day emend); but, even if we accept Hanna and Lawton's reading, it remains possible that the verb may have been trisyllabic (*handeleþ*). A syllabic plural inflexion (*faucones* rather than *faucouns* is possible at 892 (cf. the b-verse readings at *SJ* 43, 72, 76, 103, 118 *etc.* and note Hanna and Lawton's emendation at 686). The proper name *Tadde* at 150 could well have had a disyllabic or even trisyllabic form (*Thaddeus*). Several short a-verses have majority readings which would result in at least one long dip:

106 as[2]; PAUDEC *as þe*
418 and; A *and with*; UDEC *and of*[27]
442 harnays; A *thaire hanayse*; UDEC *her herneys*[28]
909 flowe; PADEC *fled* (with possible inflexional –*e*); U *fledden*

The situation in *B* is also clear. Assuming final –*e* in the usual contexts, there are just a couple of exceptions — 'wordliche wisdam' (102), 'þat wantede wisdam' (263) — both of which we think are

[25] A pronounced infinitive ending is a regular requirement in the b-verse (see e.g. *SJ* 343, 411, 432, 641). Hanna and Lawton regularly emend such final –*e*s to –*en*, but the evidence does not suggest that this is necessary in non-eliding position (see pp. 91–96 above)

[26] At *SJ* 299, for instance, all manuscripts except L have *callede* for L *callen* (the original was probably *calleden*); at 576 *dascheden* appears as *daschen* in P and A (the scribes add *doune* and *thaire* respectively to maintain the b-verse metre), while UC and D have *dasshed* (in the case of U and C with added *the*); at 793, L *dropeden* appears as *droppen* in PD, while in the b-verse Hanna and Lawton emend to *dryeden*, the manuscripts reading variously *dryed* and *dryen* and, in the case of L, *dyed*.

[27] Note also that PA read 'selcouth werke' for L 'sendel'.

[28] As Duggan observes ('Aspects of A-Verse Rhythms', p. 484) this reading also raises questions about the authenticity of the reading at 514 (Duggan uses the Kölbing-Day edition and so refers to these lines as 438 and 510).

genuine a-verses, since there is evidence to suggest that the *B* poet could still pronounce final *–e* after preterites in *–ed*, and that *wordlyche* was trisyllabic in both weak and strong flexion.[29]

There is only slender evidence, then, that verses without a long dip were in any way acceptable;[30] and since a-verse exceptions are considerably fewer than b-verse ones, the position that short verses are unmetrical should apply *a fortiori* to the a-verse. It is therefore regrettable that editors have adopted that position only towards b-verses.

## A-verses without two long dips

It is much more difficult to judge exactly what the rules might be beyond this point. Two approaches seem to be worth considering. Does the metrical pattern of the a-verse have to be distinct from that of the b-verse (and, if so, in what ways?); and, given the fact that in b-verses that the form of one dip determines that taken by the other, is the form a given a-verse dip in any way dependent on that found in the other two dips in the a-verse? Clearly, given that two long dips are the norm, the principle of rhythmic dissimilation cannot be operative within the a-verse, but there may be other ways in which the a-verse dips are interdependent. The observations by Duggan and Turville-Petre on extra-long a-verse dips in *WA* (which tend to occur in that poem only when the other two dips have two or fewer unstressed syllables)[31] suggest that it may be fruitful to explore the possibility that alliterative poets deliberately wrote longer dips when the other dips in the a-verse are short. What happens, then, in a-verses that do not contain a long initial and long medial dip?

In such abnormal a-verses we almost always find one or other of the following three features:

[29] See pp. 111, 236.

[30] Similar arguments can be made about lines in *B* which at first sight appear to have no long dip. Thus a pronounced plural verb inflexion, regularly necessary in the b-verse (see 20, 33, 35, 51, 61, 119, 123, 136, 146, would restore a long medial dip to 19, 500; pronunciation of final *–e* on *mihte* would restore a long initial dip to 264 (cf. the b-verse of the following line).

[31] Duggan and Turville-Petre (eds), p. xx.

1) extra-long dips (by which we mean dips of four or more unaccented syllables). Note that in normal a-verses and in b-verses such dips are anomalous and probably unmetrical.[32]
2) heavy elements at verse ending, such as suffixes *–dam*, *–man*, *–chef*, *–ing*, *–les*, *–ly*, which retained secondary stress,[33] monosyllabic adverbs, and verbs such as 'be' and 'do', as in 'Þrow Pylat pyned he was' (*SJ* 8)
3) sequences of two or more weakly stressed syllables at a-verse ending, as in *SJ* 24, 'Or princes presed in hem' or *B* 60, '& kennen þe conquerour'. (It is possible that the final syllable in some of these sequences, e.g. 'conquerour', carries secondary stress.)

We shall call the final dips with a single secondary stress 'heavy' and those with two or more unaccented syllables 'long'.

The notion of a 'heavy' dip requires some justification, for in the metrical analysis of ME alliterative verse it is usually thought that secondary stress is irrelevant, and that words or syllables count simply as being either stressed or unstressed. That this mode of analysis is inadequate is indicated by the fact that at line ending one *unstressed* syllable is *mandatory*, while a syllable with *secondary* stress is *impermissible*.[34] Of course, long final dips are not permitted at line ending either. In a-verses that have heavy or long final dips, we therefore encounter endings that would be impossible in the b-verse:

Whyle Pylat was provost (*SJ* 3)
Þey Sesar sakles were (*SJ* 7)
A pyler py3t was doun (*SJ* 10)
Whyppes of quyrboyle (*SJ* 11)
To þe athel emperour (*SJ* 50)[35]
Alle ben þey endeles (*SJ* 117)

Þe princes and þe prelates (*SJ* 161)
Of Crist and þe kerchef (*SJ* 211)
Þe kny3tes with þe kerchef (*SJ* 218)
Þe wede fram þe womman (*SJ* 229)
Of Iosophat þer Ihesu Crist (*SJ* 431; PAUDEC omit *Crist*)

[32] See Noriko Inoue, 'The A-Verse', pp. 121–5. Inoue concludes: 'My findings suggest that in the b-verse the [*Gawain*] poet always avoids producing a dip of more than three syllables by selecting from doublet forms' (p. 125). The doublet forms examined by Inoue are various prepositional phrases which gave the poet the option of using either *on* or *vpon*.

[33] See Ten Brink, *Chaucer's Language*, pp. 194, 197–8.

[34] For a characterisation of the kinds of unstressed syllables permitted at line ending, see above, p. 24–25. As we observe there, *Piers Plowman* and *Destruction of Troy* are exceptions.

[35] Note that *athel* belongs to a class of disyllabic adjectives (in *–en*, *–el*, *–er*) that did not take final *–e* (see p. 116 n. 108 and pp. 234–6 below).

Ful raþe rommede he (*B* 2)
Þanne weies of worshipe (*B* 18; *þanne* (conj.) = monosyllabic)
Kairus cofli til hem (*B* 48)
By ludus of þe langage (*B* 56)
Of me þat miȝteles am (*B* 74)
Whi farest þou so fihtinge (*B* 79)
Of erþe to be emperour (*B* 86)
In cost þere þe kyng was (*B* 141)
Hit wasteþ no wisdam (*B* 238)
But if we ony enemis (*B* 343)
Þer-for we al ouur comen (*B* 345)
And to miche mischef (*B* 372)
Where-wiþ we mihte mis-do (*B* 464)
Þat in kinde colour (*B* 482)
But oure kinde konninge (*B* 583)
No no sory sacrifice (*B* 639)
As a burn bereþ now (*B* 644)
þat ȝe auowen verraie (*B* 671)
But of hur owne offringe (*B* 743)
For ȝour ydil idolus (*B* 754)[36]
And seggus for ȝe so don (*B* 760)
And ludus ȝif hem loþ be (*B* 768)
Of clergie þat clene is (*B* 899)
But whan þe daies dimme ben (*B* 928)
But we ben pore pilegrimus (*B* 983)
For gold þouh it gay be (*B* 1028)

What is interesting about the above examples is that in all cases the heavy or long final dip follows a short initial or medial dip (or sometimes both, as in the case of *SJ* 7, 24, *B* 2, 48, 74). This pattern is standard in both *B* and *SJ*: long or heavy final dips occur in a-verses when one of the preceding dips is short. By contrast, when both the initial and medial dip are long, a final heavy or long dip is suspiciously rare. In the whole of *B* and in *SJ*[37] we find only six exceptions, and none of these is convincingly authorial:

And weren [inwardly] endeles (*SJ* 118; *sic* A, L *endeles euer*)
þe fifþe of his felawys (*SJ* 146; L *and þe*)
With engynes to Ierusalem (*SJ* 324; PDC *gynnes*)
Saue [an an]lepy olyfaunt (*SJ* 583; *sic* A; L *olepy*)
We no recche of no richesse (*B* 369)
ȝe ne herien nouht herteli (*B* 641)

*SJ* 118 is an emendation by Hanna and Lawton, resulting in an a-verse with three long dips. The original L reading does not present the same problems, and seems to us altogether superior to the reading of MS A. At *SJ* 146 L has an a-verse with three long dips, but this not the case in the majority of the manuscripts and the verse is correctly emended by Hanna and Lawton. At *SJ* 324 PDC have *gynnes* for *engynes*. At *SJ* 583 the verse as emended by Hanna and Lawton has three long dips, but the

[36] Final *–e* after *ydil* is again impossible. See the note above.
[37] In the case of *SJ* we record lines as printed in Hanna and Lawton's edition, with readings from L.

original L reading omits *an*,[38] thus giving a short initial dip. The P reading (*anely an*, i.e. 'only an'), which would have the same effect, is also a possibility. The only two lines from *B* both result from the use of a double negative, a construction which often appears to be scribal in this poem.[39]

It is also worth noting that there appears to be a relationship between the length of the final dip and the number of short dips which precede it. A *long* final dip can be preceded by either one or two short dips (contrast *SJ* 3 and 211 with *SJ* 117 and 161) but in the case of a *short*, heavy final dip one of the preceding dips must be long (see *SJ* 7, 10, 245 etc.). This pattern maintains the rule that the a-verse must have at least one long dip,[40] but militates aginst Cable's argument that two long dips are an a-verse requirement.

Once we have noticed the interrelationship between a-verse dips, it is easy to notice also that extra-long medial or initial dips (i.e. dips with four or more unaccented syllables) appear to occur in similar situations, that is a four-syllable medial dip will occur in conjunction with a short initial dip and vice versa (although the pattern with the extra-long medial dip is by far the more common):[41]

Blyndfelled as a be (*SJ* 14; *sic* PAUDEC, L *hym as*)
þat souȝt oft ouer þe se (*SJ* 46)
þat kneleþ doun to þat cloþ (*SJ* 171)
With processioun and pres (*SJ* 220)
Veronyk and þe vail (*SJ* 235)
þe body suþ al aboute (*SJ* 254)
My sone is next to myself (*SJ* 970)
Comyn in here owen kynd (*SJ* 1054)
Fellen doun for defaute (*SJ* 1077)
Batail aboute þe borwe (*SJ* 1085)
ȝit beter were at o brayde (*SJ* 1099)
To worchyn vndere þe wal (*SJ* 1109)
As Tytus after a tyme (*SJ* 1113)

[38] Kölbing and Day retain L. As they point out in their note to this line, the construction without article is exactly paralleled in *Havelok*; see also *Cursor Mundi*, ed. R. Morris, 7 vols, EETS OS 57, 59, 62, 66, 68, 100, 101 (London 1874–93), IV, 27939 (Vesp.).

[39] See *B* 742b, 'nor no mastrie on erþe', *B* 784b, 'ye ne soffre no paine', and *B* 980b, 'we ne wone nouht euer'. See also below, p. 230.

[40] Once again, there are rare exceptions (at *SJ* 727, 758 and 1256), but we have already discussed these (see above p. 223) and found that, in each case, there is evidence to suggest that the second dip was in fact initially long.

[41] Many extended b-verses such as 'To quélle þe emperour qúyk' (*SJ* 904) show the same structure on our two-beat scansion. Another possible example of an a-verse with an extra-long dip is *SJ* 483, 'Whan Pharao and his ferde', assuming trisyllabic pronunciation of 'Pharao', as in Chaucer (*BD* 282) and Gower (*CA* 5.1654).

þey setten vpon eche side (*SJ* 305)
A fauchyn vnder his feet (*SJ* 396)
þey wolle no3t þe heþen here (*SJ* 636)
By þat was many bold burne (*SJ* 663)
By þat was þe day don (*SJ* 729)
[Bot] Waspasian þe wile (*SJ* 797; L omits *Bot*)
Assaylen on eche a side (*SJ* 802)
Frosletes fro þe ferst (*SJ* 835)
Suþ euereche a segge (*SJ* 853)
Comen forþ with þe kyng (*SJ* 859)
Louten alle to þe lord (*SJ* 960)
Bot wenten with hem to þe walle (*SJ* 1153)
With Symond þat oþer segge (*SJ* 1160)
[G]oren euereche a gome (*SJ* 1171; L *Toren*)
Tyen out of þe toun (*SJ* 1182)
3ernes now of my 3ift (*B* 67)
& hem þat in þi bodi ben (*B* 342)
& derely wiþ-oute deþ (*B* 364)
& deliten in no dede (*B* 505)
3e ben to þe helle-hond (*B* 792)
3e witen wel whan a wolf (*B* 860)
We faren alle to þe flod (*B* 1024)

As was the case with extra-long or heavy final dips, four-syllable dips do not usually occur in these particular poems unless the norm of a long initial and a long medial dip is broken, i.e. an extra-long initial dip usually only occurs in conjunction with a short medial dip and vice versa. Of course, there are some possible exceptions; the following occur in the base manuscript L and/or in Hanna and Lawton's edition:

Vmbecasten with a cry (*SJ* 18; L *hym with*)
Oþer chauntementes or charmes (*SJ* 100)
Þerof Waspasian was ware (*SJ* 209)
Or Y to þe walles schal wende (*SJ* 355)
Was neuer Waspasian so wroþe (*SJ* 375)
Þus han þey certifiet þe [to sey] (*SJ* 384; L omits 'to sey')
Ouer al þe cite to se (*SJ* 420)
Weren tourmented on a tre (*SJ* 710)
Þerouer he casteþ a cote (*SJ* 750)
Alle assenteden to þe sawe (*SJ* 883)
Bot alle ouertourned and tilt (*SJ* 1020)
Þan Titus toward his tentis (*SJ* 1133; if 'than' is disyllabic)
And oþer Symound of his assent (*SJ* 1138)
And whan þe temple was ouert[ilt] (*SJ* 1293; L *ouertourned*)

But the authenticity and the precise syllabic form of many of the a-verses listed above are uncertain. At *SJ* 18, L *hym* is present in only two manuscripts and is removed by Hanna and Lawton. At *SJ* 100, the four-syllable medial dip would depend on both the medial *–e–* and the *–es* ending of *chauntementes* being syllabic, and there is, in any case, considerable manuscript variation, including the omission by AUDEC of *Oþer*. At *SJ* 355, only one of the manuscripts which actually have a reading (three, including Thornton's copy, do not) shares the L reading that results in the four-syllable dip; P, for instance reads 'Or to þe walles sall I wend'. At *SJ* 384, PU lack *þe.* At *SJ* 710, the four-syllable dip depends on the past participle *tourmented,* which in PAU appears in the French form *turment* (perhaps a deliberate attempt to avoid a four-syllable dip),[42] and something similar may account for *SJ* 883, where U has *assent.* At *SJ* 1138, PAVC lack *his* and therefore have a trisyllabic medial dip. In a number of other cases, the actual syllable count is doubtful: in four cases (*SJ* 420, 750, 1020 and 1293), the four-syllable dip is dependent on disyllabic rather than monosyllabic 'over' and in two (*SJ* 209 and 375) on a four-syllable pronunciation of 'Vaspasian'.

This exclusive use of extra-long dips in a-verses without a long initial and medial is equally striking in *B*, where only the following a-verses can be counted as exceptions:

And ȝif þei ne hadde none holis (*B* 57)
I ne haue no lordschipe of lif (*B* 76)
Þat i ne am temted ful tid (*B* 98)
Þanne þe mascedonius men (*B* 145)
Hit ne is no leue in our land (*B* 311)
We ne haue fere of no fon (*B* 346)
To maken hem comelokuer corn (*B* 407)
We ne faren to no philozofrus (*B* 457)
ȝe ne vndurstonde nouht þat stounde (*B* 609)
ȝe holden hure a goodesse god (*B* 695)
ȝe ne leuen not on a lord (*B* 706)
But eueri wile of a wehy [*sic*] (*B* 736)
Whan þei ne han miht of no mor (*B* 742)
& euerich pinchen his part (*B* 751)
So wheþur þei graunte hit or gruche (*B* 770)
We ne said noukt king be þou sur (*B* 991)

However, at *B* 145, 736 and 751, possible four-syllable dips would depend on non-contracted pronunciations of *Mascedonius*, *eueri* and *euerich*, while at 770 a monosyllabic form of 'whether' is a possibility. All the remaining lines involve either an inflectional *–en* (*B* 407, 695), where the poet may have written *–e*, or a double non-contracted negative, and the way in which this particular unusual combination of long dip plus extra-long dip clusters round this particular construction suggests that it may

[42] Compare the metrically motivated variation between *depaynt* and *depaynted* in the Cotton Nero poems (see above, p. 39)

have been scribal, as b-verse evidence confirms (see above, n. 39). Contracted negations are evidently possible in a number of these a-verses, and would be entirely consistent with the poet's dialect (Gloucestershire), which is recognised as a core area for contracted negation.[43]

The restriction of both extra-long initial or medial dips and long or heavy final dips to positions where the norm of long initial and medial dips has been broken implies a motivated relationship between these phenomena. Possibly, this relationship is simply permissive, that is, an extra-long initial or medial dip or a long or heavy final dip is only allowed where the norm of a long initial and a long medial dip has been breached. Looked at like this, the pattern can be seen as reflecting a restriction on a-verse length: only when the earlier part of the verse is shorter than would normally be expected are extra-long dips or a long or heavy final dip permissible. This view of the relationship receives support from the fact that the two patterns outlined above appear to be mutually exclusive: a four-syllable dip does not normally occur in conjunction with an extra heavy or long final dip. The following are apparent exceptions:

> And Y schal þe redly rewarde (*SJ* 92; PUDC omit 'And'; PA *redly þe* )
> Receyued hit myd reuerence (*SJ* 230)
> þe vernycle after Veronyk (*SJ* 261; *sic* PAUDEC, L *veronycle*)
> Ierusalem and Ierico (*SJ* 302)
> [C]hoppyn ouer þe cheuentayns (*SJ* 329;L *Thoppyn*)
> Assembleden at þe cite (*SJ* 647; P *Assemblede*)
> To hold þat þey byhot han (*SJ* 1024, if the infinitive ending is syllabic)
> Tri-ce[r]berus þe tenful (*B* 793)

Once again, these exceptions are unconvincing. At *SJ* 92, line-initial *And* is not present in PUDC, a grouping which includes manuscripts from two branches of the stemma and the early manuscript P, while the word order of PA reduces the syllable count. At *SJ* 647, the P reading would

[43] Richard Hogg, 'The Spread of Negative Contraction in Early English', in A. Curzan and K. Emmons (eds), *Studies in the History of the English Language II: Unfolding Conversations* (Berlin, 2004), pp. 459–82 (p. 473). Hogg tries to explain the unusual number of uncontracted negatives in *B* by suggesting it was a comparatively late work written at a time when such forms were in the process of being lost. The metrical evidence we outline suggests instead that many non-contracted forms listed are scribal (the dialect of the scribe belonging not to Gloucestershire but to the East Midlands, see above, p. 11).

result in elision which would reduce the syllable count (it is impossible to tell from H&L's apparatus whether other MSS share P's reading). At *SJ* 1024, PAVUEC read *heght* for L *byhot* and D has *hit*. The four-syllable dip at *SJ* 230 depends on a trisyllabic pronunciation of *Receyued*; that at *SJ* 329 depends on a disyllabic pronunciation of 'ouer'; while that at *B* 793 depends on a four-syllable pronunciation of *Tricerberus*. At *SJ* 261, elision would normally operate to reduce the medial dip to three syllables.

**A-verse and b-verse asymmetry**

We have argued so far that the poets of *SJ* and *B* wrote a-verses with at least one long dip. Two long dips are not a requirement in a-verses but a norm. When that norm is broken the poets wrote either extra-long dips (with four or more unaccented syllables) or a heavy or long final dip; poets do not seem to have introduced such variations into a-verses with two long dips. In this section we would like to take our argument one step further by exploring the possibility that extra-long dips and heavy or long final dips are not merely *permissible* in a-verses without a long initial and medial dip but may in fact be *mandatory*: they provide compensation in order to maintain the distinction between the a- and the b-verse. Although we fundamentally agree with Cable's claim that the 'rhythmical patterns of the two halves of the line are mutually exclusive',[44] we would insist that the use of two long dips in the a-verse is only one of a number of ways in which this dissimilation can be achieved.[45] Since b-verses must end in one and only one unstressed syllable, the introduction of a long or heavy final dip into the a-verse may also have served to maintain the distinctiveness of a-verse metre. And since dips of four or more unaccented syllables seem to be unmetrical in b-verses, their introduction into a-verses would be yet another way of securing asymmetry between the half lines. That extra-long dips are an effective way of marking that asymmetry may be surmised from the rhythms of actual speech, where a two- or three-syllable dip is normally the upward limit in the English

[44] Cable, *English Alliterative Tradition*, p. 86.

[45] Geoffrey Russom's research is uncovering some other unexpected asymmetries between the two hemistichs. See G. Russom, 'The Evolution of the A-Verse in Middle English Alliterative Meter', in *Studies in the History of the English Language* III (Berlin, 2007), 63–87. We are grateful to Professor Russom for allowing us to read this article in typescript.

language.[46] A four-syllable dip is therefore likely to be perceived as a salient prosodic feature; and we think that the point of its use in alliterative metre is to make the a-verse sound markedly longer than the b-verse. Our theory, then, is that a-verse metre is distinct from b-verse metre, normally because the a-verse has two long dips (forbidden in the b-verse); where that norm is broken, extra-long dips or heavy or long final dips (also forbidden in the b-verse) are essential forms of compensation.

The manuscripts of *SJ* and *B* contain various a-verses that appear to infringe our a-verse rules (i.e. a-verses where the absence of a long initial and medial dip does *not* seem to result in these forms of compensation), just as they contain various b-verses that contradict the b-verse rule. What convinces us that our a-verse rules are nevertheless correct is the fact that these apparent exceptions have features in common with unmetrical b-verses. We distinguish several of these common features, and give a representative selection of examples under different headings.

*Words with long and short forms*

As Hoyt Duggan has observed,[47] scribes of alliterative poems were apt to interchange longer and shorter forms of the same word. This fact explains various unmetrical b-verses, such as the following:

> *syþen* wyȝeȝ wyl torne (*P* 518)
> (Duggan suggests emendation to *syn*)
> *amyd* þe face (*SJ* L 30)
> (Hanna and Lawton emend to *inmyddis*, after PUDC)
> *aȝen* ȝour wille (*SJ* L 1219)
> (Hanna and Lawton emend to *agenes*; most MSS have forms with final –*s*)

A number of a-verses that are unmetrical by our understanding cluster around the same prepositions and conjunctions:

> Becroked *aȝens* kynde (*SJ* 1033; *aȝenes*)
> A calf *aȝen* kynde (*SJ* 1227; D *al agayn*; *al ayenes*)
> *Suþ* britaged aboute (*SJ* 338; *Syþen*)
> *Syþ* he þe lede haþ lost (*SJ* 1206; *Syþen*)[48]

[46] See Richard Hogg and C. B. McCully, *Metrical Phonology: a Coursebook* (Cambridge, 1987), pp. 224–5.
[47] Duggan, 'The Shape of the B-Verse', pp. 579–80.
[48] See also *SJ* 543, 685, 721, 747.

*SJ* 1033 and 1227 can be regularised with the same emendation that Hanna and Lawton make to the b-verse of 1219. In the case of *suþ*, the Kölbing-Day edition[49] clearly shows that in the majority of cases scribal variants suggest a possible alternative disyllabic reading for *Suþ* (*sethen*, *sythen* etc.) in *SJ*.[50] If the poet used the longer forms *syþen* and *aȝenes* (with addition of *al* at *SJ* 1227), these a-verses would be metrically regular.[51]

*Combinations of disyllabic premodifier+noun, where the premodifier (adjective or genitive plural in* –n*) has justified final* –e.

Various b-verses with these combinations are problematic, unless one assumes inflectonial –*e*. For example,

| | |
|---|---|
| with *carful* wordes (*SJ* 1014) | *corsede* þouhtous (*B* 767) |
| with *rewful* wordes (*SJ* 1083) | on *folken* wyse (*C* 271) |

Duggan has argued that in b-verses such combinations are metrically regular.[52] In his view, this is so not because final –*e* was retained after disyllabic adjectives, but because it had once been acceptable and survived as a relic in the practices of poets who themselves no longer pronounced schwa after paroxytonics. As our discussion of adverbs and adjectives in –*lyche* will have made clear, we do not find this argument convincing, not least because almost all of the disyllabic adjectives in this

[49] The apparatus in Hanna and Lawton's edition is inadequate for these purposes.

[50] The fact that the b-verses in *SJ* provide no evidence to support such a-verse emendations simply reflects the syntactic structure of the line: no b-verse in *SJ* contains the word 'since'.

[51] In the case of *SJ* 13, which appears in the Hanna and Lawton edition as 'Suþ stoked on a stole', the original L reading (with *hym on* for *on*) provides a 4-syllable medial dip to compensate for the short initial dip. However, if, as seems likely, Hanna and Lawton's emendation is correct, this is a further example of the use of a monosyllabic form of the conjunction where a disyllabic form is required. In the case of *SJ* 945, the line as it appears in Hanna and Lawton's edition (*Suþ gored the gorel*) may perhaps contain adequate final dip compensation for the short initial dip, but Hanna and Lawton admit to emending to *gorel* from L (and all other manuscripts except E) *gome* only 'with some trepidation' and the majority reading suggests an original disyllabic conjunction to provide a long inital dip.

[52] See Duggan and Turville-Petre (eds), *Wars*, p. xxii, and Duggan 'Final –*e*'.

grammetrical position have grammatically justified *–e*.[53] In other words, where final *–e* is needed for a long dip it tends to be historically justified. The solution to unmetrical b-verses such as the four above-cited examples is therefore to add the final *–e* omitted by the scribe (*carful[le]*, *rewful[le]*, *folken[e]*). Various a-verses appear unmetrical for the same reason, namely scribal loss of *–e*. We include some examples where written final *–e* has been preserved:

| | |
|---|---|
| For þat *mansed* man (*SJ* 158) | Of þe *fletinge* fihs (*B* 491) |
| And þat *worliche* wif (*SJ* 165; L *wordlich*) | & þe *guldene* ger (*B* 522) |
| For þe *doylful* deþ (*SJ* 226) | Wiþ þat *vnblisful* blod (*B* 543) |
| Of þis *wlon[k]fulle* worde (*SJ* 397) | Of brem *briddene* song (*B* 503) |
| & to þe *schamlese* schalk (*B* 20) | & for no *bestene* blod (*B* 611) |
| To oure *painede* peple (*B* 268) | After *ludene* lif (*B* 773) |

Note that in all these cases final *–e* is historically correct: the adjectives are weak, the premodifying nouns (shown in the last three examples) have the plural genitive ending in *–ene* < OE *–ena*.[54] In *B* that genitive *–e* is systematically retained in spelling.[55]

[53] See also *SJ* 485, 496, 550, 554, 556 (on which, see also discussion above, p. 223), 597, 768, 818, 872, 912 (and see also the discussion of *–ande* words below; similarly 1018, 1194, 1259), 978, and *B* 126, 387, 523, 529, 547, 559, 566, 603, 621, 772, 908, 970, 980, 999, 1085, 1087. The a-verse of *SJ* 54 ('over the Grekys grounde') may well also fall into this category, if *Grekys* is read as a form of 'Greekish' (cf. DEC *grekissh*). This appears to be the interpretation of Kölbing and Day, who record this word in the glossary as an adjective meaning 'Greek'. Hanna and Lawton, however, see it as a genitive. The same problem of construal is posed by *WA* 2795b, 'þe Grekis maistir' (A *Grekyn*) and 3745b, 'of Grekis kniȝtis'. Duggan and Turville-Petre gloss these as genitives. If *–e* was retained after paroxytonics, as we believe, the poet must have intended the adjective. Because disyllabic adjectives with stems in *–el*, *–er*, *–en*, *–y* joined the strong flexion, we regard as anomalous *SJ* 994, 'And to þe douȝti duke' (read *vnto*?) and possibly *B* 682, 'And þat folie fur', where, however, *folie* could be the noun (with final *–e*, as in *B* 654b, 'folies manye' and *B* 633a, 'Wiþ oþur folies fale').

[54] See also *B* 286, 522, 559, 566, 603, 615, 621, 908, 1087. Here also belongs *B* 547, 'Þorou þe, *prouede* prince, ful *proude* ben woxe'. With regard to *prouede*, Skeat could not decide between *proved* ('experienced',) and *proud*. Metre confirms the former: alliterative poets did not mechanically repeat the same stave, and *prouede* (with vocative *–e*) puts in place the metrically-required long dip.

[55] See also *B* 320, 640.

There are in *SJ* only four a-verses with an adjective+noun combination where an additional syllable is needed but where final *–e* cannot be supplied in accordance with historical grammar:

Þer is a *worlich* wif (*SJ* 95)
Hit was a *doylful* dede (*SJ* 163)
With a *tenful* toure (*SJ* 414)
Þis is a *comlich* kyng (*SJ* 768)

At *SJ* 95, ME *worthily* rather than *worthly* is possible, and MS D has *dolorous* at *SJ* 163.

In *B* we find the following counter-examples:

Whan no *wordliche* wele (B 32)
For oþur *wordiche* won (*B* 72)
*Worldiche* wisdam (*B* 102)
Wiþ no *scharpede* schar (*B* 294)
We han a *sertaine* somme (*B* 321)
Or in *erþliche* ese (*B* 360)
& to no *wikkede* werk (*B* 378)
Of ony *wikkede* werk (*B* 387)
ȝou wantus *worldiche* won (*B* 891)
And oþur *wordliche* werk (*B* 913)
We wonde *wikkede* werk (*B* 990)

The examples with the noun *werk* are unclear since the neuter noun *werk* retained an uninflected plural in ME.[56] The adjective *wordlich* (worldly) also behaves exceptionally in b-verses: we have drawn attention to this curiosity (and the comparable anomaly of *eorþlich* in Orm; cf. *erthlich* at *B* 360) in an earlier chapter (see above, p. 111). At *B* 294 the poet may have intended the plural *schares*, and at *B* 321 the plural *hauen* is possible (cf. 951, 956).

Our assumption, therefore, is that alliterative poets continued to pronounce historically justified *–e*. This assumption is further supported by the fact that this type of disyllabic adjective+noun combination is not accompanied by a long or heavy final dip, except in the case of disyllabic adjectives with stems (*–en*, *–er*, *–el*, *–y*) that disallow final *–e*, as in

To þe *athel* emperour (*SJ* 50)
For ȝour *ydel* idolus (*B* 754)
Þe *aþel* king alixandre (*B* 822)

These same disyllabic adjectives are found in alliterative verse in b-verses after a long dip:

and þe *reken* fyþel (*C* 1082)
to þe *neþer* houe (*SJ* 365)
for his *luþer* dedes (*SJ* 950)
ȝour *unsely* wombe (*B* 797)
of ȝoure *luþur* fare (*B* 878)
þat ȝe been *leþur* alle (*B* 1100)

[56] See Brunner, *Outline*, p. 50.

The implications of this pattern for Duggan's views on final *–e* are significant. Duggan believes that, by the late fourteenth century, final *–e* was no longer pronounced after disyllabic adjectives and that the use of the syntactic structure weak or plural disyllabic adjective+noun reflects an evolution in metrical requirements: as final *–e* was lost, b-verses without a long dip became acceptable in this particular syntactic context. But the evidence outlined makes this argument less convincing. If we were to accept it, we would also need to accept that alliterative poets considered not only the adjective's syntactic status (weak or strong?) but also its phonetic details: did the disyllabic adjective have a stem in *–el*, *–er*, or *–en*? These additional levels of complexity seem to us to make Duggan's explanation less likely and the alternative assumption that final *–e*s were pronounced rather more so.

*The word* eche

In the b-verses of *SJ*, this word is a regular troublemaker:

> *eche* gome hadde
> (*SJ* L 1167; Hanna and Lawton emend to *ilka* after U)
> *eche* freke hadde
> (*SJ* 1187; Hanna and Lawton emend to *ilka* after U)[57]

The same word crops again up in number of metrically irregular a-verses:

> *Eche* grayn is o god (*SJ* 111)
> And lord[chip] of *eche* londe (*SJ* 512; L *lord sup* for *lordschip*)
> Tille *eche* dale with dewe (*SJ* 628)[58]

As comparable b-verses suggest, the form *eche* in L often covers a disyllabic form, such as *ech a*, *ilka*, or possibly *echë* in datives.[59]

*The adverb* þanne

This adverb is historically disyllabic (< OE *þenne*, *þænne*), and its use at line ending in alliterative verse (see *B* 175, *SJ* 337, *C* 347, *etc*) and in the rhymes of Chaucer and Gower indicates that disyllabic pronunciation

[57] See also *SJ* 128b and 590b. At *SJ* 412a, Hanna and Lawton emend *eche* to *eche a*, the majority reading of the manuscripts.
[58] The verse may belong in the section on p. 238 below, since disyllabic *dale* is possible (and regular in Orm, Chaucer and Gower).
[59] As in Chaucer (see Ten Brink, *Language*, p. 168).

must also have been a possibility in later Middle English.[60] In alliterative verse, various infringements of the feminine-line-ending rule are due to the scribal omission of the final *–ne*. For example, at *WA* 1943b, 'said þe kyng þen', the poet is likely to have written *þenne* or *þanne* (this spelling is carefully observed in the Cotton Nero MS and in *B*, but only exceptionally in the MSS of *WA*).[61] The same scribal error is evident in *SJ*, where, at the end of line 181, the L scribe wrote *þan* (read *þanne*). In the a-verses of *SJ*, too, various lines with 'þan' create unmetricalities:

*þan* bygan þe burne (*SJ* 225)
*þan* with a liouns lote (*SJ* 1001)[62]
*þan* melys þe man (*SJ* 1305)

The scribe of *B* was more careful in his spelling:

*Þanne* raþe let þe rink (*B* 21)
*Þanne* weren from hem went (*B* 53)

Disyllabic pronunciation (*þanne*) would regularise these a-verses.

*Other words with historically justified final* –e *(etymological, organic, and analogical)*
As we have argued in the first two chapters, we think that final *–e* was still pronounced by alliterative poets in many more contexts than has generally been thought. It is for this reason that we encounter b-verses such as:

and *rennande* teris (*SJ* 230; D *and with*)
*aboute* four myle (*SJ* 292b; all MSS except A: *all abowte*)[63]
to *serche* your wylle (*SJ* 343; *sic* LPDC; E *wetyn*, U *serchen*;
(Hanna and Lawton emend after U)

[60] According to Wild, *Eigentümlichkeiten*, p. 13, *thanne* is only disyllabic in Chaucer at line ending; we are not sure of this: it was clearly optionally disyllabic in Gower's verse (*CA* 1.213, 2.623) and there are some lines in Chaucer where disyllabic *thanne* seems likely (*CT* IV.1486, *CT* VI.326, VI.772, VII.3276).
[61] See *WA* 1837, where *A* has *þene*, D *þen*.
[62] Disyllabic 'than' would result in a verse with a four-syllable initial dip providing compensation for a short medial dip. The other possibility is that *liouns* is trisyllabic (*liounes*). However, it is unusual in this poem for the adverb 'than' to be used in a position where a disyllabic reading would give a four-syllable initial dip, except in cases where the medial dip is short, though see 1093, 1237 (the latter evidently corrupt).
[63] Hanna and Lawton suggest, implausibly, that *foure* may be disyllabic after the preposition. Cf. *B* 282b, 'aboute þe werre'.

hem *grace* to sende (*SJ* 1023; *sic* LPVDC; E omits)
(Hanna and Lawton emend after AU *forto*)
and *seide* þis wordes (*SJ* 1295; *sic* LADEC; VU *seiden*;
(Hanna and Lawton emend after VU)
*rydinge* þedirre (*B* 2)
at *wille* we haue (*B* 72)
ȝe *saide* þis wordus (*B* 1006)

Verbal inflections were still syllabic, as some of these examples show;[64] before vowels poets wrote *–en* in plurals and infinitives to guard the inflection against elision.[65] Scribal omission of *–e* or *–en* probably accounts for irregular b-verses such as the following:

þey *drow* vp tentis (*SJ* 1337; *sic* LD; AUDE *vp payr*; VU *drowen*)
(Hanna and Lawton emend after VU).
to *say* þe truþe (*B* 275)
*shining* rede (*B* 479)
and *wrout* ful foule (*B* 1065)

If we asssume such b-verses to have been metrically regular in the original spelling, then the following a-verses would also be regular by our a-verse rules:

(a) a-verses with present participles and present participial adjectives in *–ande* (the usual form in *SJ*)[66] and *–inge* (*B*):

Þat in þis *wastinge* word (*B* 980)
And he *gronnand* glad (*SJ* 199)
þat alle *dasschande* doun (*SJ* 812)

(b) a-verses with finite verbs with inflectional endings (*–e* or *–en*), endings not always reflected in scribal spellings:

*Hadde* byr at þe bake (*SJ* 294)

[64] As Luick argued, (see *Historische Grammatik*, I, 511), in *B* at least this includes final *–e* and *–en* in preterites after *–ed*, as shown by b-verses such as *B* 15, 88, 217 and comparable a-verses (*B* 39, 263). There are various verses in the Cotton Nero poems that might suggest the same was true for alliterative poets (as perhaps for Chaucer; see above, p. 117 n. 109).

[65] For example, *B* 10, 20, 36, *etc.* See also our discussion of *–en* in infinitives, pp. 77–101 above.

[66] The present participle normally ends in *–ande* , but L has a few examples in *–yng*, e.g. *growyng* (*SJ* 42), *wepyng* (*SJ* 1097, emended by Hanna and Lawton to *wepande*), *fedyng* (*SJ* 1330), and once *–ynde* (469). The rarity of *–yng* and *–ynde* casts doubt on their authenticity.

Whan þey *sey* hym so (*SJ* 1034; cf. *seyen SJ* 903)
Forþ þey *went* for wo (*SJ* 1097; cf. *wenten SJ* 1339)
We *schulle* us kepe on-cauȝt (*B* 38; cf. *schullen B* 720)
*Scholde* talken hem til (*B* 148)
We ne *doute* none douhtie (*B* 349)
þat we no *wante* no wite (*B* 354)[67]

(c) a-verses with infinitive endings (*–e* or *–en* before vowels):

And Y schal *buske* me boun (*SJ* 187)
To *affray* þe folke (*SJ* 672)
*Strike* doun with a ston (*SJ* 874)
& for to *winne* þe word (*B* 80)
So wolde i *reste* me raþe (*B* 93)
þat i mai *stinte* no stounde (*B* 97)
*Ride* miȝte nouht þe rink (*B* 151)[68]

d) a-verses containing other words with pronounced etymological, analogical or grammatical *–e*:

*Pore* men and noȝt prute (*SJ* 142)
Er alle þe *sege* was sette (*SJ* 339)
*Faste* toward þe feld (*SJ* 458)
*Heye* bonked aboue (*SJ* 667)
Alle *aboute* þe burwe (*SJ* 682)
*Boþe* blowyng on bent (*SJ* 744)[69]
þat euer *stede* bystrode (*SJ* 1208)
For what *richesse* rink (*B* 31)
*Faste* heiede þei to holis (*B* 51)
For we no *dede* no don (*B* 380; cf. *B* 394)
*Boþe* blessed & blyþe (*B* 624)
& þis *sawe* ȝe said (*B* 646)
A ful *derworþe* douue (*B* 721)[70]
Þat þus *tidynge* tolde (*B* 1077)[71]

[67] See *SJ* 295, 306, 359, 885, 1110, 1119, 1139, 1212, *B* 6, 120, 312, 350, 367, 368, 384, 401, 538, 709, 758, 763, 832, 834, 852, 886, 1018, 1121.
[68] See *SJ* 877, 997, 1104, 1105, *B* 299, 322, 326, 336, 509, 514, 854, 857, 1119.
[69] The adverb and adjective *bothe* is optionally disyllabic in Chaucer (see e.g. *CT* III.1241, VII.2813), and also appears to be so within the b-verse in alliterative verse (see e.g. *E* 194, *G* 828, *C* 824); at line ending it is always disyllabic. See above, p. 29.
[70] The adjective has etymological *–e* (and also medial *–e–* in Orm: *deorewurrþe* < OE *deorwyrþe*).

Þat here to *schame* ben schape (*B* 1109)[72]

*Weak medial vowels*

A number of b-verses appear to be unmetrical because the scribe omitted a weak medial *–e*. This is particularly marked in *SJ* (b-verses from *SJ* are cited with Hanna and Lawton's emendations in square brackets):

*diȝ[ed]en* sone (*SJ* 581)
þe *kirnel[e]s* vder (*SJ* 686)
of *metal[le]s* fele (*SJ* 1269)
in *contres* manie (*B* 26; read *contre[e]s*)
*soffre* paine (*B* 635; read *soffere*)

A number of a-verses with words historically containing weak medial *–e–* are likewise irregular by our a-verse rules. For example:

Croked and *cancred* (*SJ* 129; *cankered*)
Bot *walwyþ* and wyndiþ (*SJ* 739; *walowyþ*; cf. C *wallowede*)
Men *seþ* wel þat þe se (*B* 91; *seeþ*; cf. *saien* 146b)
And þat ȝour *doctours* dere (*B* 223; *doctoures*; cf. *B* 778b)
Þat þou might *trystli* say (*B* 513; *trystily*)[73]

A final example, which shows *en passant* how our a-verse rules may help to recover the poet's words, is *B* 941, 'Hoe [= 'who'] wole a cherched child chese for hardy' (*B* 941). Skeat thinks the word 'cherched' means 'churched, i.e. baptised'), but 'cherished child' (= spoilt child) would fit the context much better: emendation to *cher[y]ched* is also indicated by a-verse metre.

*Past participles*

On a number of occasions in *SJ*, regular b-verse metre depends on past-participial prefix *y–*. In their Introduction to *SJ* (p. xcv), Hanna and

[71] The verbal noun ending in *–ing* is optionally disyllabic in Chaucer and apparently in Langland and *B* (see *PP* B 3.198b, 'and mournynge lette', and cf. 5.305, and *B* 240, 755, 887). There is good evidence that it acquired analogical *–e* in EME. See Moore, 'Earliest Morphological Changes'. In Moore's list of words with unetymological *–e*, we find items such as *witegunge* and *gitsunge*.

[72] And see also *SJ* 179, 234, 708, 740, 857, 928, 952, 1007, 1150, 1294, *B* 111, 535, 537, 690, 905.

[73] See also *SJ* 286, 549, 669, 782, 839, 1116 (cf. Gower, *CA* 1.349), 1220, *B* 368, *B* 941(read 'cherýched' not 'cherched').

Lawton acknowledge such dependence at line 559, but the *y–* prefix occurs elsewhere and must have been a feature of the poet's language:

> scheldes *ydressed* (282; D *dressid*)
> and scheldes *yþrelled* (1121; AVCEx *thirllede*)[74]

As the variants show, the prefix was vulnerable to scribal omission. A number of a-verses with past participles are suspect on grounds of metre:

> For we ben *diȝt* today (*SJ* 521)
> For or þis toun be *tak* (*SJ* 865)

The poet may well have written these forms with *y–*. In *B* the prefix *y–* is also frequently needed for the sake of metre in both a- and b-verses (e.g. 394a, 454a, 497a, 666b, 864b). At *B* 118, the scribe seems to have replaced it with a word he picked up from the next line:

> & als so sone as þe sonne sesede to schine,
> Þat *siȝt* don was þe day fordon of þe cloudus.
> Þat frekus seseden of *siȝht* & sonken to gronde … (*B* 117–19)

Skeat emends *siȝt don* to *don*: *y-don* is preferable in view of the poet's normal rhythm. The use of the prefix would also regularise *B* 588: 'And þe erþe is called'.

Outside of these seven categories, the only significant grouping of possible exceptions in *SJ* consists of a-verses with contested manuscript readings. Of course, these are lines which call for editorial judgement, and it seems to us that our a-verse rules can be of considerable help to editors in making the right judgement. A good example is *SJ* 769, where L reads: 'He boweþ to the barres', but AUD read *barrers*. Hanna and Lawton follow their copy-text since they find the variation 'incapable of resolution'. Semantically, there is indeed nothing to separate these readings, but rhythmically the AUD reading is superior, for *barrers* (< OF *barrière*) compensates for the short opening dip with a heavy final dip. The pattern can be confirmed with reference to *Cleanness*, 'Betes on þe *barers*' (1263), and *Morte Arthure*, 'Brittenes thaire *barrers*' (2469).

There are many other cases where a-verse metre may help to discriminate between manuscript readings. In the following cases, the readings offered by L are contradicted by metrically superior readings in other manuscripts (given in brackets):

[74] See also *SJ* 418, 487.

And ȝo a *mayde* vnmarred (*SJ* 105; A *mayden*)
*As* sone was þe Sone (*SJ* 119; P *Als*; E *Also*,
suggesting a disyllabic initial conjunction)[75]
And or þis wordes *were* (*SJ* 177; PD and Kölbing-Day *war wele*)
*Þe* lawe and þe lore (*SJ* 206; PAUD *Of þe*)
*For* confort of þe cloþ (*SJ* 248; A *And alle for*, UDE *And for*)
Hewen on þe *heþen* (*SJ* 561; A *harde stele*;
parallel with *gild schroud*, *burnee* in the next line)
*Þe* caste was so kene (*SJ* 630; PAUDEC *For þe*)
And bygonnen with *bir* (*SJ* 656; PA *a bir*, giving a
four-syllable medial dip, assuming the beat falls on *by*–)
Tysen at þe *toures* (*SJ* 659; A *torettis*, and cf. *SJ* 337)
*Riȝt* wicked to wynne (*SJ* 668; PAUDC *And wonder*)
*With* stockes and stones (*SJ* 691; P *Both with*)
*Bet* on with þe brond (*SJ* 770; C *beteth*, present
tense consistent with previous and following lines)
*Al* wery of þat werk (*SJ* 848; PUDEC *Wonder*)[76]
Alle þe knyȝthod *clene* (*SJ* 860; A *full clene*)
Torn[ei]en, *trifflyn* (*SJ* 895; A *truffelynge*; UDE *tarying*)[77]
And oþer frendes *fele* (*SJ* 972; AV *fulle fele*)[78]
*Was* lyþy as a leke (*SJ* 1032; *Weryn* VDE, U *Waxen*,
following plural subject) .
*With* condit as he come (*SJ* 1066; AV *Bot with*;
UE *With sauf*; C *Safe with þe*, suggesting that the
original had something meaning 'except')
*A* wye on þe wal (*SJ* 1229; A *And a*; DE *Also a*)

[75] It appears from the Cotton Nero poems that poets made deliberate use of correlative *also+as*. The poet's unmarked form is *a(l)s+as* but *also+as* appears uniquely at *C* 984a, '*Also* salt as ani se', *C* 1045a, '*Al so* red and so ripe', *C* 1792a, 'Now is a dogge *also* dere', *P* 291a, 'Þer he sete *also* sounde'. The scribal reduction of *also* explains the irregular b-verse at *C* 1516, 'As sonet out of sauteray songe *als* myry'.
[76] Hanna and Lawton describe this as scribal secondary alliteration, but poets evidently did write lines of this kind: 'For wonder wroth is þe wyȝ' (*C* 5a).
[77] For other likely cases of scribal misreadings of –*yng* as –*yn* in *SJ*, see above, pp. 93 and 95.
[78] Cf. Hanna and Lawton's emendation of *SJ* 743b. At 920, 'þat þe colke to clef', A reads 'þat þe colke al toclef', which gives a perfectly regular line, but it is difficult to be confident that this is the correct reading given Thornton's predilection for adding syllables. It is possible that Thornton is compensating for the loss of pronounced final –*e* on *colke*. Since the suffix –*hod* is optionally disyllabic in e.g. Gower, the a-verse of *SJ* 860 may be metrically regular in L.

Fourty *to fyȝten* (*SJ* 779; P *Fourty to defende*,
Hanna-Lawton *Fourty to defenden*; ADU *Fourty to fende off*;
ADU provide compensation for
the missing initial dip).[79]

In a few cases, metrical abnormalities are the result of editorial intervention. *SJ* 162, 'Alle þei ha[tt]e in h[er]te', is the product of emendation by Hanna and Lawton; the original LUDEC 'Alle þei hadde hem in hate' gives a line with long initial and medial offbeats, as do the variant readings of A and P. *SJ* 256 in Hanna and Lawton's edition, 'Þat er [w]as lasar-l[ic]he', is unmetrical on our terms but this is the result of an emendation based on DE ('Þat arst was lasar-liche'); the reading of the majority of manuscripts including L ('Þat er lasar was longe') does not cause this problem. *SJ* 376 in L reads, 'Þat were scorned and schende'. Hanna and Lawton conjecturally emend to p.p. *shorne* to avoid alliteration of /ʃ/ and /sk/: the weak form *shaued* is preferable on metrical grounds and can more readily explain the MS variants (E *yschaue*; UC *shamed*; D *shamefully*). At 832, L is regular, ' And was born vp as a bal'; Hanna and Lawton's emendation, 'Born vp as a bal' (*sic* PUDE) is not. The same is true for *SJ* 1062, which is regular in L, 'And þer graunted hym grace', but not in Hanna and Lawton's emendation, 'And graunted hym grace' (based on AVUDEC).

Hanna and Lawton, then, sometimes emend metrically regular lines in L to readings that are prosodically less plausible. On other occasions, MS L offers metrically irregular readings, with other manuscripts indicating plausible emendations. From the point of our metrical theory, this manuscript variation is significant, for it shows that the witnesses cannot usually be found to agree on unmetrical a-verses. There are in *SJ* only eleven a-verses that are irrregular in all the manuscripts witnesses — assuming possible variation between short and long forms and assuming historically justified final and medial *e*.[80] For purposes of comparison, there are eight lines in *SJ* without regular *aa/ax* alliteration in any of the manuscripts,[81] the reason being (as Hanna and Lawton argue) that these manuscripts descend from a corrupt archetype.

[79] See also *SJ* 106, 138, 333, 551, 557, 592, 600, 619, 632, 695, 703, 737, 752, 817, 821, 837, 854, 858, 884, 909, 927 (see U and *MED* s.v. *yomeren*), 1126, 1151, 1264.
[80] These are *SJ* 181, 393, 411, 540, 557, 570, 590, 831, 1072, 1214, 1333.
[81] These figures are based on Hanna and Lawton (eds), *Siege*, pp. xciii –xcv.

*Alexander and Didimus*, being a single-manuscript poem, does not offer us the benefit of variant manuscript readings, but because it is a careful copy it nevertheless offers us an excellent basis for studying alliterative metre. Assuming historically justified final or medial *e/en* (whether reflected in spelling or not), we count nineteen b-verses that are unmetrical by Hoyt Duggan's b-verse rules,[82] and twenty-seven a-verses that are irregular.[83] Another sixteen lines do not have *aa/ax* alliteration.[84] The statistical evidence for our a-verse rules is therefore qualitatively comparable with the evidence for the rules governing b-verse metre and alliterative patterning.

## Avoidance Strategies

There are several other points that argue in favour of the a-verse rules we have posited. First, it is striking that many anomalous verses are suspect on other grounds. Thus *SJ* 68, 78, 412, 665, 684, 784, 948, 1237 are all emended by Hanna and Lawton, and, as they note, 611 'looks corrupt': in all these cases their suspicions are independently confirmed by the metrical criteria we have outlined. In *B*, lines 769 and 815 have irregular a-verse metre: our suspicion that the poet did not write them can in both cases be confirmed by the defective alliterative patterning. *B* 138, 'He did him forþ to flod þat phison is called' is clearly suspect for a different reason: the restrictive relative clause presupposes the article ([þe] flod), and both grammar and metre call out for emendation. Second, lines that have a short initial or medial dip and no form of

[82] They are (with possible emendations in brackets): 32 (read *wiþ us*), 93 (see above, p. 30), 216 (supply *to*), 236 (read *unwasted y–*), 371 (supply *many*), 395 (supply *fram*), 506 (the possessive pronoun is not, we think, disyllabic; perhaps *aren*?); 579 (or disyllabic *þorou*?), 580 (supply *in*), 602 (supply *to*), 675 (*bowen*), 742 (delete *no*), 784 (delete *ne*), 847 (supply *no*), 910 (read *corde*), 980 (delete *ne*), 982 (read *bide*), 1000 (read *aboue*), 1086 (*euerechon*?)

[83] Namely: 34 (supply *&*), 84 (read *þe goddes*; cf. *þei*, 85), 114 (*vpon*) , 130 (*adoun*), 138 (supply *þe*), 190 (*how þat*), 237 (*Also*), 294 (*schares*), 321 (*hauen* for *han*), 386, 432 (*Forwhi*), 488 (unless *here* is disyllabic), 588 (*y-called*), 610, 769, 778, 794 (*vpon*), 815, 862 (or hiatus?), 871, 914 (*Sithen*), 923, 942 (*Oþer*), 997 (*Maked*), 1021 (*noþer*), 1025, 1126.

[84] 11 (*gentil*), 22 (supply *tid*), 81, 127 (supply *buskede*), 201 (*eren*), 229 (*gome* for *man*), 302 (*bireue*), 437 (*boldus*), 592 (*lodlich*), 635, 769, 773 (*wille*), 815, 925 (*seen* for *fain*), 1075, 1082 (*a-selede*, cf. 286). The pattern at 194, 825, and 1083 is curious; we assume the preposition alliterates, though perhaps the poet wrote *Ongat*).

compensation do appear to be deliberately avoided. For instance, where the final dip consists of zero or a weak *–e* ending, poets adopt deliberate strategies to ensure that both the initial and the medial dips are long. In this section, we would like to show some of these strategies in action.

A good example of this evasive action is the use of the pleonastic 'that' after the conjunction 'when'. This pairing is found twice in *SJ*. At *SJ* 933a, 'whan þat' maintains the long dip:

Whan þat Gabba was gon[85]

This is a strategy only employed elsewhere by the poet in order to maintain the b-verse metre:

whan þat Crist deyed (*SJ* 6b)[86]

We find something similar at *B* 775, the only example in this poem of a pleonastic 'that':

Whan þat burnus are bured

In the case of *SJ* in particular, it is also interesting to consider the use of the conjunction 'and' as it is used at the beginning of the line linking two main clauses. It is not *necessary* to use 'and' in this position — beginning a new sentence would do equally well — and the evidence suggests that the use or non-use of the conjunction was normally determined by the metre. Let us compare, for example, lines beginning with the subject pronoun 'he' and lines beginning with 'and he':

And he fraynes how fer (*SJ* 82)
And he gronnand glad (*SJ* 199)
And he grаunteþ to go (*SJ* 1040)
And he ferkiþ hym forþ (*SJ* 1046)
And he grаunteþ hem grace (*SJ* 1164)
And he frayneþ þe freke (*SJ* 1302)

but

He hadde a malady vnmeke (*SJ* 30)
He commaundiþ kny3tes to come (*SJ* 263)

[85] It is true that L reads 'And whan', which would make the use of pleonastic *that* unnecessary, but this seems unlikely to have been original. It is not found in any other manuscript and is rejected by both Kölbing and Day and by Hanna and Lawton.
[86] At *SJ* 404, as the note in Hanna and Lawton's edition explains, and as the readings of manuscripts other than L indicate, 'that' is a definite pronoun, not, as L interprets it, an extension of the conjunction *tille*.

He schal vs fynde in þe felde (*SJ* 371)
He strey3t vp a standard (*SJ* 389)
He say þe wrake on hem wende (*SJ* 585)
He boweþ to þe barres (*SJ* 769; AUD *barrers*)
He chargeþ hem chersly (*SJ* 887)
He wexe marchaunte amys (*SJ* 1310)
He made inmydde[s þe] ost (*SJ* 1317; L *in myddel of*)

It is clear from these examples that initial 'and' is used in lines which would otherwise have an initial short dip with no compensation in the remainder of the a-verse. Where this is not the case, 'he' is used without the conjunction. The only exception is 769, 'He boweþ to the barres', where, however, the reading found in AUD would provide adequate compensation.

Likewise, in *B*, short initial dips without subsequent compensation are often avoided by the use of 'for to' rather than the usual 'to' plus infinitive:

For to fihche on þe fom (*B* 204)
For to wirchen our wil (*B* 427)
For to rome vndur ris (*B* 501)
For to libbe in 3our land (*B* 843)
For to sowe & to sette (*B* 912)

The *y*– past participle seems to perform a similar function:

Ben y-punched in paine (*B* 395)
Ben y-demed to do (*B* 909)

Short medial dips without a four-syllable or final dip compensation are also purposely avoided by the use of 'for to' rather than 'to':

Ho did calle ffor to come (*B* 166)
As men han wit for to wite (*B* 1002)
By lowere pris forto passe (*SJ* 1316)

As Duggan has pointed out, [87] it is certainly not the case that alliterative poets consistently used *for to* rather than *to* to avoid short initial or medial dips, but his conclusion, that variation between *to* and *for to* is of little diagnostic value in the study of a-metre is unduly pessimistic, as a quick glance at Duggan's copious examples immediately shows:

[87] 'Some Aspects', pp. 490–91.

'To clayme his kingdome' (*A* 80); 'Too preche as a prophet' (*A* 604); 'Too traie them untruly' (*A* 933), 'Too catche sum cunnyng' (*A* 1048), 'Too burye þat burn' (*A* 1106), 'To carpe of his konninge' (*B* 230), 'To witen of þe wisdam' (*B* 242), 'To haunte hure in hordom' (*B* 565), 'To legge in ȝour licam' (*B* 592), 'To lyue þer in lykyng' (*C* 239), 'To vouche on avayment' (*C* 1358), 'To teche of þe techal' (*C* 1733), 'To chese hom a cheftan' (*DT* 8952), 'To fyghte wyth thy faamen' (*MA* 303), 'To trete with this tyraunt' (*MA* 991), 'To ryde with þat reall' (*MA* 1656), 'To helpen thaire hawkes' (*P3A* 227), 'To wayue vp þe wicket' (*PP* B 5.611), 'To do what he dempte' (*SJ* 138), 'To worchyn vnder þe wal (*SJ* 1109), 'To joyne wyth hym in iustyng' (*G* 97), 'To herber in þat hostel' (*G* 805), 'To welcum þat ilk wyȝ' (*G* 819), 'To wynne hit on eche [wyse]' (*SJ* 1178), 'To knaw by his clergi' (*WA* 54), 'To buwne furth with all þe burȝe' (*WA* 1634), 'To fighte furthe with oure folke' (*WW* 245).

This list demonstrates convincingly that two long dips were not a metrical requirement in the a-verse, but it also bears out our theory that poets compensated for this either with a heavy or long final dip or with an extra-long dip of four or more unstressed syllables. The only verses that do not exemplify our a-verse rules are *A* 80 (read *claimen*?), *A* 1106 and *SJ* 138 (but note A *al that* for *what*). At *G* 819 and *SJ* 1178, *ilk[e]*[88] and *echë* (dative) or *ech a* would create extra-long dips. The fact that so many a-verses without two long dips maintain asymmetry from b-verses in the ways we would predict is suggestive. There are at least twenty-four additional examples in *B* and the Cotton Nero poems of a-verses (without long initial and medial dips) that begin with *To* rather than *for to*.[89] Yet in *only one* of them do we find no metrical compensation. The line in question is *B* 1119, 'To lenge aftur ȝour lif', where loss of final *–n* is possible.[90]

[88] That the form (< OE *ilca*) was disyallabic for the poet is evident from its use at line ending (e.g. *C* 511, *G* 173) and within the b-verse (e.g. *C* 1755b, 'þat ilk derk after').

[89] See *B* 338, 362, 789, 800, 1119, *C* 400, 870, 917, 1370, 1371, 1584, 1500, 1600, 1750, 1804, *P* 58, 363, *G* 547, 976, 1243, 1253, 1405, 1575, 2421.

[90] Exactly the same pattern can be seen in *MA*. Here *for to* is used for the sake of metre in the a-verse just as surely as it is in the b-verse. Discounting lines with irregular alliteration (867, 2349, 2415, 2779), *for to* is regularly used in line initial position to provide a long opening dip when there is no compensation in the form of an extra-long medial dip or an extra-heavy final dip, see 58, 302, 404, 696, 936, 898, 2194, 2427, 3237, 3548, 358, 3720. At 3580 it is possible that compensation may be provided by the second syllable of *beryne*, but that form

Inverting the word order can also have the effect of creating forms of metrical compensation. For instance, in *SJ* the particle 'up' is normally placed after the verb,[91] and it therefore seems likely that when the particle precedes the verb, as in *SJ* 1241, 'Bot vp ȝeden her ȝates', the motive is metrical, to provide long first and second dips in a position where the final dip provides no compensation (cf. **Bot ȝeden vp her ȝates*).[92] Variation in the form of particular prepositions can also be used for this purpose. The usual preposition for *to/towards* in *SJ* is *to*, but *towards* can be used to provide an additional metrically necessary syllable:

Tourned toward þe toun (*SJ* 598) Faste toward the feld (*SJ* 458)

Here *toward* rather than *to* is necessary to provide a four-syllable rather than a three-syllable medial dip, as compensation for the lack of initial dip.[93]

In *SJ*, the use of *euereche* or *euereche a* rather than simple *eche* or *eche a* (or, as Hanna and Lawton have it, *ilka*) provides a four-syllable dip where necessary:

And clayme of euereche kyng (*SJ* 502)
Aȝen euereche ȝate (*SJ* 650)
Stoppen euereche a streem (*SJ* 690)
Knyt to euerech clerke (*SJ* 711)
And bren[n]en euereche bon (*SJ* 720; L *brenten*)
Suþ euereche a segge (*SJ* 853)
[G]oren euereche a gome (*SJ* 1171; L *Toren*)

appears to be restricted to Northumbrian dialects (see Luick, *Historische Grammatik*, §450) and there is no evidence for it elsewhere in the poem. The use at line end of forms such as *berynes* (*MA* 655, 1012, 3531, 3534, 3562, 3696, 3765, 3780, 3933, 4027, 4124) suggests that the stem was normally monosyllabic. A similar syllable-count problem probably explains the presence of *for to* rather than *to* at *MA* 3915, 'Dighte hir ewyne for to dye', where *ewyne* could be monosyllabic.

[91] As in *SJ* 293, 565, 619, 621, 652, 670, 832, 995, 1169, 1213.

[92] It is possible that something similar is happening at *SJ* 1200 where the a-verse reads 'And vp stondiþ for ston', but this may instead be an instance of the verb 'upstand'. See also *SJ* 1116, discussed above, p. 241 n. 73.

[93] In Hanna and Lawton's emended version of *SJ* 68 (*Toward [c]ostes vncouþ*), the disyllabic pronoun is likewise used to provide a long initial a-verse dip in a position where there is no final-dip compensation. Compare the use of *froward* rather than *fro* to maintain the b-verse metre in the previous line.

It is difficult to be certain of the syllable count of *euereche*[94] and it may be that in some of these cases the reading should in fact be *euereche a* (as the variants often suggest). What is clear, however, is that this particular form, which is only used in the a-verse in the examples cited, represents a deliberate attempt to provide an extra-long compensatory dip.[95]

In the Cotton Nero poems, the use of *þis ilk* rather than simply *þis* follows the same pattern. Usually, *þis* is used on its own. The word *ilk* is only added where metrically necessary. Compare e.g. these a-verses with bare *þis* in *Gawain* —

> Ande quen þis Bretayn watȝ bigged (*G* 20)
> If ye wyl lysten þis laye (*G* 30)
> Þis kyng lay at Camylot (*G* 37)
> For al waty þis fayre folk (*G* 54)[96]
> þe gouernour of þis gyng (*G* 225)

— with the following containing *þis ilk(e)*:

> To welcum þis ilk wyy (*G* 819)
> Where ye wan þis ilk wele (*G* 1394)
> Þis day wyth þis ilk dede (*G* 1468)
> Bot wered not þis ilk wyye (*G* 2037)
> & ryde me doun þis ilk rake (*G* 2144)
> With glopnyng of þat ilke gome (*G* 2461)

The use of *ilke* before the demonstrative pronoun in *Cleanness* and *Patience* is similarly motivated by metre. Only once does it create a hypermetrical syllable: 'Wher-so wonyed þis ilke wyȝ' (*C* 675).[97] Elswehere it is used for the sake of metre: once to provide alliteration (*C* 782a), once to create one of two long a-verse dips ('Þat ilke skyl for no scaþe', *C* 569), and on all other occasions *ilke* contributes to an extra-

[94] In datives at least disyllabic *eche* must be taken into account as a possibility.

[95] It seems probable that the production of a compensatory extra long dip is the reason for the isolated use of the form *euerilk a* at *MA* 212, where the a-verse reads, *In euerilk a party pyghte*. The only other use of such a form in this poem (*In eueriche a viage*, 2037) is more difficult to judge, because of uncertainty about the placement of the beat.

[96] And see also 100, 221, 225, 253, 257, 280, 283, 285, 289, 316, 344, 358, 382, 383, 450, 491, 500, 546, 556, 631, *etc.*

[97] The suffix *–so* is suspect: *wher* refers back to Mamre, and the generalising sense that *–so* normally adds is inappopriate.

long dip in the absence of two long dips, as in 'Prestly at þis ilke poynte' (*C* 628).[98]

These patterns suggest that poets composed a-verses with our rhythmical rules in mind.

**Conclusion**

There is, then, a clear relationship between the presence of a long or heavy final dip or an extra-long dip and the presence in the same a-verse of a short initial or medial dip. Why should this be the case? Our explanation is that extra-long dips and heavy or long final dips were used as a means of maintaining the distinction between a-verses and b-verses. Where such forms of compensation are not present, the poets went to some lengths to maintain long initial and medial dips. These observations cast doubt on Cable's claim that all non-extended a-verses had to have at least two long dips. In fact the minimum metrical requirement is one long dip; when either the initial or the medial dip is short, a-verse and b-verse asymmetry is maintained in other ways. A short initial or medial dip can be compensated for by a final heavy syllable such as a suffix, while a long final dip can provide compensation for two preceding short dips, thus making it the only long dip in the a-verse. Moreover, where compensation is provided instead by a medial or initial extra-long dip of four syllables or more, this too will provide the only long dip in the a-verse.

Readers are entitled to worry how our theory stands up when appplied to other alliterative poems, so we would like to end by looking much more briefly at *Patience*, once again ignoring a-verses that are extended or have only one alliterating stave. Short a-verses do not occur in this poem, with the possible exceptions of 'what lede moȝt lyue' (259), where *moȝt* has historical *–e*, 'Alle faste frely' (390), where *alle* is plural, and 'Vch prynce, vche prest' (389), where 'vch a' is possible.

The majority of a-verses in *P* have a long opening and long medial dip, and where that is not the case we usually find the forms of compensation we have described:

(a) extra-long dips, e.g:

Sunderlupes for hit dissert (12)
Much ȝif he me ne made (54)
And lyȝtly when I am lest (88)

[98] See also *C* 105, 195, 571, 573, 930, 1669, 1756, *P* 131, 361, 414.

(b) a long or heavy final dip, e.g.:

For hores is þe heuen-ryche (14, 28)
Þay ar happen also (15, 17, 19, 23, 25, 27)
I schal me poruay pacyence (36)
And als in myn opynyoun (40)
Thus pouerte and pacience (45)
What grayþed me þe grychchyng (53)
To sette hym to sewrte (58)

Assuming inflectional *–e* in verbs[99] and adjectives (monosyllabic and disyllabic),[100] optionally pronounced final *–e* in *þenne* and *boþe*,[101] and etymological/analogical *–e* in some other words,[102] we find the following exceptions to our a-verse rules:

O folez in folk (121)
ȝet coruen þay þe cordes (153)
Saf Jonas þe Jwe (182)
What seches þou on see (197)
With sacrafyse vpset (239)
What lede moȝt lyue (259)
And þrew in at hit þrote (267)
Ay hele ouer hede (271)
Þaȝ I be fol and fykel (283)
I calde and þou knew (307)
And for þe drede of dryȝtyn (372)
And of a hep of askes (380)

In a few of these lines the suspicion of scribal error is strengthened by other evidence. For instance, if we consider that the poet's normal form is *called* and next compare *P* 307 with *C* 1583b, 'and calde hem chorles', we may reasonably deduce that *calde* is scribal in both verses. The word *dryȝtyn* is involved in a number of other irregular b-verses in this MS (*C* 243, 1065, *G* 1999), probably because the scribe omitted the definite article which elsewhere accompanies the word for the sake of metrical regularity (e.g. *C* 669, 1007). At 239, the MS has *sacrafyce* singular, while the Bible has plural (*hostias*). At 267, the context strongly favours a past participle (*þrowen*), parallel with 'lachched' (266), and at 183 one expects the adjective *folé* (parallel with 'fykel'). Plausible emendations are possible

[99] E.g. 'Hit bitydde sumtyme' (61), 'Bot I trow[e] ful tyd' (127), 'For to layte mo ledes' (180).
[100] E.g. 'Bot if my gaynlych[e] God '(83), 'In his glowande glory' (94), 'Lo þe wytles[e] wrechche' (113), 'Of þat schended[e] schyp' (246).
[101] E.g. 'Þen[ne] hurled on a hepe' (149), 'Boþe burnes and bestes' (388), 'Þenne wakened þe wyȝ' (446).
[102] E.g. *wodebynde* (< OE *wudubinde*) at 459, 480, 486 (note also at line ending, 446), *nedeles* 220 (also trisyllabic in Chaucer), *joy[e]les* (cf. *joyeful* in Chaucer) at 146, and *wel[e]wed* at 475 (< OE *wealwian* but also *wealuwian* and *wealowian*).

in some other cases: *o ȝe* for *O* (121), *Saf for* for *Saf* (182, cf. 291b), *þe se* for *se* (197), *For what* for *What* (250).

It therefore seems to us likely that the relationship between extra-long dips and long or heavy final dips on the one hand, and short initial or medial dips on the other was meaningful, and that the *Gawain* poet, too, used the former to compensate for the latter in order to ensure that the metrical form of the a-verse remained distinct from that of the b-verse. That we find exceptions is only to be expected: in poems transmitted by scribes there are bound to be some. What is surprising is how few there are. Statistically, the evidence for our a-verse rules is of similar quality as the evidence for Duggan's b-verse rules. Making the same kinds of allowances for the b-verse that we have made for the a-verse in *P*, i.e allowing for historical *e*,[103] we count eleven exceptions to the rule that b-verses should contain one and only long dip;[104] this compares with twelve a-verses that are unmetrical by our a-verse rules.

In other respects, too, the evidence in favour of our a-verse rules is on a par with that underpinning b-verse metre. 'Strategies of avoidance' explain lexical and syntactical choices in both the a-verse and the b-verse, and on both sides of the caesura the rhythmical rules have the power to confirm scribal error in lines that are suspect on other grounds. A good example of this diagnostic power in a b-verse is *P* 118, 'Þat oft kynd hym þe karp    þat kyng sayde', of which Anderson writes, 'the sense would require a *þat þat* or *þat þe* construction'; since that construction is also required by the metre, editors ought to emend. We have already referred to some lines in *B* and *SJ* that are not only corrupt by our a-verse rules but also defective in other respects.[105] An additional example from *Cleanness* might illustrate the point further:

> Sayde þe lorde to þo ledeȝ:    'Laytes ȝet *ferre*
> *Ferre* out in þe felde,    and fecheȝ mo gesteȝ ...' (*C* 97–8)

Anderson defends the MS reading, with its clumsy repetition of *ferre*, suggesting that the second *ferre* may be the positive 'far' (as distinct from the first *ferre*, comparative 'further'). However, this is unlikely, because *far* is always spelt *fer* in this MS, except once at line ending where the poet

[103] As in *P* 13, 143 (*breëde* = terrified), 166 (read *derue*, weak flexion before proper name), 178, 269, 297 (*wyld[e]ren*), 337, 447, 491.

[104] These are 61 (delete *þe*), 85 (*proche*), 118 (supply *þat*), 230 (*luchen*), 344 (*renayd*) 410 (*towardes*), 411, 432 and 463 (*or* for *oþer*), 499 (delete *&*), 518 (*syn*).

[105] See above, p. 244–5.

chooses special forms *metri causa* (*G* 1093). The emendation to imperative *ferkeȝ*, due to Gollancz, would bring the verse in line with the source, Luke 14.23: 'Go out [*exi*] into the highway and hedges'. For editors who accept our findings the problems with the manuscript reading are metrical as well semantic: the a-verse lacks a long initial and medial dip, and the emendation *ferkeȝ* puts in place the extra-long dip that the poet typically uses to compensate for that lack.

We conclude that the rhythms of the a-verse, like those of the b-verse, are rule-governed. What has made the a-verse rules hard to detect is their dependence on two factors that have been rather overlooked in the analysis of alliterative metre. One of these factors is the syllabic status of a long dip: is it *long* (two or three unstressed syllables, permitted in the b-verse) or is it *extra-long* (four or more unstressed syllables, used in a-verses in the absence of a long initial and long medial dip)? The other factor concerns the degree of stress vested in a short dip: is the dip unstressed or does it have secondary stress? The former (an unstressed syllable) is mandatory at line ending; the latter (a heavy dip) is taboo at the end of the b-verse but clearly favoured by alliterative poets at the end of an a-verse without two long dips.

Once these factors are taken into consideration, it will be found that a-verses and b-verses are asymmetrical. This asymmetry has been noticed by other scholars, and Thomas Cable has gone furthest towards specifying its nature: the a-verse, he contends, must have two long dips while the b-verse must have one and only one long dip and must end in an unstressed syllable. This particular specification of dissimilation can no longer be maintained. A long initial and a long medial dip was not a metrical *rule* but a *norm*. When poets broke that norm, as they assuredly did, they made use of other means to maintain the distinction between a-verse and b-verse rhythms: in a-verses with one long dip they either wrote an extra-long dip (not allowed in b-verses) or a long or heavy final dip (also not allowed in b-verses).

The question of how and why such rules might have developed is one that we will address in the general conclusion below.

# CONCLUSION

We would like to use the conclusion both to summarize our main findings and to indicate some areas that merit further investigation. We must again begin by emphasising the limits of our corpus. We have focused on later Middle English poems in the unrhymed alliterative long line, and have said very little about *Piers Plowman* (which many scholars believe to be *sui generis*) and poems with extremely irregular alliteration such as *Joseph of Arimathie* and *Cheualere Assigne*.[1]

In the poems that we have considered, with the exception of *Destruction of Troy* and *Piers Plowman*, the alliterative long line must end in one and only one unstressed syllable: a final syllable with primary or secondary stress is unmetrical. In the extant texts, the line-ending rule has often been obscured by scribal omission of final *–e*, but the evidence that alliterative poets obeyed the rule is strong. The avoidance of masculine line endings is clearly shown in the Cotton Nero poems and *Saint Erkenwald* by lexical variation (e.g. *now/nowþe*, *to/tille*, *two/twayne*) and grammatical variation (e.g. between regular/irregular weak preterite, inflected/uninflected forms, subjunctive/indicative). Furthermore, an analysis of words at line ending in *Alexander and Dindimus* shows that feminine line endings are systematically observed. Where the final unstressed syllable depends on final *–e* (as it often does), that *–e* is with very few exceptions both reflected in the spelling and justified by grammar (including, apparently, the dative), etymology, or by the development of analogical *–e* in EME. In this and other respects, *Alexander B* is one of the more reliable witnesses for the study of alliterative metre.

The development of analogical *–e* in nouns and adjectives (such as *bare*, *mind*, *skill*, *way*) is a complicating factor. Because the issue has largely been neglected in scholarship,[2] the question of whether a particular noun at line ending could or could not have pronounced final *–e* can be a hard one to answer. Some evidence is available from Orm, Chaucer and Gower, but usages are likely to have differed from dialect to dialect and many uncertainties remain.

[1] By 'extreme' we mean that the poems show no clear preference for any alliterating pattern (indeed many lines contain no alliteration at all).

[2] But see McJimsey, *Chaucer's Irregular –E*.

In the second chapter, we considered the question of inflectional final *–e* within the alliterative long line, using the earliest extant poems (i.e. the Cotton Nero poems, *Alexander and Dindimus*, *Siege of Jerusalem*, and *William of Palerne*) as our corpus. Our findings run counter to the general assumption that final *–e* was more or less defunct in the dialects of the alliterative poems, an assumption in accordance with which texts of these poems are currently being emended. That this assumption is mistaken is shown by the distribution of variant forms (*–e* and *–en* in infinitives, *–ly* and *–lyche* in adverbs and adjectives) which were evidently selected to meet different metrical demands. In the case of infinitives it is plain that alliterative poets frequently counted on inflectional *–e* to provide them with an unstressed syllable where metre required it; they did not normally write *–en* except to prevent elision of the metrically required syllable (though in some poems we also find final *–n* to avoid hiatus). In the case of adverbial *–ly* and *–lyche*, we also find evidence of purposeful variation: *–ly* is monosyllabic, while *–lyche* is disyllabic (in non-eliding position, of course), so the latter normally occurs where the b-verse demands a long dip; in adjectives the suffix *–lyche* also normally occurs in long-dip position, with justified final *–e* (i.e. in the weak inflection). In this connection, there are two further questions that we have not ourselves addressed with any thoroughness. The first is whether final *–e* was also possible in other grammatical contexts (e.g. in strong past participles, present and past tense plurals, other disyllabic adjectives, regular weak past tenses, nouns with organic or analogical *–e*). The second is whether final *–e* in these different categories was regular, optional, rare, or simply impossible. Further work is needed to make such discriminations possible.

In the third chapter, we have directed attention to alliterative patterning in the *Alliterative Morte Arthure* and the Cotton Nero poems. We cannot claim any originality for our assertion that many non-*aa/ax* (or non-*aa/aa*) lines in these poems are likely to be scribal. That argument has already been made by Thorlac Turville-Petre and Hoyt Duggan, who point to the evidence of multiple-manuscript poems (*Wars of Alexander*, *Siege of Jerusalem*, *Parliament of Three Ages*).[3] In these poems, non-*aa/ax* readings are frequently contradicted by variants that contain regular patterns. However, we are more confident than previous scholars have been that single-manuscript poems, too, can yield evidence about

[3] Turville-Petre, 'Emendation', and Duggan, 'Alliterative Patterning'.

the poet's metrical system. Careful study of irregularly alliterating lines in *Morte Arthure* and the Cotton Nero poems shows that many such lines are suspect in other ways. A significant number of these non-*aa/ax* lines have light a-verses with only one obvious candidate for the beat: in such lines one may reasonably suspect scribal omission or simplification. It is also significant that many of the irregular lines involve prosaic words for 'man' (*man*, *lord*, *knight*) and for verbs of movement (*come*, *go*). It is known that alliterative poets had in these semantic fields a specialised vocabulary which they used to meet alliterative requirements: this is evidently the case in the *Morte Arthure* and the Cotton Nero poems, where such specialised words (e.g. *freke*, *wyȝe*, *gome*, *renk* for 'man/knight' and *cayren*, *busken*, *hyȝen*, *helden* for 'go') are found in lines with perfectly regular alliterative patterning. This fact raises the distinct possibility that many non-*aa/ax* lines are due to the scribal substitution of a poetic word by a prosaic one. We are occasionally fortunate enough to have external evidence to confirm that diagnosis. In the case of *Morte Arthure*, copied by Robert Thornton, we can use his copy of *Siege of Jerusalem* to gain further insight into his scribal habits; we can also consult Malory's *Morte Darthur*, which borrows heavily from a version of the alliterative *Morte* and can therefore function in some ways as an independent witness to the archetype. In the case of the Cotton Nero poems, the poet's biblical source occasionally confirms scribal error. While editors of multiple-manuscript poems have obvious bases for restoring regular alliteration, editors of single-manuscript poems have not generally had the inclination or courage to do the same; we hope to have shown that the latter may not be quite without evidence that might allow them also to distinguish between scribal and authorial practice.

The shape of extended verses, i.e. verses with more than two open-classed words, also deserves further systematic study of the kind that we have begun. That the current rules of 'stress-assignment' are unworkable and empirically false has, we hope, been shown in sufficient detail. Open-class words do not automatically take metrical stress, and close-classed words plainly can take the beat (even in the presence of two other open-class words in the same verse). If existing theories of stress are untenable, what theory is to take its place? Our own understanding is that, in language as in poetry, stress is dependent on many factors, and we have argued that the same complex factors that influence accentuation in normal language should also be taken into account when we are reading and scanning verse. In the area of accentual-syllabic verse, this principle is now widely accepted. For example, Marina Tarlinskaja's research has shown that, in the verse of Shakespeare and his contemporaries, nouns of wide and general sense are much more likely to occur in off-beats than are other more concrete nouns. This statistically demonstrable fact corresponds with normal stress patterns in the English language. Rhythmical tendencies are also important. In English, there exists, for example, a 'rhythm rule' which dictates that, in a noun phrase consisting of two adjectives followed by a noun (e.g. 'bíg bad wólf'), the second adjective will generally be more weakly stressed. This phenomenon is likewise reflected in accentual-syllabic verse, as in 'fýn blak sátyn' and 'a stréight flat bák' (*Book of the Duchess*, 253, 957). Our analysis of extended b-verses suggests that contextual rules for stressing and de-stressing also operate in alliterative verse. We discussed examples of contrastive stress and its opposite, lexical presupposition (leading to the de-accenting of words that are contextually expected or occur in predictable collocations). We have also shown that certain words (such as quantifiers, intensifiers and adverbs of degree, anaphoric pronouns (including reflexives), high-frequency and 'stative' verbs, and indefinite nouns) are of lower accentual rank than other kinds of adverbs, adjectives, verbs, deictic pronouns and nouns. Nor is it always the case that closed-class words cannot be strongly stressed. Sometimes grammatical words can be beat-preferred over open-class words of low accentual rank. For example, deictic pronouns, prepositions derived from open-classed words and prepositions of time and place do not really behave in the same way as do other pronouns and prepositions. It is true that the 'rules of stress' we propose are much more complicated than those described by Duggan and Cable; but we believe that they offer a closer fit both with the evidence and with the way we actually speak. Their complexity is therefore simply the complexity of the linguistic competence that we naturally possess as speakers of the English language.

Much more work remains to be done in this area. For example, if, as we suggest, some verbs (stative verbs, common verbs of speech and motion, and verbs with senses similar to 'have' and 'be') are of lower accentual rank than others (and were so in the language of alliterative poets), one would expect to see this reflected in the accentual-syllabic verse of the period. A cursory inspection of Book I of *Troilus and Criseyde* reveals many verbs in weak position (in the abstract metrical pattern

WSWSWSWSWS), including: *go* (52+),[4] *know* (68), *wit* (76+), *take* (79+), *come* (142+), *hear* (197+), *wax* 'become' (232+) *trow* (240+), *think* (264+), *fall* 'happen' (320), *find* (659+), *lie* (772+), *call* (873), *rise* ('arise', 944), *bear* (947),[5] *work* (959), and *stand* (969). In the area of alliterative verse, it would be instructive to examine extended a- and b-verses in order to ascertain the nature and context of words which are routinely passed over for alliteration. Of course, we should not assume that all extended verses that meet the basic alliterating requirements are authorial; but systematic study of the kind we have begun may in due course allow us to distinguish between extended a-verses that are well formed and ones that are not.

The syllabic code of the a-verse has not so far been cracked, but we do not share the assumption that the a-verse has no precise syllabic constraints. For instance, it is clear that a-verses, too, must have a long dip. Indeed, the evidence for this is actually much better than that for the long-dip requirement of the b-verse. That being so, modern editors of alliterative poems should not compile their textual apparatus on the assumption that variant readings that could affect the syllable account need to be recorded only for b-verses.[6] This would result in editions on which students of a-verse metre cannot safely rely. Thomas Cable has made the claim that a-verses must have two long dips (as distinct from the b-verse, which must have one and only one long dip). Although this claim is false, we take seriously Cable's suggestion that a-verses and b-verses are asymmetrical. However, our study of the *Siege*, *Alexander B*, and *Patience* suggests that this asymmetry can take several forms, and that a long initial and medial dip in the a-verse is only the most common one. Asymmetry with the b-verse can be maintained in other ways: by an extra-long dip of four or more unstressed syllables; or by a long final dip (two or more unstressed syllables) or a heavy one (consisting of a syllable with secondary stress), both of which endings are restricted to a-verses, since b-verses must end in a single unstressed syllable. One important implication of our findings, which now need to be tested on a wider corpus, is that the alliterative long line is rule-governed, not merely as far

[4] We use the symbol + to signal words that occur more than once in off-beats.

[5] Lexical presupposition may have a role to play here; compare stressed and unstressed 'bereth' in 'For thilke grownd that *bereth* the wedes thikke / *Bereth* ek thise holsom herbes, as ful ofte' (946–7)

[6] As do Hanna and Lawton in their recent edition of the *Siege*: 'This apparatus includes ... all syllabic variants in b-verses' (p. lxxxviii).

as the distribution of accented and unaccented syllables is concerned, but also with regard to the placement of syllables with secondary stress. It is striking that alliterative poets did not tolerate syllables with secondary stress (e.g. suffixes in *–ly*, *–ship*, *–dom*, and compound elements) at the end of b-verses but were happy to do so at the end of a-verses, particularly in a-verses with only one long dip (that is, in a-verses that in all other respects look just like b-verses). To explain such phenomena, it is necessary to move beyond the simple binary of 'stressed' and 'unstressed syllables', and to introduce yet another complexity that is a simple fact of the English language: there are levels of stress; and we may need some notion of 'secondary stress' or 'heavy dips' to understand the subtleties of alliterative verse.

If the alliterative line is rule-bound in the way we have described, then the following metrical constraints apply to the poems of the alliterative corpus that we have studied:

(1) the *aa/ax* pattern is the minimum alliterative requirement (except apparently in *Piers Plowman*).

(2) the long line has four beats: two in the a-verse and two in the b-verse. This applies also to extended a- and b-verses (by which we mean verses with three or more open-class words). In extended verses, open-class words combine in predictable structures (e.g. quantifier + noun, classifying adjective + noun of wide denomination, noun preceded by two premodifiers) that tend to determine which open-class words take the beat and which ones do not.

(3) The long line must end in one and only one unstressed syllable. Final syllables with primary or secondary stress are not permitted (except in *Piers Plowman*, where secondary stress and long dips do occur, and in *Destruction of Troy*, where both masculine and feminine line endings are permitted.

(4) The b-verse must have one and only one long dip.

(5) The a-verse must contain at least one long dip, and its syllabic structure must be dissimilar from that of the b-verse: that is, it must contain either a long initial and medial dip or, failing that, an extra-long dip (four or more unstressed syllables) or a long or heavy final dip.

These rules are likely to prompt one further question which we have not so far addressed. How and why did Middle English alliterative metre develop this particular set of rules? The rules of Old English alliterative verse were comparatively speaking much looser. Of the five rules listed above only the second, the requirement of four beats, also applies to Old English verse. Short verses (x/x/), outlawed by rules 4–5, are in fact the norm in the a- and b-verses of *Beowulf*; one alliterating stave in the a-verse (though there can be two) often suffices in that poem; and there was no requirement that lines should end in an unstressed syllable or that a- and b-verses should have a different rhythmical structure (though Old English poets do seem to have preferred such asymmetry).[7] Geoffrey Russom has recently made some persuasive suggestions about why and how the metre of a poem like *Beowulf* could have morphed into classical Middle English alliterative metre.[8] To simplify a complex argument, he points out that the pattern (/x/x), as in 'feascaft funden' (7a), or 'gomban gyldan' (11a) had normative status in Old English verse because it replicated the prevailing word patterns (with 'trochaic' compound stress) of the language. The linguistic decline of compounding — which led to more complex word groups and different stress patterns[9] — and the inevitable increase of function words (due to the decay of the case system) would have made long dips normative, and may eventually have led poets to reanalyse preponderating tendencies as rules.

Russom's account is the most sophisticated attempt to explain the peculiarities of Middle English alliterative verse as part of an evolution-

[7] See Jakob Schipper, *History of English Versification* (Oxford, 1910; repr. New York, 1971), p. 45.

[8] Geoffrey Russom, 'The Evolution of Middle English Alliterative Meter', in *Studies in the History of the English Language II: Unfolding Conversations*, Topics in English Linguistics 45 (Berlin, 2004), pp. 275–304.

[9] On this point see also Christopher B. McCully and Richard M. Hogg, who argue in 'Dialect Variation and Historical Metrics', *Diachronica*, 11 (1994), 13–34, that 'left-strong' patterns of word stress in the language were weakened in ME by a new phrasal stress rule (the Nuclear Stress Rule), generating 'right-strong' patterns. According to McCully and Hogg, the native 'left-strong' patterns, favourable to alliterative verse, persisted longest in the conservative western dialects — which would explain why alliterative verse flourished in this area. It should also be noted that McCully and Hogg doubt that classical ME alliterative metre is a continuation of OE metre; they argue (as others have done) that 'later forms of alliterative writing were … a reinvention' (p. 18), ultimately derived from OE alliterating prose.

ary process from Old English verse.[10] And given the complexity of the metrical system as we have described it, we agree with Russom that '[i]t is difficult to imagine how anything like this meter could have been invented or learned independently of tradition. The hypothesis of continuity seems to be required by the very nature of rules 1–4.'[11] Since the four rules mentioned by Russom comprise only some of the rules we have posited above, his argument for the likelihood of an evolutionary process applies *a fortiori* if any of our further rules are accepted. The study of that evolutionary process also needs further work.

We shall hazard one suggestion. It may be beneficial to consider the development of Middle English alliterative metre not only in relation to its native progenitor (Old English verse or, as some have argued, prose[12]) but also in relation to the non-native species of accentual-syllabic metre with which it had to compete. Here it is worth looking briefly at the first commentator on alliterative metre, James VI, King of Scotland. His remarks on the subject in *Ane Short Treatise Conteining Some Reulis and Cautelis to Be Obseruit and Eschewit in Scottis Poesie* (printed 1584) deal with rhymed alliterative verse, but since that verse continued to be practised in Scotland under James VI's own patronage,[13] and appears to obey some of the same metrical rules that operate in the unrhymed long line (our rules 2, 4, and possibly 5),[14] James's comments are as close as we are likely to get to an 'insider's view' of the metrical system as we have described it. This is what James VI had to say:

[10] Again Luick was a pioneer in this regard. In his 'Die Englische Stabreimzeile' he tried to derive permissible a- and b-verse patterns in Middle English alliterative verse from Sievers's five types.

[11] Russom, 'Evolution', p. 297. By rules 1–4 he means the following: 1): 'A b-verse must contain a long dip'; 2) 'A b-verse must not contain more than one long dip'; 3) 'A b-verse must contain exactly two stressed syllables'; and 4) 'A b-verse must end with a trochaic element' (p. 275).

[12] See above, n. 9.

[13] See David Parkinson, 'Alexander Montgomerie, James VI, and *Tumbling Verse*', in *Loyal Letters: Studies on Mediaeval Alliterative Poetry and Prose*, ed. L. A. R. J. Houwen and A. A. MacDonald (Groningen, 1994), pp. 281–95.

[14] See Ruth Kennedy, 'New Theories of Constraint in the Metricality of the Strong-Stress Long Line, Applied to the English Rhymed Alliterative Corpus, *c.* 1400', in *Métriques du Moyen Age et de la Renaissance*, ed. Dominique Billy (Paris, 1999), pp. 131–44, and also Kennedy's edition of *Three Alliterative Saints' Hymns*, EETS OS 321 (Oxford, 2003), pp. xxxiii–xxxviii.

> Let all your verse be *Literall* ... speciallie *Tumbling* verse for flyting. Be *Literall* I meane that the maist pairt of your lyne sall rynne vpon a letter, as this tumblyng lyne rynnis vpon F.
>
> *Fetching fude for to feid it fast furth of the Fairie*[15]
>
> Ye man obsuerue that thir *Tumbling* verse flowis not on that fassoun as vtheris dois. For all vtheris kepis the reule quhilk I gaue before, to wit, the first fute short, the secound lang, and sa furth. Quhair as thir hes twa short and ane lang throuch all the lyne, quhen they keip ordour: albeit the maist pairt of thame be out of ordour, and kepis na kynde nor reule of *Flowing*, and for that cause are callit *Tumbling* verse: except the short lynis of aucht in the hinder end of the verse, the quhilk flowis as vther verses dois, as ye will find in the hinder end of this buke, quhair I giue exemple of sindrie kyndis of versis.[16]

Certain terminological differences may obscure the perceptive points that James VI is making. By 'literall' James VI obviously means 'alliterative' and by 'letter' he means the alliterating sound. We may recall here the *Gawain* poet's homage to his source, a 'stori stif and stronge, / With lel letteres loken' (*G* 34–5) and Chaucer's Parson, who says he is a southern man and cannot 'geeste "rum, raf, ruf" *by lettre*' (*CT* X.43). (Incidentally, the Parson's derogatory comment about alliterative verse might suggest that Chaucer, too, thought of alliterative verse as having *three* alliterating sounds.)[17] By 'verse' James means sometimes 'poetry' and at other times 'stanza'. The 'short lines' at the end of the stanza are of course the iambic lines of the bob-and-wheel, which in the 'flyting' in question (as in *Gawain*'s bob-and-wheel) indeed consist of *flowing* verse. In *flowing* verse, the first 'foot' (i.e. syllable) is normally short (i.e. unstressed), the second 'long' (i.e. stressed) and so on. James, however,

[15] This seems to be a garbled recollection of Alexander Montgomery's *Flyting of Montgomerie and Polwart*, 476: 'Syne fetcht food for to feid it, / foorth fra the Pharie', as noted by Schipper, *History of English Versification*, p. 89, n. 1.

[16] James VI, *Ane Short Treatise Conteining Some Reulis and Cautelis to Be Obseruit and Eschewit in Scottis Poesie*, in *Elizabethan Critical Essays*, ed. Gregory Smith (Oxford, 1904), 2 vols., I, pp. 208–25 (218–9).

[17] Note also *Winner and Waster*, 24–25, which (in Gollancz's emended version) read:

> Bot now a childe appon chere, with-owtten chyn-wedys,
> Þat neuer wroght thurgh witt th[ree] wordes togedire' [MS *thies*].

It is perhaps not too far-fetched to think of these lines as a defence of 'proper' alliterative verse where three alliterating 'wordes' must be brought together.

has noticed that the rhythm of the alliterative long line is predominantly anapaestic: i.e. he would scan his sample line as xx/xx/xx/xx/x. Significantly, then, James did *not* hear this extended a-verse as having three beats: the 'routine' verb *fetch* does not attract the beat, and as far as he and we are concerned the alliterative long line has four beats.[18]

What is more, James discerns not one but two fundamental differences between flowing and tumbling verse. First, the characteristic rhythm of the former is iambic and that of the latter anapaestic; and, second, the rhythm of flowing verse 'keeps order', while that of tumbling verse is 'out of order', keeping 'neither the kind nor the rule of flowing verse.' Tumbling verse therefore differs from flowing verse not only in its preference for long dips but also in its avoidance of recurrent rhythmical patterns. James touches here on what Cable calls the principle of 'dissimilation'.[19] This principle obtains in alliterative verse at various levels:

(a) *within* the b-verse, where *x/x/x and *xx/xx/x are both outlawed;

(b) *between* the two hemistichs, which are always asymmetrical in terms of their rhythm;

(c) in terms of the alliterative pattern, which is normally *aa/ax* (although *aa/aa* appears to be a genuine, though rare, variant).

The final unstressed syllable at line ending is potentially an important marker of that asymmetry, for in a-verses that otherwise look like b-verses (e.g x/xx/x) a heavy or long final dip maintains the asymmetry. The final unstressed syllable at the end of the b-verse becomes, in these circumstances, the guarantor of rhythmical dissimilation, and it should not therefore surprise us that a weakly stressed syllable should have become mandatory at line ending.

When we ask why alliterative metre is the way it is, it is perhaps worth taking seriously James's point that 'tumbling verse' is designed to be different from 'flowing verse'. For rhyme it substitutes alliteration, normally in a form that 'keeps no order' (*aa/ax* rather than *aa/aa*). For iambic rhythm it substitutes anapaestic rhythm, and for the regular recurrence of rhythmical patterns it substitutes rhythmical dissimilation. The evolution of the species we have called 'classical alliterative metre'

[18] Cf. the pattern of extension at *G* 1084a, 'Lét þe ládieȝ be fette', and *PP* B 18.350, 'Thow fettest mýne in mý place [máugree] alle résoun'.

[19] See Cable, *Alliterative Tradition*, p. 86.

should perhaps be understood, not simply *diachronically* in relation to historic forms of that species, but also *synchronically* in relation to the species of accentual-syllabic verse which was contemporary with it (and which was in the end to displace it). The metrical rules as we have described them may have served the purpose of contra-distinguishing the native metre from the foot-counted metres. Strong-stress metre may have developed with an 'anti-iambic' teleology.

Ralph Hanna has recently emphasised that alliterative verse was not written by poets who were isolated from or ignorant of the rhymed syllabic verse composed by their contemporaries. 'Alliterative poetry', he writes, 'had a vital circulation in Chaucerian surroundings', and, although some scholars have seen alliterative verse as the Other of Chaucerian verse, 'this Otherness essentially occupies a space of consciousness, not of geography.'[20] It would be worth exploring whether Hanna's observation sheds any light on the evolution of the alliterative long line, and on the question of why its metre changed to become, in so many respects, the 'conscious Other' of Chaucerian verse.

20 Ralph Hanna, 'Alliterative Poetry', in *The Cambridge History of Medieval English Literature*, ed. David Wallace (Cambridge, 1999), pp. 488–512 (p. 511).

# BIBLIOGRAPHY

**Primary Sources**


*ABC of Aristotle*, in *The Babees Book: Early English Meals and Manners*, ed. F. J. Furnivall, EETS OS 32 (London, 1868), pp. 9–10.

*Alexander A*, ed. Francis Peabody Magoun, *The Gests of King Alexander of Macedon: Two Middle-English Alliterative Fragments* (Cambridge, Mass., 1929).

*Alexander and Dindimus*, ed. W. W. Skeat, EETS ES 31 (London, 1878).

Andrew, Malcolm, and Ronald Waldron (eds), *The Poems of the Pearl Manuscript*, 4th edn. (Exeter, 2002).

Brewer, D. S., and A. E. B. Owen (eds), *The Thornton Manuscript (Lincoln Cathedral MS. 91)* (London, 1977).

*Castle of Love*, in *The Middle English Translations of Robert Grosseteste's 'Chateau d'Amour'*, ed. Kari Sajavaara (Helsinki, 1967).

Chaucer, Geoffrey, *The Legend of Good Women*, ed. Janet Cowen and George Kane (East Lansing, Mich., 1995).

—, *The Riverside Chaucer*, gen. ed. L. D. Benson, 3rd edn. (Boston, 1987).

—, *The Works of Geoffrey Chaucer*, gen. ed. Alfred W. Pollard (London, 1913).

*Cleanness*, ed. Israel Gollancz, Select Early English Poems (London, 1921).

*Cleanness*, ed. J. J. Anderson (Manchester, 1977).

*Cursor Mundi*, ed. R. Morris, 7 vols, EETS OS 57, 59, 62, 66, 68, 100, 101 (London 1874–93).

*Death and Liffe*, ed. Joseph M. Donatelli, Speculum Anniversary Monographs (Cambridge, Mass, 1989).

*Destruction of Troy*, ed. George A. Panton and David Donaldson, EETS OS 39, 56 (London, 1869, 1874).

*Destruction of Troy: a Diplomatic and Color Facsimile Edition*, ed. Hiroyuki Matsumoto, Society for Early English and Norse Electronic Texts (Ann Arbor, Mich., 2002).

Duncan, Thomas G. (ed.), *Late Medieval English Lyrics and Carols, 1400–1530* (London, 2000).

*Genesis and Exodus*, ed. Richard Morris, EETS OS 7 (London, 1865).

Gower, John, *Confessio Amantis*, ed. G. C. Macaulay, *John Gower's English Works*, 2 vols, EETS ES 81–82 (London, 1900–01).

Hoccleve, Thomas, *Complaint of the Virgin Mary*, in *Hoccleve's Minor* Works, ed. F. J. Furnivall and I. Gollancz, rev. J. Mitchell and I. Doyle, EETS OS 61, 73 (London, 1892–1925, repr. 1970).

James VI, *Ane Short Treatise Conteining Some Reulis and Cautelis to Be Obseruit and Eschewit in Scottis Poesie*, in *Elizabethan Critical Essays*, ed. Gregory Smith (Oxford, 1904), 2 vols., I, pp. 208–25.

Kennedy, Ruth (ed.), *Three Alliterative Saints' Hymns: Late Middle English Stanzaic Poems*, EETS, OS 321 (Oxford, 2003).

Laȝamon, *Brut*, ed. W. R. J. Barron and S. C. Weinberg (Harlow, 1995).

Langland, William, *Piers Plowman, B-Text, Prologue and Passus I–VII*, ed. J. A. W. Bennett (Oxford, 1972).

—, *Piers Plowman: the A Version*, ed. George Kane (London, 1960).

—, *Piers Plowman: the B Version*, ed. George Kane and E. Talbot Donaldson (London, 1975).

—, *Piers Plowman: the C Version*, ed. George Russell and George Kane (London, 1997).

—, *The Vision of Piers Plowman*, ed. A. V. C. Schmidt (1978, repr. London, 1995).

Magoun, Francis P. (ed.), *The Gests of King Alexander of Macedon: Two Middle-English Alliterative Fragments* (Cambridge, Mass., 1929).

Menner, Robert J. (ed.), *Purity* (New Haven, Conn., 1920).

*Morte Arthure*, ed. Eric Björkman (Heidelberg, 1915).

*Morte Arthure*, ed. Valerie Krishna, *The Alliterative Morte Arthure* (New York, 1976).

*Morte Arthure: a Critical Edition*, ed. Mary Hamel (New York, 1984).

*Mum and the Sothsegger*, in *The Piers Plowman Tradition*, ed. Helen Barr (London, 1993).

Orm, *Ormulum*, ed. Robert Holt, notes and glossary by R. M White, 2 vols (Oxford, 1878).

*Parlement of The Thre Ages*, ed. M. Y. Offord, EETS OS 246 (London, 1959).

*Patience*, ed. J. J. Anderson (Manchester, 1969).

*Pearl*, ed. E. V. Gordon (Oxford, 1953).

*Saint Erkenwald*, in *A Book of Middle English*, ed. J. A Burrow and Thorlac Turville-Petre, 2nd edn. (Oxford, 1996).

*St. Erkenwald*, ed. Henry Savage (New Haven, Conn., 1926).

*Siege of Jerusalem*, ed. Eugen Kölbing and Mabel Day, EETS OS 188 (London, 1932).

*Siege of Jerusalem*, ed. Ralph Hanna and David Lawton, EETS OS 320 (Oxford, 2003).

*Sir Gawayne and the Green Knight*, ed. Richard Morris, EETS OS 4 (London, 1864).

*Sir Gawain and the Green Knight*, ed. Israel Gollancz, EETS OS 210 (Oxford, 1940).

*Sir Gawain and the Green Knight*, ed. J. R. R. Tolkien and E. V. Gordon, rev. Norman Davis (Oxford, 1967).

*Sir Tristrem*, ed. George P. McNeill, Scottish Text Society 8 (Edinburgh, 1886).

Turville-Petre, Thorlac (ed.), *Alliterative Poetry of the Later Middle Ages: an Anthology* (London, 1989).

Wace, *Roman de Brut*, ed. and trans. Judith Weiss, rev. edn. (Exeter, 2002).

*Wars of Alexander*, ed. Hoyt N. Duggan and Thorlac Turville-Petre, EETS SS 10 (Oxford, 1989).

*William of Palerne*, ed. G. H. V. Bunt (Groningen, 1985).

*Winner and Waster*, ed. Israel Gollancz, Select Early English Poems (London, 1920).

*Wynnere and Wastoure*, ed. Stephanie Trigg, EETS OS 297 (Oxford, 1990).

**Secondary Sources**

Aertsen, Henk, 'The Infinitive in *Sir Gawain and the Green Knight*', in *This Noble Craft: Proceedings of the Xth Research Symposium of Dutch and Belgian University Teachers*, ed. Erik Kooper (Amsterdam, 1991), pp. 3–28.

Allerton, D. J., and A. Cruttenden, 'Three Reasons for Accenting a Definite Subject', *Linguistics*, 5 (1979), 49–53.

Amodio, Mark C., *Writing the Oral Tradition: Oral Poetics and Literate Culture in Medieval England* (Notre Dame, Ind., 2004).

Andrew, S. O., 'The Dialect of *Morte Arthure*', *Review of English Studies*, 4 (1928), 418–23.

Attridge, Derek, *The Rhythms of English Poetry* (New York, 1982).

Bache, Carl, *The Order of Pre-modifying Adjectives in Present-day English* (Odense, 1978).

Bailey, James, 'Linguistic Givens and Their Metrical Realization in a Poem by Yeats', *Language and Style*, 8 (1975), 21–33.

Barney, Stephen A., *Studies in 'Troilus': Chaucer's Text, Meter, and Diction* (East Lansing, Mich., 1993).

—, 'Langland's Prosody: the State of Study', in *The Endless Knot: Essays on Old and Middle English in Honor of Marie Borroff*, ed. M. Teresa Tavormina and R. F. Yeager (Cambridge, 1995), pp. 65–85.

Bihl, Joseph, *Die Wirkungen des Rhythmus in der Sprache von Chaucer und Gower* (Heidelberg, 1916).

Bolinger, Dwight, *The Phrasal Verb in English* (Cambridge, Mass., 1971).

—, 'Accent is Predictable (if you're a mind reader)', *Language*, 48 (1972), 633–44.

—, *Intonation and Its Parts* (London, 1986).

—, 'Two Views of Accent', in Carlos Gussenhoven, Dwight Bolinger, and Cornelia E. Keijsper, *On Accent* (Bloomington, Ind., 1987), pp. 51–107.

—, *Intonation and Its Uses* (London, 1989).

Borroff, Marie, '*Sir Gawain and the Green Knight*': *a Stylistic and Metrical Study* (New Haven, Conn., 1962).

Brewer, D. S., 'The Arming of the Warrior in European Literature and Chaucer', in *Chaucerian Problems and Perspectives: Essays Presented to Paul E. Beichner. C.S.C.*, ed. E. Vasta and Z. P. Thundy (Notre Dame, Ind., 1979), pp. 221–43.

Brink, Bernhard ten, *The Language and Metre of Chaucer*, rev. F. Kluge, trans. M. Bentinck Smith (London, 1901).

Brunner, Karl, *An Outline of Middle English Grammar*, trans. G. K. W. Johnston (Oxford, 1963).

Burnley, David, 'Inflexion in Chaucer's Adjectives', *Neuphilologische Mitteilungen*, 83 (1982), 169–77.

Burrow, J. A., *A Reading of 'Sir Gawain and the Green Knight'* (London, 1965).

—, '*St Erkenwald*, line 1: "At London in Englond"', *Notes and Queries*, n.s. 40 (1993), 22–3.

—, 'Hoccleve's Questions: Intonation and Punctuation', *Notes and Queries*, n.s. 49 (2002), 184–8.

Cable, Thomas, *The English Alliterative Tradition* (Philadelphia, 1991).

Chatman, Seymour, *A Theory of Meter* (The Hague, 1965).

Chomsky, Noam, and Morris Halle, *The Sound Pattern of English* (New York, 1968).

Cooper, Helen, 'Textual Variation and the Alliterative Tradition: *Canterbury Tales* I.2602–2619, the D Group and Takamiaya MS 32', in *The Medieval Book and A Modern Collector: Essays in Honour of Toshiyuki Takamiya*, ed. Takami Mastuda, Richard A. Linenthal, and John Scahill (Cambridge, 2004), pp. 71–81.

Crystal, David, *The English Tone of Voice* (London, 1975).

Dobson, E. J., *English Pronunciation 1500–1700*, 2 vols, 2nd edn. (Oxford, 1968).

Doyle, Ian, 'The Manuscripts', in *Middle English Alliterative Poetry and Its Literary Background*, ed. David Lawton (Cambridge, 1982), pp. 88–100.

Duggan, Hoyt N., 'The Shape of the B-Verse in Middle English Alliterative Poetry', *Speculum*, 61 (1986), 564–92.

—, 'Alliterative Patterning as a Basis for Emendation in Middle English Alliterative Poetry', *Studies in the Age of Chaucer*, 8 (1986), 73–105.

—, 'The Authenticity of the Z-Text of *Piers Plowman*: Further Notes on Metrical Evidence', *Medium Aevum*, 56 (1987), 27–45.

—, 'The Evidential Basis for Old English Metrics', *Studies in Philology*, 85 (1988), 145–63.

—, 'Final -*e* and the Rhythmic Structure of the B-Verse in Middle English Alliterative Poetry', *Modern Philology*, 86 (1988), 119–45.

—, 'Langland's Dialect and Final *–e*', *Studies in the Age of Chaucer*, 12 (1990), 157–91.

—, 'Stress Assignment in Middle English Alliterative Poetry', *Journal of English and Germanic Philology*, 89 (1990), 309–29.

—,'The Role and Distribution of *–ly* Adverbs in Middle English Alliterative Verse', in *Loyal Letters: Studies on Mediaeval Alliterative Poetry and Prose*, ed. L. A. R. J. Houwen and A. A. MacDonald (Groningen, 1994), pp. 131–154.

—, 'Libertine Scribes and Maidenly Editors: Meditations on Textual Criticism and Metrics', in C. B. McCully and J. J. Anderson (eds), *English Historical Metrics* (Cambridge, 1996), pp. 219–237.

—, 'Some Unrevolutionary Aspects of Computer Editing' in *The Literary Text in the Digital Age*, ed. Richard J. Finneran (Ann Arbor, Mich., 1996), 77–98.

—, 'Meter, Stanza, Vocabulary, Dialect', in *A Companion to the Gawain Poet*, ed. Derek Brewer and Jonathan Gibson (Cambridge, 1997), pp. 221–242.

—, 'Extended A-Verses in Middle English Alliterative Poetry', in *Medieval English Measures: Studies in Metre and Versification*, ed. Ruth Kennedy, special issue of *Parergon*, 18 (2000), 53–76.

—, 'Some Aspects of A-Verse Rhythms in Middle English Alliterative Poetry', in *Speaking Images: Essays in Honor of V. A. Kolve*, ed. R. F. Yeager and Charlotte Morse (Asheville, NC, 2001), pp. 479–503.

—, 'Notes on the Metre of *Piers Plowman: Twenty Years On*', forthcoming in *The Metres of Alliterative Verse*, ed. Judith Jefferson and Ad Putter, Leeds Studies in English (2008).

Einenkel, Eugen, *Geschichte der englischen Sprache: II: Historische Syntax*, Grundriss der Germanischen Philologie (Strasbourg, 1916).

Eitrem, H., 'Stress in English Verb + Adverb Groups', *Englische Studien*, 32 (1903), 69–77.

Field, P. J. C., *Malory: Texts and Sources* (Cambridge, 1998).

Finlayson, John, 'Formulaic Technique in "Morte Arthure"', *Anglia*, 81 (1963), 372–93.

Fischer, Joseph, *Die stabende Langzeile in den Werken des Gawaindichters*, Bonner Beiträge zur Anglistik, 11 (1901), 1–64.

Fischer, Olga, 'Infinitive Marking in Late Middle English: Transitivity and Changes in the English System of Case', in Jacek Fisiak, *Studies in Middle English Linguistics* (Berlin, 1997), pp. 109–34.

Forsström, Gösta, *The Verb 'To Be' in Middle English: a Survey of the Forms* (Lund, 1948).

Gadamer, Hans-Georg, *Truth and Method* (London, 1975).

Gordon, E. V., and Eugène Vinaver, 'New Light on the Text of the Alliterative *Morte Arthure*', *Medium Aevum*, 6 (1937), 81–98.

Gussenhoven, Carlos, *On the Grammar and Semantics of Sentence Accents* (Dordrecht, 1984).

Hagen, Karl, 'Adverbial Distribution in Middle English Alliterative Verse', *Modern Philology*, 90 (1992), 159–71.

Hamel, Mary, 'Scribal Self-Corrections in the Thornton *Morte Arthure*', *Studies in Bibliography*, 36 (1983), 119–37.

Hanna, Ralph, 'Alliterative Poetry', in *The Cambridge History of Medieval English Literature*, ed. David Wallace (Cambridge, 1999), pp. 488–512.

Hayes, Bruce, 'A Grid-based Theory of English Meter', *Linguistic Inquiry*, 14 (1983), 357–393

Hogg, Richard, 'The Spread of negative contraction in Early English', in A. Curzan and K. Emmons (eds), *Studies in the History of the English Language II: Unfolding Conversations* (Berlin, 2004), pp. 459–82.

—, and C. B. McCully, *Metrical Phonology: a Coursebook* (Cambridge, 1987).

Holthausen, F., Review of Mennicken's 'Versbau und Sprache', *Englische Studien* 30 (1902), 271–5.

Inoue, Noriko, 'The A-Verse of the Alliterative Long Line and the Metre of *Sir Gawain and the Green Knight*' ( PhD Dissertation, University of Bristol, 2003).

—, 'A New Theory of Alliterative A-Verses', *Yearbook of Langland Studies*, 18 (2005), 107–32.

—, 'The Metre of Middle English Alliterative Verse: *–ly* and *–lych(e* Adverbs and Adjectives', forthcoming in *Modern Philology*.

Jakobson, Roman, *Language and Literature* (Cambridge, Mass., 1987)

Jefferson, Judith A., 'The Hoccleve Holographs and Hoccleve's Metrical Practice', in *Manuscripts and Texts: Editorial Problems in Middle English Literature*, ed. Derek Pearsall (Cambridge, 1987), pp. 95–109.

Jordan, Richard, *Handbuch der Mittelenglischen Grammatik: Lautlehre*, 2nd edn. (Heidelberg, 1934).

Kane, George, 'Music Neither Unpleasant nor Monotonous', in *Medieval Studies for J. A W. Bennett* (1981), repr. in his *Chaucer and Langland: Historical and Textual Approaches* (London, 1989), 77–89.

Kellog, Allen Bond, 'The Language of the Alliterative *Siege of Jerusalem*' (PhD Dissertation, University of Chicago, 1943).

Kelly, Michael, and David C. Rubin, 'Natural Rhythmic Patterns in English Verse: Evidence from Child Counting-Out Rhymes', *Journal of Memory and Language*, 27 (1988), 718–40.

Kennedy, Ruth, 'New Theories of Constraint in the Metricality of the Strong-Stress Long Line, Applied to the English Rhymed Alliterative Corpus, *c.* 1400', in *Métriques du Moyen Age et de la Renaissance*, ed. Dominique Billy (Paris, 1999), pp. 131–44.

Kingdon, Roger, *The Groundwork of English Intonation* (London, 1958).

Knigge, F., *Die Sprache des Dichters von 'Sir Gawain and the Green Knight'* (Marburg, 1886).

Koziol, Herbert, *Grundzüge der Syntax der mittelenglischen Stabreimdichtungen*, Wiener Beiträge zur englischen Philologie (Vienna, 1932).

Lawton, David, 'The Idea of Alliterative Poetry: Alliterative Meter and *Piers Plowman*', in *'Such Werkis to Werche': Essays on 'Piers Plowman' in Honor of David C. Fowler*, ed. M. F. Vaughan (East Lansing, Mich., 1993), pp. 147–68.

Lehnert, Martin, *Sprachform und Sprachfunktion im 'Orrmulum'* (Berlin, 1953).

Luick, Karl, 'Die englische Stabreimzeile im XIV., XV. und XVI. Jahrhundert', *Anglia*, 11 (1889), 392–443, 553–618.

—, Review of Mennicken, *Versbau und Sprache in Huchowns 'Morte Arthure'*, *Beiblatt zur Anglia*, 12 (1901), 33–49.

—, 'Der mittelenglische Stabreimvers', in *Grundriss der Germanischen Philologie*, ed. Hermann Paul, 2 vols (Strasbourg, 1905), II, 141–80.

—, *Historische Grammatik der englischen Sprache*, 3 vols (Leipzig, 1921–29).

Luttrell, Claude, 'Three North-West Midland Manuscripts', *Neophilologus*, 42 (1958), 38–50.

Marckwardt, Albert H., *Origin and Extension of the Voiceless Preterit and the Past Participle Inflections of the English Irregular Weak Verb Conjugation* (Ann Arbor, Mich., 1935).

Matthews, William, *The Ill-Framed Knight* (Berkeley, Cal., 1966).

McCully, Christopher B., and Richard M. Hogg, 'Dialect Variation and Historical Metrics', *Diachronica*, 11 (1994), 13–34.

McIntosh, A. I. 'The Textual Transmission of the Alliterative *Morte Arthure*', in *English and Medieval Studies Presented to J. R. R. Tolkien*, ed. Norman Davis and C. L. Wrenn (London, 1962), pp. 231–40.

—, 'A New Approach to Middle English Dialectology', *English Studies*, 44 (1963), 1–11.

—, M. L. Samuels, and Michael Benskin, with the assistance of Margaret Laing and Keith Williamson, *A Linguistic Atlas of Late Mediaeval English*, 4 vols (Aberdeen, 1986).

McJimsey, Ruth, *Chaucer's Irregular –E* (New York, 1942).

Mennicken, Franz, *Versbau und Sprache in Huchowns 'Morte Arthure'*, Bonner Beiträge zur Anglistik, 5 (1900), 33–144.

Minkova, Donka, *The History of Final Vowels in English: the Sound of Muting*, Topics in English Linguistics 4 (Berlin, 1991).

Minkova, Donka, and Robert Stockwell, 'Against the Emergence of the Nuclear Stress Rule in Middle English', in J. Fisiak and W. Winter (eds), *Studies in Middle English Linguistics* (Berlin, 1997), pp. 301–35.

Moore, Samuel, 'Loss of Final *n* in Inflectional Syllables of Middle English', *Language*, 4 (1927), 232–59.

—, 'Earliest Morphological Changes in Middle English', *Language*, 4 (1928), 238–66.

Moriya, Yasuyo, 'The Meter of the Verse Line of the Middle English *Pearl*', *Studies in Medieval English Language and Literature*, 11 (1966), 49–79.

—, 'Identical Alliteration in the *Alliterative Morte Arthure*', *English Language Notes*, 38 (2000), 1–16.

—, 'The Role of the Sound *r* in *The Alliterative Morte Arthure*', *Poetica*, 53 (2000), 1–13.

—, 'Alliteration Versus Natural Speech Rhythm in Determining the Meter of ME Alliterative Verse', *English Studies*, 6 (2004), 498–507.

Mossé, Fernand, *Handbook of Middle English*, trans. James A. Walker (Baltimore, 1952).

Mustanoja, Tauno F., *A Middle English Syntax. Part I: Parts of Speech* (Helsinki, 1960).

Nakao, Toshio, *The Prosodic Phonology y of Late Middle English* (Tokyo, 1978).

Oakden, J. P., *Alliterative Poetry in Middle English*, 2 vols (Manchester, 1930–35).

—, 'The Scribal Errors of the MS Cotton Nero A.x', *The Library*, 4th series, 14 (1932), 353–58.

Ohye, Saburo, 'Metrical Influences in the Grammar of the Four Poems Preserved in MS. Cotton Nero A.x,', *St Paul's Review* (Tokyo) 11 (1962), 75–97

O'Loughlin, J. L. N., 'The Middle English Alliterative *Morte Arthure*', *Medium Aevum*, 4 (1935), 153–68.

Parkinson, David, 'Alexander Montgomerie, James VI, and *Tumbling Verse*, in *Loyal Letters: Studies on Medieaval Alliterative Poetry and Prose*, ed. L. A. R. J. Houwen and A. A. MacDonald (Groningen, 1994), pp. 281–295.

Putter, Ad, Review of Hanna and Lawton (eds), *Siege of Jerusalem*, *Speculum*, 81 (2006), 524–6.

—, 'Weak *e* and the Metre of Richard Spalding's *Alliterative Katherine Hymn*', *Notes and Queries*, n.s. 52 (2005), 288–92.

—, 'Chaucer's Verse and Alliterative Poetry: Grammar, Metre, and Some Secrets of the Syllable Count', *Poetica*, 67 (2007), 19–35.

—, and Myra Stokes, 'Spelling, Grammar and Metre in the Works of the *Gawain Poet*', in *Medieval English Measures: Studies in Metre and Versification*, ed. Ruth Kennedy, *Parergon*, 18 (2000), 77–95.

—, and Myra Stokes, 'The Linguistic Atlas and the Dialect of the *Gawain* Poems', forthcoming in *Journal of English and Germanic Philology*, 106 (2007), 468–91.

Quirk, Randolph, Sidney Greenbaum *et al.*, *A Grammar of Contemporary English* (London, 1972).

Quirk, Randolph and Sidney Greenbaum, *A University Grammar of English* (London, 1973).

Reed, David, *The History of Inflectional N in English Verbs Before 1500* (Berkeley, 1950).

Russom, Geoffrey, 'The Evolution of Middle English Alliterative Meter', in *Studies in the History of the English Language II: Unfolding Conversations*, ed. A. Curzan and K. Emmons, Topics in English Linguistics 45 (Berlin, 2004), 275–304.

—, 'The Evolution of the A-Verse in Middle English Alliterative Meter', in *Studies in the History of the English Language III*, ed. C. M. Cain and G. Russom, Topics in English Linguistics, 15 (Berlin).

Sakai, Tsuneo, 'On Some Aspects of the Infinitive in ME *Sir Gawain and the Green Knight*', *Bulletin of Kochi Women's University* 11 (1962), 1–15.

Samuels, M. L., 'Langland's Dialect', *Medium Aevum*, 54 (1985), 232–47, repr. in *The English of Chaucer and His Contemporaries*, ed. J. J. Smith (Aberdeen, 1988), pp. 70–85.

Sapora, R. W., *A Theory of Middle English Alliterative Meter with Critical Applications*, Speculum Anniversary Monographs (Cambridge, Mass., 1977).

Sauer, Hans, *Nominalkomposita im Frühmittelenglischen mit Ausblicken auf die Geschichte der englischen Nominalkomposition* (Tübingen, 1992).

Schipper, Jakob, *History of English Versification* (Oxford, 1910; repr. New York, 1971.

Schmerling, Susan F., *Aspects of English Sentence Stress* (Austin, Texas, 1976).

Schumacher, Karl, *Studien über den Stabreim in der mittelenglischen Alliterationsdichtung*, Bonner Studien zur englischen Philologie 11 (Bonn, 1914).

Scott, Kathleen L., *Later Gothic Manuscripts, 1390–1490*, 2 vols (London, 1996).

Selkirk, Elizabeth O., *Phonology and Syntax: the Relation Between Sound and Structure* (Cambridge, Mass., 1984).

Smithers, G. V., 'The Scansion of *Havelok* and the Use of ME *–en* and *–e* in *Havelok* and Chaucer', in *Middle English Studies Presented to Norman Davis*, ed. Douglas Gray and E. G. Stanley (Oxford, 1983), pp. 195–234.

Solopova, Elizabeth, 'Metre and Scribal Editing in the Early Manuscripts of *The Canterbury Tales*', in *'The Canterbury Tales' Project: Occasional Papers*, vol. II, ed. Norman Blake and Peter Robinson (London, 1997), pp. 153–65.

Steffens, Heinrich, *Versbau und Sprache des mittelenglischen stabreimenden Gedichtes 'The Wars of Alexander'*, Bonner Beiträge zur Anglistik, 9 (Bonn, 1901), 1–104.

Suzuki, Eiichi, 'Notes on Lexical Substitution in *The Siege of Jerusalem*', in *Philologia Anglica: Essays Presented to Professor Yoshio Terasawa*, ed. Kinshiro Oshitari (Tokyo, 1988), pp. 184–94.

Sweet, Henry, *A New English Grammar, Logical and Historical*, 2 vols (Oxford, 1892–8).

Tarlinskaja, Marina, *Shakespeare's Verse: Iambic Pentameter and the Poet's Idiosyncrasies* (New York, 1987).

—, 'General and Particular Aspects of Meter', in *Rhythms and Metre*, ed. Paul Kiparsky and Gilbert Youmans, special issue of *Phonetics and Phonology* 1 (1989), 121–54.

Thomas, Julius, *Die alliterierende Langzeile des Gawayn-Dichters* (Jena, 1908).

Tobler, A., and E. Lommatzsch, *Altfranzösisches Wörterbuch* (Berlin, 1915–).

Turville-Petre, Joan, 'The Metre of *Sir Gawain and the Green Knight*', *English Studies*, 57 (1976), 310–29.

—, *The Alliterative Revival* (Cambridge, 1977).

—, 'Emendation on the Grounds of Alliteration in *The Wars of Alexander*', *English Studies*, 61 (1980), 302–17.

—, 'The Author of *The Destruction of Troy*', *Medium Aevum*, 57 (1988), 264–9.

—, '*Wynnere and Wastoure*: When and Where?', in *Loyal Letters: Studies on Mediaeval Alliterative Poetry and Prose*, ed. L. A. R. J. Houwen and A. A. MacDonald (Groningen, 1994), pp. 155–166.

Western, August, *On Sentence Rhythm and Word-Order in Modern English*, Videnskabs-Selskabet Skrifter 2 (Christiania, 1908).

Wild, Friedrich, *Die sprachlichen Eigentümlichkeiten der wichtigeren Chaucer-Handschriften und die Sprache Chaucers* (Vienna, 1915).

Wilson, Edward, 'John Clerk, Author of the *Destruction of Troy*', *Notes and Queries* n.s. 37 (1990), 391–6.

Woodrow, Herbert, 'Time Perception', in *Handbook of Experimental Psychology*, ed. S. S. Stevens (New York, 1951), 1223–36.

Wright, Joseph, and Elizabeth Mary Wright, *An Elementary Middle English Grammar*, 2nd edn. (Oxford, 1967).

# INDEX OF WORDS AND TOPICS

ME words are cited in ModE spelling, except when they do not have obvious or closely-resembling equivalents in ModE.

www.ingramcontent.com/pod-product-compliance
Ingram Content Group UK Ltd.
Pitfield, Milton Keynes, MK11 3LW, UK
UKHW042007190726
13854UKWH00005B/2201

9 780907 570189